ON
THIS
DATE

Also by Carl M. Cannon

The Pursuit of Happiness in Times of War

Reagan's Disciple: George W. Bush's Troubled Quest for a Presidential Legacy
(with Lou Cannon)

Circle of Greed (with Patrick Dillon)

ON THIS DATE

FROM THE PILGRIMS TO TODAY, DISCOVERING AMERICA ONE DAY AT A TIME

CARL M. CANNON

TWELVE

New York   Boston

Twelve
Hachette Book Group
1290 Avenue of the Americas, New York, NY 10104
twelvebooks.com
twitter.com/twelvebooks

First Edition: July 2017

Twelve is an imprint of Grand Central Publishing. The Twelve name and logo are trademarks of Hachette Book Group, Inc.

The publisher is not responsible for websites (or their content) that are not owned by the publisher.

The Hachette Speakers Bureau provides a wide range of authors for speaking events. To find out more, go to www.hachettespeakersbureau.com or call (866) 376-6591.

Library of Congress Cataloging-in-Publication Data has been applied for.

ISBNs: 978-1-4555-4230-7 (paper over board), 978-1-4555-4228-4 (ebook)

Printed in the United States of America

LSC-C

10 9 8 7 6 5 4 3 2 1

This book is dedicated to all Americans—past, present, and future—who were not born in the United States, but who made, or who will make, this nation their own.

Introduction

Spanish-born American philosopher George Santayana is known for expressing a sentiment that has become a cliché: Those who cannot remember the past are condemned to repeat it. This quote is accurate—it comes from his book *The Life of Reason*—but he was not only making a negative point. The passage begins with an upbeat expression of the same idea. "Progress," he wrote, "far from consisting in change, depends on retentiveness."

I would add to that sentiment an idea expressed by author David McCullough. Speaking at the 2003 Jefferson Lecture at the National Academy for the Humanities, McCullough defended historical books written for the mass public, and not just other academics.

"No harm is done to history," he said, "by making it something someone would want to read."

This admonition was somewhat self-serving, in that David McCullough has a gift for writing books that millions of people want to read. But his point is right. The approach used in this book, taking a digestible event from any given day—366 given days—was done with that in mind. The format comes out of a newsletter I send to some nineteen thousand subscribers five mornings a week in my capacity as Washington bureau chief and executive editor of RealClearPolitics.

Our online news site, devoted to politics and government, is assiduously nonpartisan. I'm aware that most journalists say similar things, and that for too many their work belies that claim. But at RCP our very business model depends on not taking sides in the great national argument between Republicans and Democrats—and Independents. In any event, I'm nonpartisan naturally, as the contents of this work will demonstrate.

Yet, it would be facile to claim that no guiding principles about America's place in the world inform this work. Many loyal readers of my "Morning Note" are already familiar with my underlying approach to writing about American history. I believe they can be distilled in a couple of sentences. The first is that notwithstanding the degraded condition of our dysfunctional, rude, hair-on-fire politics—and not minimizing the violence roiling the globe—through the years Americans have lived through similarly trying times, often facing even graver challenges.

My second point, which flows naturally from the first, is that we have usually prevailed. When we didn't prevail, we muddled through. Often, though not always, we learned something along the way. In researching this book, I stumbled across supporting evidence for this attitude in a 1921 essay by a Washington newspaperman and magazine writer named Edward G. Lowry. Well-known in his day and utterly forgotten now,

Lowry helped popularize the famously taciturn nature of then vice president Calvin Coolidge. Lowry dubbed Coolidge the "Foster-Child of Silence," writing in one essay that the vice president was "a politician who does not, who will not, and who seemingly cannot talk."

The essay that caught my eye, however, was one in which he writes about how political life in Washington "proceeds from one crisis to another." He continued:

> But do not despair of the Republic. The only thing one can be sure about in a crisis or situation or condition in Washington is that it is not unprecedented; it has happened before.... Certainly the sons and descendants of Jeremiah have rended their garments, beat their breasts, and made such loud lamentation before the Capitol and the White House after each of our war periods. They sat about in bewilderment as they sit now, and will again, saying to one another, 'Was there ever such an extraordinary situation? Was there ever such another mess as we find ourselves in now? Was there ever such another set of dolts, knaves, and incompetents in command of our destinies?' The answer is: There was. This is not the first time that the wind has moaned through the rigging.

My first book, *The Pursuit of Happiness in Times of War*, was an examination of how American presidents and other national leaders employ the language in the Declaration of Independence to rally their countrymen in times of war or national peril. It was published after September 11, 2001, about the time of the U.S. invasion of Iraq, and landed me on C-SPAN's *Booknotes* program, hosted by C-SPAN founder Brian Lamb. Brian is the rare on-air host who reads a book before interviewing its author. This is not always good for the writer. Brian noted during our interview that as far as he could tell, I didn't have a bad word to say about any U.S. president. There was an answer to this observation, but I didn't give it.

"You'll notice that Richard Nixon's not in it," I quipped.

This was supposed to be a laugh line, except that Brian Lamb—who is disinclined to indulge his guests by playing the straight man—barely cracked a smile. In time, I came to see that there was something else wrong with my jibe: It was a cheap shot. To atone, Nixon *is* mentioned in this book. I'll do it right now, because on April 13, 1972, he said something pertinent to this project. Speaking in Ottawa at a formal dinner hosted by the Canadian president, President Nixon told a self-deprecating story about playing golf in Canada when he was vice president and how their group went to a pub afterward without changing clothes—and without the presence of Secret Service agents.

"We went in and sat down," Nixon recalled. "The waiter looked us all over, and some way he seemed to think he recognized me, but he wasn't sure."

"After we had finished—he was a very polite waiter—and were ready to leave, the waiter came up and said, 'Sir, if you don't mind, I have a bet with the bartender, and you can help me win it or I might lose it.'

"What is the bet?" Nixon asked.

"I bet him five dollars that you are Vice President Nixon."

"Well, call him over and we will confirm it," Nixon recalled.

The bartender paid the bet, but as Nixon left the pub, the bartender mumbled to the waiter, "You know, he doesn't look near as bad in person as he does in his pictures."

Richard Milhous Nixon, speaking two years before he would resign from office to avoid impeachment, then summed up the moral of his vignette. "Maybe none of us look quite as bad in person as we may in our pictures," he said. "We must never miss the opportunity to see each other in person, to discuss our differences."

These are words to live by, especially in today's politically divided America where the election returns that don't go our way prompt rival inauguration weekend parades and #NotMyPresident campaigns on social media. Anyway, Nixon also told his audience about speaking in Guildhall in London in 1958 and how the most eloquent speech, and the briefest one, ever made in that storied venue had been delivered by a British prime minister 150 years earlier.

After Lord Nelson's victory at Trafalgar, William Pitt the Younger was toasted at a banquet in his honor as the savior of Europe. He rose to respond, answering in these words: "I return you many thanks for the honor you have done me; but Europe is not to be saved by any single man. England has saved herself by her exertions, and will, as I trust, save Europe by her example."

Nixon, speaking without notes, had the quote almost exactly right. This is also a timely sentiment, in the wake of Britain's election to part with its Continental neighbors. It's timeless, too. When Germany fell on May 8, 1945, Winston Churchill stood on the balcony of a government building overlooking Whitehall and told the huge crowd serenading him below, "God Bless you all. This is your victory."

"No," roared back the adoring crowd, "it is yours!"

It was Churchill who had it right. To extrapolate to the United States of America, certainly our nation has been served in its time of utmost need by marvelous men and wonderful women, but mostly, it was built by all of us, one day and one deed, at a time—and not only by the "Greatest Generation."

Speaking of that dwindling cohort, just before the sixtieth anniversary of the 1944 Normandy invasion, I visited Pointe du Hoc, where the U.S. Army Second Ranger Battalion used ropes and knives to scale the cliffs on D-Day. The Rangers' bravery has been immortalized in forums ranging from a 1962 movie classic starring John Wayne called *The Longest Day* to a stirring June 6, 1984, speech at Normandy by onetime Hollywood leading man Ronald Reagan.

"Behind me is a memorial that symbolizes the Ranger daggers that were thrust into the top of these cliffs—and before me are the men who put them there," President Reagan said while looking upon the aging citizen-soldiers who'd returned to the site of their former glory.

"These are the boys of Pointe du Hoc," Reagan added. "These are the men who took the cliffs. These are the champions who helped free a continent. And these are the heroes who helped end a war."

The Americans and their Allies were not the only fighting men at Normandy on D-Day. Those foreboding cliffs were defended that day by the Wehrmacht's 352nd Infantry Division, a veteran-studded force under the overall command of Field Marshal Erwin Rommel. In *The Longest Day*, an officer named Werner Pluskat is the first German soldier to spot the huge American and British armada as it appears out of the dawn mists. He frantically calls headquarters on the field phone from his concrete bunker as it's being shelled.

"You know those five thousand ships you say the Allies haven't got?" he yells into the phone. "Well, they've got them!"

The real-life Major Pluskat may or may not have been on the beach that morning. Some of his men later claimed he was carousing in Caen the night before and slept late. But Pluskat survived the war and was a paid consultant to Daryl Zanuck and Cornelius Ryan on *The Longest Day*, so in the film version he is not only there, and sober, but in full uniform with his faithful German shepherd by his side when the Allied invasion commences. Some of Normandy's concrete bunkers still stand; while a White House correspondent I went to see them in advance of President George W. Bush's 2004 visit. When I arrived, a German family was inside the structure looking around. Recognizing me as an American, the father, a middle-aged man my own age, became agitated.

"*Lass uns gehen,*" he said to his wife. Let's leave.

She seemed unsure, as did their children. I had smiled at them, and certainly had not been unfriendly.

"*Hinausgehen!*" he told his family with more urgency. Go out. And they did.

The encounter was slightly unsettling. It was the flip side of the warmth bestowed on me six decades after the invasion by appreciative French residents in the coastal Normandy towns of Colleville-sur-Mer and Sainte-Mère-Église. Although I appreciated pro-U.S. sentiment—especially coming from people who had so much to be thankful for—I hadn't personally done anything to merit their gratitude, any more than the German man who felt embarrassed by my presence in the bunker had done anything to feel shame. When I hiked up the bluff from Omaha Beach to the Normandy American Cemetery and Memorial, no enemy machine guns fired away at me. Quite the contrary: Old men in their berets deferentially stepped off the footpath to let me pass.

"*Américain,*" one Frenchman told his grandson as I walked by. The little boy saluted me.

John McCain once wrote that he learned to love his country—truly love his country—while a prisoner of war in North Vietnam. I think I know what he means. I had always been proud to be American, but hadn't really done anything to merit that pride. United States citizenship was conveyed on me at birth, a gift from the cosmos, on account of being born in San Francisco to American-born parents. Not an accomplishment; an act of good fortune.

After my visit to Normandy, I began to see this happy accident as an obligation. To do what? Pay my taxes, and be thankful for the opportunities this country has given me and my family? To exhibit a welcoming attitude toward immigrants? To vote, and recycle, and volunteer, and make charitable donations? Sure, all of that.

But I also felt called do my part by aiding in the task of telling America's story—to ourselves, and the rest of the world. This book is an effort to fulfill that duty. It tells individual stories, one day at time, a snapshot of an event or person that I hope will flesh out a constantly changing marvel that a friend of mine once dubbed "the American Identity."

Carl M. Cannon
Arlington, Virginia
July 4, 2017

ON
THIS
DATE

January 1, 1915

Everybody Stopped and Stared

At 10 a.m. on the first day of the New Year, a New York City taxicab headed east on Fiftieth Street before turning right onto Broadway. It was parked to await the day's first fare. Nothing unusual, even a century ago, except for a couple of details about the driver, whose appearance stopped traffic and prompted a story in the *New York Times* under the headline:

WOMAN TAXI DRIVER INVADES BROADWAY.

Even before it was apparent that the cabbie was wearing a skirt, the new taxi attracted attention on account of the driver's headgear—"a huge hat of leopard skin, and around her neck and over her shoulders the yellow and black spotted pelt of the same animal."

Don't let the costume fool you. The driver, "Miss Wilma K. Russey," worked as an auto mechanic in a Manhattan garage. While passersby stopped and stared she approached an NYPD patrolman, Philip Wagner, who was directing traffic. She showed her chauffeur's license to the police officer, who informed her there was no reason she shouldn't take her place in the cabstand. (Below is a photograph of Miss Russey, courtesy of the National Archives.)

A first hurdle cleared, a second presented itself—the male cabdrivers. Forming impromptu discussions groups, they discussed "the feminine invasion of their business," the *Times* reported, before a quick consensus emerged: When it did, they walked over to her car to congratulate her and offer words of encouragement.

One final obstacle remained. How would passengers react? The answer came quickly. A group of men approached Russey, asking if her cab was engaged.

"Where do you want to go?" she asked.

"No place in particular," answered one. "Just take us down Broadway a-ways. All we want is to have the first ride in your taxi."

January 2, 1620

Absolute Quiet

The Pilgrims aboard the *Mayflower* began gathering the materials to build their settlement on this date. The site they chose was near a hill they dubbed Plymouth Rock, which rose 165 feet from the shoreline. A nearby stream they called Town Brook had good fishing, and the topography made it a natural fortress. In addition, native people had already cleared the surrounding land before leaving the area, which the Pilgrims considered a sign from God.

Although they didn't know it, this emptiness was the work of disease, not Providence. French explorer Samuel de Champlain had seen hundreds of wigwams here in 1605, with some two thousand people occupying the land. Fifteen years later, they were all gone. An uneasy silence settled over the *Mayflower* passengers as they contemplated their new home.

No fireworks or gaiety had greeted the New Year. Pilgrims didn't celebrate like that. Their calendar didn't turn over on this day anyway. These settlers used the old Julian calendar, not today's Gregorian calendar, meaning that by their calculations, it was only December 21. Their calendar year began March 25. Not that any of this mattered to them; they didn't celebrate March 25, either. For that matter, they didn't observe Christmas. December 25 was important to them that year because it was when they framed their first wooden house in the New World.

"What would have astounded a modern sensibility transported back to that Christmas Day in 1620 was the absolute quiet of the scene," wrote *Mayflower* author Nathaniel Philbrick. "Save the gurgling of Town Brook, the lap of waves against the shore, and the wind in the bare winter branches, everything was silent as they listened and waited."

That silence would give way in the four ensuing centuries to the cries of millions of newborn babies, the shrieking of charging warriors of all colors and ethnicities, the screams of wailing widows, and the babel of every language spoken on Earth.

Other sounds would include the buzzing of saws, the pounding of hammers, and the reverberations of industrialization's noisy machines, accompanied by the endless buzz of a contentious, martial, industrious, loud, litigious, inventive, violent, spiritual, and preternaturally self-confident people.

January 3, 1938

The March of Time

Polio mostly struck children in the early twentieth century, but Franklin Delano Roosevelt was thirty-nine when he contracted the dreaded disease that cost him use of his legs. In a rare concession to his condition, FDR championed research into polio and other childhood afflictions and celebrated his birthday by raising money from wealthy donors at the Presidential Birthday Balls for Crippled Children.

But the man who hosted "fireside chats" over the radio realized he could reach millions of potential donors via the airwaves. In 1937, he announced creation of the National Foundation for Infantile Paralysis, and turned to Hollywood pals to help devise a nationwide pitch. At a meeting to plan the campaign, comedian and singer Eddie Cantor wisecracked, "We could call it the 'March of Dimes.'"

This was a pun based on a popular newsreel called *The March of Time*. But Cantor's quip was too catchy to ignore and by the time Roosevelt reincorporated his family charity into the NFIP on this date in 1938, the name had stuck.

"The March of Dimes will enable all persons, even the children, to show our president that they are with him in this battle against this disease," Cantor proclaimed. "Nearly everyone can send in a dime, or several dimes. However, it takes only ten dimes to make a dollar and if a million people send only one dime, the total will be $100,000."

This estimate proved conservative. By Roosevelt's birthday, 2.5 million dimes had flooded into the White House. An ailing FDR made his final March of Dimes radio appeal on January 30, 1945, his last birthday, asking First Lady Eleanor Roosevelt to read it to their fellow Americans.

"The success of the 1945 March of Dimes in the campaign against infantile paralysis does not come as a surprise to me," FDR wrote. "We are a nation of free people, and free people know how to go over the top—whether it's a Nazi wall, a Japanese island fortress, a production goal, a bond drive, or a stream of silver dimes."

By April, Franklin Roosevelt was dead, but the March of Dimes lived on. Four years later, former Roosevelt law partner Basil O'Connor used money from the fund to underwrite promising research being done by a University of Pittsburgh virologist.

His name was Jonas E. Salk.

January 4, 1896

The Saints Go Marching In

A wagon train emerges from the Utah mountains carrying 148 pilgrims, including Brigham Young, leader of the Church of Jesus Christ of Latter-day Saints. It is midsummer 1847 and the "saints" are seeking a new Zion. As he gazes on the great Salt Lake valley, Young realizes he's found it. "This is the place," he proclaims simply.

America's first home-grown religion had burgeoned since 1830, when Joseph Smith published *The Book of Mormon*, which told of a lost Hebrew text claiming that Jews had lived in the New World. The country was full of self-proclaimed prophets preaching the "Old Time Religion," but this was a new faith altogether. However odd its tenets seemed to traditional Christians, Smith's teachings attracted adherents in droves, many of them farmers from Northern Europe.

What made Mormonism a target was its approval of polygamy. Plural marriage was practiced in the Old Testament, but in nineteenth-century America it could get you killed, which was what happened to Joseph Smith and his brother at the hands of an Illinois lynch mob in 1844.

Smith's successor led the saints westward in search of a place they could live in peace. Brigham Young and his followers weren't afraid. They were biding their time until their persecutors couldn't easily overpower them.

"If the people of the United States will let us alone for ten years," Young vowed, "we will ask no odds of them."

Ten years later, when LDS church membership reached 55,000, President James Buchanan removed Young from his position as governor of the Utah Territory—Young's twenty wives were a sticking point—and ordered federal troops to march on the redoubt the Mormons called the "State of Deseret." This time the saints girded for a fight.

The shooting war envisioned by both sides never materialized, however, and in 1890 then Mormon leader Wilford Woodruff issued "The Manifesto" renouncing polygamy. This set the stage for Utah statehood, which came on this date in 1896. President Grover Cleveland signed the proclamation, and word was telegraphed to Salt Lake City. A battery of the Utah National Guard unleashed a twenty-one-gun salute, shopkeepers closed their doors, American flags were unfurled, and spontaneous celebrations erupted.

"Thank God Utah is a state after fifty years of struggle," Woodruff wrote to his son. "We have conquered."

January 5, 1643

Purify or Separate?

The Pilgrims who sailed on the *Mayflower* were followed a decade later by an armada of Puritans led by John Winthrop aboard the flagship *Arabella*.[1] Divorce was disallowed by the Church of England, but these people had sailed to America in protest against their mother country's official church. (For the difference between Pilgrims and Puritans, here's a rule of thumb: Pilgrims were *separatists* who broke away from the Church of England; Puritans wanted to *purify* the church from within—hence the name—but still felt impelled to leave England.)

Questions governing marriage inevitably arose in the colonies. The first case involved Elizabeth Luxford, who petitioned the courts in December 1639 on grounds her husband James was married to another woman when he wed her. James was fined and sent packing to England. The real precedent came on January 5, 1643,[2] when Denis Clarke abandoned his wife, Anne, and their two children to take up with another woman, with whom he also had two children. In an affidavit to John Winthrop Jr., the son of the colony's founder, Denis acknowledged what he'd done, while refusing to return to Anne, who was granted a divorce for desertion.

Although their doctrinal differences would determine New England's state borders, Pilgrims and Puritans both were Protestant sects. Martin Luther, Protestantism's founder, had written about divorce as early as 1519, two years after he sparked the Reformation. Luther's opposition to celibacy helped prompt the split with Rome, but that wasn't all he had to say about marriage. Luther counseled that marital unions existed for love and companionship, not solely procreation. This was a far-reaching idea—literally. It traveled across the ocean, touching the nonseparatist Puritans who came to believe that in marriages and politics sometimes separation *was* the answer. Luther also described marriage as a civil contract, not a sacrament, consigning it to the purview of secular, not ecclesiastic, authorities. Here was another idea with profound ramifications. The seeds containing the legal basis for gay marriage, in other words, were planted in the early sixteenth century by a German priest and carried across the ocean on ships named *Mayflower* and *Arabella*. They lay dormant for four and a half centuries, but not forever.

---

1. John Winthrop spelled the name of his flagship "Arbella," but since its name was changed (from *Eagle*) to honor Lady Arabella Johnson, Winthrop was most likely using a common contraction.
2. This is a Julian calendar date, not one reconfigured to the Gregorian calendar, but for convenience in the rest of this book, we will use dates that would have been used contemporaneously by the events' participants.

January 6, 1913

Seeking a Permit, Not Permission

The first issue of the *Women's Political World* appeared on this date. An in-house organ of the New York-based Women's Political Union, headed by Harriot Stanton Blatch, its objective was gaining the vote for women in the Empire State. The publication also kept readers apprised of the sisterhood's efforts in the rest of the country. And on this day, feminist dynamo Alice Paul made a formal request to Richard Sylvester, police chief in Washington, D.C.

Writing on the stationery of the National American Woman Suffrage Association, Ms. Paul informed Major Sylvester that she had "the honor to request that a permit be granted for a woman suffrage procession, to be held on the 3rd day of March, 1913."

She described the proposed route: from the base of the Capitol steps, down Pennsylvania Avenue, between the Treasury and Executive Mansion back to Pennsylvania Avenue and down Seventeenth Street to Continental Hall, when the procession would end in a mass meeting.

But March 3, 1913, was the day before Woodrow Wilson's inauguration as president, as Alice Paul knew only too well. So did the police chief, who cited it as a pretext for denying the permit. The women's proposed march route was the same as the traditional inauguration parade, which was the point of the entire exercise. In a letter to fellow suffragist Mary Ware Dennett, Paul termed this route women's rightful "place." A local newspaper, the *Washington Times*, took up the cause, noting in an editorial that "men's processions have always marched there."

Sylvester was forced to relent. Alice Paul's march took place and President-elect Wilson, arriving in the capital that afternoon by train, expressed surprise by the sparseness of the crowd greeting him at Union Station.

"Where are all the people?" he inquired.

Watching the women's parade, Wilson was told.

This answer was true, but incomplete. What they were really watching was the march of history. As for Sylvester, he was hauled before a congressional committee to defend his officers for standing idly by while women marchers were pestered by jeering hooligans who tore their signs and engaged in what newspapers termed "ribaldry." Two years later, he resigned under pressure. Alice Paul was just getting started.

Then All the Reindeer Loved Him

On this date, an unlikely ditty topped America's pop music charts. The cast of characters behind the song includes a Chicago ad man, a four-year-old girl, a popular wartime president, and a mythical reindeer with a physical oddity.

Christmastime during the Great Depression could be a source of stress for financially strapped parents. To counter Americans' impulse to scrimp, retailers instituted customer giveaways. At Chicago-based Montgomery Ward, this meant coloring books for kids. Then one foggy Christmas Eve (actually, autumn 1939), word went out to the marketing department: Replace the coloring books with an original Christmas story. The task of creating it fell to copywriter Robert L. May—the man with the four-year-old girl. Printed versions of the story he concocted, "Rudolph the Red-Nosed Reindeer," were given to her and 2 million other children.

Later, May's brother-in-law, professional songwriter Johnny Marks, wrote an accompanying tune. After the story was shortened to a four-verse, sixteen-line narrative, Gene Autry, Hollywood's "Singing Cowboy," was enlisted to sing it. This happened after World War II, when Americans were again receptive to happy endings. The war years had been tumultuous for Montgomery Ward's chairman, Sewell Lee Avery. A free-market champion hostile to taxes, labor unions, and the New Deal, Avery openly clashed with Franklin Roosevelt. Matters came to a head in 1944 when FDR invoked the National Recovery Act and ordered Montgomery Ward to extend lapsed union contracts or face seizure by the federal government.

Avery did not kneel to this threat, but Roosevelt wasn't bluffing. An iconic *Chicago Tribune* photograph shows Avery being carried out of his boardroom by two U.S. Army soldiers. That part of the story was well-known to Americans at the time. What is known by only a few is that Sewell Avery was no Ebenezer Scrooge. By Christmas of 1949, when "Rudolph" topped the charts, Robert May was a widowed father of a teenage daughter and facing hospital bills he couldn't pay. They'd been incurred by medical treatment of his wife's terminal illness.

The same Sewell Avery who called labor leaders and their political patrons "robbers of liberty" signed over to May the copyright to "Rudolph." He certainly wasn't obliged to do so: May was a paid employee under contract to Montgomery Ward when he wrote the song. But Avery did it, and May paid off his debts and lived off the royalties for another three decades.

January 8, 1946

A Gift to Us All

A mother in Tupelo, Mississippi, takes her only son shopping for his birthday. The kid had been lobbying for a bicycle, or maybe a rifle—memories later differed—but this much is certain: he didn't get either one. What that mother brought her son at the Tupelo Hardware Store was a guitar that retailed for $6.98.

That was the present Elvis Presley took home on his eleventh birthday.

Elvis's musical bent was evident early in life, his mother, Gladys, was always proud to report. As a toddler, he'd wiggle out of her lap in the pew at Tupelo's First Assembly of God Church to scoot down during Sunday services and position himself in front of the choir.

This was a time and place in history where a variety of distinctly American genres—bluegrass, country and western, gospel, jazz, R & B, and big band music—were all poised to collide in a way that would produce a new sound altogether. Nowhere was the confluence more creative than in the Mississippi Delta and surrounding towns and cities.

As Elvis Presley biographer Peter Guralnick would note, Elvis was born within five years and five hundred miles of James Brown, Little Richard, Carl Perkins, Jerry Lee Lewis, and Sam Cooke, all of whom helped produce the new sound: rock 'n' roll.

Sometimes all it takes to ignite a cultural revolution is a spark or two. One of them was lit on this date by a thirty-three-year-old mother who wanted to protect her son from bicycle crashes and the hazards of firearms. The guitar she bought her boy would do more than protect him. It was a present to the whole world.

January 9, 1493

Sirens

Christopher Columbus was plying the waters off what is now the Dominican Republic when he recorded in his diary that his crew had spotted something unusual in the ocean.

The famous sea captain, not someone given to flights of fancy, described "three mermaids who came quite high out of the water." The creatures he described were hardly sexy nymphs. They are not, he lamented, "as pretty as they are depicted, for somehow in the face they look like men."

The life-forms being described in Columbus's captain's log on this date were almost certainly manatees or Steller's sea cows, a slow-moving marine mammal hunted to extinction by the mid-eighteenth century. Both are *sirenians*, an aquatic order of herbivores deriving their name from the "sirens" of the sea—mermaids in the parlance of myth—whose presumed presence in the world's oceans dates at least to ancient Greek mythology.

Centuries later that fable was being put to good use in efforts to prevent manatees from going the way of their sea cow cousins. The Environmental Protection Agency, signed into law by Richard Nixon (whose birthday is also on January 9) is entrusted with saving manatees, a goal the thirty-ninth U.S. president explicitly lauded while signing the Marine Mammal Protection Act on October 28, 1972.

During Barack Obama's presidency, the EPA also approved a plan developed by Florida to protect the state's waterways from the discharge of excess nitrogen and phosphorus, which produce toxic algae blooms. These efforts are necessarily bolstered by local authorities such as Palm Beach County, which launched "Operation Mermaid" in 2016. It's a campaign to educate boaters—and ticket them, if necessary—to avoid striking and killing manatees.

One day, a posse of Palm Beach sheriff's deputies showed up in force at Riviera Beach, educational brochures—and citation books—in hand. They were joined by twenty-year-old Palm Beach State College student Trina Mason, wearing her $3,000 mermaid costume. Trina normally charges for appearances, but she did this one for free, to help her fellow sirenians.

"It's something I'm passionate about," she explained.

Gusher

Although the discovery of deposits of Texas crude coincided with the dawn of the automobile age, humans had known the stuff was in the ground there for centuries. Spanish explorers caulked their ships with oil that oozed from the ground near Sabine Pass in the 1500s. In the 1700s, settlers near present-day Nacogdoches used seeping oil to lubricate farm implements.

After the Civil War, drilling activity commenced all over Louisiana and Texas. The two men responsible for finding oil in southeastern Texas represented an improbable pairing: The first was Pattillo Higgins, a quarrelsome roughneck with a fourth-grade education and one arm—he'd lost the other in a gunfight with local sheriff's deputies—who then found Jesus and mended his ways. He partnered up with a Croatian immigrant originally named Anton Lucic who'd served in the Austrian navy, moved to America, anglicized his name to Anthony Francis Lucas, and became a mechanical engineer with a family ensconced in Washington, D.C.

One of the drilling companies operating in the Spindletop area was Higgins's outfit, the Gladys City Oil, Gas and Manufacturing Company. Several dry holes led to financing problems and a falling-out among the partners. Higgins was kicked out of his own company. When it was nothing but a shell, he returned—still convinced that oil was in the ground there, but not knowing exactly where to look. He ran ads in local magazines and mining periodicals, one of which was answered by Anthony Lucas, who'd been drilling on the Louisiana coast. One look at the geography near Beaumont convinced Lucas that this was the place.

"I was attracted by an elevation, then known locally as Big Hill, although this hill amounted merely to a mound rising only twelve feet above the level of the prairie," he wrote. "This mound attracted my attention on account of its contour, which indicated possibilities for an incipient dome below. This...suggested to me, in the light of my experience at Belle Isle, that it might prove a source of either sulphur or oil, or both."

Lucas's hunch would prove correct, but he ran out of money before his crews struck pay dirt. But Lucas had connections "back East," as the saying went, and he set out to convince them to invest. In Pittsburgh, he found willing partners who had access to Mellon money. They wanted in (provided Higgins was stripped of his 10 percent of the company), and drilling resumed. On this date, it bore results. The ensuing gusher revealed at the outset the good, the bad, and the ugly of the oil industry: The physical danger, the environmental degradation, the greed, the wealth, the thrill of discovery—it was all there at the very beginning. Lucas's crew consisted of A. W. "Al" Hamill, along with his brother Curt, and Henry McLean, and a man named Peck Byrd. The men addressed the boss as

"Captain Lucas" in deference to his naval experience, and they worked hard. Drilling had begun on October 27, 1900, and by December 9 they began to reach the oil field as they hit soft sand at a depth of 880 feet.

On this date, at more than 1,000 feet, they hit a crevice. Then things got wild. Here's the account of Al Hamill:

> We put the new bit on, and had about 700 feet of the drill pipe back in the hole when the rotary mud began flow up through the rotary table....
>
> Soon the 4-inch drill pipe started up through the derrick, knocking off the crown block and shooting through the top of the derrick and breaking off in lengths of several joints at a time as it shot skyward. After the mud, water, and pipe were blown out, gas followed, but only for a short time. Then the well was very quiet....
>
> We started shoveling the mud away—when, without warning, a lot of heavy mud shot out of the well with the report of a cannon....In a very short time oil was going up through the top of the derricks, and rocks were being shot hundreds of feet into the air. Within a very few minutes, the oil was holding a steady flow at more than twice the height of the derrick.

A man was sent to fetch "Captain Lucas," who arrived in his buggy, horses at full trot. Even this was too slow for him. Lucas leaped from his wagon, fell to the ground, picked himself up, and raced up to the men shouting in excitement.

"Al, Al, what is it?" he yelled.

"Oil, captain!" came the answer.

In reply, Lucas grabbed Hamill in a happy bear hug and exclaimed, "Thank God!"

January 11, 1908

America's Best Idea

Invoking a power delegated to the president by Congress, on this date Theodore Roosevelt designated 800,000 acres in and around the Grand Canyon as a national monument. "Let this great wonder of nature remain as it now is," Roosevelt said in words that became a battle cry for conservationists. "You cannot improve on it. But what you can do is keep it for your children, your children's children, and all who come after you, as the one great sight which every American should see."

In the 1830s, English poet William Wordsworth described Britain's mountainous Lake District as "a sort of national property, in which every man has a right and interest who has an eye to perceive and a heart to enjoy." It was in the United States that this vision was first realized. Not having royalty, Americans had no royal jewelry to display. America's physical wonders—Yellowstone, Yosemite, the Grand Canyon, and many others—formed the basis of a national park system that became known as America's "crown jewels." The first national park in the world was Yellowstone, set aside on March 1, 1872, when President Ulysses S. Grant placed the area under federal protection as "a public park or pleasuring-ground for the benefit and enjoyment of the people." In 1916, J. Horace McFarland, president of the American Civic Association, amplified on Congress's description, calling the parks national "restoring places."

"There is nothing so American as our national parks," President Franklin Roosevelt added two decades later. "The fundamental idea behind the parks...is that the country belongs to the people, that it is in process of making for the enrichment of the lives of all of us."

Yellowstone was only the beginning. Today, nearly four hundred parks, historic sites, seashores, and other entities make up the crown jewels overseen by the National Park Service. President Obama, in his last year in office, signed legislation creating Pinnacles National Park, a twenty-six-thousand-acre redoubt ninety miles southeast of San Francisco boasting majestic rock spires, hidden caverns, and soaring California condors. Pinnacles was first set aside by Theodore Roosevelt in 1908, the same year as the Grand Canyon, and has been protected ever since, although Obama made it official. Western writer Wallace Stegner, who lived most of his life in Northern California, would have approved. "National parks are the best idea we ever had," he wrote. "Absolutely American, absolutely democratic, they reflect us at our best rather than our worst."

January 12, 1969

Broadway Joe

Years before Police Commissioner William Bratton, Mayor Rudy Giuliani, and the NYPD helped make New Yorkers safe on their streets, a cocky quarterback named Joe Willie Namath gave the city its swagger back. With his unusual accent—half Beaver Falls, Pennsylvania, where he starred in every sport, and half Alabama, where he played college football under Bear Bryant—Joe Namath was an unlikely spokesman for New York City.

But he was the right guy at the right time.

On this date, his New York Jets team was representing the upstart American Football League in Super Bowl III. After the AFL champions had been routed in the first two Super Bowls by the powerhouse Green Bay Packers, the Jets were huge underdogs.

That year, the older league was again represented by National Football League royalty in the form of the Baltimore Colts. Joe Namath didn't care. In a pregame appearance at the Miami Touchdown Club, he said, "We're gonna win the game, I guarantee it."

Namath was an All-America in college at 'Bama, and had been lured to the newer league a couple of years earlier by a $400,000 contract. That's less than pro football's annual minimum salary now, but it was unheard-of money then. Namath was worth every penny, which he proved by leading the Jets to a Super Bowl victory as he'd promised. And that was only half the story. As good as he was on the football field, Namath was better off of it, setting records for, well, the indoor sports. His playboy persona and partying ways earned him the moniker "Broadway Joe," but columnist Jimmy Breslin wrote that, if anything, the nickname undersold the man.

"He comes with a Scotch in his hand at night and a football in the daytime and last season he gave New York the only lift the city has had in so many years it is hard to think of a comparison," Breslin wrote after the Jets backed up Namath's guarantee. But Breslin did come up with a comparison: Babe Ruth.

"When you live in fires and funerals and strikes and rats and crowds and people screaming in the night, sports is the only thing that makes any sense," he added. "And there is only one sport anymore that can change the tone of a city and there is only one player who can do it. His name is Joe Willie Namath and when he beat the Baltimore Colts he gave New York the kind of light, meaningless, dippy and lovely few days we had all but forgotten."

January 13, 1982

The Bridge

A snowstorm was snarling rush-hour traffic all over the Washington area, especially on the suddenly icy Fourteenth Street Bridge connecting Arlington, Virginia, and the nation's capital city between the Pentagon and Washington National Airport.

Air traffic controllers were still trying to keep things moving. Among the planes cleared for takeoff was Air Florida Flight 90, bound for Fort Lauderdale. Although pilot Larry Wheaton and first officer Roger Pettit were veterans, they had little experience flying in winter weather. After they taxied to the airport's only open runway that afternoon, they were left sitting on the tarmac for forty-nine minutes after their plane had been de-iced. They should have returned to the gate for more de-icing, an NTSB investigation found. An incoming pilot taxiing past them remarked to his crew, "Look at the junk on that airplane."

It was snowing heavily at 3:59 p.m. when the Boeing 737 took off laboriously. It was airborne only thirty seconds before crashing with a tremendous roar into the bridge. Several vehicles were swept into the icy river, along with the plane itself, which quickly sank.

Among those trapped on the bridge was a local television crew. They soon began filming what *Washington Post* reporter Ashley Halsey III described as "the horror and the heroism for which the day is remembered."

Four people trapped in cars died on that bridge. Among the seventy-nine crew members and passengers aboard Flight 90—three of whom were infants—all but five died. One valiant passenger, Arland D. Williams Jr., handed lifelines to others before slipping below the frigid water himself. A bystander on the bridge, seeing a woman struggle to hold a lifeline, dove into the freezing river to save her. His name was Lenny Skutnik.

Two weeks later, Skutnik, an office assistant in the Congressional Budget Office, found himself sitting in the House chamber as a guest of the president during the State of the Union address. Ronald Reagan had won office by running against Washington's bureaucracy, but when he paid homage in this way to an everyday American hero—one who happened to be a government bureaucrat—he began a precedent followed by every succeeding U.S. president. As for the only Air Florida passenger to die by drowning, he was immortalized in another way: Most Washingtonians don't know it, but when they cross the Fourteenth Street Bridge—as thousands do so each day—they are crossing the Arland D. Williams Jr. Memorial Bridge.

January 14, 1919

Great Pandemic

On this date, it was clear to local health officials across the country that a worldwide influenza epidemic was overwhelming them. New Orleans reported 524 new cases in a single day. In Port Jefferson, New York, the flu swept through a Catholic home for disabled children, killing six children and a nun. Nearly every community had similar horror stories.

Although called the "Spanish flu" because it spread so rapidly in Spain, the influenza epidemic of 1918–1920 probably did not start in Europe. The current theory is that it began in the United States, literally circled the globe, undergoing a catastrophic genetic shift as it did so. As if to compound mankind's sins, its spread was aided by war. As horrifying a toll as World War I took, the flu was deadlier. Worldwide, an estimated 50 million people died in the two-year pandemic, 675,000 of them were Americans—six times as many U.S. deaths as in the "Great War."

The first wave was mild, but after soldiers shipping out from Fort Riley, Kansas, took it to Europe, it mutated as it spread through the trenches. The strain that returned from Europe with them was frighteningly lethal. At Chelsea Naval Hospital overlooking Boston Harbor, Navy doctor J. J. Keegan examined returning sailors and found flu symptoms of shocking severity: it often killed its victims within hours. After three Bostonians died, Massachusetts Department of Health officials warned that "unless precautions are taken the disease in all probability will spread to the civilian population of the city."

It was too late. The deadly contagion was already racing along the Eastern Seaboard and migrating to every corner of the country. This grim pattern was repeating itself all over the globe. But science was teaching health-care professionals how to fight it. On this date in 1920, when an official of Chicago State Hospital—a person who'd had no contact with patients—contracted the flu, the entire facility was placed under quarantine. By then, the crisis had begun to wane. Was it implementing such precautions, or something else?

"If the epidemic continues its mathematical rate of acceleration," U.S. Surgeon General Victor Vaughan warned, "civilization could disappear from the face of the earth within a few weeks." But the pandemic began to ebb as fast as it had arrived. "It probably ran out of fuel," Los Angeles County public health official Dr. Shirley Fannin said eight decades later. "It ran out of people who were susceptible and could be infected."

January 15, 1870

Donkeys, Elephants, Father Christmas

The donkey as a symbol for the Democratic Party had been around sporadically since Andrew Jackson's presidency. But it was permanently etched in the nation's collective political memory with a wood engraving called "A Live Jackass Kicking a Dead Lion," which appeared on page forty-eight of *Harper's Weekly* on this date.

The depiction wasn't a compliment. The donkey (or jackass) stood for Northern Democrats known as "Copperheads." More precisely, the donkey in the drawing represented newspapers loyal to the Copperheads. The lion they were kicking was Edwin M. Stanton, the secretary of war in Abraham Lincoln's cabinet. Nonetheless, the image solidified the Democrats as donkeys. Four years later, Thomas Nast returned the compliment to the opposing political party by employing an elephant to lampoon the Grand Old Party. This *Harper's* cartoon was titled, "Third-Term Panic." Once again, the satirist's target were partisan newspapers.

The *New York Herald*, which Nast depicts as hysterically terrified over the mere possibility of a third term for President Ulysses Grant, is the donkey wearing lion's skin. "Caesarism," it cries. Although the donkey-in-a-lion's skin is transparently counterfeit, he still manages to stampede other timid animals, that is, the *New York Times* and the *New York Tribune*.

Meanwhile, a raging rogue elephant is standing over a cliff labeled "Chaos," while breaking its restraints, which are platform planks.

The elephant is "the Republican vote," which reminds us that the challenges facing the GOP in the twenty-first century are nothing new. Nast's busy cartoon was captioned, "An Ass having put on the Lion's skin, roamed about the Forest, and amused himself by frightening all the foolish Animals he met with his wanderings."

The Bavarian-born cartoonist bequeathed another famous image to the world: From 1863 through 1886, Nast drew thirty-three Christmas drawings for *Harper's Weekly,* all but one including Santa Claus. Nast's 1881 illustration became almost an official Santa portrait.

"A sketch in *Harper's Weekly* from 1858 shows a beardless Santa whose sleigh is pulled by a turkey," noted the *New York Times*. "Nast was instrumental in standardizing and nationalizing the image of a jolly, kind, and portly Santa in a red, fur-trimmed suit delivering toys from his North Pole workshop."

January 16, 1920

Prohibition

On this night, the streets of San Francisco were packed with people eager to score one last drink—or take home a stash of beer, wine, or stronger stuff. New York City, by contrast, seemed more subdued: Liquor store owners put their wares in wicker baskets on the street at going-out-of-business prices. Hotels draped their restaurant tables in black cloth.

In Norfolk, Virginia, the scene was jubilant, at least at a revival meeting featuring fiery evangelist Billy Sunday. Some ten thousand ecstatic "drys" came to hear the famous baseball player-turned-evangelist preach a mock funeral service for "John Barleycorn." A peerless showman, the Reverend Sunday arranged for a twenty-foot coffin to be brought to the doors of the church, conveyed by horses and trailed by a dejected-looking man in a devil costume.

"Good-bye, John!" Sunday shouted. "You were God's worst enemy. You were hell's best friend!"

"The reign of tears is over," Sunday added. "The slums will soon be a memory. We will turn our prisons into factories and our jails into storehouses and corncribs. Men will walk upright now, women will smile, and the children will laugh."

Prohibition was now the law of the land.

At the First Congregational Church in Washington, D.C., a service took place nearly as theatrical as Billy Sunday's performance—and with its own wildly inaccurate predictions. Congressman Andrew Volstead, the Minnesota Republican who authored the legislation that produced Prohibition, was there, along with Howard Hyde Russell, founder of the Anti-Saloon League, and Anna Gordon of the Woman's Christian Temperance Union. Former Democratic presidential candidate William Jennings Bryan delivered a Scripture-quoting sermon comparing the Eighteenth Amendment to deliverance of the baby Jesus and the death of King Herod.

"They are dead that sought the young child's life!" Bryan thundered. "They are dead!"

Secretary of the Navy Josephus Daniels took the pulpit, vowing that Prohibition was the law of the land forever. "No man living will ever see a Congress that will lessen the enforcement of that law," he proclaimed. "The saloon is as dead as slavery."

January 17, 1706

In Vino, Veritas

Benjamin Franklin was born on this date, in Boston, where his brother James became a pioneering newspaperman. Ben liked the news business but not his big brother's autocratic ways, so he made his way to Philadelphia, where he launched the *Pennsylvania Gazette* in 1729. The city already had a newspaper, but it was quickly eclipsed by Ben Franklin's innovative intruder.

The May 9, 1754, *Pennsylvania Gazette* included a Franklin-devised political cartoon, the first of its kind. As the Library of Congress points out, Franklin also initiated America's first subscription library, volunteer fire department, insurance company, public hospital, and scholarly association. He founded Pennsylvania's first college, now the University of Pennsylvania. Not to mention bifocals, the Franklin stove, and electricity. And freedom. Yes, Ben Franklin helped forge a new nation—he was probably the only editor Thomas Jefferson would have accepted as he drafted the Declaration of Independence. Americans today might remember Franklin mainly for his wit. Not a bad thing, though it's a bit much to see his folk wisdom rendered on T-shirts as "BEER IS PROOF THAT GOD LOVES US AND WANTS US TO BE HAPPY."—BENJAMIN FRANKLIN.

Is that an accurate Ben Franklin line? Not really. The actual Franklin quote is so much more eloquent, and concerns wine, not beer. In a 1779 letter to his friend André Morellet, Franklin opens with a famous observation, and takes it from there:

"In vino veritas, says the wise man—*Truth is in wine*. Before the days of Noah, then, men, having nothing but water to drink, could not discover the truth. Thus they went astray, became abominably wicked, and were justly exterminated by water, which they loved to drink....

"The good man Noah, seeing that through this pernicious beverage all his contemporaries had perished, took it in aversion; and to quench his thirst God created the vine, and revealed to him the means of converting his fruit into wine....

"We hear of the conversion of water into wine at the marriage in Cana as of a miracle. But this conversion is, through the goodness of God, made every day before our eyes. Behold the rain which descends from heaven upon our vineyards; there it enters the roots of the vines, to be changed into wine; a constant proof that God loves us, and loves to see us happy. The miracle in question was only performed to hasten the operation, under circumstances of present necessity, which required it."

January 18, 1996

Good-bye, Dolly

Seven U.S. presidents served in office in the time between when Carol Channing first took Broadway by storm with *Hello Dolly!* and when she made her final adieu to her signature role. An adaptation of Thornton Wilder's brilliant play *The Matchmaker*, the musical version featured a title number bound to be a hit. The show did not disappoint, winning ten Tony Awards.

Born in Seattle and raised in San Francisco, Channing wasn't the producers' first choice. They wanted Ethel Merman. Mary Martin declined the title role, too. Then Carol Channing came along and made Dolly Gallagher Levi part of the American identity. After out-of-town trial runs in Detroit and Washington, D.C., *Hello Dolly!* had its Broadway debut on January 16, 1964, at the St. James Theater. The show, wrote *New York Herald Tribune* critic Walter Kerr, "is a musical comedy dream, with Carol Channing the girl of it. . . . She is glorious."

It wouldn't close until December 27, 1970—2,844 performances later. It was revived in 1978 and again in October 1995, playing to sellout crowds again. It closed for the last time on this date. Did Ethel Merman and Mary Martin regret turning it down? Apparently, because they both took their turns at playing Dolly (Martin opened the London version of the show) as did Ginger Rogers, Martha Raye, Betty Grable, Phyllis Diller, Dorothy Lamour, Eve Arden, and Edie Adams. Pearl Bailey sang Dolly in an all-African-American production that featured Cab Calloway and an up-and-coming young thespian named Morgan Freeman.

Channing had become a star on the strength of her performance as Lorelei Lee in *Gentlemen Prefer Blondes* in 1949. Her father was a Seattle newspaperman and a Christian Science practitioner in San Francisco whose duties included handing out church literature. One day, her mother asked Carol if she wanted to distribute copies of the *Christian Science Monitor* in the city's thriving theater district. A little girl at the time, Carol found herself backstage at San Francisco's storied Curran Theatre.

"My mother went to put the *Monitor*s where they were supposed to go for the actors and the crew and the musicians, and she left me alone," Channing later recalled. "And I stood there and realized—I'll never forget it because it came over me so strongly—that this is a temple. This is a cathedral. It's a mosque. It's a mother church. This is for people who have gotten a glimpse of creation and all they do is re-create it. I stood there and wanted to kiss the floorboards."

Tokyo Rose

Gerald R. Ford began his presidency by pardoning Richard Nixon, an act of mercy that probably cost him his 1976 election against Jimmy Carter. Yet on the last full day in the White House, Ford issued a little-remembered presidential pardon that righted an old wrong. The recipient was a woman named Iva Toguri D'Aquino.

Known to American audiences in her day as "Tokyo Rose," she was portrayed by the government and the media as one of the most nefarious traitors in World War II. The truth was nearly the opposite. She was born on July 4, 1916, in Los Angeles. Having a loyal daughter who shared America's birthday thrilled her immigrant parents. Iva took tennis lessons, played swing music on the piano, and attended Methodist Church services. Her parents spoke English at home, so she never learned Japanese. After graduating from UCLA in 1941, she planned to go into nursing.

When an aunt in Japan took ill, Iva's family thought it would be good experience for her to travel there to care for her. Iva had no passport, but the State Department issued an emergency travel certificate. When war broke out in December, she found herself in a strange country, and without papers that would facilitate her trip home. When Iva expressed pro-U.S. sympathies, her uncle kicked her out of his house. Pressed into service as a Japanese radio deejay broadcaster—one of many nicknamed "Tokyo Rose"—she played American music along with a steady dose of propaganda designed to sap the morale of U.S. servicemen.

It did no such thing, of course, and Toguri's over-the-top and tongue-in-cheek comments signaled U.S. Navy sailors not to take the broadcasts too seriously. She also smuggled food and clothes to Western prisoners of war. Nonetheless, after the war, U.S. officials decided to make an example of her. She was brought to San Francisco and tried for treason. An all-white jury convicted her; a federal judge gave her ten years. After serving her sentence, she was deported to Japan, which had never been her home. Along the way, she lost a baby and her husband.

Eventually Toguri settled back in the United States, living anonymously in Chicago, working for her father until his death in the early 1970s. Grateful for her pardon by President Ford, Ms. Toguri expressed only one regret: that her dad had not lived to see it happen. When a sympathetic American reporter asked her about her ordeal, she cited her father's pride in her, specifically for never giving up on her country.

"You were like a tiger," he told his daughter. "You never changed your stripes, you stayed American through and through."

January 20, 1937

Happy Valley

The first president to give a January 20 inaugural address was Franklin D. Roosevelt, who was also the last president to take the oath of office on March 4. On this date, FDR spoke to an American public still in the throes of the Great Depression.

"Let us ask again," said FDR. "Have we reached the goal of our vision of that fourth day of March, 1933? Have we found our happy valley?"

Most Americans had not reached a happy place in 1937, but four years later, Roosevelt's third inaugural took place amid an even more frightening crucible: world war.

"Democracy is not dying," FDR assured his countrymen on January 20, 1941. "We know it because democracy alone, of all forms of government, enlists the full force of men's enlightened will."

John F. Kennedy's January 20, 1961, inaugural address was so remarkable that LP records were made of this speech and sold commercially. To be sure, there were some duds along the way. "I have no new dream to set forth today," Jimmy Carter proclaimed glumly at his sober inauguration. George H. W. Bush spoke of a "new breeze" blowing in the world, an allusion that proved forgettable and inaccurate. Twelve years later, though, Bush's son delivered an inaugural speech judged by prominent liberal journalist Hendrik Hertzberg as "shockingly good."

This was more than generous praise: Hertzberg had helped draft Jimmy Carter's inaugural speech. "We have a place, all of us, in a long story—a story we continue, but whose end we will not see," Bush intoned. "It is the story of a new world that became a friend and liberator of the old, a story of a slave-holding society that became a servant of freedom, the story of a power that went into the world to protect but not possess, to defend but not to conquer.

"It is the American story—a story of flawed and fallible people, united across the generations by grand and enduring ideals. The grandest of these ideals is an unfolding American promise that everyone belongs, that everyone deserves a chance, that no insignificant person was ever born."

January 21, 1957

Sweet Dreams

Decades before *America's Got Talent* and other similar shows captivated reality television fans, ubiquitous TV personality Arthur Godfrey ruled the airwaves. And on this date, Godfrey introduced Patsy Cline to the American public.

Arthur Godfrey's Talent Scouts—that was the show's formal name—had an impressive track record during its 1948–1958 run. Among the gems unearthed by the scouts were Tony Bennett, Lenny Bruce, Marilyn Horne, Rosemary Clooney, Connie Francis, Pat Boone, and Jonathan Winters.

On this night, the avuncular, red-haired Godfrey brought out on stage a twenty-five-year-old Virginian with perfect pitch and a new song she'd just recorded. Patsy Cline had been performing professionally for years by then, and had appeared on television once or twice. But if you could deliver the goods, Arthur Godfrey's stamp of approval could make you a national star overnight. And Patsy did so. Wearing a cocktail dress supplied by Godfrey's staff instead of her typical cowgirl outfits, she sang, "Walkin' After Midnight." The audience loved it.

Other hits followed in rapid succession, including "I Fall to Pieces" and "Crazy," a song kept alive by Willie Nelson for successive generations of country music fans after Patsy Cline's 1963 death in a plane crash. Two decades later, she was immortalized in *Sweet Dreams*, a film in which Jessica Lange portrays Patsy. That movie includes a nice exchange between Patsy and her future husband Charlie Dick, played by Ed Harris.

CHARLIE: Hey, I want you to get your coat. I want to drive you some place for
a drink. I want us to dance a while. Then I want us to get to know each other
a lot better.
PATSY: You want a lot, don't you?
CHARLIE: Yeah, I do, baby.
PATSY: Well, people in hell want ice water. That don't mean they get it.

January 22, 1981

All You Need Is Love

An issue of *Rolling Stone* magazine hits the newsstands featuring John Lennon and Yoko Ono on the cover. That photo, taken by the great Annie Leibovitz, answered for the last time any lingering question about the bond between the famous couple.

Leibovitz arrived at the Dakota, the apartment building west of Central Park where John Lennon and Yoko Ono lived on December 8, 1980. Although *Rolling Stone* publisher Jann Wenner "never told me what to do" on a photo shoot, Leibovitz recalled, this time he did: "Please get some pictures without her," he said.

Fortunately, that order was ignored. Yoko Ono was still considered by some rock fans as the interloper who had broken up the Beatles. John Lennon obviously never saw it that way. He'd never felt about anyone the way he felt about Yoko Ono. "It's called love," he told journalist Howard Smith. "It's a precious gift."

"I thought it was an abstract thing, you know," Lennon added. "When I was singing about 'all you need is love' I was talking about something I hadn't experienced."

A month before Leibovitz arrived at the Dakota, the couple had released *Double Fantasy*, an album that included the song "(Just Like) Starting Over" and cover art that showed the couple in a romantic kiss. Leibovitz was intrigued by it. "This was the 1980s—romance was a little dead," she recalled later. "And I was so moved by that kiss."

For her photo shoot, Leibovitz suggested that John and Yoko disrobe. "It wasn't a stretch to imagine them with their clothes off, because they did it all the time," she noted. For some reason Yoko balked. She offered to take her top off, but by then Lennon and Leibovitz had hit on another idea: John naked, Yoko fully clothed, with him cuddling up to her, as if for warmth. Leibovitz took a Polaroid of the pose, which all three people in that room immediately knew was the image they wanted.

Twelve hours later, John was dead, shot outside the Dakota by a deranged fan. Six weeks after that, on January 22, 1981, *Rolling Stone* gave grieving music fans the famous image. It was John Lennon's parting gift to us. When Annie Leibovitz had arrived that morning, John made it clear he wanted his wife in the pictures.

Pointing at Yoko, he insisted simply, "I want to be with *her*."

January 23, 1959

The Day the Music Lived

It was billed as the Winter Dance Party, which was clever, but if the promoter had been as equally creative with the buses he rented as for the band's performance schedules, it wouldn't have ended in tragedy. The star of the tour was Buddy Holly. He was joined by talented cohorts: J. P. Richardson Jr., who performed under the name "the Big Bopper"; Dion and the Belmonts; seventeen-year-old Ritchie Valens, the Mexican-American prodigy from Southern California; and band members Tommy Allsup (lead guitar), Carl Bunch (drums), and Waylon Jennings (bass guitar).

The first show happened on this date, in Milwaukee, where six thousand teenagers braved subzero temperatures to converge on George Devine's Million Dollar Ballroom. For the next ten days, the tour crisscrossed Wisconsin, Minnesota, and Iowa, without any geographical logic, on poorly heated buses that sometimes broke down. On January 27, they played the Fiesta Ballroom in the western Minnesota town of Montevideo. A local musician named Bob Bunn, who revered Buddy Holly, saw the performance and got it in mind to have his idol sign his guitar. After the show ended, Bunn drove to the Highway Cafe, where he heard the band planned to eat. Approaching the table, he found Holly friendly enough—but chilled to the bone.

"Is it always this damn cold in Minnesota?" Holly asked.

"No," Bunn quipped. "It gets a lot colder."

Buddy Holly had been contemplating chartering a small plane. But who would fly with him was the question—they couldn't all fit—and the capriciousness of the answer would haunt the band members' families for years.

After their wildly well-received show in Clear Lake, Iowa, Holly found a pilot with a four-seat Beechcraft B35 Bonanza who said he could take them to Fargo, North Dakota, that night. Holly chose Waylon Jennings and Tommy Allsup to ride with him, but neither ended up making the trip. Jennings graciously gave his seat to J. P. Richardson because the Bopper was coming down with the flu. When beseeched by Ritchie Valens, who didn't even own a winter coat, Allsup agreed to flip a coin for the last seat on the doomed airplane. Ritchie won.

Fargo's airport was closed because of a blizzard, but twenty-one-year-old pilot Roger Peterson didn't know that. It would cost $108 for the trip, Peterson told Holly, who agreed instantly. "He was," Tommy Allsup recalled later, "determined to fly."

January 24, 1848

Eureka!

The men at Sutter's Creek east of Sacramento were not even mining when they found gold. They were constructing a sawmill. Yet, New Jersey–born James Wilson Marshall had spent enough time in the Sierra Nevada foothills to know the soil, rocks, and streams of that region—and he had an inkling something was about to happen.

The day before, Marshall had confided in one of the young men from the famed "Mormon Battalion" who had marched from Utah to California, and been hired to build the mill. His name was James Stephens Brown. A recent convert to the LDS faith, Brown would live to see the twentieth century. On this day, though, he was still a teenager who'd seen a lot of country, but not much gold.

"Mr. Marshall called me to come to him," Brown later wrote in his memoirs. "I went, and found him examining the bedrock. He said, 'This is a curious rock, I am afraid that it will give us trouble,' and as he probed it a little further, he said, 'I believe that it contains minerals of some kind, and I believe that there is gold in these hills.'"

Yes, James Marshall said those words: *gold in these hills*. At the time, it wasn't a laugh line, although the next morning Brown and the other men joked that Marshall—who awoke earlier than usual—had gone out to find his gold mine. That was exactly what he had done.

Carrying his old wool hat in his hand, Marshall approached the men and showed them what it contained: a dozen or so pieces of gold nuggets.

"Boys," he exclaimed, "I have got her now!"

The men were sworn to secrecy, but it was not a secret they kept. Marshall and his men weren't even successful in retaining their claims over their own creek bed. Sam Brannan, a Mormon businessman who visited the mill, started the stampede by literally running through the streets of San Francisco shouting "Gold from the American River!"

Back East, these reports were dismissed as the product of overactive imaginations by California's civic boosters. All that changed in December when President James K. Polk noted in his State of the Union address that "explorations already made warrant the belief that the supply is very large and that gold is found at various places in an extensive district of country."

The Gold Rush was on.

January 25, 1890

Around the World in 72 Days

Police held back the crowds pushing past rope lines to glimpse the daring celebrity who'd returned to New York City ten weeks after setting sail east from New York across the Atlantic Ocean. The heroine's name was Nellie Bly, and for a shining moment she was perhaps the most famous woman in the world.

Born Elizabeth Cochrane in Pennsylvania in the waning days of the Civil War, Bly first made her name as an investigative reporter who exposed conditions of cruelty toward the poor, the mentally ill, and the downtrodden. Gutsy and photogenic, she also possessed a gift for self-promotion that would do the Kardashians proud. Seeking to capitalize on the popularity of Jules Verne's popular 1873 novel *Around the World in 80 Days*, Nellie Bly proposed to her editors at the *New York World* a great publicity stunt: Send her on a quest to beat the record of Verne's fictional Phileas T. Fogg.

The editors went for it, and the race was announced. *Cosmopolitan* promptly declared it was dispatching one of its star correspondents, Elizabeth Bisland, around the world on the same day, November 14, 1889. The chase was on. But breaking Jules Verne's mythical record was Nellie Bly's idea, and she had no intention of losing to another woman—or anyone else.

"I would rather," she said, "go back to New York dead than not a winner."

So to her, it was a real race, conducted with the fastest conveyances of the day: steamships, trains, horses, burros, sampans, and even rickshaws—all of it documented for the rapidly rising readership of the *New York World*. Bly certainly understood the ultimate goal was to sell newspapers, but she wasn't entirely unsentimental. In China, she visited a leper colony, which evoked her roots as a crusading reporter. In Singapore, she bought a monkey because, well, because she was Nellie Bly. One of the most touching moments on her journey came when she detoured in Paris to lunch with Jules Verne and his wife, both of whom were charmed by their young American guest.

After steaming across the Pacific Ocean (days ahead of the *Cosmo* reporter, whom she would beat by four days), Bly alit in San Francisco. Leaving nothing to chance, the *World* chartered a train for her. Bly arrived in New York exactly seventy-two days, six hours, and eleven minutes after leaving.

January 26, 1980

Missing Moscow

The Cold War still dominated global politics during Jimmy Carter's presidency, even when it came to international athletics. On this date, the U.S. Olympic Committee, adhering to Carter's request, asked the International Olympic Committee to cancel that year's Olympic Games—or move them from Moscow.

The U.S. gambit, which the IOC ignored, came in protest of the Soviet Union's invasion of Afghanistan the month before. Fifty-five nations joined the Americans' subsequent boycott of the 1980 Summer Games, and in retaliation, the Soviets and their allies boycotted the 1984 Olympics in Los Angeles.

The Afghanistan invasion did not turn out well for anyone. It's difficult to overstate its failure and pivotal point as a world event: It was one of the precipitating events in the collapse of the Soviet Union, and it prompted the CIA to prop up the mujahedeen forces in Afghanistan. Those rebels welcomed into their ranks many so-called Afghan Arabs, among them a Saudi engineer named Osama bin Laden.

Although it's minor by comparison, the 1980 U.S. boycott also had harmful effects on athletes who had no hand in politics. Among those who had trained most of their lives for the Summer Games only to be forced to stay home were two American distance runners in their midtwenties, Craig Virgin and Tony Sandoval. Both men were at the top of their game that year and 1980 was their chance for an Olympic medal. Virgin was the world record holder in the 10,000-meter, and the best American distance runner since the great Steve Prefontaine. Sandoval, a marathoner, had set a U.S. Olympic trials record of 2:10:19 that spring while the American athletes were hoping for a reprieve, which did not come.

For those runners, and a thousand others, their heyday had passed by the time of the 1984 Games. Sandoval failed to make the team for Los Angeles; Virgin did qualify, but was eliminated in the preliminaries.

For one U.S. track star, however, the Moscow boycott was merely a minor speed bump on the road to immortality. His name was Carl Lewis.

Gut Punch to a President

Lyndon B. Johnson was presiding over a signing ceremony in the East Room when news reached the White House. LBJ had succeeded in negotiating a pact with Great Britain and the Soviet Union that would ban nuclear weapons from outer space. "This treaty means that our moon and sister planets will serve only the purposes of peace and not of war," President Johnson said. "It means that astronaut and cosmonaut will meet someday on the surface of the moon as brothers and not as warriors for competing nationalities or ideologies."

LBJ told his wife, Lady Bird, that he considered it one of the signature achievements of his presidency. Meanwhile, down at Florida's Cape Canaveral, the crew of Apollo 1—Virgil "Gus" Grissom, Edward H. White II, and Roger B. Chaffee—were going through their launch pad safety checks.

John F. Kennedy had warned that there might be days like this. In explaining why human beings should pursue the expensive and daunting challenge of space exploration when there were so many problems on Earth, President Kennedy recalled the simple logic of famed British explorer George Mallory. Asked why he wanted to climb Mount Everest, Mallory replied, "Because it is there." Invoking Mallory was more than a rhetorical flourish. The climber had died on Everest, which Kennedy noted in his speech. Now, less than three and a half years later, JFK was buried in Arlington, Cape Canaveral had been renamed Cape Kennedy, and the space program was proceeding apace under President Johnson.

After the nonproliferation signing ceremony, LBJ was in the White House family quarters when an aide handed him a note: "The first Apollo crew was under test at Cape Kennedy and a fire broke out in the capsule and all three were killed," it stated. "Grissom, White, and Chaffee." Gus Grissom, who had nearly drowned in a Mercury spaceflight splashdown, was especially cognizant of the dangers of his chosen profession. Like Kennedy, he had warned his countrymen of the peril. "We're in a risky business and we hope that if anything happens to us, it will not delay the program," Grissom had said. "The conquest of space is worth the risk of life."

Brave words, but they were of scant consolation that night to Lyndon Baines Johnson. "The shock," he recalled later, "hit me like a physical blow."

January 28, 1986
Touching the Face of God

Two decades after Lyndon Johnson absorbed the news from Cape Kennedy, Ronald Reagan was hit with a similar gut-punch. By then, the job description of the presidency had expanded to include the duty of mourner in chief. Reagan's challenge was complicated by the presence aboard the doomed space shuttle *Challenger* of a civilian, a beloved New Hampshire social studies teacher named Sharon Christa McAuliffe, whose mantra to her students was, fittingly, "Reach for the stars."

Unaffected and likable, she'd beat out eleven thousand other applicants who had vied to become the first schoolteacher in space. The ceremony to announce the winner—all ten finalists were present—was broadcast live from the White House.

"We had this cute little curly-headed teacher in that blue astronaut outfit, and we had dragged in every kid in America to write her letters before the launch, so it was like Christmas Eve," recalled Sally Karioth, a Florida State professor who studies grief counseling. "Then it blows up in the sky—and that's the Grinch."

On this date, which was also supposed to be the date of the president's State of the Union Address, House Speaker Thomas P. "Tip" O'Neill Jr. decided the Grinch in Washington was Reagan. O'Neill had emerged from an Oval Office meeting fuming over what he considered Reagan's lack of sympathy for the unemployed. But then the unthinkable happened, and the two men joined forces. O'Neill agreed to postpone the State of the Union while Reagan's speechwriters drafted an alternate address. It is considered one of the rhetorical highlights of Reagan's presidency.

"The future doesn't belong to the faint-hearted, it belongs to the brave," Reagan told his fellow Americans. "The *Challenger* crew was pulling us into the future, and we'll continue to follow them."

He ended his 648-word homily by borrowing a passage from a World War II–era sonnet: "We will never forget them, nor the last time we saw them, this morning, as they prepared for their journey and waved good-bye and slipped the surly bonds of earth to touch the face of God."

Tip O'Neill would later write that he had seen the worst of President Reagan, and the best, in just a few hours' time. "It was a trying day for all Americans," O'Neill wrote, "and Ronald Reagan spoke to our highest ideals."

W. C. Fields

William Claude Dukenfield (you can see why he changed his name) was born on this date in a working-class borough five miles southwest of Philadelphia. His parents appear to have been normal people, but their son was a restless lad. He ran away constantly, taught himself to juggle, dropped out of school young, and was off to vaudeville by the time he was eighteen.

His career as a juggler took off when Fields discovered that what animated his audiences were snarky asides that made them laugh. He occupied a niche as a comedic juggler, but what he craved was to be considered a serious comedian, an oxymoron that would have delighted Fields's sense of the absurd. With the help of a new medium, motion pictures, Fields honed his comedic genius into an archetype: the pompous, hard-drinking misanthrope.

"I am free of all prejudice," he'd deadpan in his famous drone. "I hate everyone equally."

The drinking part was real enough, though. Booze helped kill "Uncle Claude," as his friends called him, at sixty-six. The misanthrope bit was more nuanced. The infamous quip often attributed to Fields ("Any man who hates dogs and babies can't be all bad") was actually said in jest *about* Fields by humorist Leo Rosten at a 1939 roast.

In real life, Fields owned dogs and doted on his friends' children. Fields biographer James Curtis also said that he answered all the fan letters sent by kids, and was invariably encouraging to boys who wrote about their interest in juggling.

W. C. Fields's politics were also hard to pin down. He poked merciless fun at blue noses, censors, and busybodies. He despised the "social conservatives" of his day, which is to say anti-alcohol activists. Yet he bristled at political correctness and "nanny-state" types, which would have made him a pariah on today's excessively sensitive college campuses. Most of all, Fields detested high taxes, and occasionally needled New Deal excess in his films, which took gumption at the height of Franklin Roosevelt's popularity.

In 1940, he went so far as to announce his own whimsical presidential campaign, one built around a slogan that combined actual U.S. campaign history with one of his best-known films: "A Chickadee in Every Pot."

January 30, 1933

"Hi-Yo, Silver! Away!"

As Americans awaited Franklin Roosevelt's inauguration while the banking situation in the country deteriorated, radio listeners in Michigan were treated to the debut of a new serial, *The Lone Ranger*. The drama was the brainchild of George Washington Trendle, owner of Detroit radio station WXYZ, and writer Fran Striker.

An instant hit, *The Lone Ranger* was syndicated nationally by the Mutual Radio Network. By 1939 it was being broadcast three times a week to 20 million Americans. In 1949, it made the jump to television, starring Clayton Moore, with Jay Silverheels as his sidekick, Tonto. In both mediums, the hero would appear to the stirring strains of the William Tell Overture and his signature shout-out, "Hi-yo, Silver! Away!"

Loyal listeners knew that their hero wore a mask to protect his identity from the gang that ambushed him. They also knew the Lone Ranger did not use alcohol or tobacco, refrained from coarse language, and never shot to kill. About Tonto, less was known. Radio audiences were told he belonged to the Potawatomi tribe, although television viewers later assumed from his garb that he was Apache. The scout was astute, brave, and loyal, but what is remembered about him today is his much-parodied pigeon English.

Some of this was to be expected. Neither Trendle nor Striker had real-life associations with cowboys or Indians, and the exigencies of radio required someone the hero could talk to. Television didn't fundamentally alter that dynamic, but on-screen Tonto and the Lone Ranger also needed to be physically impressive. In casting Clayton Moore and Jay Silverheels, the show's producers got what they wanted. Silverheels was neither Potawatomi nor Apache. He was a Canadian-born Mohawk who starred in lacrosse and wrestling—competing under his birth name, Harold Smith—and had boxed as a middleweight. Clayton Moore performed as an acrobat as a young man and was a gifted horseman. But what really made the show work was the actor's total embrace of the role. It's not too much to say that Clayton Moore *became* the Lone Ranger.

After the series was canceled in 1957, Moore kept in character, donning his mask, hat, and frontier attire for everything from shopping mall openings to Western rodeos. In 1979, the corporation that had bought the rights to the Lone Ranger—a new movie was in the works—secured a legal injunction forbidding Moore from appearing as the masked man. They might as well have tried to get water to flow uphill. Moore took to wearing wraparound sunglasses in place of a mask, but that was his only concession. After the movie flopped, the producers relented, and at age seventy, the Lone Ranger rode again.

"This country needs heroes, and there aren't many left," Moore said while explaining his reluctance to abandon the role. "For many Americans, the Lone Ranger is a hero, and people don't want to see their heroes shot down."

January 31, 1848

Pathfinder

On this date, John C. Frémont, the military governor of California, was court-martialed after losing a power struggle to Army general Stephen Kearny. It seemed that the meteoric rise of Frémont—a man dubbed "the Great Pathfinder" by the popular press—was over. But it wasn't. Captain Frémont had one more trail to blaze for his country.

John C. Frémont was always on the move. A noted explorer and mapmaker, he solidified his colorful sobriquet as a pathfinder when, as the leader of the famed California Brigade, he led his troops through the Santa Ynez Mountains on Christmas Eve, 1846, and surprised the Spanish garrison at Santa Barbara. Frémont's trip to California had the personal blessing of President James K. Polk, whom he visited at the White House before heading out West. Once there, he clashed with General Kearny, who court-martialed him. Polk, whose own conflicting orders had caused the problem, upheld the verdict against Frémont, but commuted his sentence to a dishonorable discharge.

In the end, the controversy only propelled Frémont's career. He settled with his wife on a ranch in California, got rich in the Gold Rush, and became one of California's first U.S. senators. By then, he'd embraced the cause of abolition, which made him a pariah in the Democratic Party. He served in Washington less than a year, and by the mid-1850s, was in the vanguard of a new political movement: He was the Republican Party's first presidential nominee. John Frémont didn't win the presidency. History would reserve that honor four years later for a man who truly had the temperament for it.

Nonetheless, the Republicans' 1856 platform set the stage for Abraham Lincoln, and its campaign slogan was one of the most memorable in history: "Free soil, free men, and Frémont!"

Sitting In

Franklin McCain, Ezell Blair Jr., Joseph McNeil, and David Richmond each took a seat at the diner in the Woolworth's store in Greensboro, North Carolina. African-Americans could shop at Woolworth's, but the diner was known to be "whites only."

The young men, soon to be immortalized as the "Greensboro Four," were freshmen at North Carolina A&T, a historically black college. While returning from his family's home in New York after the Christmas break, Joseph McNeil had received a reminder of the world he inhabited: He'd been denied food service at Greensboro's Greyhound bus depot. By way of response, McNeil and his three friends entered Woolworth's at 4:30 p.m., and politely ordered a cup of coffee. They were refused service and told to leave.

They returned to campus that evening and told their story, electrifying their fellow students. The next day they returned—with twenty-five others. By Wednesday, sixty students, some from nearby Bennett College and a local high school, took every available seat. Responding to media inquiries, Woolworth's issued a statement saying company policy was "to abide by local custom." On Thursday, the number of protesters had swelled to three hundred. By the end of March, lunch counter sit-ins had spread to fifty-five cities in every state in the old Confederacy.

Years later, Franklin McCain explained how he knew from the start that they were making history. On the sit-in's first day, a female patron sat at the counter, a few stools away from the four students. Described by McCain as "a little old white lady," she eyed the protesters silently. After finishing her doughnut and coffee, she paid her bill and started to leave. McCain briefly let his imagination run wild: Was she hiding knitting needles and scissors in her purse? Were they about to be stabbed in the neck as she walked behind them? Instead, she stopped and put her hands gently on McCain's and McNeil's shoulders.

"Boys, I am so proud of you," she said. "I only regret that you didn't do this ten years ago." Well, ten years earlier, they were small boys, but McCain appreciated her support.

"What I learned from that little incident was, don't you ever, ever stereotype anybody in this life until you at least experience them and have the opportunity to talk to them," he explained years later. "I'm always open to people who speak differently, who look differently, and who come from different places."

Groundhog's Day

It's an odd little custom imported to this country from Germany in the nineteenth century and seized upon by small-town burghers for the dual purposes of civic pride and tourism. The largest celebration is in Punxsutawney, Pennsylvania, where a groundhog named Punxsutawney Phil emerges from his tree-trunk cage on this day each year.

For a generation of modern Americans, their frame of reference for this quaint tradition is the 1993 film *Groundhog Day,* starring Bill Murray and Andie MacDowell. Murray plays the role of Pittsburgh television station weatherman Phil Connors. MacDowell is Rita, his TV producer. Murray is a jerk. Rita is as sweet as she can be. The karma of this juxtaposition propels the plot, which revolves around Bill Murray reliving Groundhog Day over and over.

Some people—serious film critics, mind you—consider *Groundhog Day* one of the great theological masterpieces in the Hollywood canon. A wonderful exploration of that idea can be found in Jonah Goldberg's *National Review* essay, a minor classic published each Groundhog's Day. "He is a thoroughly postmodern man," notes Goldberg, "arrogant, world-weary, and contemptuous without cause." When Rita reminds Phil that people love the annual groundhog rite, he's unmoved. "People are morons," he sneers. So, the question arises: Was Phil Connors Donald Trump in 2016? Or maybe that was the role of the elites who scoffed at Trump.

Either way, an interesting thing happens to Bill Murray's character as he reexperiences the same day endlessly. He eventually becomes *less* jaded, not more. That doesn't often happen with presidential candidates. Yet, when Trump, a man who famously hates "losers," came in second in the Iowa caucuses to launch the primary season, his reaction was surprising.

"Iowa, we love you!" Trump exclaimed enthusiastically. "You're special. I think I might come here and buy a farm."

Not as heartwarming as falling in love with Andie MacDowell, for sure. Yet the idea of buying a local place was straight out of the ending to *Groundhog Day.* As the star-kissed couple embraces and Bill Murray gazes around the bucolic little town that is no longer his personal purgatory, he declares, "Let's live here!"

As the closing music builds and just before the credits roll, however, Murray adds the movie's last line: "We'll rent to start."

February 3, 1931

Southern Belle to the Rescue

Baltimore Sun columnist H. L. Mencken was another misanthrope who liberally applied the word *moron* to his fellow citizens. "Nature abhors a moron," Mencken often quipped, and in 1931 he'd offended nearly all of Arkansas by anointing it "the apex of moronia." In response, the state legislature passed a motion on this date urging lawmakers to pray for Mencken's soul.

Southerners and people of faith weren't the only objects of H. L. Mencken's caustic wit. He pronounced Christian Science an oxymoron, denounced chiropractic medicine as quackery, and routinely characterized politicians as dim bulbs and thieves. Although Hollywood would make him an iconic figure in *Inherit the Wind* (Mencken's character was played by Gene Kelly), the columnist spent a summer in Southern California, and was unimpressed.

The movies "need a Shakespeare," he groused, not that they'd recognize the bard if he appeared in their midst. "If he is in Hollywood today, he is probably bootlegging, running a pants pressing parlor, or grinding a camera crank," Mencken wrote.

What softened Henry Louis Mencken, eventually, was love. In his case Eros turned out to be a Southern beauty. In the 1920s, the man dubbed "America's Best-Known Bachelor" met a teacher from Goucher College named Sara Haardt. She was a writer, too, eighteen years Mencken's junior, who hailed from Alabama. Their marriage made headlines, in part because the Bard of Baltimore had previously pronounced the institution of matrimony "the end of hope."

Having mocked contemporaries who'd taken the plunge, Mencken found himself on the receiving end of the barbs. "Bachelors of the nation are aghast," wrote one columnist, "like a sheep without a leader."

Mencken's explanation? "The Holy Spirit informed and inspired me," he proclaimed. "Like all other infidels, I am superstitious and always follow hunches: this one seemed to be a superb one."

Had those prayers that emanated from the state capitol in Little Rock performed a miracle? If so, H. L. Mencken's bliss was short-lived. Sara succumbed to tuberculosis at thirty-seven, just five years after marrying. The man she left behind would outlive her for twenty-one heartbroken years.

February 4, 1941

The Great Hope

On this day, the United Service Organizations came to life. The idea, which was to create social clubs catering to those in uniform, was Franklin Roosevelt's. It was launched just in time. Less than a year later, the United States was plunged into world war, and some three thousand existing recreational clubs and organizations—supplemented by 1 million civilian volunteers—organized USO clubs and functions for the nation's military personnel.

Among those who answered their nation's call were movie stars, entertainers, athletes, politicians, and other celebrities who performed at USO functions around the world. But one performer separated himself from the crowd. "Where there's death, there's Hope," he would quip at the start of his shows. And on cue, the soldiers, sailors, Marines, and airmen stationed from Da Nang to Berlin would forget war for an hour and start to laugh, which was the whole idea.

He was born in England, and named Leslie Hope, but came to Ohio as a boy. He got a laugh out of other kids by introducing himself, British style, as "Hope, Leslie," knowing they'd make it into "Hopelessly," and, soon enough, "Hopeless." It was his own joke, but he tired of it and as a vaudevillian renamed himself "Lester" Hope, and ultimately, simply Bob, as he sang, danced, and acted his way into Americans' hearts until he died at one hundred years of age. He never won an Academy Award, although he hosted the Oscars and his pictures did well enough at the box office. His iconic song, "Thanks for the Memory," still evokes that crooked smile and ski-jump nose that Hope used as a sight gag in his comedy. Mostly, we remember his running patter.

"Have you heard about President Kennedy's new youth Peace Corps to help foreign countries?" he'd say. "It's sort of *Exodus* with fraternity pins."

When Dwight Eisenhower was in the White, Hope joked, "I played golf with him yesterday. It's hard to beat a guy who rattles his medals while you're putting. Ike uses a short Democrat for a tee."

Hope himself identified with the GOP, but he teased them all, Republicans or Democrats. He really did golf with them, and he considered some of them friends. He supported Thomas Dewey in 1948, but when Harry Truman surprised nearly everyone by winning reelection, Bob Hope sent him a one-word telegram, "UNPACK."

Truman cherished it.

They Liked It Hot

On this day, three extraordinary women had lunch together. Writer Carson McCullers was the hostess. The guests of honor were Marilyn Monroe, who had recently completed filming of *Some Like It Hot*, and Baroness Karen Blixen, better known by her pen name, Isak Dinesen.

The idea of the lunch party was so that the seventy-three-year-old Blixen could meet the thirty-two-year-old Monroe. No one was disappointed.

The lunch shared by the three female powerhouses came about more or less spontaneously at the annual dinner of the American Academy of Arts and Letters. Blixen was the keynote speaker that year. McCullers, the Georgia-born author of *The Heart Is a Lonely Hunter* and other acclaimed novels and short stories, was a dedicated devotee. About to turn forty-two, McCullers had read Blixen's *Out of Africa* every year for two decades. She explained later that she considered Blixen something of an "imaginary friend," a woman who was always present "in her stillness, her serenity, and her great wisdom to comfort me."

So, at the Arts and Letters dinner, McCullers had arranged to be seated beside Blixen.

At one point in the dinner, Marilyn Monroe's name came up. Blixen said she'd like to meet the young movie star. Monroe wasn't in attendance that night, but her husband, playwright Arthur Miller, was present, seated at a table not far away. McCullers called him over, filled him in, and the lunch was soon scheduled at McCullers's New York home.

The three women, none of whom had very long to live, hit it off famously. Marilyn, accompanied by Miller, arrived late, of course, but no one minded. The movie star told a disarming story of finishing off noodles for a dinner party with a hair dryer. The three women danced on the table, McCullers later wrote. Maybe that happened, maybe it didn't. But there's no reason to doubt McCullers's characterization of the lunch as the best party she'd ever hosted. For her part, Karen Blixen was charmed by Monroe, whom she described as "almost incredibly pretty," with "unbounded vitality" and "unbelievable innocence."

"I have met the same in a lion cub that my native servants brought me in Africa," Blixen added in a prescient warning for Arthur Miller. "I would not keep her."

February 6, 1911

A Communicator Is Born

On this day Nelle and Jack Reagan of Tampico, Illinois, welcomed their second son into the world. They named him Ronald, although as he grew they called the boy Dutch.

As a radio announcer, Dutch Reagan became a familiar handle to listeners in the Midwest. In Hollywood, he was allowed to keep his real name by Warner Bros., the studio that signed him, after a comical conversation around a table that amused the future star. As a stateside military officer in World War II—he was deemed unsuitable for combat due to poor eyesight—he was "Captain Reagan" by the end of the war.

His pals called him Ron, his second wife, Nancy, called him Ronnie, and a generation of Californians in the 1960s and 1970s knew him as Governor Reagan. (Jack Warner, upon hearing of Reagan's intention to run for governor, is reputed to have quipped, "No! Jimmy Stewart for governor, Ronald Reagan for best friend.") To this day, many Reaganites fondly call him "the Gipper," after his memorable film portrayal of doomed Notre Dame football star George Gipp. Democrats uninspired by his presidency called him other names, some of which, in the old city room phrase, are unsuitable for a family newspaper.

In his farewell address as president, Ronald Wilson Reagan took note of another appellation he acquired along the way. In discussing it in that January 11, 1989, speech Reagan revealed one of the unsung traits of effective communicators: humility.

"In all of that time," Reagan said after briefly recounting the journey of the previous eight years, "I won a nickname, 'the Great Communicator.' But I never thought it was my style or the words I used that made a difference. It was the content."

"I wasn't a great communicator," Reagan continued, "but I communicated great things, and they didn't spring full bloom from my brow, they came from the heart of a great nation—from our experience, our wisdom, and our belief in the principles that have guided us for two centuries. They called it the 'Reagan Revolution.' Well, I'll accept that, but for me it always seemed more like the great rediscovery, a rediscovery of our values and our common sense."

With that, he left the place he called "the Puzzle Palace on the Potomac," returning with Nancy Reagan to California, the place that had given rise to his dreams.

Imagine All the People

Pan Am's Yankee Clipper flight 101 landed in New York. It was a daily route from Heathrow Airport, but the ground crew at John F. Kennedy International Airport never had an arrival like this one. Six weeks earlier, Capitol Records had released "I Want to Hold Your Hand," a hit that topped the charts instantly—and brought three thousand shrieking fans, most of them teenage girls, to mob the terminal when the Beatles stepped off the plane.

Not able to actually hold hands with any of the Fab Four, the giddy female fans contented themselves with screaming hysterically. Beatlemania had announced itself.

The Beatles were the vanguard of the so-called British Invasion, but it was more accurately described as a reimportation than an invasion. The Beatles and other U.K.-based rock groups, including the Rolling Stones, were always quite open about who their musical influences had been: Elvis Presley, Jerry Lee Lewis, Carl Perkins, along with Chuck Berry, Bo Diddley, T-Bone Walker, and a host of other African-American rhythm and blues players.

Although in the post–Beatles phase of his career John Lennon was known for poignant ballads like "Imagine" and "Woman," as a young musician he quipped: "If you tried to give rock 'n' roll another name, you might call it 'Chuck Berry.'"

Keith Richards has explained that when he first heard Muddy Waters, he found it to be "the most powerful music...and the most expressive" he'd ever heard. The Stones took their name from the title of a Muddy Waters song.

What's the moral of such stories? Perhaps it's that transcontinental cross-pollination often works this way in the arts, and in politics and business, too. In Detroit, Ford Motor Company pioneered mass production of automobiles. Many years later, the Japanese perfected it, in part by incorporating the theories of brilliant American management guru W. Edwards Deming, the intellectual father of what has been described as "the quality revolution."

Today, excellent cars are built in factories all over the world, including Korea, while Nissan builds pickup trucks in Tennessee. Meanwhile, as Eminem and Clint Eastwood reminded us in Super Bowl ad campaigns in successive years, Detroit was getting its act together again. The point here is that global competition, much maligned in the politics of the twenty-first century, also entails transnational creativity—and worldwide sharing. Imagine that.

February 8, 1924

"They Should Get It Over With"

Nevada employed a new method of executing prisoners on this date. It was called cyanide gas. The first condemned prisoner to die this way was Gee Jon, a Chinese-born gang member from San Francisco who shot an elderly member of a rival tong just across the Nevada state line.

This method of killing, originally considered a reform, was adopted by neighboring California as well. In the ensuing five decades, thirty-one more men would go to the Carson City prison gas chamber. The last was Jesse Walter Bishop in 1979.

Bishop earned a Purple Heart as a paratrooper in Korea where he also picked up a heroin habit and a dishonorable discharge, after which he embarked on a life of robbery and drug dealing. At forty-four, he committed a crime for which there would be no reprieve. On December 29, 1977, he strode up to a female teller at the old El Morocco on the Las Vegas strip, told her he had a gun, and demanded money. She screamed, a casino pit boss drew his revolver. David Ballard, a twenty-two-year-old bystander from Baltimore honeymooning in Vegas, came running. Bishop whirled and fatally shot the unarmed newlywed.

Apprehended and tried, Bishop was swiftly sentenced to death. He was hoping for a life sentence, but when the judge pronounced death, Bishop chose not to appeal and he forbade his court-appointed lawyers from prolonging the case. His view was that it was sophistry to claim the death penalty constituted "cruel and unusual punishment"— because capital punishment was considered neither cruel nor unusual at the time the Bill of Rights was adopted. In Bishop's telling, what violated a defendant's Eighth Amendment rights were the interminable delays and false starts and last-minute stays for Death Row inmates. "I never asked for the death penalty," he told me. "They gave it to me. I'm only asking that they either give it to me or commute it."

He believed the system wanted him to beg for his life, which he refused to do. "Now they got me dead bang on a cold murder beef I can't beat," he added. "I'm not going to turn to God, or to snivelin' or snitchin' or rattin.' They got their gas chamber…they should get it over with."

Bishop got his wish on October 22, 1979. True to his word, he went to the gas chamber stoically. Although one of the fourteen witnesses slumped to one knee as the cyanide pellets were dropped into an acid bath, releasing the deadly fumes, Jesse Walter Bishop merely made a thumbs-down sign, took a few deep breaths, and was gone.

February 9, 1952

The Start of Something Big

The quadrennial madness known as the New Hampshire primary started on this date, when Estes Kefauver, a freshman senator from Tennessee, went north to make his case why he should be the Democrats' presidential nominee. New Hampshire's legislature had enacted election reforms in 1913 setting up a primary, but direct voting didn't take place until 1952 when Republican Robert Taft campaigned hard there but was defeated by Gen. Dwight Eisenhower. "Ike," as he was known by an adoring public, hadn't set foot in New Hampshire, but voters figured he had a good excuse: Eisenhower was still stationed in Europe.

When Kefauver spoke in Nashua's Elm Street Junior High School auditorium he blazed a trail still being followed. Among the forgettable lines quoted in the next day's *Nashua Telegraph* were Kefauver speaking of a "parallel between the code of the domestic criminal and the social philosophy of the totalitarian state." The Tennessean did better when he talked to voters one-on-one. It's a style now associated with New Hampshire, but it was a longtime staple of Southern politics and Kefauver imported the folksy charm he'd honed in local campaigns in Chattanooga.

Traversing New England's wintry environs, Kefauver sported a coonskin cap while riding around in a borrowed Chevrolet—or a rented snowmobile—and at least once, on a borrowed dogsled. An imposing six foot three inches, Kefauver would approach strangers and thrust out his large right mitt. "Hello, I'm Estes Kefauver and I'm running for president," he'd say. "I'd appreciate your vote."

All this effort paid off when Kefauver won the March 11, 1952, primary over Harry Truman, the only prominent name on the Democratic ballot. When Truman decided to forego another term, the party establishment gravitated to Adlai Stevenson, even though Stevenson lost most of the primaries to Kefauver. Party stalwarts portrayed the eventual ascension of the cerebral Stevenson as a victory of brains over brawn, but this was unfair. Kefauver was a former math teacher who went to Yale Law School, and was a Southern liberal on race relations when such a stance required foresight as well as courage.

Kefauver ran for president again in 1956, crushing Stevenson in New Hampshire's primary. Party bosses nominated Stevenson over Kefauver again, anyway. Judging by how badly Stevenson lost to Eisenhower in both 1952 and 1956, perhaps the Democrats should have heeded the voters of New Hampshire.

February 10, 1899

Meeting of the Minds

Two Stanford University graduates who'd majored in geology were married on this date in Monterey, California. The bride was Lou Henry, a natural athlete, avid outdoorswoman, and an academic star who spoke several languages fluently and whose deep religious faith translated into a lifetime of helping the least among us. The groom was future engineer and U.S president Herbert Hoover.

Lou Henry's father had evidently wanted a son, but aside from that unorthodox first name, no one in that clan ever let gender—or anything else—slow them down. Charles Henry took his daughter hunting and fishing in the woods and fields of Iowa, and she learned to skate and sled on the frozen Cedar River. When Lou was eleven, her family moved to California where she climbed trees to tie up rope swings, organized pickup baseball games, and became an expert horsewoman who eschewed sidesaddle. She collected reptiles as pets, starred as Joan of Arc in the school play, and wrote two school essays at age fourteen: "Universal Suffrage" and "The Independent Girl."

At Stanford, she was the school's first female geology major. It was in Palo Alto that she met her future husband, "Bert." They honeymooned in China, where he had accepted a job and where she set a precedent as being prepared for any kind of action.

Lou Hoover immersed herself in Chinese art, history, and culture. She learned Mandarin faster than her husband and manned the barricades with him when the Boxer Rebellion broke out. In the White House, Lou Hoover was the first First Lady to address the nation on the radio. Without fanfare, she put a stop to the antediluvian custom of not inviting pregnant women to White House social occasions. She also not-so-quietly tendered an invitation to a White House tea for congressional wives to Jessie DePriest, the wife of black congressman Oscar DePriest.

This simple gesture brought fierce reaction from segregationists. Southern newspapers howled. An Arkansas senator had an account of the event read into the *Congressional Record* in protest. The First Lady stood accused of "defiling" the White House.

Actually, Lou Hoover had done just the opposite: She had done the old mansion proud.

Smelling a Rat

David Lawrence passed away on this date, a man who helped define how U.S. presidents are covered by the press. A founder, at age twenty-five, of the White House Correspondents' Association, Lawrence lived another six decades in which he helped invent the political column and became a friend—and critic—of eleven presidents from William Howard Taft to Richard Nixon. He founded various publications, including *U.S. News & World Report*, and the Bureau of National Affairs.

"When he smelled news," said the *New York Times*'s Arthur Krock, "he was unrelenting until he found its origins." In 1919, he created the Consolidated Press Association and became the first syndicated columnist. He also was the first to distribute his column by wire instead of mail. His growing influence put him in the orbit of a succession of presidents, including Woodrow Wilson, whom he knew from his days as a Princeton student.

Personal ties to presidents never changed the strong conservative leanings that often put him on the wrong side of history. He opposed the civil rights movement, viewing desegregation as unconstitutional, and called the Vietnam War an example of American "philanthropy." But he never imposed his views on his own reporters, ordering them not to read his column so they wouldn't be swayed. He was also uninterested in personal enrichment. Before his death he donated a magnificent tract of land he owned in Fairfax County, Virginia, for a park.

In 1970, President Nixon presented him the Medal of Freedom. When Lawrence suffered a heart attack at age eighty-four and died in 1973 shortly after finishing that day's column, Nixon hailed him as "not only a dean of his profession but also one of our most distinguished patriots." But Nixon was not finished. Two months later at that year's White House Correspondents' Association dinner, Nixon recalled Lawrence once telling him, "There is only one more difficult task than being president of this country when we are waging war, and that is to be president of the nation when it is waging peace."

Thanks to the White House tapes, we later got a Nixonian footnote to those grace notes.

"What did you think of the Lawrence quote?" the president asked aide Robert Haldeman.

"Appropriate," responded Haldeman.

"I made it up," said Nixon.

February 12, 1943

From Liberia, with Love

Franklin D. Roosevelt hadn't attended the correspondents' dinner since the United States had entered World War II—until this date. "It is nearly two years since I attended the last dinner of our White House Correspondents' Association," FDR began. "A great deal of water has flowed over the dam since then. And several people have flown over the water."

He was referring to hundreds of thousands of U.S. pilots and fighting men—and to their commander in chief. Only a month earlier, Roosevelt met Winston Churchill in Casablanca, then traveled to West Africa and on to South America. In a press conference held earlier on the day of the dinner, Roosevelt had discussed his travels.

"I had the president of Liberia to lunch with me at our camp," Roosevelt said. "I flew back to Gambia in the afternoon.... It's an amazing thing: Wednesday in Liberia, Thursday in Brazil! And I don't like flying!"

FDR also explained that he'd invited that Liberian president, Edwin Barclay, the grandson of Kentucky slaves, to visit Washington. One White House reporter saw the important symbolism in the visit of an African president to a U.S. capital that was, in many important ways, still segregated. The man who saw the big picture was University of Wisconsin journalism school graduate Harry McAlpin, who would cover Barclay's impending visit for the *Chicago Defender*, a black weekly—but only after the intervention of White House press secretary Steve Early. As an African-American, McAlpin was prevented by the White House Correspondents' Association from covering presidential press conferences.

Many years later, former WHCA president George E. Condon Jr. unearthed this sordid story. Condon did more than write about it. He proposed that the association name a scholarship after Harry McAlpin. Condon also tracked down McAlpin's son, Sherman, and invited him to the 2014 dinner.

There, WHCA president Steve Thomma introduced Sherman to Barack Obama. From the podium, President Obama repeated the story unearthed by George Condon. The forty-fourth U.S. president also quoted the words of the thirty-second president to Harry McAlpin, on the occasion when he was finally ushered into a presidential press conference on February 8, 1944.

"I'm glad to see you, McAlpin," said Roosevelt as he flashed his famous smile and stuck out his hand to the correspondent. "And very happy to have you here."

February 13, 1919

Little Time for Baseball

One of Gen. John J. "Black Jack" Pershing's famous "doughboys" who marched off to France in 1917 was named Leon Cadore. Before the war—and afterward, too—he was a professional baseball player. On this date came the announcement that Cadore was trading the khakis of the U.S. Army for his old uniform as a member of the Brooklyn Dodgers.

He was met in New York by his father and Wilbert Robinson, the Dodgers' manager and a future Hall of Famer. Although Cadore is not enshrined in Cooperstown, he put on a performance on May 1, 1920, that is considered one of the most untouchable feats in major-league history. That day Cadore dueled Boston Braves hurler Joe Oeschger for twenty-six innings—with each pitcher throwing well more than three hundred pitches. The game, which ended in a 1–1 tie, was called because of darkness by the umpires despite entreaties from players on both teams who wanted to be able to say they'd played the equivalent of three full games.

"Joe Oeschger and Leon Cadore were the real outstanding heroes among a score of heroes in the monumental affray of this afternoon," wrote the *New York Times* beat reporter. "Instead of showing any signs of weakening under the strain, each of them appeared to grow stronger. In the final six innings neither artist allowed even the shadow of a safe single."

This story is a reminder that civilians often try to forget war as soon as it is over. It was only one year earlier, however, that New York journalists were interviewing Cadore about genuine heroism, a conversation he tried to deflect.

"Lt. Cadore is the same modest, unassuming chap he was before he won his shoulder straps and the French cross of war," reported George B. Underwood of the *New York Sun*.

How did he win the Croix de Guerre?

"Oh, a couple of us went out into No Man's Land one night and bagged a few prisoners that gave us a little valuable information," Cadore replied. "None of us were killed or wounded. It wasn't much, you know...."

"Needless to say, when we were in the thick of the fighting in the Vosges and the Champagne we got mighty little time for baseball," he added matter-of-factly. "We had to play it with hand grenades."

Lighting a Fire

Frederick Douglass celebrated his birthday on this date, although in truth he wasn't sure of the year, let alone the month or exact day. He celebrated it on Valentine's Day because that was the last time he saw his mother's face. She brought him a heart-shaped cake.

The man we know as Frederick Douglass was born on a Talbot County, Maryland, plantation. His mother was a slave and his father, Douglass later wrote, "was a white man." His name as a boy was Frederick Augustus Washington Bailey. He was raised by his maternal grandmother. His mother was a field hand lent to a farm twelve miles away. Douglass never once recalled seeing her face in the light of day. Sometimes she'd walk from her farm at night, lie down beside him in bed, and be gone by sunrise.

At six, the boy was also separated from his grandmother. At eight, he was taken to another plantation where his fortunes changed. A white woman, Lucretia Anthony Auld, chose him as a companion for her son. Fred, as he was called by whites, began to closely observe the odd and evil social restrictions of his circumstance. Two years later, having been sent to Baltimore to Lucretia's in-laws, young Douglass observed a young woman named Sophia Auld reading the Bible aloud. Delighted by this "wonderful art," he asked her to teach him to read.

Breaking with custom—and the law—Sophia did so. Her husband warned Sophia that this was not only unsafe, but impractical. Being literate "will forever unfit him to be a slave," Hugh Auld told his wife. "If you teach him how to read, he'll want to know how to write, and this accomplished, he'll be running away with himself."

This speech cowed Mrs. Auld, but lit a fire in the heart of the boy who called it "the first decidedly anti-slavery lecture" he'd heard. Working on the docks at Fells Point, Douglass had learned something else: the lingo of the seagoing men. This, too, proved invaluable. On September 3, 1838, true to Hugh Auld's prediction, he donned the apparel of a free black sailor, went to the Baltimore terminal, and hopped on a northbound train.

Questioned briefly about his destination, he adopted the manner

of a merchant seaman headed toward his next port of call. It worked. Frederick Douglass changed trains in Philly and was in New York by morning, happy and fearful, but on his way to fulfilling his destiny, which was playing a momentous role in America's greatest drama— the long fight to end slavery. He never answered to "Fred" again. Once, while in the East Room of the White House, he overheard a woman say to a friend, "There's Fred Douglass." He turned to her, made a courtly bow, and said, "*Frederick* Douglass, if you please."

February 15, 1903

Teddy's Bears

Theodore Roosevelt disliked the nickname Teddy, but it's hard to stop a spontaneous fad. The teddy bear as America's iconic stuffed animal dates to November 1902, when TR decided he needed a break from the White House. For Roosevelt, a holiday meant hunting, so he traveled to a Mississippi town named Onward, about thirty miles north of Vicksburg.

The choice of locale had a dual purpose. First, it was bear season in the Mississippi Delta. Second, Roosevelt wanted to bolster the prospects of the reform-minded Andrew Longino, the first Mississippi governor elected since the Civil War who had not served in the Confederate Army. Yet, a Confederate veteran was hired as a guide. His name was Holt Collier, and he was a character in himself. A freed slave who rode as a cavalryman under Confederate general Nathan Bedford Forrest, Collier had reportedly killed some three thousand bears.

With the president, the governor, and a traveling caravan that included trappers, horse wranglers, servants, journalists, and four dozen hunting dogs, Collier set out into the swamps. On the second day of the hunt, the hounds picked up a scent. This animal, an aging, 235-pound black bear, was cornered in a watering hole where it killed one of the snarling hounds. Collier came to his dogs' aid by clubbing the bear in the head and tying it to a tree. When the rest of his party caught up, they found the bear disabled and surrounded by other hunters waiting for the president to make the kill. Collier cautioned Roosevelt against shooting the bear while it was tied up, but he needn't have bothered. TR refused to even shoulder his gun.

Although the bear was euthanized by Collier, the reporters' stories made the president seem merciful. This wasn't wrong, as far as it went, although a modern sensibility might recoil from a president who hunted bears for sport at all. Later, *Washington Post* cartoonist Clifford Berryman immortalized Roosevelt's gesture with a November 16, 1902, drawing showing the bear as a cub and the president waving his arm as though he wanted nothing to do with it.

"Drawing the line in Mississippi," it read.

The cartoon was seen by Brooklyn candy and curio shop owner Morris Michtom. After his wife Rose sewed two stuffed-animal bears, Mitchtom sought and received Roosevelt's permission to call them "Teddy's bears," and they went on sale on this date. They caught on quickly, and were mass-produced. They still are.

February 16, 1945

MacArthur's Return

Japan's December 7, 1941, attack on Pearl Harbor was not an isolated military event. As Franklin Roosevelt told Americans in his "day of infamy" speech, the Japanese simultaneously invaded Hong Kong, Guam, Wake Island, Malaysia, and the Philippines. The U.S. garrison on the Philippine islands fought bravely, but were surrounded, cut off, and finally overwhelmed by superior numbers. U.S. Army general Douglas MacArthur was ordered by Roosevelt to evacuate himself from Corregidor and make his way to Australia. It was no easy feat, but as he left the Philippines, the fiery general uttered his famous vow, "I shall return."

MacArthur made good on his promise on October 20, 1944, wading ashore at Leyte while the newsreel camera crews filmed the scene. They captured the theatrical general in all his preening glory, bravado, and physical bravery. Dressed in a recently pressed uniform, MacArthur made his way past the grunts on the beach and into the jungle to a makeshift microphone where he gave a short and dramatic speech that was broadcast over the radio.

"I have returned," he proclaimed. "By the grace of Almighty God our forces stand again on Philippine soil—soil consecrated in the blood of our two peoples. We have come, dedicated and committed, to the task of destroying every vestige of enemy control over your daily lives.... The hour of your redemption is here."

Bataan was fully subdued on this date. The final cost was frightful. Of the seventy thousand Filipinos and Americans taken prisoner in 1942, twenty-one thousand perished on forced marches or in Corregidor's brutal prison camps. Under Japanese commanding general

Masaharu Homma, these prisoners of war died of hunger or thirst, were bayonetted or shot by their captors, run over by tanks, or left to die in ditches of tropical disease or heat stroke. Those that survived were sent on "hell ships" to forced labor camps in Japan. Of the twelve thousand Americans taken prisoner in the spring of 1942, only four thousand survived the war.

President Truman would boast of repaying Japanese cruelty "with interest," but when it came to the Bataan Death March, the execution of General Homma for his war crimes never seemed to the men who survived the horrors of the Philippines as being nearly sufficient.

February 17, 1904

Good Vibrations

A new opera by composer Giacomo Puccini opened on this date at La Scala in Milan. *Madama Butterfly* was taken from a popular London play, which itself was adapted from a short story by Philadelphia lawyer John Luther Long. It's a tragedy about doomed love, and honor and a mother's love—though modern operagoers might say it was about sexism and racism.

The La Scala crowd didn't much like it. Puccini had been inspired by Verdi's masterpiece *Aida* as a young man and had already produced two works destined to become classics of their own, *La Bohème* and *Tosca*. But the original score in *Butterfly* seemed too similar to the audience. Some patrons hissed. Others yelled at the stage or left early.

Horrified, Puccini pulled the opera and went back to work, retooling the staging and the music. Four months later, it was rereleased—to thunderous acclaim. It opened at the New York Metropolitan Opera three years later, and has been a fan favorite ever since.

Six decades later to the day, an American composer also known as something of a perfectionist rolled tape for a new song destined to become a classic of its genre. On February 17, 1966, Brian Wilson of the Beach Boys began working on "Good Vibrations." The song was supposed to round out the group's cutting-edge new album, *Pet Sounds*, but Wilson had trouble getting it just right. Small wonder: No song had ever been recorded quite like this one. Wilson employed dozens of instruments, ranging from the cello and harpsichord to the electric theremin, an early synthesizer mainly used to convey futuristic sound in science fiction movies.

Six months and ninety hours of tape later, Wilson had the sound he wanted—a veritable symphony in three minutes and thirty-nine seconds. But if "Good Vibrations" was a new sound, it was about an old theme: Love. Audree Wilson, mother of Beach Boys members Brian, Carl, and Dennis, had told her boys that people gave off invisible "vibrations"—good or bad—which was why dogs bark at some people, but not others.

As a boy, Brian found this idea frightening. As a man, he turned the concept into an upbeat song about the possibilities of hidden connections between people, and love at first sight. In 2004, when *Rolling Stone* issued its list of the top five hundred rock hits of all time, "Good Vibrations" came in at number six, two spots ahead of the highest-ranking Beatles song, and only three spots behind John Lennon's "Imagine."

February 18, 1967

Destroyer of Worlds

Famed physicist J. Robert Oppenheimer—the "father" of the atom bomb—died in New Jersey on this date. Although Japan was the nation that suffered the brunt of the frightening new weapon, at the outset of the Manhattan Project the scientists assembled in the New Mexico desert believed they were in a race with Nazi Germany.

When the Third Reich collapsed in April 1945, Oppenheimer's all-star team of physicists, chemists, and engineers kept going. "It was an enormous project," physicist Roy Glauber recalled. "We were all deeply involved in finding out whether the darn thing would work."

Oppenheimer had been a brilliant scholar everywhere he went—Harvard, Cambridge, Caltech, UC Berkeley, Leiden University in the Netherlands—but something of a misfit socially. He'd tackled Harvard in three years, graduating first in his class, and devoured the curriculum, immersing himself in chemistry, physics, and calculus while also studying English and French literature, along with Western and Eastern philosophy. For relaxation, he wrote poetry. It was, he later said, "the most exciting time I've ever had in my life.... I almost came alive."

He'd spent some time in the high desert of New Mexico—his family owned a small ranch there—and it was a place that gave him great solace. "My two great loves," Oppenheimer wrote to a friend in 1929, "are physics and the desert. It's a pity they can't be combined." The Manhattan Project, undertaken in tremendous secrecy at Los Alamos, did combine them. The moral dilemma of dropping such a weapon on an unsuspecting population would come later. For the scientists, it was a race against Nazism, time, physics, and Japanese aggression. On July 16, 1945, the race was won with the detonation of the bomb. Oppenheimer named the test site "Trinity," but more fitting—as he knew from his days in New Mexico—was the site's location at the end of a road called Jornada del Muerto (Journey of the Dead) commemorating another death march, this one of Spanish during the Pueblo Revolt of 1680. Later, after he became known as a peace activist who favored disarmament, Oppenheimer wrote that what came to him as he saw the flash of light and the mushroom cloud he'd helped create were words from the Bhagavad Gita: *"Now I am become Death, the destroyer of worlds."*

Did he really say this? It's possible: One of the subjects he studied at Harvard was Hindu thought. But that day, recalled those present (including his own brother), what Robert Oppenheimer said aloud was: "It works."

Internment

On this day, Franklin Roosevelt issued Executive Order 9066 authorizing the forced relocation of persons of Japanese descent living on the West Coast into internment camps. It is a date which will also live in infamy: Most of the men, women, and children covered by the edict were naturalized or American-born citizens. The rationale cited in the order was espionage, but the true causes were wartime hysteria, overt racism, and latent jealousy over the commercial and agricultural success of Japanese immigrants and their descendants. From Washington state to Arizona, 120,000 innocent people were rounded up under this order.

Donald Trump didn't invent the threat from ISIS or from murderous Muslim radicals living in the United States. The San Bernardino couple who worked among peaceful Southern Californians before slaughtering them at a Christmas party were a second-generation Pakistani Muslim and his immigrant bride. But how America responded two months after Pearl Harbor provides a valuable history lesson. Was the government being vigilant? Or hysterical? In this instance, the verdict has been officially rendered, although it took forty-six years.

That judgment came in the form of the Civil Liberties Act of 1988. Signed by President Reagan, it compensated all those still living who had been interned in the "relocation" camps with $20,000 and an apology from their government. "The legislation that I am about to sign provides for…restitution," Reagan said. "Yet no payment can make up for those lost years. So, what is most important in this bill has less to do with property than with honor. For here we admit a wrong; here we reaffirm our commitment as a nation to equal justice under the law."

Reagan paid homage in his statement to Norman Y. Mineta, a Democratic congressman from California instrumental in enacting the Japanese-American redress legislation. "This is not about the past—this is about the future," Mineta said at a 2011 dedication of the Heart Mountain Interpretive Learning Center in Wyoming, where he was incarcerated as a boy. "And the reason it's about the future, is that history always has the ability to repeat itself." Mineta then recalled that on 9/11 he was transportation secre-

tary in George W. Bush's cabinet and was hearing talk of preventing Muslims from boarding airplanes. At a later White House meeting with congressional leaders, David Bonior of Michigan told President Bush that his district had significant Arab-Americans who were disturbed by the rhetoric they were hearing.

"David, you are absolutely correct," Mineta recalled Bush saying. "We are equally concerned, and we don't want to have happen today what happened to Norm in 1942."

February 20, 1962

John Glenn's Wild Ride

As a U.S. Marine Corps pilot, John Glenn had flown 149 combat missions in World War II and Korea, so he was already a war hero by the time he climbed into *Friendship 7*. But when he climbed out of that capsule in the Atlantic Ocean, he was a national icon.

Until then, the Soviet Union had been ahead of the United States at every step in the space race. Was the American space program even ready to send a man into orbit? That's debatable—*Friendship 7* experienced serious problems during Glenn's flight—but NASA certainly picked the right man for the job. Easing into orbit at seventeen thousand miles per hour, Glenn radioed back to Mission Control: "Zero G and I feel fine. Man, that view is tremendous."

By the end of the first orbit, the ship's automated controls malfunctioned, but the astronaut calmly switched to manual power and regained control of the craft. During the third and final orbit, NASA engineers at Mission Control received a signal from the spacecraft's sensors that the capsule's heat shield might be loose. As *Friendship 7* began its fiery reentry into the Earth's atmosphere, the straps for the retrorockets flapped wildly against the spacecraft just as it lost radio contact with Mission Control.

Remember those white-knuckle scenes in the movie *Apollo 13*, where everyone waits nervously to reestablish contact with the spaceship? That was what it was like. Nearly three minutes later, Glenn's voice rippled through Mission Control. Asked how he was doing, the astronaut said, "Oh, pretty good." And after being picked up in the Atlantic Ocean, his first words to the sailors of the USS *Noa* were, "It was hot in there."

He had spent nearly five hours in space. An estimated one hundred thousand spectators jammed onto the beaches and observation points around Cape Canaveral, and millions watched on television. President Kennedy pinned a medal on Glenn, Congress invited him to speak, and New York City held a ticker-tape parade in his honor. Given the precarious condition of its rocketry, NASA couldn't risk the life of such a popular astronaut, meaning that Glenn's days of space travel were essentially over—at least then. Champing at the bit, Glenn left NASA and announced his candidacy for a U.S. Senate seat in his native Ohio.

"John came out of the heart of the country . . . and he stole America's heart," said Vice President Joe Biden at Glenn's December 17, 2016, funeral. "He knew by his upbringing that ordinary Americans can do extraordinary things."

February 21, 1848

Stifling Debate in Congress

John Quincy Adams literally gave his life to the cause of abolition. More than a decade before John Brown's raid at Harper's Ferry, Adams suffered a stroke on the floor of the House of Representatives on this date. He died two days later, having served seventeen years during his postpresidency in Congress, where he emerged as a leader in the fight against slavery.

The first son of a president to attain the White House, Adams did not start the abolitionist movement in Congress. Quaker-sponsored petitions to end slavery were regularly sent to Congress beginning in 1790. House Democrats from the Southern states grew so tired of them, and so powerful, that in 1836 they succeeded in passing a rule automatically tabling such petitions. It was this infamous "gag rule" that Adams devoted his career to fighting.

The Senate had rejected a similar rule, but the response of powerful South Carolina senator John C. Calhoun revealed just what Adams and his fellow abolitionists were up against.

On March 16, 1836, after losing a gag rule vote, Calhoun angrily stomped out of the chamber. In a fiery speech delivered days earlier, Calhoun warned his colleagues against interfering with the South's complex system of slave labor.

"The relation which now exists between the two races has existed for two centuries," Calhoun said. "It has entered into and modified all our institutions, civil and political. We will not, cannot, permit it to be destroyed." Adams, who considered slavery a "foul stain" on the still-new nation, was mystified by such intransigence. In private entreaties to Calhoun, he invoked the preambles to the Constitution and the Declaration of Independence and asked the senator how he could possibly find such language compatible with slavery. Calhoun's response, as recorded in Adams's diary, was chilling in its circular simplicity: "Calhoun...said that the principles which I had avowed were just and noble: but that in the Southern country, whenever they were mentioned, they were always understood as applying only to white men."

Plantation owner John Randolph, who represented Virginia in the House and later in the Senate, put it this way: "I am an aristocrat. I love liberty. I hate equality."

George Mason, a wiser Virginian, had seen this coming. He had warned his fellow Founders (and fellow slave owners) much earlier that slavery was a "poison" that was producing in the South a society of "petty tyrants" in which "every generous" or "liberal" sentiment on race was being extinguished.

February 22, 1732

Spare the Rod, Save the Child

George Washington's birthday, in the days before Presidents Day, was widely celebrated in this country, along with the famous story of a certain cherry tree. The tale, told through the ages, is that the boy cut down a cherry sapling, and when confronted by his father, confessed with a version of "I cannot tell a lie." The parable, which comes from an 1800 book by biographer Mason Weems, is not an incidental one in the American canon. Young Abraham Lincoln devoured Weems's *The Life of Washington*, and internalized its lessons about Washington's high moral character. His "Honest Abe" nickname predates his presidency, as does the vignette of Lincoln walking miles as a store clerk to return a few cents' change to a customer.

Modern historians, even those at Mount Vernon, airily dismiss the chopping-down-the cherry tree story as a myth. These revisionists don't know what they are talking about. For starters, Mason Weems didn't write that young George "chopped down" a tree. He reported that the six-year-old lad "barks" the young tree, meaning he idly swung his hatchet and gouged it—a lesser offense, suggesting carelessness, not malice. Second, Weems cites a source, although he doesn't name her, which is more than his detractors do for their smug rebuttals. Weems says the story comes from an "aged lady," presumably an aunt who lived on the farm.

Finally, modern cynics miss the entire point of Weems's anecdote. It wasn't about young George's innate honesty. The hero of this story was the boy's father, Augustine Washington. Weems is providing a window into the enlightened home in which George Washington was raised, one where little boys weren't whipped for absentmindedly gashing a tree.

One of the few modern historians who grasps this point is Garry Wills. Weems, Wills noted, abhorred corporal punishment, and the point of his story was that parents who beat their children essentially are forcing them to lie.

"Weems was a natural educator," Wills wrote. "The most famous tale—that of the cherry tree—is almost always printed in a severely truncated form, which destroys its point. The moral, aimed at children, becomes: Never tell a lie. But that was not Weems's moral."

George Washington can tell his father that he gashed the cherry tree, perhaps fatally, because he isn't terrified at the consequences of the truth. "The conclusion of the tale makes it clear," Wills writes, "that the hero is Washington's father, who teaches a lesson to parents."

February 23, 1954

Polio Fighter

As a young physician, Jonas E. Salk worked on the vaccines that helped protect U.S. soldiers and sailors in World War II from the deadly flu that had caused such heartbreak and havoc in the First World War.

In 1947, he accepted an appointment at the University of Pittsburgh medical school, where he was contacted by Harry Weaver, research director of the National Foundation for Infantile Paralysis, which ran the annual March of Dimes campaign. Would Dr. Salk take aim at polio, he was asked, the disease that had put Franklin Roosevelt in a wheelchair as an adult but which usually struck children?

The answer was yes; Salk signed on for the fight, and on this date, he first went into the field with a trial for his polio vaccine. It's hard to overestimate the fear that this disease engendered in people at that time. It crippled thousands of children every year and was often fatal, and in the early part of the twentieth century no one knew how it spread. During epidemics in 1914 and 1919, medical professionals went door-to-door seeking answers.

In 1954, a Gallup poll showed that more Americans knew about the polio field tests Dr. Salk was conducting than could provide the full name of the president. That was something of a trick question, as Americans knew the popular Dwight Eisenhower as "Ike." Nonetheless, the fact remains that on this date, the attention of parents around the world was riveted on Arsenal Elementary School in Pittsburgh's Lawrenceville neighborhood.

In that school's tiny school gymnasium, 137 youngsters lined up to receive injections of the serum that would become the vaccine. Participation was a matter of choice: They and their parents were among five thousand Pittsburgh volunteers. The field test was a success, and the following year 9 million such vaccines were purchased by the National Foundation for Infant Paralysis.

Soon it would be delivered orally, in sugar cubes, which kids lined up to take happily. A final point to make—and to consider in light of how expensively medicines are priced and how handsomely pharmaceutical companies are recompensed in the twenty-first century: Jonas Salk never personally profited from his vaccine, a decision he made consciously. He was honored for this selflessness by presidents and Congress; his name was praised by parents around the world.

February 24, 1868

Profile in Courage

The first act in the great civil drama of the nineteenth century is concluded. Andrew Johnson, President of the United States, stands impeached of 'high crimes and misdemeanors.'"

So wrote the *New York Times* in its Washington-datelined story.

The underlying issue was Reconstruction. The dominant Senate faction opposing Johnson, "Radical Republicans," held views few Americans would consider radical today: They believed the white Southern political structure was reasserting itself in ways that disenfranchised blacks and was essentially attempting to reconstitute slavery by another name—with the president's acquiescence. For his part, Andrew Johnson, who'd been sworn in as vice president just weeks before Abraham Lincoln's assassination, believed he was carrying out Lincoln's wish to reincorporate the vanquished South into the fabric of the nation as quickly as possible.

To thwart him, Congress passed a bill barring the president from replacing cabinet members without congressional approval. Johnson vetoed it, but Congress overrode him. The stage was set for a confrontation, which Johnson precipitated by firing Secretary of War Edwin M. Stanton. This led to Johnson's impeachment in the House and the looming Senate trial.

On the eve of the trial, one of the few undeclared senators was Edmund G. Ross, a former newspaperman representing Kansas, a hotbed of abolition. To remove Johnson from office, all thirty-six Republicans in the Senate would have to hold together. But in a preliminary straw vote, one of them withheld his verdict: Senator Ross.

"I did not think that a Kansas man could quibble against his country," groused Sen. Charles Sumner of Massachusetts. But Ross was neither quibbling nor standing against his country. He was taking his oath of office seriously, weighing the merits of the articles of impeachment, and considering the effect conviction would have on the country. Then he cast the decisive vote against conviction.

Although Johnson's presidency was spared, Ross's political career was not. He was voted out of office in the next election, and he left the Republican Party, and Kansas, altogether. He ended up in New Mexico, seeking office as a Democrat. He lost, but was later appointed territorial governor by President Grover Cleveland. Ross would be forgotten today except that his principled stance was resurrected by a future U.S. president who devoted a chapter to this crucible in a book with an evocative title: *Profiles in Courage*.

February 25, 1870

Dispensing a Putrid Precedent

Hiram Revels was born of mixed-race lineage in North Carolina in the 1820s. He was never a slave and apprenticed in the barbershop of his brother, also a free black man, before gravitating north to attend theological seminary.

When the Civil War broke out, Hiram Revels was an ordained minister in the African Methodist Episcopal Church and an educator in Baltimore. He helped recruit troops for Maryland's first colored regiment and was later commissioned in "Mr. Lincoln's Army" as a chaplain. Stationed in Mississippi after the war, Revels emerged as one of the nation's most able and eloquent administrators during Reconstruction. He was appointed as an alderman for the city of Natchez and then ran successfully as a Republican candidate for state senate. That body promptly elected him a United States senator.

February 23, 1870, was swearing-in day, but Hiram Revels was not administered the oath of office. Senate Democrats chose to litigate with arcane arguments that cited, among other things, the *Dred Scott v. Sandford* decision while questioning whether a black man was eligible for such a post. Other Democrats were not so legalistic. Sen. Garrett Davis of Kentucky simply asserted that Revels's race precluded him from serving in the Senate. Republicans were outraged. Nevada senator James Nye rebuked his colleagues for even invoking such a discredited judicial fiat as *Dred Scott*. Michigan Republican Jacob Howard pronounced himself "nauseated."

As usual, Massachusetts's abolitionist warhorse Charles Sumner was the most acerbic lawmaker in the chamber. In the Hollywood hit *Lincoln*, it's a bit disconcerting at first to hear the passionate invective of the Boston-born Sumner delivered in a Southern accent. Tommy Lee Jones may have attended Harvard, but he never lost the twang of his native Texas. Yet Jones perfectly captured Sumner's disgust at racist argument, even those gussied up in legal niceties.

The *Dred Scott* decision, Sumner said on the Senate floor on this date, was "a putrid corpse" from the day it was born and should "be remembered only as a warning and a shame." With that, the vote was called and on a party-line roll call, Revels's appointment was accepted. As he approached the front of the chamber to take the oath of office, the packed audience in the Senate gallery rose to watch. During the debate, there had been two outbursts among the crowd. Now, those in the gallery were utterly silent as they watched history being made.

The Man in Black

Johnny Cash was born on this day in 1932. The self-assigned moniker referred to Cash's clothes, not his skin color. When asked why he dressed that way, Cash gave an answer that still inspires seekers of social justice of all generations and musical genres.

The outlines of his life are known to country music fans. He was born in Kingsland, Arkansas, one of seven children in a family that farmed twenty acres of cotton and other crops and made music together when the workday was done. He left the South for the lure of work in Michigan's auto plants, enlisted in the Air Force, married a woman he met while stationed in Texas, and shipped out to Germany, where he organized his first band.

He settled in Memphis while trying to break into the music business with a local band. Over the years, he had several run-ins with the law, most of them related to drug and alcohol abuse, and although he spent numerous nights in local jails, Cash made his name performing at Folsom Prison and San Quentin and not, contrary to rumor, for serving time in the penitentiary.

Johnny married a second time, to June Carter—herself a daughter of country music royalty—tamed his addictions, and reconnected with his Christian faith, all while writing and recording one hit after another. A thread runs through most of these songs: empathy for those left behind. Cash performed, always, dressed head to toe in black. He was asked about this often. By 2002, he must have become tired of the question because he gave a puckish reply to Larry King.

"You know, I wrote a song about why I wear black, but maybe that's not quite it," he deadpanned. "I wear black because I'm comfortable in it. But then in the summertime, when it's hot, I'm comfortable in light blue."

That song he mentioned was written in 1971 before a performance at Vanderbilt University, in Nashville, where Johnny Cash remains popular. He said he was inspired by the students he talked to. "The Man in Black" is a protest song. Against war and illiteracy. Against excessive incarceration and rampant materialism.

"I wear the black for the poor and the beaten down, living in the hopeless, hungry side of town," he sang. "I wear it for the prisoner who has long paid for his crime, but is there because he's a victim of the times."

February 27, 1914

The Babe

The St. Mary's Industrial School for Boys had done what it could for George Herman Ruth. And on this date, the Xaverian brothers who ran the Baltimore institution knew that it was time to see what nineteen-year-old George could do for himself.

"I was listed as an incorrigible, and I guess I was," he later noted in his autobiography. "I chewed tobacco when I was seven, not that I enjoyed it especially, but, from my observation around the saloon it seemed the normal thing to do."

St. Mary's was an orphanage and reform school. The idea was to show the boys how to behave, while also teaching them a trade. The priests and other instructors had tried to teach George how to be a tailor, but outside the classroom he was in training for another pastime, one denoted in a simple line on his school record: "He is going to join the Balt. baseball team."

From Baltimore, he went to the Boston Red Sox and then, to immortality as a New York Yankee. To say that Babe Ruth never forgot where he came from is certainly true, although imprecise. He couldn't recall the names of longtime teammates—or even good friends. But friends he made nonetheless, from the rich and famous to street urchins. "Affable, boisterous and good-natured to a fault," wrote Murray Schumach in his lyrical *New York Times* obituary of the Babe, "he was always as accessible to the newsboy on the corner as to the most dignified personage in worldly affairs."

Much was made at the time—and, later, in movies and books—of a sick Long Island boy named Johnny Sylvester, to whom Ruth signed a baseball and promised a 1926 World Series home run if he would get better. Years later, the boy's uncle ran into Ruth and thanked him. The New York Yankees star was gracious enough, but when the uncle left, he asked a sportswriter, "Who the devil is Johnny Sylvester?" The real point is that the Babe loved children, did many charity events for them, and always had a kind word and an affectionate pat for his littlest fans.

As he became more and more famous, Ruth devised a strategy for aiding his spotty memory. If he met someone who seemed familiar—and that person looked, say, under forty years old—the Babe would just say warmly, "Hello, kid, how are you?"

If the guy seemed older than him, Ruth would alter his greeting slightly: "Hello, doc!" he'd say. "How's everything going?"

February 28, 1827

From Babe to Behemoth

On this date, the Baltimore & Ohio Railroad became the first railway chartered in this country. From a business standpoint, the idea was to open up western trade routes—at a time "the West" referred to the Ohio Valley. From that modest ambition grew an industry that settled a continent. It's easy to forget now, but the advent of the railroad was probably the greatest technological success story of the nineteenth century.

And it was one romanticized—and criticized—in songs and literature. Frank Norris's novel, *The Octopus*, documented the predations of the Southern Pacific Railroad and helped fuel the Progressive movement. The song "Casey Jones," included by the Library of Congress on an album called *California Gold: Northern California Folk Music from the Thirties*, paid homage to the men who worked on the railroad.

Put in your water, shovel in your coal,
Put cha head out the window and watch the drivers roll
I'll run her 'til she leaves the rail
For I'm eight hours late with the western mail.

But there was a lot more than mail being carried on those trains. The most valuable cargo wasn't mail or coal, lumber, or buffalo hides—it was people. The patent for a steam engine was granted in 1815, a year after a British engineer built a steam locomotive that hauled eight railroad cars up a grade at four miles per hour. No infrastructure existed to support the invention, however, and a decade later the United States still had only twenty-three miles of railroad tracks.

A year later, America had nearly fifty miles of track, and a couple of years after that, more than ninety miles—and so on. In one decade, the miles of rail lines doubled nearly seven times, so that by 1840 the country boasted 2,800 miles of track. As author Joel Garreau notes in *Radical Evolution*, between 1840 and 1910 the amount of railroad track doubled fourteen and a half times. It would be hard to overstate the effect this had on the country.

"The railroads changed whatever they touched," wrote Garreau, a demographer and futurist at Arizona State University. "It changed cities; it changed families; it changed businesses; it changed this country," he added. "A struggling, backward, rural civilization mostly hugging the East Coast was converted into a continent-spanning, world-challenging, urban behemoth."

"Oh, Mammy!"

At the Academy Awards ceremony, *Gone with the Wind* reaped eight Oscars, plus two special awards given out that year. The winning categories included best picture and best director, and both female acting categories. Hattie McDaniel won for best supporting actress, the first time the Motion Picture Academy bestowed its highest honor on a black woman.

The NAACP complained, even then, that Margaret Mitchell's epic Southern romance and the screenplay adapted from her novel idealized the Old South while glossing over the horrors of slavery. This was a fair critique, although Hattie McDaniel didn't write the script. She did, however, turn in a nuanced performance as an independent-minded housemaid doing her best to maintain her human dignity. Audiences recognized that, as did her peers in the profession. Yet even while honoring her, the Academy revealed how far it, and the country, had to go: McDaniel was seated at a segregated table, away from her fellow cast members.

Born in Wichita, Kansas, in 1895, Hattie McDaniel had always known what she was up against. She viewed her talent as a path to a better life for herself and other African-American women. To those who sniped at her for playing subservient roles, McDaniel had two answers.

The first was a practical one: If she wasn't being paid handsomely to play a maid on the screen, she'd be paid poorly to be an actual maid in real life. Her second response to her critics was more subversive. Although specializing in the role of genial, if sometimes sassy, cooks or household servants, she subtly undermined the very stereotype she was playing. That attitude was the key. She did more than repeat the humorous asides written into the scripts of the films she made. She asserted the character's, and her own, independence and resilience.

Asked about *Gone with the Wind* the year after it was made, McDaniel revealed how hard she worked at her craft. "I read that book three times through," she said, recalling how thoroughly she prepared for her audition: "Not for weeks have I been Hattie McDaniel. I just been going through the house all the time, peeping and peering like Mammy does after Miss Scarlett." She was paired with Vivien Leigh during her screen test. Producer David O. Selznick didn't know he was looking at two future Academy Award winners when he viewed the test, but he knew he had something special on his set.

"Save your overhead, boys," he instructed his crew. "We can start shooting tomorrow."

March 1, 1961

Peace Corps

The idea for the Peace Corps, John F. Kennedy's biographers say, came from a 1958 novel, *The Ugly American*, set in Southeast Asia. The book was a best seller, and the title phrase entered the language as a term of derision denoting loud and ostentatious Americans traveling or living abroad. That shorthand explanation is misleading. Actually, "ugly American" was the tag given by villagers to one of the novel's main characters, engineer Homer Atkins, because of his unlovely physical appearance. The description more accurately applies to ham-handed U.S. foreign policy bureaucracies. Atkins, no matter how homely, is doing beautiful work abroad. One of the book's pivot points is when he uses a bicycle to fashion a water pump for the village.

Also, a year before *The Ugly American* was published, Wisconsin congressman Henry Reuss returned from Southeast Asia convinced that the United States needed to send armies of volunteers overseas. Reuss knew what war could do: Like Kennedy, he was a hero in World War II. Better, he thought, to intercede in a way that made war unnecessary. Two Senate Democrats, including Kennedy rival Hubert Humphrey, sponsored legislation to fund such an effort.

"Traditional diplomats," Humphrey said, "quaked at the thought of thousands of young Americans scattered across their world." He was right: Opposition from the foreign policy establishment derailed his legislation. In June 1960, with a presidential race taking place, Humphrey tried again. His legislative proposal made the first mention of a "Peace Corps"—and impressed one influential Senate colleague. In the last weeks of the presidential campaign, Kennedy began talking it up—to enthusiastic reception.

At an impromptu 2 a.m. rally in Ann Arbor, Michigan, he asked students, "How many of you, who are going to be doctors, are willing to spend your days in Ghana?"

The reaction was electric; a spontaneous petition produced a thousand volunteers. In San Francisco, two weeks later, JFK invoked "a peace corps of talented men and women" who would dedicate themselves to progress in developing countries. After the election, his transition team received twenty-five thousand letters responding to this call. In response to the Bay of Pigs fiasco, Kennedy quipped that victory has a hundred fathers while defeat is an orphan. But this idea had many fathers and (and mothers) and what they gave birth to, in a pilot program created with an executive order by President Kennedy on this date, was a shared victory called the United States Peace Corps.

March 2, 1904

The Cat in the Hat

Ted Geisel, as his family and friends called him, was born on this day in Springfield, Massachusetts, a town that gave his father a job when he needed one. Geisel's father had the bad timing to inherit the family brewery the year before Prohibition outlawed the sale of beer. So, Dad became head of the public parks in Springfield, the city that inspired Geisel's first book, *And to Think That I Saw It on Mulberry Street*. After twenty-seven rejections from publishers, Vanguard Press released that book in 1937, the same year Geisel and his wife, Helen, learned they couldn't have children. The author's public reaction to this news about kids?

"You make 'em," Dr. Seuss quipped to his fans, "I'll amuse 'em."

The name Dr. Seuss wasn't entirely whimsical. Seuss was his middle name and his mother's maiden name, and he began using it as a nom de plume while at Dartmouth after being banned from extracurricular activities—including writing for a campus humor magazine—for drinking gin in his dorm room with nine friends. After college, he went into advertising and then political cartooning, something he never stopped doing. While holding to his promise to amuse America's children, Geisel also perfected the trick of appealing to kids and their parents at the same time. *The Cat in the Hat*, the book that made him rich, was in part a story about the Red Scare. *The Cat in the Hat Comes Back* had allusions to nuclear winter.

As a political cartoonist and occasional commentator, his views were aligned with the liberal wing of the Democratic Party, perhaps to a fault: Even while remonstrating against isolationism and racism in the 1940s, he casually accepted the Roosevelt administration's disparagement of Japanese-Americans. In the summer of 1974, as Watergate came to a head, Dr. Seuss sent liberal newspaper columnist Art Buchwald a copy of a 1972 book he wrote called *Marvin K. Mooney Will You Please Go Now!*

In the new version, the author had replaced "Marvin K. Mooney" with "Richard M. Nixon" and Buchwald reprinted it in his column:

Richard M. Nixon will you please go now!
You can go on skates.
You can go on skis.
You can go in a hat.
But
Please go . . .

March 3, 1887

Who's Blushing Now?

Helen Keller was a bright and precocious baby when, at nineteen months of age, she was stricken by a disease—scarlet fever or meningitis, most likely—that left her blind, deaf, and unable to speak. As it turned out, Helen was still a bright and precocious person *after* her illness, and would remain so all her life. Sensing this, Helen's parents arranged for her to meet Anne Sullivan, the teacher who would change her life. It happened on this date when Helen was six.

Miss Sullivan, later celebrated as the "Miracle Worker," helped reorient this "half-wild Southern child trapped in a world of darkness." Helen Keller would go on to learn to read (in three languages), graduate with honors from Radcliffe College, and become an advocate for those with disabilities. She would also embrace numerous progressive causes, employing both a heartfelt passion and a droll wit in service of her ideas.

One hundred years ago, Helen Keller also was on the receiving end of impolite invective, believe it or not, by some of the editorialists of her day. It happened after she embraced various left-leaning causes. Let's not gloss over it: She espoused socialism. This didn't sit right with the reigning newspapers at the time. One of them, the *Brooklyn Eagle*, sought to excuse her—and blame Anne Sullivan and her husband for this apostasy—by reminding its readers, without irony, that Helen Keller's faculties of observation were limited.

In a 1912 rebuttal in the *New York Call*, Keller dispensed with that argument in prose simultaneously erudite, puckish, and outraged.

"I like newspapermen," Keller wrote, adding that she'd met the *Brooklyn Eagle* editor at a benefit for the blind. "At that time the compliments he paid me were so generous that I blush to remember them," she recalled. "But now that I have come out for socialism he reminds me and the public that I am blind and deaf and especially liable to error. I must have shrunk in intelligence during the years since I met him. Surely it is his turn to blush. . . .

"Oh, ridiculous *Brooklyn Eagle*! What an ungallant bird it is!" she continued. "When it fights back, let it fight fair. . . . It is not fair fighting or good argument to remind me and others that I cannot see or hear. I can read. I can read all the socialist books I have time for in English, German, and French. If the editor of the *Brooklyn Eagle* should read some of them, he might be a wiser man and make a better newspaper."

Inauguration Day

The Founders chose March 4, not January 20, as the date for inaugurating U.S. presidents. Even accounting for vast differences in travel times and modes of communication, it was a long gap between winning an election and taking office. Today, it would be an eternity. Actually, it seemed too long in 1933, when dozens of banks were failing daily, and the American people had lost confidence in their president. So Congress moved it up.

But some of the nation's greatest oratory was spoken on March 4. And even though most of them predate the existence of radio, let alone television, the power of a well-crafted speech has a way of surviving the attritions of Father Time. Here are passages from five of them:

We have called by different names brethren of the same principle. We are all Republicans, we are all Federalists.   —Thomas Jefferson, 1801

I am loath to close. We are not enemies, but friends. We must not be enemies. Though passion may have strained, it must not break our bonds of affection. The mystic chords of memory, stretching from every battlefield and patriot grave to every living heart and hearthstone all over this broad land, will yet swell the chorus of the Union, when again touched, as surely they will be, by the better angels of our nature.   —Abraham Lincoln, 1861

With malice toward none, with charity for all, with firmness in the right as God gives us to see the right, let us strive on to finish the work we are in, to bind up the nation's wounds, to care for him who shall have borne the battle and for his widow and his orphan, to do all which may achieve and cherish a just and lasting peace among ourselves and with all nations.   —Abraham Lincoln, 1865

If we fail, the cause of free self-government throughout the world will rock to its foundations, and therefore our responsibility is heavy, to ourselves, to the world as it is today, and to the generations yet unborn.   —Theodore Roosevelt, 1905

This great nation will endure as it has endured, will revive and will prosper. So, first of all, let me assert my firm belief that the only thing we have to fear is fear itself—nameless, unreasoning, unjustified terror which paralyzes needed efforts to convert retreat into advance.   —Franklin D. Roosevelt, 1933

March 5, 1946

Missouri Card Sharps

Winston Churchill made one of the most momentous speeches of the twentieth century on this date, at Westminster College in Fulton, Missouri. "An iron curtain has descended across the continent," Churchill intoned. The Cold War was declared.

After being voted out of office in 1945, Churchill had become restless and melancholy. He turned to painting and traveled, seeking sun and a change of scenery. He found both in Florida. But the world wasn't done with Churchill, nor he with it. The following year, White House military aide Harry Vaughan came up with the idea of giving Churchill an honorary degree. President Truman himself suggested Westminster College, and personally accompanied the British lion on the train from Washington, D.C.

An Anglo-American railroad trip meant drinking and cards. After the train pulled out of Union Station, Truman served drinks. As Truman aide Clark Clifford wrote later, "Churchill drank scotch, with water, but no ice, which he viewed as a barbaric American custom." But the former prime minister was half American, so he fancied himself a poker player. Over dinner, Churchill told Truman he'd first played stud poker during the Boer War and inquired if a game might be conjured up. These were magic words to the Missourians.

"Winston," Truman said, "the fellows around you are all poker players, serious poker players, and would be delighted to provide you with a game." When Churchill excused himself briefly after dinner, Truman told his cronies that if their guest had been playing poker for forty years, he was probably a cagey player. The honor of American poker was at stake, Truman said, and they must do their duty. After about an hour of playing, however, it was clear that Churchill was in over his head. During a break, while Churchill was away from the table, Truman changed his tune.

"Now look here, men. You are not treating our guest very well," he said, gazing balefully at Churchill's dwindling pile of chips. "I fear that he may have already lost close to $300."

Hearing this, Vaughan started laughing. "But boss," he said, "*this guy's a pigeon!*"

Vaughan added that if Truman really wanted them to play poker for the nation's honor, Churchill would be sitting at the table in his underwear long before they reached Fulton. So, they eased back on the throttle a bit. Churchill wasn't allowed to win, but he didn't lose any more. An alliance, if not an empire, was preserved.

March 6, 1947

Storybook Love

On this date, two talented New Yorkers welcomed the first of their three children into the world. Carl and Estelle Reiner, both talented Broadway performers who sang and acted, named their boy Robert and eventually moved their family to California.

There, the Reiner clan achieved great success, including Rob's directing of what many people consider the perfect family movie. *The Princess Bride* achieved modest success when it was released in 1987, grossing nearly $31 million in the United States and Canada, on a $16 million budget. It might have been forgotten after that but for a new industry that came along about the same time: the home video rental business.

With parents on the prowl in their local Blockbuster stores for something to show their kids, *The Princess Bride* gradually achieved an audience—then a cult following. The film has everything: giants, pirates, castles, humor, swordplay, love, and a beautiful princess named Buttercup. Her role was played flawlessly by Robin Wright, then a little-known daytime soap opera actress.

The cast assembled by Reiner began with two recognizable television stars, Peter Falk and child actor Fred Savage, and included a brilliant ensemble: Mandy Patinkin, Chris Sarandon, Christopher Guest, Wallace Shawn, Andre the Giant, Billy Crystal, Carol Kane, Cary Elwes. British thespian Peter Cooke was cast as the clergyman whose "Mawage" ceremony is as funny the ninth time you see the movie as it is the first.

Patinkin, who played the aggrieved Spaniard Inigo Montoya, has said that no day goes by that he's not approached by a stranger who recites his character's signature line: "My name is Inigo Montoya. You killed my father—prepare to die." Patinkin, who filmed a physically taxing sword-fighting scene, has also said that the only time he got hurt making the movie was bruising a rib while trying to stifle a laugh during Billy Crystal's hilarious cameo as "Miracle Max."

It all started with an inspired screenplay by William Goldman, based on a novel Goldman had written earlier. The icing on the cake was the film's soundtrack, courtesy of the great Mark Knopfler, whose score includes the theme song, "Storybook Love." The upshot is celluloid magic.

To quote Cary Elwes's character Westley, "Think that happens every day?"

March 7, 1974

The Dick and Pearl Show

The pressure was closing in on Richard Nixon. A grand jury had indicted seven former administration officials in the burgeoning Watergate scandal and named the president himself an unindicted coconspirator. Talk of impeachment was being heard on Capitol Hill. And though Dick Nixon was no favorite in Hollywood, he was a native Southern Californian and possessed the sensibility that the show must go on. He did his best on this evening at a White House dinner by personally supplying the piano accompaniment to the great Pearl Bailey.

Pearl Bailey was a longtime Nixon supporter, and this night she stood by her man, while showing Washington how she earned her nickname, "Ambassador of Love."

The president was hosting the midwinter conference of the National Governors Association, and Ms. Bailey was wrapping up her solo performance when the singer got the idea to have the president join her onstage. Like Harry Truman before him, Nixon's piano playing was passable, but this wasn't entertaining friends in his living room. This was accompanying a legendary singer before an audience that included political allies and rivals (as well as three future presidents).

"You don't play as well as I sing," Bailey said while coaxing Nixon to start playing, "but I don't sing as well as you govern."

When the president drummed out a few bars of "Home on the Range," Bailey quipped, "Mr. President, I wanted to sing a song, not ride a horse." Getting into the swing of things, Nixon mentioned that St. Patrick's Day was coming, and played "Wild Irish Rose" which made Bailey laugh. For their finale, she suggested, "God Bless America."

Sadly, only a portion of the session was filmed, but contemporaneous witnesses provided reviews of the music—and the banter between the president and the first lady of torch singing:

"Absolutely tops!" pronounced California governor Ronald Reagan.

"I laughed so much I cried," added Vice President Gerald Ford.

Georgia governor Jimmy Carter's reaction was not recorded for posterity, but the *Washington Post*, where the most damaging investigative reporting on Watergate had been published, put down its swords for the evening. "President Nixon and Pearl Bailey," it noted, "performing as an impromptu 'Dick and Pearl Show,' momentarily upstaged Watergate, the energy crisis, troubles in the Middle East and the economy."

March 8, 1782

Massacre on the Tuscarawas

One of the most shameful events in U.S. history occurred on this date: the slaughter by Pennsylvania militiamen of ninety-six defenseless Indians who were kneeling in prayer at a Christian mission in present-day Ohio. The native people belonged to the Lenape tribe, an offshoot of the Delaware Indians. Those killed were Christians living in a Tuscarawas River village called Gnadenhutten. They were executed by being bludgeoned from behind, twenty-eight men in one "killing house," twenty-nine women and thirty-nine children in another. They were praying to Jesus as they were murdered. Their bodies were then burned.

Although the killings were carried out in retaliation for murderous raids by Indians, there is little reason to believe that those murdered were the same people who had taken up arms against whites. Even so, it would hardly have justified what took place. This atrocity sparked reprisals by surviving Lenape, some of whom resumed the practice of ritually torturing captives. It also entered the collective consciousness of Indians living in the region. Shawnee chief Tecumseh was only fourteen when the massacre occurred, but it was on his mind two decades later when he met territorial governor and Army officer William Henry Harrison at the Wabash River town of Vincennes in 1810. Tecumseh came with four hundred armed braves who had accompanied him down the river in canoes, sporting full war paint, and armed for battle. Land swindles and murder had proved to the Indians that they never could trust whites. As Tecumseh told Harrison, "When Jesus Christ came upon the earth you killed him and nailed him upon a cross."

Harrison was so alarmed by Tecumseh's defiance that at one point he drew his sword, while others in his negotiating team silently cocked their pistols. Violence did not break out that day. But the following year, Harrison decided to act. While Tecumseh was away recruiting southern tribes to the pan-Indian cause, Harrison marched on a Shawnee band camped on the Tippecanoe River headed by Tecumseh's brother.

Outgunned and outnumbered, the Shawnee were repelled, but the skirmish had sustaining ripple effects. Tecumseh became the undisputed leader of the Shawnee-led federation, which then sided with the British in the War of 1812. And in the white world, his victory at Tippecanoe made Harrison a national hero. It also set the stage for his successful presidential campaign three decades later, along with its memorable campaign phrase, "Tippecanoe and Tyler, too."

March 9, 1959

Barbie Doll

The star of Mattel Toys made her debut on this day at the American Toy Fair in New York City. Mattel gave Barbie a full name (Barbie Millicent Roberts), a fictional hometown (Willows, Wisconsin) and a boyfriend (Ken, who first appeared in 1961), but it was always Barbie herself—and those endless outfits—that held American girls in such thrall.

Mattel's marketers understood early on that their profits were not dependent on Barbie's WASP-ish identity. Barbie spoke Spanish as early as 1968, the year after her African-American friend, Francie, hit the toy shelves. But one didn't have to be a "bra-burning feminist," in the parlance of the day, to worry that Barbie's figure (it was estimated that if she were life-sized her measurements would be 36-18-38) might give young girls unrealistic expectations about their bodies. Also, what was with all the designer clothes?

The idea for Barbie came to Ruth Handler, a cofounder of Mattel with her husband, Elliot, by watching their daughter Barbara play with dolls. The girl and her friends gravitated toward adult paper dolls, not baby dolls, giving Ruth the insight that girls wanted to play with dolls that depicted kids older than themselves, not younger. On a trip to Europe in the mid-1950s, Ruth saw such a doll and bought three of them. This doll was named Lilli and was originally sold as kind of a gag gift in tobacco shops for German men. But German husbands had German little girls at home, and it soon became apparent, as Ruth Handler had noticed in California, that girls preferred this kind of doll.

Although Barbie was once programmed to say, "Math class is tough," a Miss Astronaut Barbie appeared as early as 1965 (when Sally Ride was fourteen). In addition, Mattel produced Barbie the Olympic Athlete (in 1975, before Title IX regulations were adopted by the federal government); Barbie, Ambassador for Peace (in 1986, ten years before Madeleine Albright became the first female U.S. secretary of state); Marine Corps Officer Barbie (in 1991, a year before Gunnery Sgt. Melody Naatz became the first woman to don the flat brimmed "Smokey Bear" as a U.S. Marine drill instructor); and a Barbie for President (in 1992, when Hillary Clinton was seeking only to become First Lady). To quote a famous ad campaign, American women and girls have come a long way since Mattel's doll first appeared. Barbie was with them each step of the way—sometimes showing the way.

March 10, 1927

Intermittent Flash of Genius

Robert W. Kearns had reason to be philosophical: His greatest invention occurred to him because of a minor personal calamity on his wedding night in August 1953. Born on this date in Gary, Indiana, and raised near Ford Motor Company's sprawling River Rouge complex, Kearns grew up wanting to help build cars. During World War II, he served in the OSS, the forerunner of the CIA. After the war, he earned engineering degrees from Detroit-area colleges and a doctorate from Case Western Reserve University. He began amassing patents for several inventions and innovative mechanical tweaks to help U.S. automakers.

His Big Idea followed from a bit of bad luck, which about sums up Kearns's life. After his wedding reception in 1953, he opened a champagne bottle and the cork struck him in the left eye. He eventually lost the sight in the eye, but in 1962, while driving in Detroit during a rain shower, his incessant blinking got him to wondering if he could produce windshield wipers that operated under the same principle—working at intermittent intervals as the need arose. He experimented for many years on his own family automobiles. "If it rained," his former wife recalled, "we would stop whatever we were doing, run out to the car, turn the wipers on, and drive around."

This determination paid off eventually: Robert invented a windshield wiper that drivers could set at the intervals of their choosing. He was awarded several patents in 1967. When this technology subsequently showed up in cars, Kearns sued. And sued and sued and sued. He refused an out-of-court settlement with Ford Motor that would have made him a rich man, although many years later he won a $10.2 million trial verdict against Ford and then won nearly $20 million in a suit against Chrysler. By then, however, the crusade had cost Kearns his perspective and his marriage.

"It had become an obsession," ex-wife Phyllis Hall recalled after her first husband passed away. "I told him, 'I can't stand this life.' He said, 'This *is* my life.'"

Three years after Kearns's death in 2005, a movie, *Flash of Genius* starring Greg Kinnear, was made about his life. To the *Wall Street Journal*, the man's obsessiveness went hand in hand with "the kind of inspiration that separates inventors from ordinary people."

Kearns himself once put it this way: "Bob Kearns is not somebody's lackey."

March 11, 1989

Bad Boys

On this day, a show named *COPS* appeared for the first time. The idea that you could get Americans to look and act ridiculous if you point a camera or microphone at them—and that people would willingly watch—was not new. The notion predates television. Its pioneer was Allen Funt, an Ivy League–educated New York native who learned to record sound in the U.S. Army Signal Corps during World War II.

After the war, Funt took his idea to ABC. In June 1947, it debuted as a radio show called *Candid Microphone*. The following year, the format migrated to television, along with a signature line that would become a cultural touchstone: "Smile, you're on *Candid Camera*." A genre was born. Over the years, the format ranged from *An American Family* to "Jaywalking." The former was a 1973 reality show featuring the Loud family of Santa Barbara, California; the latter was Jay Leno's sporadic *Tonight Show* forays into streets where he quizzed the citizenry about its (comically tenuous) grasp of history, culture, and current events.

But *COPS* was a new frontier. Producers John Langley and Malcolm Barbour found a receptive audience for their concept among Fox network executives because a writers' strike had left the network in the lurch. Set in Florida, and heralded by the reggae tune "Bad Boys," the show followed the Broward County sheriff's deputies as they made actual arrests.

This show didn't require writers, saving money in the process, and it attracted strong ratings. Other networks were following suit, launching a craze that didn't abate when the writers' strike ended. You can draw a line from *Candid Camera* to *Keeping up with the Kardashians*, stopping along the way for *Divorce Court*, *The Bachelor*, *The Cougar*, *The Biggest Loser*, and *19 Kids and Counting*. At some point, the genre began to defy parody.

It was the long-running TV series *Happy Days* (not a reality show) that gave rise to the expression "jump the shark," signifying the moment when a show's decline was irreversible. The reality TV craze had a whole industry jumping the shark. Everybody had their favorite example. For some it was *Celebrity Wife Swap* or *My 600-Pound Life*. For others, it was *Toddlers & Tiaras* or its infamous spinoff, *Here Comes Honey Boo-Boo*.

The reality show with the biggest cultural impact, however, was launched in January 2004. It was a network program with high production values and a host whom people loved or hated. It was called *The Apprentice*.

March 12, 1901

Surplus Wealth

Scottish-born Andrew Carnegie announced a $5.2 million donation to the city of New York for construction of sixty-five new branches of the city's public library system on this date. One of the most successful turn-of-the-century industrialists, he amassed an immense personal fortune in an age before income taxes were levied on anyone, let alone the rich.

To his critics, this wealth was piled up on the backs of working people: Carnegie was one of the most prominent moguls known as "robber barons." But the committed capitalist who wrote a book called *The Gospel of Wealth* also believed that a successful person should spend the first third of his life acquiring education, the second third acquiring wealth, and the last third giving that money away to worthy causes. And this was exactly what he did.

No cause was more worthy to Andrew Carnegie than education; hence the gift to the libraries. By the time of his death, he'd given $5 billion (in today's dollars) to charity, the arts, and education—founding some 2,500 libraries in the United States and other English-speaking nations. This money is the gift that keeps on giving. Public libraries, with their reliance on government funding, volunteers, and philanthropy, are a testament to an ethos of cooperation.

Examples abound by the thousands. If you are benefitting from the English as a Second Language program, listening to lectures on First Ladies at the Kansas City Library, or availing yourself of the volunteer-propelled programs such as financial management, nutrition, poetry workshops, and online learning at the Bernardsville Public Library in New Jersey, you are benefitting, at least in part, because of Andrew Carnegie. Ditto if you live in Centerville, South Dakota, where the library's entire annual budget is less than $80,000, yet offers a webinar, extended hours of operation, school homecoming festivities, and a Christmas parade.

On summer nights, the library lawn on Block Island off the coast of Rhode Island is aglow with handheld devices and laptops courtesy of the Island Free Library's twenty-four-hour Wi-Fi access. "Libraries will get you through times of no money," writer Anna Herbert once observed, "better than money will get you through times of no libraries."

Andrew Carnegie would have approved of the fruits of his seed money. He called surplus wealth a "sacred trust" that a rich man was obliged to dispense in his lifetime for the good of the community. "The man who dies rich," he added, "dies disgraced."

March 13, 1908

Ancient Superstition

The idea of bad fortune accruing to the thirteenth day of the month, provided it falls on a Friday, is a melding of two old superstitions: that thirteen is an unlucky number and that Friday is an unlucky day. University of Delaware professor Thomas Fernsler, affectionately known as "Dr. Thirteen," says the number gets bad press because it follows twelve, which numerologists consider a "complete" number. Disparate societies over the millennia produced twelve months in a year, twelve signs of the zodiac, twelve gods of Mount Olympus, twelve tribes of Israel, and twelve Apostles of Christ. In the Christian tradition, the thirteenth person to sit at the Last Supper, Judas Iscariot, betrayed Jesus.

Friday has also long been considered in the folktales of many cultures to be the wrong day to begin a venture, lay the keel of a new boat, harvest a crop, begin a long journey—whatever. At some point in the twentieth century, these two superstitions merged.

Not everyone subscribed to these phobias, notably a turn-of-the-century U.S. senator and Democratic presidential candidate from Oklahoma named Robert L. Owen. On March 13, 1908—a Friday—Senator Owen sponsored thirteen bills in Congress. "Friday the 13th holds no terrors for Senator Owen," reported the *New York Times*. "The senator from Oklahoma is a Cherokee Indian, and he places the Indian sign on the ancient superstition."

Actually, Robert Owen's ethnic heritage was not so easily defined. Born in Virginia prior to the Civil War, his father was a Southern gentleman of Welsh origin who worked as a civil engineer and railroad executive.

The father lost his family's fortune in the Panic of 1893, the same year he died. Robert and his mother, Narcissa, moved to Oklahoma, where she had kinsmen. Narcissa claimed some Cherokee blood, but not much. Tracing her own family tree, she deduced she was one-sixteenth Cherokee, although the editor of her memoirs thinks she might have skipped a generation or two. This suggests that Robert Owen was perhaps one sixty-fourth Cherokee.

That was close enough for the *Times* and for the Cherokee Nation elders, who recognized Owen as one of their own. And wouldn't they? After moving to Oklahoma, Owen taught at the Cherokee orphanage, published a reservation newspaper, and served as a union agent for the "Five Civilized Tribes." In 1920 he sought his party's presidential nomination at the Democrats' San Francisco convention. Senator Owen's luck held out through the thirteenth ballot—until he finally lost on the forty-fourth.

March 14, 1879 (and 1948)

Albert and Billy

Genius comes in many guises, sometimes revealing itself in the musings of those who contemplate gravity, space travel, and the limits of physics; other times it manifests itself in the whimsical comedy of movies. This date is Albert Einstein's birthday—and Billy Crystal's.

Born in Manhattan and raised on Long Island, Billy Crystal is one of America's most beloved comedians. Albert Einstein was born in Ulm on the Danube River, raised in Munich, and became the world's most revered intellectual. Einstein traveled the world as he earned fame as a scientist and lecturer, and he came to the United States for good in 1933 as Adolf Hitler rose to power in Germany.

Crystal's father owned a music store, and their house was an eclectic gathering place for the greats of Dixieland jazz. But Billy Crystal idolized Mickey Mantle and dreamed of turning his high school baseball success into a career at Yankee Stadium. Although there aren't many five-foot-seven-inch center fielders, baseball's loss was the arts' gain. But the funny man has a serious side. Visitors to the Simon Wiesenthal Center's Museum of Tolerance in Southern California are greeted by a video of Billy Crystal welcoming them to the genealogical wing.

Like Crystal, Albert Einstein was raised by Jewish parents, but they were ecumenical enough to send their boy to Catholic school when he was young. Some of that education stuck. Einstein is remembered as the scientist who alerted Franklin Roosevelt to the possibility of building an atomic bomb, but he had a spiritual side all his life. Religion is pitted against science, but Einstein suggested that this is a false choice.

"Strenuous intellectual work and the study of God's Nature," he wrote to a female friend in 1897, "are the angels that will lead me through all the troubles of this life with consolation, strength, and uncompromising rigor."

"I want to know God's thoughts," Einstein also told author Esther Salaman. "The rest are details."

And if Billy Crystal can be serious, Einstein could be funny. In 1913, commenting on his famously rumpled appearance, he told Elsa Lowenthal, "If I were to start taking care of my grooming, I would no longer be my own self."

Late in life, Einstein also quipped to the *New York Times*, "Why is it that nobody understands me, yet everybody likes me?"

March 15, 1965

LBJ Takes the Bully Pulpit

After civil rights marcher Jimmie Lee Jackson was fatally shot by state troopers in Marion, Alabama, a protest was called for March 7, 1965. The planned destination: the state capital in Montgomery. Two years earlier, Gov. George Wallace had delivered a fiery inaugural address from the spot where Jefferson Davis had been sworn in as president of the Confederacy. Wallace made that historical connection in his speech, which he punctuated with the now-infamous declaration: "I say segregation now, segregation tomorrow, segregation forever!"

To this, civil rights leaders offered a succinct rejoinder, "We shall overcome!" This was more than a hymn. It was a call to action. But on March 7 at the Edmund Pettus Bridge the civil rights marchers were attacked by a mob armed with clubs and whips. Alabama state troopers either stood by and did nothing or participated in the attack.

"Bloody Sunday" generated national outrage and prompted a direct challenge from Student Nonviolent Coordinating Committee leader John Lewis, who was severely beaten that day, to the man in the White House: "I don't see how President Johnson can send troops to Vietnam," Lewis said. "I don't see how he can send troops to the Congo... and can't send troops to Selma."

In Washington, Lyndon Johnson was having similar thoughts. Meanwhile, religious leaders poured into Alabama from around the country, and two days later, Martin Luther King led a crowd four times as large on the same route. Again, they were turned back by police, who had barricaded State Route 80, the road into Montgomery. Johnson had seen enough. On this date, the president took to the airwaves to announce a new voting rights act.

"Their cause must be our cause, too, because it is not just Negroes, but really it is all of us, who must overcome the crippling legacy of bigotry and injustice," Johnson said. "And we shall overcome." Six days later, the marchers tried again. This time, they were escorted by U.S. Army troops and federalized members of the Alabama National Guard. They crossed the Edmund Pettus Bridge and continued on State Route 80.

A federal judge had limited the number of marchers to three hundred, but by the time they reached the steps of the capitol in Montgomery on March 25, their ranks had swelled to twenty-five thousand. How long must they wait for justice? King asked the audience in his famous call-and-response.

"How long? Not long."

March 16, 1947

Margaret Truman Hits the Big Time

As a girl growing up in Missouri, Harry and Bess Truman's only child, Margaret, performed as a soloist at Trinity Episcopal Church in Independence. Impressed, the choir director encouraged Margaret to get professional voice lessons, advice she followed before and after graduating from George Washington University in the nation's capital.

By that time, her father was president and Margaret would learn that the opportunities were greater—and the spotlight brighter—than back home in Missouri. When she made her professional debut on this date, singing with the Detroit Symphony, some 15 million Americans heard the ABC radio broadcast. Two and a half years later, she packed Constitution Hall in Washington for an audience that included her parents. Also in the theater that night was a young man named Paul Hume, who studied piano and organ as a child and, like Margaret, took professional voice lessons. In hindsight, we can note that Hume probably had a better voice and ear for classical music than Margaret Truman; he was certainly destined for a more distinguished career in the field of music.

At the University of Chicago, Hume had majored in English while taking courses in music theory and music history. After World War II, he became the music critic for the *Washington Post* while teaching music classes at Georgetown and Yale, hosting a popular classical-music radio program, and writing books on Catholic church music and biographies of influential musicians ranging from Verdi to Irish tenor John McCormack. Hume also moonlighted as a cocktail pianist at the Mayflower Hotel, was a baritone soloist and organist at the Washington National Cathedral, and directed the Georgetown glee club.

On December 5, 1950, he was seated in Constitution Hall in his capacity as a newspaper music critic—and was underwhelmed with how Margaret Truman handled her program of Schumann, Schubert, and Mozart.

"Miss Truman is a unique American phenomenon with a pleasant voice of little size and fair quality," Hume wrote in his review. "She is extremely attractive on stage. Yet Miss Truman cannot sing very well. She is flat a good deal of the time—more so last night than at any time we have heard her in past years."

President Truman read these words in his morning newspaper the following day, and they did not go down well. What happened next will be revisited on December 5.

March 17, 1762

The Wearin' of the Green

On St. Patrick's Day each year, Ireland's prime minister visits the White House to drop off shamrocks symbolizing America's bond with the Irish people. It's a tradition that has grown more elaborate over time. When the first shamrocks were delivered on this date in 1952, President Truman wasn't even home. A modern president would be tone-deaf to miss such an opportunity now. Not only do 40 million Americans claim Irish ancestry, but St. Patrick's Day is, in a very real sense, an American original.

The first St. Patrick's Day parade was held in New York City, not Dublin. Fourteen years before the Declaration of Independence was signed, homesick Irishmen serving in the British Army marched out of their barracks in celebration. New York's parade is still the largest in the world, making it a magnet for politicians and social activists as well as Irish-Americans—and those without a drop of Irish blood.

This is oddly fitting. Patrick himself was not Irish. His parents were Roman citizens who lived in present-day Scotland where Patrick was born and his father served as a government official at the western outpost of the Roman empire. Kidnapped by Irish raiders, Patrick's faith was strengthened in captivity, and he dreamed of spreading Christianity to Druid and pagan Ireland. After escaping and returning to Britain, he studied for the priesthood, was made a bishop, and sailed back across the Irish Sea. Patrick's gift wasn't an ability to perform miracles such as driving snakes from Ireland. It was how he spread the gospel. He had no armies to force the issue, but he did speak the local language, and he incorporated local traditions into his ministry. The great bonfires the Irish liked to burn to herald the arrival of spring were appropriated by Patrick for Easter celebrations. He used the island's ubiquitous three-leaf clovers to illustrate the Holy Trinity.

That teaching prop might be why he is remembered still. For more than a millennium, his memory was kept alive by those shamrocks, as his life was celebrated as a distinctly religious, and distinctly local, holiday. As the Irish diaspora spread throughout the world, immigrants spread the word of St. Patrick, just as he had spread the word of the Gospel. Those who complain that New York's parade has been marred by culture wars infighting—specifically, the desire of gays to march—should remember two things:

First, there was an overtly pro-Irish political agenda in the very first St. Paddy's parade. Second, the overriding purpose of the event was social: The men who marched in 1762 weren't heading into battle—and didn't wind up at any cathedral. They marched to a tavern.

March 18, 1837

A Prescient President

On this date, in Caldwell, New Jersey, a Presbyterian minister named Richard Cleveland and his wife, Ann, welcomed a son into the world. They named him Stephen Grover Cleveland. He would serve as mayor of Buffalo, governor of New York, and president of the United States twice—the only person to serve nonconsecutive terms. His name is not heard much in American civic life these days, which is a shame: His career should be a source of inspiration for anyone with political ambitions—or who has ever suffered career setbacks.

In 2016, Hillary Clinton became the fifth presidential candidate to win the popular vote and lose the presidency. The third was Grover Cleveland, who recovered from his 1888 loss to Benjamin Harrison by running again in 1892 and winning the rematch.

George W. Bush (the fourth president to prevail in the Electoral College while failing to win the most votes) described himself as a "Reformer with Results," a dig at John McCain's tenure in the Senate, where little work ever seems to get done. But the real reformer with results was the president born on this date. Tapped in 1881 by Buffalo's business leaders to run for mayor, Cleveland promptly cleaned up City Hall. His reputation for good government led upstate Democrats to push his gubernatorial candidacy. In Albany, Cleveland tackled Tammany Hall, New York City's powerful Democratic Party machine, even though Tammany had supported his election.

Remember the horrid economy inherited by Barack Obama when he assumed office in 2009? Cleveland faced a much worse one in 1893. Cleveland succeeded because Americans trusted him. This reputation for probity did not extend to his personal life. To win the presidency, Cleveland withstood a sex scandal far more salacious than the Little Rock dalliances that nearly derailed Bill Clinton's 1992 campaign. As president, Cleveland shocked the country by courting a twenty-one-year-old woman, which evokes a subsequent Clinton sex scandal that took place in the White House. A bachelor, Cleveland had a course of action unavailable to Bill Clinton. He could (and did) marry beautiful Frances Clara Folsom.

If Cleveland is remembered today, it is usually on the anniversary of the 1886 dedication of the Statue of Liberty. Speaking without notes, in a clear voice heard two hundred feet away, President Cleveland said that the American people "will not forget that liberty here made her home; nor shall her chosen altar be neglected."

March 19, 1916

Flying After Pancho Villa

The Mexican Revolution, which broke out in November 1910, is remembered today for its frightful carnage: More than 1 million people died, most of them noncombatants, in a nation of 15 million souls, during a civil war that lasted until 1917. For the United States, that gruesome conflict south of the border produced a series of well-meaning, but inept, missteps—a template that would be repeated in many future foreign conflicts: the U.S. taking sides in an uncertain way; arming one faction, then another; all the while giving misleading diplomatic signals.

Among those who took umbrage at counterproductive American policies was a ruthless Mexican commander named José Doroteo Arango Arámbula. He fought under the pseudonym Francisco Villa, and is known to this day by his nickname: Pancho Villa.

On March 9, 1916, Villa and his troops rode across the U.S. border under cover of darkness and attacked Columbus, New Mexico. The target was Camp Furlong, which housed the Thirteenth U.S. Army Cavalry Regiment. Ten American officers and soldiers were killed in the ensuing skirmish and eight civilians were slain. Coming on the heels of a raid that killed seventeen Americans aboard a train from Chihuahua, the Columbus raid put U.S. public opinion at the boiling point. Woodrow Wilson ordered the U.S. Army to capture Pancho Villa.

This it could never do in nine months of trying. Why did the Army stop looking? Well, the general tasked with the job, John J. Pershing, was given a more pressing command in Europe. Yet the Villa campaign provided two military precedents. The first came on May 14, 1916, when one of Pershing's junior officers led the first motorized military ground assault in the history of U.S. warfare. The lieutenant directing the attack was named George S. Patton.

A second footnote is that the Villa campaign saw the first combat-related mission by U.S. military aircraft. The planes, eight in all, were flying reconnaissance, albeit ineptly. They were late taking off, putting them in darkness quickly; one of them had engine problems; the aviators' maps were inaccurate; each plane carried a different kind of compass. They were scattered around the desert the following morning. One American pilot suffered a broken nose when he crash-landed, but none of them died, and none were captured. Although they never so much as glimpsed Pancho Villa, on this date, U.S. Army pilots ushered in a technological revolution that added a transformative new dimension to how Americans waged war.

March 20, 1979

Brian Lamb's Big Idea Comes to Life

Morning newspapers reported the debut of full-time, national, not-for-profit public affairs programming. The concept behind C-SPAN was that news coverage didn't have to be sexy, it could simply be informative. So, when the *New York Times* headline on this date blared, First TV Broadcast of House Session Isn't High Theater, Brian Lamb didn't fret. He smiled.

Lamb first came up with the idea in the 1970s as Washington bureau chief for *Cablevision* magazine. His idea was to get cameras on the floor of the House of Representatives. This was before CNN (or Fox News) existed, at a time the three major networks' nightly news shows cornered two-thirds of the nation's viewing audience. When Lamb introduced his plan at an industry-wide conference—for a nonprofit to be funded by the cable broadcasters themselves—just one cable executive, Bob Rosencrans, embraced it. He wrote a check for $25,000 in seed money. Lamb proved to be one of those rare visionaries who is enough of a detail man to successfully implement his own idea. In an industry about to be convulsed by economic and ideological upheaval, the key was C-SPAN's obsessive nonpartisanship, epitomized by Lamb's own deadpan interviewing style. It was a sensibility emanating directly from the nation's heartland.

Lamb attended high school in his hometown of Lafayette, Indiana, attended nearby Purdue University, and enlisted in the U.S. Navy after graduation. By then, he'd already internalized the lessons of an educator named Bill Fraser, a teacher at Jefferson High School in Lafayette. "He taught me to stay the hell out of the way," Lamb recalled in 1989. "Too many interviewers intrude too much. They want to be the main attraction. They use inflections.... They try to make us think they're smarter than the person they're interviewing."

Criticisms about journalists' "inflections" seem quaint in the wake of another, more dubious, cable television innovation: that is, the overtly partisan network. But long before he sold one such network to Al Jazeera for $500 million, Albert Gore Jr.

was a Tennessee congressman with an expressed fascination for technology, innovation, and transparency in government.

On March 19, 1979, Gore made the first speech televised from the House of Representatives. Speaking to an audience that Lamb has joked "was in the dozens," Al Gore stood in the well of the House and said, "The marriage of this medium and of our open debate have the potential, Mr. Speaker, to revitalize representative democracy."

March 21, 2006

Tweet, Tweet

Brevity is the soul of wit," notes Lord Polonius in *Hamlet*. Shakespeare's observation is more than a timeless bit of wisdom. It's also a tacit challenge to his fellow writers, and to the innovative minded among us who like to facilitate human communication. Riffing off the Bard's prose, Dorothy Parker, a precocious ad copy-writer at *Vogue* magazine came up with this gem in 1916: "Brevity is the soul of lingerie," a line so clever it helped land her a job at *Vanity Fair*.

Ninety years later, a thirty-year-old St. Louis native and New York University dropout named Jack Dorsey was out in California trying to figure out the Internet's Next Big Thing. Dorsey was focused on two aspects of online communication: speed and brevity. Inspired in part by AOL's instant message service, Dorsey teamed up with a couple of proven Silicon Valley stars to launch an online communication service and social media vehicle with an interesting angle: It would limit users to 140 characters per message.

They initially called the thing "twttr," which proved too obscure until they changed it to Twitter. To say it took off is an understatement. Twitter quickly amassed hundreds of millions of users, among them a certain New York real estate developer with a liking for the limelight. Meanwhile, the company fixed up its founders nicely. Within eight years, Jack Dorsey was worth some $2.2 billion, according to *Forbes*, and was named to the board of directors of the Walt Disney Company.

His first tweet, disseminated on this date, wouldn't have hinted at any of this. Sending from an account simply named @jack, Dorsey pecked out, "just setting up my twttr."

Jack Dorsey was the right guy at the right time, but his success involved more than luck. Twitter's essential genius—its forced brevity—is not mere coincidence. Dorsey, it turned out, possessed a gift for explaining life succinctly. During a 2014 appearance at Harvard, he exhibited this trait. "You have to be in control of your own destiny," he said.

He also told the students: "Surround yourself with people who challenge your ideas."

This is sage advice for people of any age, especially at a time when college campuses are becoming bastions of consensns where that very concept is under direct assault. And it's only fifty-four characters long.

March 22, 1933

Carry Nation's Cause

On this date, Congress and President Franklin Roosevelt reasserted one of the privileges Americans view as their birthright: the right to drink alcoholic beverages. To do so, however, they had to buck a force of nature named Carry Nation.

"While I was at Harvard," she wrote ominously to a friend, describing her Cambridge visit, "I saw professors smoking cigarettes." But what really riled her up, and she carried a hatchet to punctuate her passions, was the proliferation of saloons in this country that had accompanied the great spike in American beer drinking in the nineteenth century.

Her signature move was to stride into a public tap house, fellow Prohibitionists by her side, order the lazy fellows at the bar out into the street, and then destroy the beer barrels that served a thirsty male population. In *Last Call: The Rise and Fall of Prohibition*, author Daniel Okrent provides a colorful description of the scourge of America's barkeeps:

Carry Amelia Moore Gloyd Nation was six feet tall, with the biceps of a stevedore, the face of a prison warden, and the persistence of a toothache. Her mother believed herself to be Queen Victoria. Her first husband was a rotten drunk. Her religious passions led her to sit on her organ bench and talk to Christ... [and] she once described herself as "a bulldog running along at the feet of Jesus barking at what He doesn't like."

Total abstinence in Jesus' name seems an unlikely tribute to the Holy Land prophet who turned water into wine. Certainly, Franklin D. Roosevelt found Carry Nation's crusade discordant. Yet she and her ilk convinced Americans to usher in Prohibition, which did not end drinking in this country, but did give organized crime a foothold. The law was the bane of a succession of U.S. presidents. Woodrow Wilson tried unsuccessfully to stop it, Herbert Hoover was booed at a baseball game by a crowd chanting, "We want beer! We want beer!"

FDR came into office hoping to be the one to sign the legislation relaxing it. On this day, Roosevelt got his wish, courtesy of a classic Washington gambit: Congress passed a law imposing a federal tax on the sale of beer and wine. To tax something, that something must be for sale, and the Beer and Wine Revenue Act of 1933 left the decision whether to legalize the sale of wine and beer up to the states. This compromise signaled the beginning of the end of Prohibition, which was repealed by the end of the year.

March 23, 1878

Caregivers

Adhering to its progressive ideals, the New England Hospital for Women and Children admitted a black woman to its nursing program on this date. Mary Eliza Mahoney was thirty-three years old, but had worked at the hospital for years. It was time well spent. Of the forty-two students admitted in her class, only four managed to complete the one-year coursework, meaning that Mary Mahoney was the first African-American professional nurse in this country.

The search for such "firsts" is not an exact science. For most of the twentieth century, the first female African-American physician was believed to be Rebecca J. Cole, a Philadelphian born in 1846 and admitted to Woman's Medical College in the same city. Cole went on to have a distinguished medical career while tangling with W. E. B. Du Bois in the process. The famed black social commentator suggested that high black mortality rates stemmed from ignorance of hygiene in African-American communities. Dr. Cole fingered another culprit: the failure of white doctors to adequately document the medical histories of their black patients.

But Cole was not the first black doctor in the United States. She wasn't even the first one named Rebecca. That distinction belongs to Rebecca Lee Crumpler, who practiced medicine before, during, and after the Civil War. Raised by an aunt who spent many of her waking hours caring for sick neighbors, and after moving to Boston in 1852, she spent eight years as a nurse. She entered New England Female Medical College in 1860, graduating from an otherwise all-white class in 1864. In a pamphlet published in 1883, she provided some bare-bones biographical information, including her motivation to go into medicine.

"It may be well to state here that, having been reared by a kind aunt in Pennsylvania, whose usefulness with the sick was continually sought, I early conceived a liking for, and sought every opportunity to relieve the sufferings of others," Crumpler wrote. She practiced in Boston before moving to Richmond after the Civil War to care for freed slaves. The fallen Confederate capital, she believed, provided "a proper field for real missionary work, and one that would present ample opportunities to become acquainted with the diseases of women and children."

"At the close of my services in that city," she added, "I returned to my former home, Boston, where I entered into the work with renewed vigor, practicing outside, and receiving children in the house for treatment; regardless, in a measure, of remuneration."

March 24, 1862

Contraband

In June 2015 when a domestic terrorist entered a venerable black church in South Carolina and murdered nine people with the goal of starting a race war, it set in motion a national conversation that included discussion about why the Civil War was really fought. Arising periodically, this is an important subject for discourse. But the answer is always the same.

In response to Southerners' professed love of liberty, Abraham Lincoln noted caustically that "the *perfect* liberty they sigh for [is] the liberty of making slaves of other people."

By the time Lincoln arrived in the White House, secession was an accomplished fact. In his first inaugural address, the new president succinctly described the battle lines: "One section of our country believes slavery is a right and ought to be extended," he said, "while the other believes it is wrong and ought not to be extended."

For the most part, the men who mustered in the respective armies of North and South knew this, too. As for the hoary debate about whether the war was fought over freeing slaves versus keeping the United States intact, those were never mutually exclusive aims. One Union soldier, Elisha Hunt Rhodes of the Second Rhode Island Volunteers, succinctly summed up all the reasons he was fighting in a passage of a letter he wrote home. "I thank God that I have had an opportunity of serving my country, freeing the slaves and restoring the Union," he wrote.

Hiram Underwood, by contrast, wasn't so sure. An officer in the Second Michigan Infantry, Underwood made known his resentment toward the politicians who'd led Americans into civil war over the question of slavery. Consequently, Underwood wasn't thought by his troops to be kindly disposed to the blacks whose condition in human bondage had forced the question.

Those perceptions changed on this date as the Second Michigan marched toward Richmond. En route, the unit encountered escaped slaves, called "contrabands" in Union Army parlance. A young enlisted man named Charles B. Haydon recorded in his diary what happened next:

"Major Underwood has always been very bitter on the Abolitionists, but tonight he worked more than 3 hours in water up to his waist to help 20 contrabands across the river & on their way to Paradise at Fort Monroe. He said they looked so frightened that he had to help them."

March 25, 1957

A Howl for Free Speech

Obscenity laws in America were so sweeping in the 1950s that Allen Ginsberg had to find a publisher in England to print *Howl and Other Poems*. On this date, 520 copies of it were seized by U.S. Customs agents. Undeterred, Lawrence Ferlinghetti, owner of the City Lights bookstore in San Francisco, stocked Ginsberg's volume on his shelves and, by June, store clerk Shig Murao was arrested for selling it to undercover cops assigned to the SFPD's Juvenile Bureau. San Francisco was a different place in the mid-twentieth century than now. Although starting to become a counterculture mecca, the city was still a maze of culturally conservative ethnic enclaves, whether Asian or heavily Catholic Irish and Italian neighborhoods. The newest wave were former servicemen who'd shipped out from California during World War II on their way to the Pacific. Fearing a San Francisco jury would deem *Howl* obscene on its face, Ferlinghetti's lawyers asked for a bench trial. The Municipal Court judge they drew was Clayton W. Horn, a Republican who spent his weekends teaching Sunday school.

He proved up to the task. Over prosecution objections, Judge Horn allowed testimony from nine literary experts, all of whom vouched for the social value of *Howl*. This testimony was countered by two prosecution witnesses, one of whom claimed that *Howl* was a poor imitation of Walt Whitman's *Leaves of Grass*, and therefore lacked literary merit. Siding with the defense, Horn noted that California's obscenity statue said nothing about minors. Horn also ruled that *Howl and Other Poems* did not violate the statute anyway. The U.S. Supreme Court had recently defined obscenity in the *Roth* case, and Horn relied on its standard in his ruling. He quoted four different Supreme Court justices, along with Thomas Jefferson and Lord Macaulay, and cut to the heart of Allen Ginsberg's work more succinctly than the defense witnesses had done.

"The first part of 'Howl' presents a picture of a nightmare world," the judge wrote. "The second part is an indictment of those elements in modern society destructive of the best qualities of human nature; such elements are predominantly identified as materialism, conformity, and mechanization leading toward war..."

"It ends in a plea for holy living," Horn added, ending on the following note: "In considering material claimed to be obscene it is well to remember the motto: '*Honi soit qui mal y pense*'" (Shame to him who thinks evil).

American Bards

To those who don't regularly read verse, poetry is considered a soothing and unthreatening mode of communication, but this is not the case, and never has been. Consider *Leaves of Grass*, the collection of Walt Whitman poems that the state of California's so-called literary rebuttal witnesses cited in Allen Ginsburg's obscenity trial. This was a powerful work when it was written, and for years after. Bill Clinton gave a copy to young Hillary Rodham when he was courting her—and to Monica Lewinsky, for the same reason, twenty years later.

It was on this date that Walt Whitman died. (It was also on a March 26, in 1874, that Robert Frost was born.) Whitman's poetry was originally considered little more than smut in some quarters. It wasn't Whitman's death that changed that view so much as it was that the Civil War toughened Americans' hides and literary sensibilities. Whitman updated *Leaves of Grass* as he went along, adding odes to Abraham Lincoln—and who could fault him for that?

> *O Captain! my Captain! our fearful trip is done;*
> *The ship has weather'd every rack, the prize we sought is won.*

Upon Whitman's death, the *New York Times* laid the old argument to rest, declaring in an editorial that to withhold from Whitman the status of "a great poet" was to "deny poetry to be an art." He had been called to this art by a Ralph Waldo Emerson essay that was a plea for a young American poet to emerge— someone to capture the nation's physical beauty, economic strength, and moral hypocrisy. Emerson was alluding, at least partly, to slavery. His piece was a paean to poetry itself ("The poets are thus liberating gods," he wrote) and it found its mark. "I was simmering, simmering, simmering," Whitman later wrote. "Emerson brought me to a boil."

By the time Walt Whitman died, the rocky soil of New England had

produced another brawny bard, and when Robert Frost passed away, the *Times* also placed him in the pantheon. The paper's obituary noted that he was the only American poet to play a touching personal role at a presidential inauguration or to "twit the Russians about the barrier to Berlin by reading to them, on their own ground, his celebrated poem about another kind of wall."

That poem is "Mending Wall," which contrasts the truism that "good fences make good neighbors" with the narrator's gut feeling—highly relevant in American politics in the twenty-first century—that he "doesn't love a wall."

March 27, 1912
Cherry Blossoms Across the Sea

In a springtime show of friendship between two great countries, Japanese cherry trees—a gift from the city of Tokyo—were on this date planted along the banks of Washington's Tidal Basin. The ceremonial planting was led by First Lady Helen Herron "Nellie" Taft and Iwa Chinda, wife of the Japanese ambassador.

The idea for planting cherry trees in our nation's capital originated with a Washingtonian named Eliza Scidmore. Eliza came to the capital as a child during the Civil War. Her father was a Union Army officer; her mother volunteered at military hospitals. Eliza spent two years at Oberlin College before becoming a Washington correspondent, a travel writer, and an explorer. In 1885, on her first trip to Japan, she was struck by how the promenades of Tokyo were lined with cherry trees. She thought they'd look wonderful in her adopted hometown, and upon returning she took her idea to a succession of Army superintendents responsible for overseeing the reclaimed Potomac River waterfront—and was ignored.

It was Nellie Taft who helped her get the project off the ground. Scidmore was in the process of raising funds privately to purchase the trees when she sent the First Lady a note explaining her vision. Having lived in Japan, Mrs. Taft knew of their beauty firsthand. The following day, she inquired of a visiting Japanese consul about the availability of cherry trees, and was promptly promised two thousand of them as a gift.

The first batch that arrived from Japan in January 1910 was infested with bugs and had to be burned, a decision that went all the way to the president's desk and involved apologies all around. By March 1912, a new shipment of three thousand Yoshino cherry trees arrived and were planted along the Tidal Basin. In the early years of Franklin Roosevelt's administration, District of Columbia schoolchildren reenacted the first planting. By 1935 the Cherry Blossom Festival was an annual event. Six years later, Japan and the United States were at war, suggesting that the cherry trees' power as a symbol of friendship were limited.

Or were they?

Among the casualties of that war of attrition fought across the Pacific were Tokyo's own cherry trees. In 1952, Japanese officials asked for American help in restoring the grove of Yoshino cherry trees in a place called the Adachi Ward in Tokyo. The National Park Service responded by sending grafts from the descendants of those same trees back to Tokyo. Today, the cherry trees survive—on both sides of the ocean.

March 28, 1969

Why We Still Like Ike

Career soldier turned statesman Dwight D. Eisenhower passed away on this date at Walter Reed Army Hospital. On NBC's nightly news show David Brinkley solemnly announced it to the nation. "His death was peaceful, and natural," Brinkley said. "He was seventy-eight years old and it was the end of a life so filled with accomplishment and achievement and honors that, even though it was a long life, it hardly could have held any more. Down to the end, he remained one of the most popular of all Americans."

After Brinkley spoke, co-anchor Chet Huntley read statements from past presidents, world leaders, and two former Army comrades, one a general, the other a mess sergeant.

"America will be a lonely land without him," Lyndon Johnson said. "But America will always be a better nation because Ike was with us when America needed him."

Charles de Gaulle announced he'd attend the funeral; UN secretary general U Thant ordered the United Nations flag flown at half-staff. British field marshall Bernard Montgomery was disconsolate. "I am very distressed," he said. "I want to be left alone now."

At the end of a decade that had seen so much loss, many Americans felt the same way Monty did. Already, the American leader who had hid his smoldering temper—sometimes from himself—with a famous grin, seemed cut from the cloth of a nobler age.

When he ran for president, the campaign slogan "I Like Ike" summed up American innocence. He came into the White House admired as the architect of D-Day, and he left warning us of the dangers of a "military-industrial complex." He was the first president to send troops to integrate a public school, and the first to sign a major civil rights bill. He kept us out of war.

"I hate war as only a soldier who has lived it can," Ike once said, "only as one who has seen its brutality, its futility, its stupidity."

The official eulogy was delivered by Richard Nixon, who described Eisenhower as a shrewd and decisive leader who kept his head. "No matter how heated the arguments were," Eisenhower's former vice president recalled, "he was always then the coolest man in the room."

In 1945, shortly after VE Day, Eisenhower spoke in Guildhall, where grateful London officials honored him with the keys to the city. In his speech that day, Eisenhower deflected the personal acclaim with a simple declaration. "I come," he said, "from the heart of America."

March 29, 1776

Hearts and Minds

Israel Putnam had proved himself in combat, so it seemed to make sense to put him in charge of the defense of New York, which George Washington did on this date. It didn't turn out well—Putnam's instincts were to retreat. March 29, as it happens, is a fateful date in the martial history of the United States. On March 29, 1945, Gen. George Patton's Third Army took Frankfurt. On March 29, 1971, Lt. William Calley was convicted for the atrocities at My Lai. Exactly two years later, the United States quit Vietnam militarily and two years after that Saigon fell.

Is there a lesson in these disparate March 29 anniversaries? If so, they don't tie neatly together. "It is fatal," Gen. Douglas MacArthur proclaimed at the 1952 Republican National Convention, "to enter any war without the will to win it." That sentiment would later be called the Powell Doctrine, after Colin Powell, but history shows that the will to win is rarely enough. Some wars cannot be won solely on the battlefield and some cannot be won at all. Sometimes the right men are in command; other times they aren't. MacArthur was the right general to retake the Philippines in World War II but the wrong one for Korea. His 1952 admonition was intended as a rebuke of President Harry Truman, but the commander in chief was trying to prevent the outbreak of World War III.

Although Israel Putnam had been a hero at Bunker Hill, his repeated retreats not only allowed the British to take New York but eroded the confidence of his men and his superiors. George Patton was a whole different story. He fought with a relentless fury and preternatural confidence that infected nearly everyone in the Third Army. "Old Blood and Guts" vowed to be the first invader to cross the Rhine since Napoleon. When Patton reached the river, he found one span intact. It was the Ludendorff Bridge, later immortalized as the "Bridge at Remagen." His men crossed it and marched a week later into the strategic hub of Frankfurt.

Like Korea, Vietnam presented a different kind of challenge. Instead of "total war," Vietnam was a war for hearts and minds. As we keep relearning—in Iraq, Afghanistan, and elsewhere—these are the hardest wars to win, especially when the enemy is willing to hide among noncombatants and disguise itself as the very citizens Americans are trying to help.

This is not an excuse for what Lt. Calley did, or for other war crimes committed by American soldiers. But it is a reminder of what war is, and what it can do to people, no matter how noble their original intentions—or which side they are on.

March 30, 1981

Profile in Courage

A mentally ill drifter with a cheap .22-caliber revolver waited outside the Washington Hilton Hotel for Ronald Reagan, who was speaking to the AFL-CIO. After "Rawhide," as the Secret Service agents called him, finished his speech and walked to his waiting limousine, shots rang out. It wasn't clear initially, even to the president, that he'd been shot. Reagan, who had turned seventy the month before, believed he'd broken some ribs when Jerry Parr, chief of the president's Secret Service detail, shoved him in the car. But when he arrived at George Washington University Hospital, it quickly became apparent that a bullet had pierced Reagan's lung.

Ernest Hemingway never articulated his famous definition of courage in his writing. It came from a 1929 Dorothy Parker profile of the great author that appeared in the *New Yorker*. She asked him what he meant by "guts" in his fiction.

"I mean," Hemingway replied, "grace under pressure."

It's doubtful this line would be remembered today except for John F. Kennedy, who liked it so much he included it in the opening pages of *Profiles in Courage*. Kennedy displayed this trait many times, not least of which was when his PT boat was sunk by the Japanese in the South Pacific and he helped his men swim to shore. Ronald Reagan spent World War II stateside, but his guts came to the fore on this date at George Washington University Hospital.

By the time he arrived, Reagan was losing lots of blood. Yet, this seventy-year-old man walked on his own power into the emergency room—before he collapsed.

"Please tell me you're all Republicans," the president quipped to the doctors as he was being prepared for surgery. When First Lady Nancy Reagan arrived, Reagan sought to reassure his wife with an old Jack Dempsey one-liner: "Honey, I forgot to duck."

Later, postsurgery, with tubes coming out of his throat, Reagan requested a note pad. To assuage the fears of his staff, he wrote out a paraphrase of an old W. C. Fields line: "All in all, I'd rather be in Philadelphia."

Reagan's grace under pressure was contagious. Dr. Joseph Giordano, the head surgeon on the team treating Reagan that day was, in fact, a Democrat. Impressed by his patient's positive attitude, however, he answered Reagan's quip. "Today," he said, "we are all Republicans, Mr. President."

March 31, 1776

Remember the Ladies

As John Adams made his way from Boston to Philadelphia to assist in the founding of a new country, he exchanged letters with his wife, who passed along a heartfelt admonition. Abigail Adams did so with a loving, even playful, touch. But her meaning was clear.

"I long to hear that you have declared an independency," she wrote. "And, by the way, in the new code of laws which I suppose it will be necessary for you to make, I desire you would remember the ladies and be more generous and favorable to them than your ancestors.

"Do not put such unlimited power into the hands of the husbands," she added. "Remember, all men would be tyrants if they could. If particular care and attention is not paid to the ladies, we are determined to foment a rebellion, and will not hold ourselves bound by any laws in which we have no voice or representation."

Abigail Adams was kidding, but she was kidding on the square. "Equal pay for equal work" wasn't yet a thing, let alone Title IX and female presidential candidates. As former slaves could explain, a fire ignited in the name of opposing tyranny is not one that easily quelled after liberty is won unless it is won completely.

"That your sex are naturally tyrannical is a truth so thoroughly established as to admit of no dispute, but such of you as wish to be happy willingly give up the harsh title of master for the more tender and endearing one of friend," Abigail wrote her husband on this date.

"Adieu," she said by way of signing off. "I need not say how much I am your ever faithful friend."

His answer may seem patronizing to modern ears. A more objective way of characterizing it is that John Adams responded in the same playful tenor as his wife, while tacitly acknowledging the truth of her counsel.

"Depend upon it, we know better than to repeal our masculine systems," Adams replied to his wife. "We dare not exert our power in its full latitude. We are obliged to go fair, and softly, and in practice you know we are the subjects. We have only the name of masters, and rather than give up this, which would completely subject us to the despotism of the petticoat, I hope General Washington, and all our brave heroes would fight."

April 1, 2016

Alternative Facts

Just before dawn on this date, Donald Trump issued a rare mea culpa, an apology so encompassing it would have been noteworthy for any public person, let alone a politician not known for public expressions of remorse.

"When I saw the video clips of me telling Chris Matthews that women who had abortions should go to prison, I wanted to punch myself in the face," Trump said in a predawn appearance outside his New York offices on Fifth Avenue.

"I did what I often do, which is wing it," added Trump. "Sad! Chris didn't entrap me, either. He was only doing his job. Believe me, nobody has more respect for the media than I do!"

Asked for a response while campaigning in Wisconsin, Ted Cruz did not attempt to score political points. "That was big of him," Cruz said softly. "I never thought I'd say this, but Donald taught me a lesson in humility today."

At a New York fund-raiser, Ohio governor John Kasich echoed this sentiment: "Who am I to talk?" he said. "I'm the guy who tried to appeal to Hispanic voters by talking about a Latina hotel maid. Remember when I mentioned women who 'left the kitchen' to vote for me? Sheesh."

The Democratic candidates were also uncharacteristically empathetic. Reached on the phone by RealClearPolitics' White House correspondent Alexis Simendinger, Hillary Clinton said that when she saw Trump's apology on C-SPAN—the only network he contacted—she headed from her Brooklyn headquarters over to Trump Tower "to give Donald a big squeeze."

Bernie Sanders told the *New York Times* that although he personally didn't like hugging other people, he was gratified to see Trump "rising above the horrible manners he learned on Wall Street." Sanders also said he missed hearing Trump's apology himself because his campaign didn't take money from super-PACs, so he couldn't afford cable television.

Asked why the other networks hadn't scrambled to cover Trump's announcement, CBS president Les Moonves expressed contrition of his own. "We've been pandering this entire election cycle, and I figured it was time our network lived up to the standard set by Edward R. Murrow," Moonves said. "I'm just hoping Chuck Todd agrees."

Reached on the set at NBC, where he was doing his fourth program of the morning, Todd said, "What is this, April Fools' Day?"

April 2, 1865

The Night They Drove Old Dixie Down

I think it is absolutely necessary that we should abandon our position tonight," Robert E. Lee wrote in a telegram to Jefferson Davis from Petersburg, where after a long siege, Ulysses S. Grant had broken the rebel army. Both Lee and Davis knew what this message foretold: the evacuation of Richmond, the South's capital, and the imminent collapse of the Confederacy.

Davis had taken his oath of office on February 18, 1861, two weeks before Abraham Lincoln's inauguration, meaning he'd been president longer than Lincoln. But on this date, Davis's time was up. The Confederate president was attending Sunday services at St. Paul's Episcopal Church on Grace Street in Richmond when informed that Petersburg had fallen. Although he'd previously sent his wife out of the city, Davis's confidence in Lee was so strong that he delayed his departure on the Danville train until nearly midnight, still hoping for better news from the battle lines, twenty-five miles away. By then, fires were burning in the city, set by Confederates incinerating documents and supplies or ignited accidentally by half-starved civilians desperate for food and other essentials. "The most revolting revelation," recalled George Pickett's wife, LaSalle, "was the amount of provisions, shoes and clothing which had been accumulated by the speculators who hovered like vultures over the scene of death and desolation."

"Taking advantage of their possession of money and lack of both patriotism and humanity," she added, "they had...bought up all the available supplies with an eye to future gain, while our soldiers and women and children were absolutely in rags, barefoot and starving."

Without the troops on the streets to keep order, the mood turned menacing. Looting broke out; fires raged out of control. The next morning, Richmond's weary populace actually felt relief when Northern troops under Maj. Gen. Godfrey Weitzel occupied the city.

"We took Richmond at 8:15 this morning," Weitzel telegrammed Grant. "I captured many guns. The enemy left in great haste. The city is on fire in two places. Am making every effort to put it out. The people received us with enthusiastic expressions of joy." After his troops had tamed the fires, Weitzel, a career Army officer and West Point man, took stock of the extraordinary spectacle before him: "The rebel capitol, fired by men placed in it to defend it," he noted, "was saved from total destruction by soldiers of the United States, who had taken possession."

The fires spared St. Paul's Church, which stands to this day.

April 3, 1968

Foreshadowing from the Mountaintop

Mason Temple in Memphis was packed with listeners eager to hear Martin Luther King Jr. He'd come in support of the city's striking sanitation workers and the audience had shown up in support of King. That night, he discussed his own mortality in a way that would prove strikingly prophetic. King recalled a book signing in Harlem a decade earlier, when a woman stabbed him in the chest with a letter opener. The blade barely missed an artery, and the *New York Times* reported that if King had sneezed in that moment, he'd have died. While recovering in the hospital, King recalled, he'd received a letter from a white ninth grader in White Plains, New York. "I'm so happy that you didn't sneeze," she wrote.

Ten years later, on the day that would prove to be his last on earth, King stood in front of supporters at that Pentecostal church in Memphis and said, "I want to say tonight that I too am happy that I didn't sneeze." If he had sneezed, King explained, he wouldn't have been around for the Freedom Ride of 1961 and events in Birmingham in 1963 that help spur the Civil Rights Act.

"If I had sneezed, I wouldn't have had a chance later that year, in August, to try to tell America about a dream that I had had," he added. "If I had sneezed, I wouldn't have been down in Selma, Alabama, to see the great movement there."

Dr. King received frequent death threats, but something about his Tennessee visit worried his staff and colleagues, he recalled in his sermon that night. "Well, I don't know what will happen now. We've got some difficult days ahead," he said. "But it really doesn't matter with me now, because I've been to the mountaintop!"

The preacher noted that, like anyone else, he'd prefer to live a long life, adding that mostly he wanted to do God's will. "He's allowed me to go up to the mountain. And I've looked over. And I've seen the Promised Land," King said, before acknowledging that he might not make it there himself.

It was as if Martin Luther King felt death knocking at his door that night. Yet he was unafraid, and undeterred.

"I'm not worried about anything. I'm not fearing any man," he proclaimed. "Mine eyes have seen the glory of the coming of the Lord!"

April 4, 1913

Muddy Waters

Although Martin Luther King Jr. was felled by hate on an April 4, fifty-five years earlier to the day another kind of prophet came into this world. His christened name was McKinley Morganfield. He, too, would take the sounds he learned in Southern churches and fuse them with worldly influences and his own talent in ways that would help African-Americans—and, later, people of all colors and creeds—cope with the vagaries of life.

"I was a good Baptist," he would recall later. "So I got all my good moaning and trembling going on for me right out of church."

We know him as Muddy Waters, and he would help create a musical genre that melded the disparate American characteristics of melancholy, rebelliousness, and an impulse to innovate into something that would become an international style of expression called rock 'n' roll.

The blues' origins, music historian David P. Szatmary has noted, entailed calculated repetitions designed to elicit a call-and-response with the audience. "[It was] often used to decrease the monotony of work in the fields, one slave would call or play a lead part, and fellow slaves would follow with the same phrase or an embellishment of it until another took the lead."

Muddy Waters is often called the father of the Chicago blues style, but he learned his craft down home, in the fecund musical fields of the Mississippi Delta, the birthplace of blues music. He worked in the actual fields, too, but found time to pick up the harmonica at thirteen, and the guitar at seventeen.

"I sold the last horse we had," he would later tell renowned music writer Robert Palmer. "Made about fifteen dollars for him, gave my grandmother seven dollars and fifty cents, I kept seven fifty and paid about two fifty for that guitar. It was a Stella. The people ordered them from Sears, Roebuck in Chicago."

By the time he was discovered by Library of Congress folklorist Alan Lomax in 1941, Waters had made the reverse journey taken by his guitar, and played the clubs in the Windy City before returning to the Delta. Lomax and his collectors were traveling the South recording musical forms that had, until then, merely passed along from one group of musicians to another.

Waters had followed the styles of bluesmen Eddie "Son" House and Robert Johnson. Lomax and his team were trying to find Johnson, who'd died three years earlier, when they came across Muddy Waters. What a consolation prize.

April 5, 1614

Powhatan Princess

Ask any eight-year-old girl in America who Susan B. Anthony was and you'll likely get a blank stare," science writer Susan Lewis once noted. "But mention Pocahontas and the child's face will light up, no doubt with a vision of Disney's beautiful 'princess' dancing in her mind."

Don't blame Disney: Pocahontas was being mythologized from the moment she came cartwheeling into the English settlers' fort as a barely clothed free-spirited teenage daughter of Chief Powhatan. John Smith was the first to stoke the legend. He penned the now-famous account of Pocahontas saving him from execution when he was captured in 1607. Is this story even true? Let's save that question for later. It is a matter of record, however, that after Smith left Jamestown for England, Pocahontas was taken hostage by settlers seeking the return of their own people. Powhatan agreed to a prisoner exchange, but having been baptized by the settlers, his daughter chose to stay among them.

Pocahontas was enthralled by one of the white men, John Rolfe, and he with her—they were married on this date. Two years later, they set sail for England where Pocahontas rebuked Smith for leaving Virginia and forsaking the promises he had made to her people. As Pocahontas and Rolfe were returning to the New World in 1617, she became seriously ill before their ship had cleared the waters of the Thames. Taken ashore, she died in Rolfe's arms, leaving him with a son. Rolfe himself was killed in an Indian attack in Virginia in 1622, so he was not around to counter the love triangle idea later exploited by writer John Davis in his book *Travels in the United States of America*.

Although we will never know what Pocahontas felt in her heart, it's clear John Rolfe loved her. It's also true that their relationship might not pass scrutiny in our more culturally sensitive time: a native girl, taken hostage, converted to a strange religion, and then taken away from her people on ships? It doesn't sound good. But Pocahontas, like her father, was no wallflower. When she lived, she had a larger-than-life personality, which got only bigger in death.

"Pocahontas is one of those characters, rarely appearing on the theater of life, which no age can claim, no country appropriate," her biographer William Watson Waldron wrote in 1841. "She is the property of mankind, serving as a beacon to light us on our way, instruct us in our duty, and show us what the human mind is capable of performing when abandoned to its own operations."

April 6, 1995

Happy Huskies

Rebecca Lobo was named the top women's college basketball player of the year after leading the University of Connecticut to a 35-0 record and the school's first national championship. It would hardly be the last. Lobo's 1994–1995 team began a period of domination for the Huskies that continued for the next two decades. The Geno Auriemma–coached UConn team would win ten more NCAA championships in the ensuing twenty seasons, evoking comparisons to the greatest dynasties in college history, especially John Wooden's storied UCLA men's teams.

UConn just kept getting better. Led by future WNBA star Diana Taurasi, the 2001–2002, 2002–2003, and 2003–2004 teams each hoisted the championship trophy. That feat was eclipsed by the 2016 class boasting Morgan Tuck, Moriah Jefferson, and the incomparable Breanna Stewart. In four years, Stewart and her teammates won 151 games to only five losses. This was the legacy Lobo started, and she did it with class, a point Connecticut's senior lawmaker made on the Senate floor.

"Young Americans are frustrated by athletic heroes who fail to lead exemplary lives off the playing field, politicians who seem focused solely on their reelection prospects or movie stars whose real-life personas pale in comparison to those of the characters they portray on screen," Sen. Chris Dodd said on this date. "In Rebecca Lobo, however, America has found a role model that not only meets our expectations, but exceeds them."

Today, her name is Rebecca Lobo-Rushin. Improbably, she married *Sports Illustrated* writer Steve Rushin in 2003. They met in a bar in 2001, soon after Rushin had mocked women's basketball in his column. Lobo, then playing pro ball, wouldn't let a simple apology suffice.

"We get fifteen thousand fans at Madison Square Garden," she told him. "How many women's games have you ever been to, anyway?" Rushin admitted never having attended one, so she invited him to one of her New York Liberty games. He accepted, and twenty-three months later they were wed at the Basketball Hall of Fame in Springfield, Massachusetts. During a tour of the museum several seasons later, Lobo told this story:

> A year and a half ago, my oldest daughter, who was four-and-a-half, and my husband [were] watching UConn men playing on the television in the living room, and my daughter...said to Steve, "Are those boys playing?"
> And I said, "Yes."
> And my daughter said, "I didn't know boys played basketball."

April 7, 1949

One Enchanted Evening

Before *Hamilton*, there was *South Pacific*, which made its Broadway debut on this date. To say that the show was an immediate hit is an understatement.

Based on *Tales of the South Pacific*, a collection of fictional stories by James Michener, the theatrical version was coauthored by Richard Rodgers, Oscar Hammerstein II, and Joshua Logan. Rodgers and Hammerstein had revolutionized the Broadway musical form with *Oklahoma!* six years earlier, and with *South Pacific* they were taking a bold step into social commentary. Logan was brought in not because he was a veteran of the theater, but because he was a veteran of the U.S. Army who could help write the parts dealing with military life.

The musical was first staged in New Haven, Connecticut, where the locals realized immediately what they had. "*South Pacific* should make history," gushed the *New Haven Register*. In Boston, the show's next port of call, playwright George S. Kaufman quipped that it was so popular that the crowds standing in line at the Shubert Theatre "don't actually want anything—they just want to push money under the doors."

By 1949, Rodgers and Hammerstein were expected to produce hits, but that hardly accounts for the reception accorded *South Pacific* when it was unveiled at New York City's Majestic Theatre. The audience included the elite of New York's art world, so the play's financial backers rented the roof of the St. Regis Hotel for an after-party. They ordered two hundred copies of the early edition of the *New York Times*, so guests could read the review. Rodgers and Hammerstein usually avoided that kind of thing. Why jinx yourself? There was no danger this time. Famed *Times* theater critic Brooks Atkinson, who sat in his customary front-row seat that night, wrote a glowing review.

The audience had already rendered its verdict. The opening night performance was delayed repeatedly because the crowd kept stopping the show with extended applause after each of the songs. Those numbers, still popular nearly seven decades later, were brilliant in their composition and sung beautifully by a cast that included Mary Martin and opera star Ezio Pinza.

Moreover, they carried uplifting social messages, the chief one being that love can thrive even in wartime—and is more powerful than racism.

April 8, 1630

A City upon a Hill

There was no turning back for the seven hundred Puritans in eleven ships who were on the open ocean on this date, heading from England to their destiny in Massachusetts. The migration was led by John Winthrop, who inspired the faithful with his "city upon a hill" sermon, a homily described more than three and a half centuries later by Harvard chaplain Peter J. Gomes as the greatest sermon in the past one thousand years. Its formal title was "A Model of Christian Charity," and it inspired generations of future Americans, including John F. Kennedy and Ronald Reagan.

"For we must consider that we shall be as a city upon a hill," Winthrop exhorted his fellow Puritans. "The eyes of all people are upon us."

Those who know their Bible recognize the "hill" imagery as being from Jesus' Sermon on the Mount. Winthrop's followers surely did, which helps explain an enduring mystery: If this sermon was the best in a millennium, why are there no contemporary accounts of it?

Historians don't even know if Winthrop delivered his sermon on the docks in England or aboard his flagship, the *Arabella*, while sailing across the Atlantic. Winthrop biographer Francis J. Bremer postulates that words that seem so profound today struck Winthrop's listeners as commonplace. In time, however, they came to mean much more than religious fealty. In his speech to the people of Massachusetts after being elected president, Kennedy invoked Winthrop, adding, "More than any other people on Earth, we bear burdens and accept risks unprecedented in their size and their duration, not for ourselves alone but for all who wish to be free."

In his farewell address as president, Ronald Reagan cited Winthrop with his own signature embellishment—America became Reagan's "shining city on a hill." Winthrop was exhorting his fellow freedom seekers to lead by example, not by military feats of arms. He was telling them they would be watched, and judged, by the world's other citizens, and that if their experiment failed—if they faltered in their faith—they would hurt the cause of religious liberty.

These words are the roots of American Exceptionalism, and Winthrop wrote them before setting foot in the New World. America, then, was from the start an idea as well as a place.

"We are called the nation of inventors," was how Mark Twain put it. "And we are. We could still claim that title and wear its loftiest honors if we had stopped with the first thing we invented, which was human liberty."

April 9, 1865

Lee's Surrender

T he time has come," Robert E. Lee told his aide-de-camp seven days after surrendering Richmond, "for capitulation."

"Well, sir," replied Col. Walter Herron Taylor, "speaking only for myself; to me, any other fate is preferable."

Those were his own feelings, Lee said, but he'd concluded that it was futile, and therefore cruel, to spill any more blood. He'd arranged to meet Ulysses Grant "with a view to surrender" and wanted Taylor to accompany him. Worried the rebels still didn't understand what they needed to do, Grant had made the terms simple and clear: "the South laying down their arms." Lee understood, and his reply to Grant on this date resulted in both generals riding with small contingents to their momentous encounter at the home of Wilmer McLean in the village of Appomattox Courthouse.[1]

"And now," wrote historian Jay Winik in his book *April 1865*, "on a spring afternoon at a small stagecoach stop, U.S. Grant, who had earlier made no bones about his intention to punish Lee and his army, would take on a most unlikely new mantle: statesman."

The details of the surrender were not punitive. Lee's men were allowed to keep their lives, their horses (if they had them), and their sidearms. In other words, they could keep their dignity. Among the arms in evidence at Appomattox was an ornate dress sword that Lee, clad in a bright and buttoned-up Confederate uniform, wore when they met at McLean's home. Grant noticed it, but never asked for it, notwithstanding the famous story of Lee proffering his sword to Grant only to have his Union counterpart respectfully hand it back. In his own memoir, Grant dismissed that account as "the purest romance." No mention of sidearms passed between the generals, Grant noted. He simply wrote out the terms of surrender, which Lee accepted.

Grant also revealed that he struggled to reconcile his respect for the bravery of Lee and his men with his complete contempt for the depraved institution, slavery, that had induced them to take up arms against their own nation in the first place.

"I felt like anything rather than rejoicing at the downfall of a foe who had fought so long and valiantly," Grant wrote, "and had suffered so much for a cause, though that cause was, I believe, one of the worst for which a people ever fought, and one for which there was the least excuse."

---

1. Wilmer McLean must have felt haunted by the Civil War: He had moved his family to the central Virginia town after his Manassas farmhouse was damaged in the first battle of the war.

April 10, 1865

Whistling Dixie

Americans awoke to the news of Lee's surrender. Spontaneous celebrations broke out across the country, at least in the North. "Joy fills every heart, in gratitude to God that the shedding of fraternal blood is about to cease," wrote a correspondent from Syracuse, where church bells began ringing at 2 a.m. In Cleveland, a two-hundred-gun salute was fired. Chicago's parade, led by the city's fire department, was three miles long. And so it went in countless cities and towns, impacted hard by four years of the Civil War.

In Washington, D.C., emotions ran especially deep. The capital had been the epicenter of the bloody fight between countrymen, and the home of the president whose election had set the machinery of secession in motion. Although it rained hard in Washington on this date, dark skies were offset by the lights illuminating the windows in homes and businesses. Along Pennsylvania Avenue, one correspondent wrote, the street formed "a line of light" nearly two miles long.

A band formed up at the Washington Navy Yard and marched toward the White House, gathering adherents as they went, shouting out hurrahs, clapping, and waving their caps. Arriving at the Executive Mansion, they sang songs played by the band, and clamored for the president, who had returned the night before from Richmond. Abraham Lincoln had no statement prepared, but he was inclined to indulge the crowd. "I see you have a band," he called from a window.

"We have three of them!" they shouted. Lincoln puckishly asked them to play "Dixie," which he described as "one of the best tunes I ever heard."

"I had heard that our adversaries over the way had attempted to appropriate it," the president added. "I insisted yesterday that we had fairly captured it."

The crowd was with him now, cheering and laughing. Lincoln was on a roll: "I presented the question to the attorney general, and he gave his opinion that it is our lawful prize."

With that the band enthusiastically played "Dixie," followed by "Yankee Doodle" and "Hail, Columbia." Cannons were fired, and three rousing cheers went up for Ulysses Grant and then for the U.S. Navy, per the commander in chief's request. Lincoln retired into his house, and the crowd headed to the War Department. But not everyone in Washington was happy. Twelve blocks away on H Street, a Southern sympathizer named Mary Surratt closed her boarding house and wept. Some of her friends were doing more than mourning. They were plotting.

April 11, 1931

Dorothy Parker's Wit and Wisdom

Directors and producers in New York City's theater district were, on this date, granted a collective reprieve: The wickedly clever—and sometimes just wicked—Dorothy Parker was stepping down as drama critic for the *New Yorker*.

Her self-described, one-woman "Reign of Terror" began at *Vanity Fair* in 1918. Now, she was decamping to California. Before going, she'd panned a play called *The House Beautiful* with this line: "*The House Beautiful* is, for me, the play lousy." No longer would a producer of a Broadway musical be forced to read a snarky Dorothy Parker review that declared, "If you don't knit, bring a book." Nor would a director who dared to stage Leo Tolstoy's *Redemption* see his efforts described thusly: "I went into the Plymouth Theater a comparatively young woman, and I staggered out of it, three hours later, twenty years older."

Although she was off for a two-decade Hollywood hiatus, Parker's spirit never really left New York, or the Algonquin, where her quotations are still featured on the hotel's walls. She lives on, too, in American literary circles, even among those who would not necessarily share her liberal politics or jaded view of men, women, love, sex, and matrimony. One reason Parker tired of drama criticism in the early 1930s was that she had found her own voice as a writer. In poems, plays, short stories—and spontaneous quips with her confederates gathered at the Algonquin bar—Parker hid personal pain and idealistic longings behind a brilliant and cynical wit.

Upon being informed that people at a Halloween party were "ducking for apples," she rejoined, "There, but for a typographical error, is the story of my life."

A 1928 hit, "Love Me or Leave Me," became in her telling, "Take me or leave me; or, as is the usual order of things, both." Parker is still quoted today, but she might be dismayed that the one-liners she tossed back like martinis are remembered better than her poems and political activism on behalf of civil rights. "There's a hell of a distance between wise-cracking and wit," she said late in life. "Wit has truth in it; wise-cracking is simply calisthenics with words."

Here, then, is a brief Dorothy Parker poem that contains both calisthenics, and wit:

Oh, is it then Utopian
To hope that I might meet a man
Who'll not relate, in accents suave,
The tales of girls he used to have.

April 12, 1877

Catching Heat

As the Civil War came to a close in 1865, Harvard fielded its first baseball team. Twelve years later, on opening day, Crimson star James Alexander Tyng was observed wearing a strange-looking contraption covering his face while crouching behind the plate against the Lynn Live Oaks. Thus armed, Tyng made only two errors in the game, far fewer than normal. Tyng had invented the catcher's mask. Or had he? The ensuing debate over this innovation would last until Tyng's death in 1931. It also foreshadowed a dispute over the paternity of another, more lucrative Harvard creation that appeared 125 years after the mask's debut.

Jim Tyng was a terrific athlete who would briefly pitch in the major leagues, but he was put behind the plate by manager Frederick Thayer after the previous catcher, Howard Thatcher, left school. Tyng was reluctant to catch. He was afraid of being disfigured back there, and told Thayer so. Recalling a game in which an opposing team's catcher had donned some sort of jury-rigged fencing mask, Thayer commissioned a Cambridge tinsmith to fashion a wire-mesh mask with eyeholes along with padded chin and forehead rests.

"To the ingenious inventor of this mask," proclaimed the *Harvard Crimson*, "we are largely indebted for the excellent playing of our new catcher." But who was that "ingenious" inventor? Some 125 years before the *Crimson* would investigate the Winklevoss brothers' claim that Mark Zuckerberg appropriated their idea for Facebook, the catcher's mask was also subject to litigation and debate. Coach Thayer, who had a law degree, was granted the patent in 1878 and proved willing to defend it in court when sports manufacturers began producing masks without paying him royalties. Meanwhile, other catchers began making claims of their own.

Howard Thatcher, then living in Maine, said he'd used one in 1876. Warren R. Briggs, a semipro catcher in New England, inserted himself into the discussion. Briggs avowed as to how he'd seen a mask in Thayer's room in 1875, suggested ways to tweak the design himself, and began using one in 1876.

"So who invented the mask: Thayer, Thatcher, Tyng, or the metalsmith who actually made it?" asks baseball historian Stephen Eschenbach. "About the only thing that can be said with any certainty, is that Thayer didn't create the mask in a vacuum, and that Tyng went to his grave believing he contributed more to the invention of the mask than he received credit for."

April 13, 1945

"Pray for Me Now"

For Thomas Jefferson's birthday, Franklin D. Roosevelt planned to deliver a radio address from his curative getaway in Warm Springs, Georgia. Two years earlier, Roosevelt had spoken at the dedication of the Jefferson Memorial, lauding Jefferson as an "Apostle of Freedom." The 1945 speech was to be an impassioned plea for postwar cooperation. FDR dictated changes to speechwriter Robert Sherwood, then went for a drive with cousins Laura "Polly" Delano and Margaret "Daisy" Suckley. Lucy Mercer, a woman with whom he had a more complex relationship, went, too. It was the Happy Warrior's last such outing. He wouldn't live to deliver the Jefferson Day speech.

News of FDR's death rocketed around the world. In a speech in the House of Commons, Winston Churchill struggled to keep his composure while eulogizing "the greatest American friend we have ever known." FDR's countrymen felt at sea, too.

"Large crowds came and stood in front of the White House," administration official Dean Acheson wrote to his son. "They merely stood in a lost sort of way."

The blow was felt most acutely by those in the man's personal orbit. "I could feel a chill in my heart," wrote Grace Tully, FDR's longtime private secretary. Eleanor Roosevelt was listening to a piano recital when she was summoned back to the White House, where she changed into a black mourning dress. Although she would ascertain that Lucy Mercer was with her husband in Warm Springs at the end, Eleanor did what she always did: rise to the occasion with dignity and decorum. The First Lady phoned her four sons, all of whom were in military service. She sent for Harry Truman, who was idling the day away in the Capitol without a single Secret Service agent present. Eleanor told Truman the news personally.

"Is there anything I can do for you?" he said.

"Is there anything I can do for *you*?" she replied. "For you are the one in trouble now."

Truman had been vice president all of three months, spent little time with FDR, and hadn't been briefed in detail on anything of consequence, including the Manhattan Project.

"Boys, if you ever pray, pray for me now," he told the White House press corps on this date. "I don't know whether you fellows ever had a load of hay fall on you, but when they told me yesterday what had happened, I felt like the moon, the stars, and all the planets had fallen on me."

April 14, 1910

Big Man Meets the Big Train

It was Opening Day in the nation's capital and America's portliest president, William Howard Taft, was there to toss out the ceremonial first pitch to Washington Senators ace Walter Johnson.

"The Big Train," as Johnson was known, pitched a one-hitter that day and it should have been a no-hitter, except for an odd glitch in the field. To accommodate the overflow crowd, the Senators' front office decided to let fans stand in the outfield near the fences. The Philadelphia Athletics' only hit came in the seventh inning, courtesy of Frank Baker, who had not yet earned his descriptive sobriquet "Home Run" Baker.

"Baker then lifted a fly ball to deep right field," baseball reporter Stephen V. Rice wrote. "This would normally have been an easy catch for Doc Gessler, but as he went back, he collided with a spectator, and all three—Gessler, the spectator, and the ball—fell to the ground. Baker had a double and broke up the no-hitter."

Walter Johnson wasn't the kind of man to complain about a minor bit of bad luck. The Big Train was pleased that in addition to his shutout and opening day win, he managed to garner a game souvenir: the ball Taft had thrown to him before it started. The Senators' ace handed it to his catcher for safekeeping, and after the game he sent it to the White House, along with a request that the president autograph it for him.

The First Fan obliged: "For Walter Johnson," Taft wrote on the ball, "with hope that he may continue to be as formidable as in yesterday's game."

Johnson fulfilled that wish. He pitched seventeen more seasons and is enshrined in the National Baseball Hall of Fame.

April 15, 1947

Jack Robinson and Jim Crow

Eighty-two years after the end of the Civil War, racial segregation was an American fact of life. Even after the United States had successfully waged a world war against racist regimes centered in Tokyo and Berlin, African-American ballplayers—even former GIs—couldn't play in the major leagues. The Brooklyn Dodgers were determined to demolish organized baseball's color barrier—and had the player to do it—but the Dodgers' brass first had to squelch a petition by five Southern players to keep Jackie Robinson off the roster. Manager Leo Durocher cussed out the rebels. General Manager Branch Rickey traded one of them to the Pirates. But after Durocher was suspended for the 1947 season because of his association with gamblers, Rickey was dependent on star shortstop and team captain Harold Peter Henry Reese, always called "Pee Wee," on a team known affectionately to its fans as "the Bums."

A Kentuckian raised under the apron of segregation, Pee Wee Reese's attitudes on race were unknown. He'd served in the Navy in World War II, though, and had seen where rampant racism led. Reese wouldn't sign the petition, explaining later he believed Robinson "had a right to be there." And so Robinson made his big-league debut on this date at Ebbets Field in Brooklyn.

Rickey long warned Jack—that was what his friends and family called him—that the worst kind of race-baiting would come his way, and he'd have to keep his cool.

Are you looking, Robinson asked Rickey, for a black man "who is afraid to fight back?"

"I need," Rickey replied, "a player who has the guts *not* to fight back."

Jack Robinson had guts, but he also needed a friend. He found one in his own shortstop. Recollections differ as to what exactly what happened or where, but during one road game the heckling got louder, the racial epithets more vicious.

"Pee Wee kind of sensed the sort of helpless, dead feeling in me," Robinson told biographer Arnold Rampersad. Suddenly, Pee Wee was on his side of the baseball diamond, standing beside Jack in solidarity. Some said Reese put his arm around the rookie. Others said he merely stood with him, as a silent rebuke to the racists. Miraculously, it seemed to Robinson, the taunts died down. "He didn't say a word, but he looked over at the chaps who were yelling at me and just stared," Robinson told Rampersad. "I will never forget it." In that simple way, in that season, Brooklyn's beloved Bums did their part to chip away at the imposing but ultimately empty edifice known as Jim Crow.

Savior and Martyr

The plot that took Abraham Lincoln's life was meant to be a coup. Vice President Andrew Johnson and Secretary of State William Seward were also to be killed. The conspirator assigned to Johnson lost his nerve; Seward was severely beaten, but not fatally. His doctors didn't tell Seward about Lincoln—they weren't sure he could take the shock. Nevertheless, on this date, which was Easter Sunday, Seward gazed out on Lafayette Square, saw the flag at half-staff, and exclaimed sadly, "The president is dead." When an attendant tried to deny it, Seward replied, "If he had been alive he would have been the first to call on me, but he has not been here."

Meanwhile, thousands of pastors tore up the Sunday sermons they had written earlier in the week. Their new homilies were about Lincoln's martyrdom. Four years earlier, Union troops marched to war to the stirring tune of "John Brown's Body Lies A-Mouldering in the Grave," a song spruced up by Julia Ward Howe into the classier "Battle Hymn of the Republic."

"In the beauty of the lilies," it intones, "Christ was born across the sea." Howe's last verse also ended with a line reminding federal soldiers of the noble cause they were fighting for: "As He died to make men holy, let us die to make men free." Now, as Abraham Lincoln's body (and not John Brown's) was being prepared for the grave, the song seemed prophetic. Lincoln had made men free, and had died for it. It was Biblical. Frederick Douglass told of a Baptist minister who encountered a freed slave in the line of mourners outside the White House. The former slave, an elderly woman, was weeping openly. "Why are you crying?" the preacher asked.

"We have lost our Moses," she replied. This was a common reaction among African-Americans. Other comparisons were made, too. Poet John Greenleaf Whittier, a prominent abolitionist, wrote

ABRAHAM LINCOLN, Pres't U. S.

Entered according to Act of Congress, by Alex. Gardner, in the year 1865, in the Clerk's Office of the District Court for the District of Columbia.

to a friend saying that if George Washington was the father of our country, then Lincoln was its savior. Thomas Nast began work on a painting called "President Lincoln Entering Richmond," depicting Lincoln arriving in the South's capital as Jesus had ridden into Jerusalem before Passover—with humility instead of exultation.

At a rally in Manhattan, a Republican congressman from Ohio made the same comparison: "It may be almost impious to say it, but it does seem that Lincoln's death parallels that of the Son of God." That congressman's name was James A. Garfield. He would become the twentieth president of the United States and the second to be felled by an assassin's bullet.

April 17, 1865

Averting a Massacre

A century and a half ago, news didn't travel instantaneously so word of Lincoln's death was still rippling out across the country on this date, the Monday after Easter. Reactions were tempered by one's politics, and by trepidations about what the assassination meant. Southern sympathizers covered their windows in black crepe out of feelings of guilt, but also out of fear: Expressing joy at Lincoln's demise could get you arrested or even killed. In San Francisco, Gen. Irvin McDowell issued an order dripping with anger at "persons so utterly infamous as to exult over the assassination of the President." The order termed such people "virtual accessories" to murder and warned they'd be arrested. Any newspaper violating the order was subject to seizure.

Meanwhile, despite Lee's surrender, Gen. William Tecumseh Sherman and his huge army remained in the field. This lethal Union fighting force was in North Carolina marching toward a Confederate army under the command of Gen. Joseph E. Johnston. Sherman was boarding a train to go meet Johnston under a flag of truce when a frantic telegraph operator relayed a message from Secretary of War Edwin Stanton revealing Lincoln's death and the attack on Secretary of State Seward, part of a conspiracy that included plans to kill other principals in the federal government, possibly including Ulysses S. Grant.

Sherman suggested in his memoirs that if news of what had happened in Washington had reached his troops before the rebels still in the field had surrendered, a frightful slaughter might have ensued. He swore the telegraph operator to secrecy, and went to see Johnston. When the opposing commanders met on this date, Sherman dismissed their adjutants to another room and handed his Southern counterpart the fateful telegram he'd received. Carefully gauging Johnston's reaction to Lincoln's murder, Sherman was satisfied with what he saw and heard.

"The perspiration came out in large drops on his forehead, and he did not attempt to conceal his distress," Sherman wrote. "He denounced the act as a disgrace to the age, and hoped I did not charge it to the Confederate Government. I told him I could not believe that he or General Lee, or the officers of the Confederate army, could possibly be privy to acts of assassination; but I would not say as much for Jeff Davis."

Johnston immediately began negotiating not only the surrender of his army, but all Confederate forces still in the field. The Civil War was truly over.

April 18, 1906

Earthquake and Fire

San Franciscans were awakened before dawn on this date by two powerful temblors that crumbled thousands of buildings, burst gas lines, and destroyed the water mains that were the only hope of containing the ensuing fires that consumed the city. When rain finally quelled the conflagration four days later, seven hundred people were dead, the city was a smoldering wreck, and the overwhelming number of the city's 350,000 residents were homeless.

"Surrender," said writer Jack London, "was complete." Not really.

Enrico Caruso and the cast of the New York Metropolitan Opera bedded down in San Francisco's finest hotel, the Palace, after performing Bizet's *Carmen* at the Mission Opera House, with Caruso singing the role of Don José. Shortly after 5 a.m., they were startled by the first of two violent earthquakes. "But what an awakening!" Caruso would relate, adding, "I wake up...feeling my bed rocking as though I am in a ship on the ocean."

Neither Caruso nor his valet lost their heads. They escaped the Palace, not forgetting Caruso's fifty-four steamer trunks of luggage, which the valet dragged down six flights of stairs. That afternoon, as the Palace was consumed by fire, the famed tenor evacuated by boat across the bay to Oakland. "I am longing to return to New York," he would write, "where I know I shall find a ship to take me to my beautiful Italy and my wife and my little boys." Yet, even as outsiders fled California, Bay Area residents immediately began rebuilding. In place of a slapdash Western boomtown rose a modern metropolis, a glorious jewel of a city, one well-built enough to withstand the 1989 Loma Prieta quake.

The Palace Hotel reopened in a new location on December 19, 1909, and the list of dignitaries who have stayed there range from Will Rogers to Ginger Rogers; Woodrow Wilson to Franklin Roosevelt; Sophia Loren to Amelia Earhart; Winston Churchill to Nikita Khrushchev; Bing Crosby to Whoopi Goldberg; Thomas Edison to Bill Gates. Warren Harding would die there, and Mark Twain had already written at the Palace. Theodore Roosevelt and Hillary Clinton both campaigned for president at the hotel.

At a 2007 Clinton rally, Hillary led the crowd by serenading legendary San Francisco Democrat Walter Shorenstein in a spirited rendition of "Happy Birthday." If the singing seemed a little too high-quality for a political crowd, could it be that the birthday revelers received some surreptitious help? Perhaps from the ghost of Caruso?

April 19, 1775

The Shots Heard 'Round the World

Alarmed about the militancy blossoming in Boston and surrounding towns, British general Thomas Gage decided to seize the Americans' cache of rifles, artillery, and ammunition stored by the Massachusetts militia in Concord. The night of April 18, 1775, Gage dispatched two regiments on the march. Before the sun rose on this date, America and Great Britain were at war.

General Gage's order set in motion the "midnight ride of Paul Revere," in which the well-connected patriot forayed out to warn Samuel Adams and John Hancock that Gage's men were on the move—and would arrest them if they could. Revere was rowed across the Charles River by fellow members of the "Sons of Liberty" committee who'd been signaled by two lanterns placed in the bell tower of Boston's Christ Church. He borrowed horses and began to ride, knocking on doors of fellow patriots—dozens of whom took to horseback themselves.

In the morning, seven hundred redcoats arrived in Lexington to find a force of American militiamen on the town green. British major John Pitcairn not only ordered the "damned rebels" to disperse, he also insisted they lay down their arms. Although American commander John Parker instructed the men to fall out, they would not part with their guns—the issue that brought the crisis to a head in the first place—so war came to these shores, not just over taxation and freedom, but over firearms. It is a subject we are still arguing about.

No one knows who fired the first shot in Lexington, but soon eight Americans lay dead, with no fatalities on the British side. Later in the day, Americans would even up the score in Concord and on the road back to Boston. As they saw smoke rising from Concord, the militiamen on the town's North Bridge faced a squad of redcoats. As in Lexington, the colonial commander, Col. James Barrett, instructed his men not to fire first. Directly questioning this order, an American lieutenant, Joseph Hosmer, shouted, "Will you let them burn the town?"

Such second-guessing would have been unheard-of in British ranks. But these were Americans, and Capt. William Smith of the Lincoln militia chimed in: He and his men were ready for battle. Colonel Barrett asked another captain, Isaac Davis, if his men were willing to be the point of the spear. Drawing his sword, Davis replied, "I haven't a man who is afraid to go."

"The New England men," wrote historian David Hackett Fischer, "were thus consulted—not commanded—on the great question before them."

April 20, 1999

Colorado Massacre

Even before the nightmare unfolded at Columbine High School, April 20 was a dark date in Colorado's history. In 1914, the Ludlow Massacre occurred in southern Colorado on that date. The victims were striking mine workers and their families, set upon by company-hired militias. The mines were owned by Standard Oil, and revulsion at the strikebreakers' violent tactics brought bitter recriminations against John D. Rockefeller and his family. The energy baron's attempt to restore his reputation has been called the birth of modern public relations.

But the horrifying events in suburban Denver on this date showed how expending too much energy spinning the press can backfire. When two Columbine High School students attacked their own school, local police, apparently fearful for their own lives, were maddeningly slow to respond. The Jefferson County sheriff's office was not tardy in trying to manage the news, however. Remember the widely disseminated narrative that Eric Harris and Dylan Klebold were normal kids pushed to the breaking point by male jocks and mean girls? It wasn't true.

The Columbine High School horror was a case of severe, undiagnosed mental illness in two young men who found each other and plotted the attack for a long time. Much of what Americans were told about Columbine massacre was simply wrong: Harris and Klebold didn't belong to a "Trenchcoat Mafia." They hadn't been bullied in school; in fact, they had picked on others. They didn't target blacks or athletes. That chilling story about the girl shot after admitting she was a Christian? Never happened.

"These are not ordinary kids who were bullied into retaliation," psychologist Peter Langman noted. "These are not ordinary kids who played too many video games. These are not ordinary kids who just wanted to be famous. These are simply *not ordinary kids*. These are kids with serious psychological problems."

Eric Harris and Dylan Klebold set out to claim thousands of lives, not the fifteen they took. They brought firearms to Columbine that day intending to shoot survivors running from a school cafeteria they tried to blow up. They rigged their cars with home-made bombs, with the aim of posthumously murdering police investigators. Although those devices didn't detonate, school officials, parents, and childhood experts were left with the disquieting realization that seemingly anonymous young men can be ticking time bombs. It's alesson learned again and again, the place names carved on the national consciousness: Virginia Tech, the Aurora Theater, Sandy Hook, Tucson, and the Boston Marathon.

April 21, 1966

Marathon

Boston, known as "the Hub," began hosting its famous marathon in 1897, a year after the event was revived by the Olympic Games held in Athens. The first to finish, two hours and fifty-five minutes later, was New Yorker John J. McDermott. Over the years, the winning times kept coming down, even as the distance got longer, the fields larger, and the makeup of the competitors more representative of the mosaic of the human family. In 1966, New England native Roberta "Bobbi" Gibb inquired about running. The response she got—that the female physiology wasn't conducive to distance running—struck her as absurd. Living in California with her husband, Gibb had been running up to forty miles a day. She flew to Boston, borrowed her brother's Bermuda shorts, and donned a hoodie. She hid in the bushes and after the starter's gun went off, joined the field. The other runners in her flight soon noticed they were running with a woman, and to a man they offered encouragement. Buoyed by their response, Gibb took off the sweatshirt. The crowds along the route began cheering her. By the time she crossed the finish line in three hours and twenty-two minutes (faster than two-thirds of the men in the race) Massachusetts governor John Volpe was waiting to shake her hand.

Gibb was pictured on this date in the *Boston Record-American* with the headline, Hub Bride First Gal to Run Marathon. The following year, Syracuse University journalism student Kathrine Switzer entered in the race after registering as "K. V. Switzer." She was given number 261. When they first noticed her at the four-mile mark, race officials lost their minds. Two of them, Will Cloney and Jock Semple, tried to physically remove her.

"Get the hell out of my race and give me those numbers!" Semple lunged at Switzer. Switzer was running with her boyfriend, Tom Miller, a muscular football player and hammer thrower, and he sent Semple flying with a body block. Switzer finished the race in four hours and twenty minutes, an hour behind Bobbi Gibb, who ran again unofficially, but it was the images of Switzer being jostled that circulated worldwide.

The famous story has a little-known postscript: Seven years later, the gruff, Scottish-born Jock Semple spotted Switzer at the starting line and kissed her on the cheek, a gesture that began an unlikely friendship that ended only when Semple died in 1988. Sitting by his side while he battled liver cancer, she heard him quip, "I made you famous, lass." The Boston Athletic Association later named an award in Semple's honor. In 2011, it went to Bobbi Gibb.

In 2017 Kathrine Switzer ran the race again, at age seventy, finishing in under four hours and forty-five minutes, wearing the same bib number they'd tried to rip away from her fifty years earlier.

April 22, 1970

Earth Day

After graduating from the University of Wisconsin Law School in 1942, Gaylord Nelson was drafted into the U.S. Army. After World War II ended, he returned to his native state and to politics, the profession he was bred to pursue. His great-grandfather was a founding member of the Republican Party. His father was a mayor. When Gaylord was nine, his dad took him to hear Progressive Party firebrand Robert M. La Follette campaign from the back of a train.

On their way home, the boy's father asked him if the experience had made him want to go into politics when he grew up.

"Yes," he replied. "But I'm afraid by the time I grow up Bob La Follette will have settled all the problems and there will be nothing for me to do."

After practicing law briefly in Madison, Nelson served in the state legislature and as governor before running for the U.S. Senate in 1962. In Washington, he found that Senator La Follette had left plenty for him to do. Nelson's passion was conservation, which he successfully urged President Kennedy to discuss on a coast-to-coast tour. Nelson's crusade was nearly drowned out by the political furor surrounding the Vietnam War, which Nelson came to oppose. But a tactic of the peace activists—campus "teach-ins"—inspired him. Why not adopt that method for environmental issues? Speaking to Seattle conservationists in 1969, Nelson called for a nationwide grassroots demonstration on behalf of the environment the following spring. He invited everyone to participate.

"The response was electric," he recalled in 2005. "Telegrams, letters, and telephone inquiries poured in from all across the country. The American people finally had a forum to express concern about what was happening to the land, rivers, lakes, and air—and they did so with spectacular exuberance."

The upshot was Earth Day, celebrated for the first time on this date, and every ensuing April. Many conservationists consider April 22, 1970, the day that signifies the birth of the modern environmental movement.

"Earth Day worked because of the spontaneous response at the grassroots level," Gaylord Nelson wrote. "We had neither the time nor the resources to organize 20 million demonstrators and the thousands of schools and local communities that participated. That was the remarkable thing about Earth Day. It organized itself."

April 23, 1956

Elvis Plays Vegas

Elvis Presley was already a big deal in 1956, so when the New Frontier Hotel booked his band (Elvis, Scotty Moore, and Bill Black) for a two-week gig on this date it was considered a coup. "The handsome 21-year-old rock 'n' roller's appearance," gushed the *Las Vegas Sun*, "is considered to be the Las Vegas entertainment scoop of the year."

This enthusiasm quickly soured. Over watered-down cocktails and lukewarm chicken cordon bleu at the hotel's dinner theater, married couples from Middle America sat mostly mute during Elvis's act, looking perplexed by such numbers as "Blue Suede Shoes," and applauding politely at the end, grateful that the din had ended. Noting that the audience "sat through Presley as if he were a clinical experiment," *Newsweek* compared the disconnect between the performer and the New Frontier Hotel clientele to "a jug of corn liquor at a champagne party."

Taking his cue from these tourists instead of young fans snapping up Presley's records nationwide, *Sun* music critic Bill Willard was also underwhelmed. "Elvis Presley, arriving here on the wave of tremendous publicity, fails to hit the promised mark," he wrote. "The brash, loud braying of his rhythm and blues catalog...is overbearing to a captive audience."

One astute subscriber felt compelled to respond. He was a Las Vegas resident named Ed Jameson, and he read the paper closely enough to know that Bill Willard usually covered the police beat. His prescient response was published as a letter to the editor a few days later.

"I will try to bravely carry on after reading the report of the *Sun*'s police reporter concerning Mr. Elvis Presley now holding forth at the Venus Room of the Hotel New Frontier," Jameson wrote. "I come not to bury Caesar, but to praise him. Despite the acid hemlock broth stirred by the *Sun*'s copy boy, methinks Mr. Presley will survive and live to sing some more."

He went on in this vein for a while, in prose that captured his own enthusiasm, along with the lingo of the age—and the spirit of the times that were just around the corner: "Perhaps this cat should have studied grand opera, the fiddle or just be satisfied herding a truck. I don't join that school of thought," Jameson wrote. "He's happy and he's making lots of other people happy doing just what he is doing naturally. You see, he's a natural. Any dope knows what a natural is."

"This cat Presley is neat, well-gassed and has the heart," he concluded. "So settle down, dad. Youth is an exuberant stage of life with the top down."

April 24, 1915

Genocide

It began on this night, when two hundred of Constantinople's most prominent Armenian civic leaders were rounded up on orders of a cabal of army officers known as the "Young Turks." The arrested Armenians were taken from the city now called Ankara to prisons in Turkey's interior and shot. The genocide of Armenians living within the old Ottoman Empire had begun.

Although the word *genocide* was not yet in use, the first of the century's horrifying episodes of racially motivated mass murder was underway. Before it was over, some 1.5 million men, women, and children would be killed. There was little armed resistance because, in a grim irony, most of the able-bodied male population of the ethnic group accused of disloyalty had loyally enlisted in the Ottoman Empire's armed forces. Those Armenian soldiers were pulled out of the ranks and either killed or forced into slave labor details. Meanwhile, their women, children, and elderly parents on death marches were attacked by armed and organized vigilante groups that raped women, kidnapped children, and randomly put people to the sword.

Facing the magnitude of the Nazi death camps after World War II, Winston Churchill said the world had been confronted by "a crime that has no name." Raphael Lemkin, a Polish Jew who survived the war, provided one, however, and *genocide* was codified as an international crime against humanity. As early as 1895, the *New York Times* had used a different word now associated with genocide: ANOTHER ARMENIAN HOLOCAUST, read a *Times* headline about a purge twenty years earlier. Theodore Roosevelt called the slaughter of the Armenians "the greatest crime" of the First World War. It was a crime denounced repeatedly by U.S. officials and covered in the American press—but not widely in Europe. Evil men took note. On the eve of Germany's invasion of Poland, Adolf Hitler invoked the Armenian slaughter to allay any qualms his military officers had about the war crimes the Third Reich was about to unleash on the Poles.

"After all," Hitler said in 1939, "who speaks today of the annihilation of the Armenians?"

The historic answer to that question—and it came in reply to shameful denials by the Turkish government—was this: Americans did. We remembered the Armenians. But Turkey is a NATO ally, and the last U.S. president to apply the word *genocide* to the Armenian Holocaust was Ronald Reagan. He did it only once, in his first year in office, before State Department officials convinced him—and every subsequent U.S. president including Donald Trump—to avoid the term.

April 25, 1983

Yuri Andropov's Pen Pal

Called out by a ten-year-old, Soviet premier Yuri Andropov sent a letter on this date to Samantha Reed Smith of Manchester, Maine, assuring her he didn't want to blow up the world. Samantha was moved to write Andropov after seeing his picture on the cover of *Time* magazine with an accompanying article on the former KGB chief's career. She asked her mother, Jane, to write to the Soviet leader and ask if he planned to start a nuclear war.

"Why don't you write to him?" replied Jane. So the girl sat down to compose a letter that would eventually be read around the world.

"God made the world for us to live together in peace," she wrote, "and not to fight."

Two months later, after President Reagan had warned of "the aggressive impulses of an evil empire," Soviet propagandists printed Samantha's letter in *Pravda*. The *Pravda* item included a patronizing aside: that Samantha could be forgiven her misapprehensions about Russians because of her age. This irritated Samantha, who sent another letter, this one to Soviet ambassador Anatoly Dobrynin, asking whether Andropov planned to answer her directly. "I thought my questions were good ones," she said, "and it shouldn't matter if I was ten years old."

This missive also made its way to the Kremlin, prompting a personal response from Andropov. It's not clear who really composed the April 25, 1983 letter, but it was warm and complimentary. It compared Samantha to Mark Twain's Becky Thatcher, and sought to assure her that the Soviet Union viewed armed conflict as a last resort. Andropov said the Russians' grievous loss of life in World War II made them fearful of total war, and that the U.S.S.R had pledged never to use weapons of mass destruction first. And he invited her to visit his country.

Samantha and her parents did so in the summer of 1983. They did not meet with Andropov, who by then was seriously ill, but Samantha met many Russians, gave speeches, attracted media attention, and became a pint-sized world ambassador for peace. In Japan, she sounded poised and unpretentious. She talked about the "beautiful and awesome" Soviet Union, but made no pretense of being an expert or even worldly in a grown-up way.

"Until last April, I had never traveled outside the eastern United States. I had never even heard of sushi!" Samantha said. "And now I will try my wish in Japanese," she added before expressing her hopes for "world peace and understanding."

April 26, 2000

Civil Union

On this date, Vermont Governor Howard Dean signed a law allowing same-sex couples to form "civil unions," conferring on gays and lesbians the same legal rights—if not necessarily the same social status—as heterosexuals who marry. Vermont's experiment was considered radical at the time, at least in the straight world. Not for long.

Until this issue was thrust upon him, Howard Dean was not only uneasy about gay marriage, he was—in his own words—"uncomfortable with gay people."

"This was a world," Dean said in 2011, "that was completely foreign to me." Dean was hardly alone among politicians of his generation. Yet, in December 1999, Vermont's Supreme Court directed the legislature to eliminate the disparity in benefits between gay and straight couples. Reading about the high court's ruling in the morning newspaper, Republican legislator Robert Edwards, a former state trooper who represented a conservative Catholic district, thought, "Oh my God, what have we done?"

Yet Edwards emerged as a key member of Vermont's House Judiciary Committee tasked with fashioning a new statute. Dean made it known that he'd veto any bill that had the word *marriage* in it, which was just as well with the members of the Judiciary Committee. After much discussion, they settled on "civil unions." As partisans on both sides descended on the tiny capital city of Montpelier, however, the raucous discourse over the measure was anything but civil. Dean was so unnerved he took to wearing a bulletproof vest.

Amidst the din emerged two lawmakers known for reasoned argument: Republican Thomas Little, Judiciary Committee chairman, and William Lippert, the ranking Democrat. Bill Lippert, as his colleagues on both sides of the aisle knew, was gay, with a partner of his own. The night the full chamber voted on the legislation, he stood on the House floor and spoke from the heart.

"I have been called names in this chamber, in this building, the likes of which I have never experienced in my life," he said, fighting back tears. "And I've watched come true what I have always known to be true—that those who stand beside gay and lesbian people as their allies...get targeted, too."

When the roll was called, the bill passed 76–69. There was a price to be paid: Of the fourteen Republicans who voted in favor, thirteen were out of office by the next election, including Tom Little and Bob Edwards. But the idea of marriage parity had taken legislative root in this country.

April 27, 1956

Going Out on Top

Boxing fans were stunned on this date when Rocky Marciano retired as the undefeated heavyweight champion of the world. He was only thirty-two. "No man can say what he will do in the future," Marciano said, "but barring poverty, the ring has seen the last of me."

Growing up in the 1930s in Brockton, Massachusetts, Rocky dreamed of becoming a baseball and football player. He was a solid athlete, good enough to earn a postwar tryout with the Chicago Cubs. And he had boxed in the Army during World War II, mainly to get out of KP duty, and had been successful, winning the 1946 Amateur Armed Forces tournament. At five foot eleven inches and 188 pounds, he lacked the classic size of a heavyweight; his short arms put him at a disadvantage, too. He was also considered old for a fledgling fighter: Rocky was in his midtwenties when trainer Charley Goodman taught him the fine points of the Sweet Science. But he had deceptively quick reflexes and thunder in each one of those fists, and in 1949 and 1950 he began amassing victories, almost all of them by knockouts.

Along the way, he acquired a loyal base of hometown fans, who piled into buses and cars to see him fight, and who yelled "Timber!" when Rocky's opponents went rubber-legged as he moved in for the coup de grace.

Marciano's big break came on October 26, 1951, when he climbed into the ring against his boxing idol, Joe Louis. The younger man sported an impressive record as a professional fighter: thirty-seven wins in thirty-seven bouts, thirty-two by knockout. But in Joe Louis, Rocky was facing perhaps the greatest fighter of all time. Louis was thirty-seven years old by then, and well past his prime. Marciano knocked him out in the eighth round.

"The reactions were not there," said the old champ, who retired after this fight. "My age counted against me."

Afterward, Marciano went to Louis's dressing room, where the victorious younger fighter wept. The Rock went on to get his title shot, which he won. He defended it successfully five times before retiring, a decision he based partly on Joe Louis's example. Rocky didn't want to go out like that—and he didn't. He died on August 31, 1969, the day before his forty-sixth birthday, in a small plane crash outside Des Moines, Iowa.

Joe Louis and Muhammad Ali attended the funeral. Louis kissed the coffin as he passed it, and said, "God is getting Himself a beautiful man."

April 28, 1915

Women of Peace

As Europe engaged in self-destructive conflagration, a delegation of forty-six Americans trekked to an international women's peace conference in the Hague to try and stop the carnage. Those attending arrived in the Netherlands from a variety of nations, some of them opposing combatants in the gruesome conflict known today as World War I. The authorities in distant capitals were not too keen on the conference, but to the women in attendance, governments run by men had already demonstrated their tragic lack of foresight.

The International Congress of Women convened on this date with 1,200 delegates from a dozen nations. French authorities refused to let its women participate, as did the governments of Japan, Russia, and Serbia. Britain suspended ferry service between England and the Dutch town of Flushing, stranding most of its 180 delegates. As the U.S. delegation's ship arrived in Holland's territorial waters, a British sailor aimed a machine gun at the bridge and refused at first to let the ship dock. The women who did make it knew that they risked being called subversives back home. But Jane Addams, leader of the American delegation, told the convention that they risked approbation from future generations if they did not address what the delegates labeled in a resolution "the madness and horror" of the Great War.

"The time may come when the survivors of the war may well reproach women for their inaction during this terrible time," Addams said in her opening-day speech. "It is possible they will then say that when devotion to the ideals of patriotism drove thousands of men into international warfare, the women refused to accept the challenge and in that moment failed to assert courageously the sanctity of human life."

Addams, who would be awarded the Nobel Peace Prize in 1931, certainly asserted herself courageously. She led a delegation across battle lines to implore European leaders to make peace and was on the Continent when a German submarine fired a torpedo into a British passenger liner, the *Lusitania*. The ship sank in eighteen minutes, killing 1,195 of the 1,959 people on board, including 123 Americans. Addams had previously met with Woodrow Wilson, urging him to remain neutral in the war, which was his inclination. But the sinking of the *Lusitania*—and the drowning of approximately the same number of civilians who had attended the women's peace conference—set President Wilson and his countrymen on a different path.

April 29, 2004

Merry Old Olds

As the last Oldsmobile rolled off the assembly line in Lansing, Michigan on this date, the assembly line workers stopped to sign the car, which was then shipped to the R. E. Olds Transportation Museum. It was a sad day for Olds lovers, who blamed General Motors. But GM produced Oldsmobiles profitably for a century, and the demise of the brand served as a reminder that technological innovation is not a national birthright. In a global economy, it is a trait that must be refreshed with each new generation.

The early car engines were powered by steam generated by gasoline, and young Ransom Eli Olds built one in his father's shop around 1886. The same year, he registered a patent for a gasoline-powered vehicle. By 1897, he incorporated the Olds Motor Vehicle Company in Lansing and produced four cars. In 1899, he moved to Detroit, lined up venture capital, and by 1901 produced 425 models of the Curved Dash Oldsmobile Runabouts. From the start, the internal combustion engine was a cultural phenomenon as well as a commercial breakthrough. The new machines not only invoked the promise of the twentieth century, they symbolized freedom itself. Freedom from the yoke of the farm, freedom to travel, freedom to escape society's binds. Seventy years before Bruce Springsteen urged "Wendy" to "strap your hands cross my engines," turn-of-the-century crooner Billy Murray sang "In My Merry Oldsmobile."

Come away with me, Lucille
In my merry Oldsmobile
Down the road of life we'll fly . . .

If it took American know-how and American imagination to mass-produce automobiles—and Ransom Olds was doing it before Henry Ford—the early years of the Olds Motor Vehicle Company revealed two great truths about capitalism. The first is that it doesn't operate on the Golden Rule. On the contrary, the man with the gold makes the rules. So Ransom Olds was forced out of his own company by his investors, who turned around and sold their stake to General Motors before the company was a decade old.

A second lesson is that the superior technology is not always easily identifiable. In 1899, Ransom built electric cars. Petroleum was cheap, however, its supply seemingly inexhaustible, so they were phased out. They were brought back many years later by a company named after Kiichiro Toyoda, a man who visited the United States in 1929 to study the auto industry.

April 30, 1975

Leaving Saigon

An unusual tune began blaring over the radio in Saigon on this date—unusual for the time of year, anyway. The song was "White Christmas." It was the signal for Americans to evacuate South Vietnam's capital.

Although the handful of U.S. Marines, embassy personnel, and American journalists stationed there knew the end of the war was near, few seemed to realize just how near. Saigon's airport had come under attack two days earlier, however, and at the White House, President Gerald R. Ford had reluctantly given the go-ahead for Operation Frequent Wind. The maneuver was badly named. This wasn't a "frequent wind." It was a rare wind, and it was a gale—a unique historical occurrence, really—the defeat of U.S. military forces on the field of battle.

"The ending was very dramatic, as everybody knows," recalled *Time* correspondent Roy Rowan in an interview with his old magazine four decades later. "I remember waking up at three in the morning and hearing 'White Christmas' and wondering what the hell it was going to be like trying to walk out of this place."

The evacuation was hectic; photos of frantic Vietnamese who'd been loyal to the United States trying to claw their way onto American military helicopters are still haunting. George Washington had helped forge a country by leading the Continental Army against the British Empire. Now, an indigenous rebel force had done the same thing to Americans. Dwight Eisenhower, another towering U.S. Army commander, had eschewed the fight in Vietnam. His successors, who had been junior officers in World War II, had not been so wise.

Gerald R. Ford inherited the Vietnam quagmire, and although opinion is still divided in the Pentagon—as it was at the time—over whether the war was winnable, by spring of 1975, the American public no longer supported the effort, meaning that it was politically unsustainable. Ronald Reagan would later call Vietnam "a noble cause," which many Vietnam veterans appreciated. Journalists who covered the war wrestled with this, too. Reporters such as Donald Kirk, who returned to Saigon (now Ho Chi Minh City) forty years later, found that the Vietnamese people, while no longer bitter at the U.S., still lack basic freedoms Americans take for granted. Vietnam was probably a mistake, it was certainly a U.S. defeat, and it may have been a waste of lives and treasure. But it was not fought over nothing.

May 1, 1961

May Day

President John F. Kennedy and First Lady Jacqueline Kennedy hosted an invitation-only soiree on this date called "An Evening with Robert Frost."

It was held in the State Department auditorium for the same reason the president often held press conferences there: Washington had few suitable venues for such events. President Dwight Eisenhower had signed legislation to create a National Culture Center in 1958—it would become the John F. Kennedy Center for the Performing Arts—but it wouldn't open until 1971. In the meantime, Jackie Kennedy made do as best she could, with help from cultured members of her husband's cabinet. Among those attending the "Evening with…" series was Secretary of the Interior Stewart Udall and his wife, Lee. It was Stewart Udall who officially cohosted the program with Robert Frost—after serving a glass of sherry to the eighty-seven-year-old poet in a private dining room.

Frost would die on January 29, 1963, two years after he recited a poem at Kennedy's inauguration. But sometime after the "Evening with…" event, the president had irked Frost's daughter Leslie by snubbing the poet for speaking out of turn to Soviet premier Nikita Khrushchev. When JFK sought to atone to the family by accepting an October 26, 1963, invitation to speak at Amherst College's dedication of its Robert Frost Library, Udall worried that Leslie would "make a scene." He warned the president that he might look from the speaker's podium to see his interior secretary "wrestling on the ground with a woman."

Kennedy smiled and quipped, "We'll give you the benefit of the doubt, Stewart."

A decade after the tragedy in Dallas, as he contemplated the hope of the Thousand Days, Udall penned a poem titled "On the Hillside at Arlington." His closing stanza evoked Jackie's lament to Theodore White that her husband's death reminded her of the signature line from the musical version of *Camelot*, which, like the book, ends in tragedy: "Don't ever let it be forgot, that once there was a spot, for one brief shining moment, that was Camelot."

There is another number from that musical, however, also sung by Julie Andrews in the role of Guinevere, that ushers in the hope of spring and the first day of May. It begins:

It's May! It's May! The lusty month of May!
That lovely month when everyone goes blissfully astray.

May 2, 1939

Iron Horse

Detroit baseball fans attending the Tigers-Yankees game witnessed something on this date that no person in any stadium had seen since June 2, 1925: a New York Yankees lineup without Lou Gehrig in it.

Until this Tuesday afternoon, the "Iron Horse" had played in 2,130 consecutive games, a testament to his work ethic and competitive desire. He'd played those games with great skill, too, batting cleanup behind Babe Ruth, while fielding first-base expertly, on perhaps the best baseball team in history. By 1939, Ruth was gone from the Yanks and the team's new superstar was Joe DiMaggio. But Lou Gehrig was still team captain, so it was his duty to trudge out to home plate and present the lineup card to the umpires—the lineup card without his name.

Gehrig wasn't hitting well, everyone could see that, but his teammates knew something was seriously wrong with Big Lou. What no one knew was that he had only two years to live. The disease that killed him, amyotrophic lateral sclerosis (ALS), is still known as "Lou Gehrig's disease."

His story is one of the most often-told in baseball lore, recounted in books, movies, and the fertile oral tradition of the great American game. The most memorable line is Gehrig's brave declaration, at a July 4, 1939, ceremony at Yankee Stadium, after his deadly disease had been diagnosed, that he considered himself "the luckiest man on the face of the earth."

But it's a life with enduring relevance. It was often said that Lou Gehrig's example inspired Americans during the Great Depression, and it turns out that is a lesson that needs reinforcing from time to time. On September 6, 1995, when Cal Ripken Jr. broke Gehrig's consecutive game streak—a record long considered unassailable—President Bill Clinton and Vice President Al Gore both went to Camden Yards in Baltimore to be there when it happened. Millions of Americans turned on their televisions to see it, too: It was one of the most widely watched games in history. Why? Clinton himself explained it nicely in a speech the following night.

"One reason that's so popular is most of the people that were in that baseball stadium last night are the same kind of people," Clinton said of Cal's feat. "They show up for work every day. They work when they don't feel good. They work when the weather's bad. They work to earn money to do right by their children. They are the people that keep this country going."

May 3, 1936

DiMaggio's Debut

Three years and a day before Lou Gehrig removed himself from the lineup, twenty-five thousand New Yorkers braved cool weather to attend a game at Yankee Stadium—and not all of them were baseball fans. "An astonishing portion of the crowd," said the *New York Post*, "was composed of strangers to the sport—mostly Italians—who did not even know the stadium subway station."

They'd come to the Bronx to see the quiet, dark-haired, twenty-one-year-old Californian they'd heard so much about. To see Joe. They weren't disappointed. Playing center field and batting third, one spot in front of Gehrig, DiMaggio scored two runs while collecting three hits, including a screaming triple. If he was a savior to Yankees fans—and DiMaggio led the Yanks to nine World Series championships in the next thirteen seasons—he was even more than that to Italian-Americans. Before a road game with the Indians, Cleveland's Italian community presented Joe with a leather traveling kit. This kind of thing happened everywhere.

From the start, "DiMag" belonged to more than just New York or even the nation's vast Italian-American diaspora. He became an American icon, celebrated in popular culture from Simon and Garfunkel's famous line in "Mrs. Robinson" to an episode of *Star Trek: Deep Space Nine*, in which his record of hitting in fifty-six consecutive games is (mythically) broken.

"I would like to take the great DiMaggio fishing," Ernest Hemingway's protagonist says in *The Old Man and the Sea*. "They say his father was a fisherman. Maybe he was as poor as we are and would understand." He was poor, this Sicilian kid from Taylor Street in San Francisco, the eighth of nine children, and although his father was indeed a fisherman, all the DiMaggio boys could play ball, not just Joe and Vince and Dom—all of whom had major league careers—but also Tom, the eldest, who ran a restaurant, and Mike who died on his fishing boat.

JOE DI MAGGIO
Salutes His Bat

© 1941..The Sporting News Pub. Co.

Long after the Giants and Dodgers moved west in the late 1950s, old-time San Franciscans still remembered the DiMaggios, especially Joe. There was resentment in those days that the boys—and other Bay Area ballplayers—had to "go back East" to fulfill their destinies. Those feelings lingered among adults even after the Giants became the darlings of the City. Northern California kids of that era, well, we would listen respectfully, but only while believing—in our hearts *knowing*—that our center fielder was better than Mickey Mantle, and perhaps even better than the great DiMaggio. Our guy was Willie Mays.

May 4, 1957

Another Willie

It was a cold, windy day in Louisville, where hot toddies were in greater demand at Churchill Downs than the traditional mint juleps. For the eighty-third running of the Kentucky Derby, Bold Ruler was made a 6–5 favorite. But John Nerud, the trainer of Gallant Man, believed his horse was faster, so he put a hotshot young rider, Bill Shoemaker, aboard the colt.

Shoemaker, who'd won the 1955 Derby, was diminutive, even for a jockey, so sportswriters called him "Willie" Shoemaker even though his christened name was "Billie." What he was called on this date, though, was every name in the book: Misjudging the finish line, Shoemaker stood in the irons prematurely—and Gallant Man was nipped at the wire by Iron Liege. Although it remains the most spectacular gaffe in Derby history, it wasn't the end of Shoemaker's story.

When he retired from riding in 1990, Bill Shoemaker had won a record 8,833 thoroughbred races. On eleven occasions, he was in the winner circle after Triple Crown races, including five times at the Belmont Stakes. His last Kentucky Derby win came aboard an 18–1 long shot named Ferdinand in 1986. He was fifty-four years old and already in racing's Hall of Fame. "Shoe" was a favorite of racing fans, partly because he eschewed the whip more than most, and because of his dignified nature. In a competitive and dangerous sport, he also earned the admiration of his fellow jockeys. In 1959, Shoe had been riding Sword Dancer, the eventual Horse of the Year, in the spring but had previously agreed to ride a horse named Tommy Lee in the Derby. He not only kept his word, but as Sword Dancer appeared to swoop past Tommy Lee in the stretch, Shoe called to rider Bill Boland, "Good luck! I hope you win it." But Shoemaker's horse held on for the win.

After Shoe retired, he achieved moderate success as a trainer. On April 8, 1991, he was driving on a deserted stretch of highway while trying to call his wife on his cell phone (he'd also been drinking). Losing control of his Ford Bronco, he plunged down an embankment. The crash left him paralyzed from the neck down. "Shoe" died in his sleep at home in San Marino, California, on October 12, 2003, leaving racing aficionados with the memories of his many remarkable rides, his consummate professionalism, and an inspiring self-delivered epitaph:

"I never gave up," he told writer Ron Flatter. "A few times I didn't think I was going to make it. But I never quit."

May 5, 1862

Cinco de Mayo

The unofficial holiday is assumed by gringos, and even many Hispanics, to be a Mexican version of July 4. That's not accurate. Although Cinco de Mayo ostensibly celebrates a temporal military victory by the Mexican Army over a French expeditionary force in the city of Puebla on this date, it was an occasion that took hold among Mexicans living north of the border as a way of commemorating their Union sympathies in America's Civil War.

News traveled slowly in the mid-nineteenth century, so Mexican miners working in California's Mother Lode region didn't learn of Mexico's victory by the Puebla defenders over the French troops dispatched to North America by Napoleon III until three weeks after the fact. Once they heard, though, the party started. In some ways, it's never stopped.

In the Gold Rush country of Northern California, fireworks were set off; rifles were fired into the air at mining camps in Nevada; spontaneous fiestas broke out in labor camps as far north as Oregon. The most organized celebrations among the vast Mexican diaspora in the West were held in Los Angeles, where Mexican-American politicians hosted rallies and delivered patriotic speeches. Many Americans believed that the French intention was to arm the Confederacy of Robert E. Lee and Jefferson Davis. This was an overblown fear, but Cinco de Mayo was a chance for Mexican-Americans living in California to revel in their loyalty to the Union.

A dozen years before, many Mexican-American politicians had changed their citizenship without changing their addresses when California was admitted to the United States as the thirty-first state. Like St. Patrick's Day, Cinco de Mayo first became an American holiday re-exported back to the country of its origin and, then, one disseminated to the four corners of the Earth.

Mexican-born Jose M. Alamillo, a professor of Chicano studies at California State University, Channel Islands, first heard of Cinco de Mayo in elementary school—after moving to the United States with his family when he was eight. "It's not a Mexican holiday, not an American holiday, but an American-Mexican holiday," Alamillo told *Time* magazine. "They had to kind of make the case for fighting for freedom and democracy and they were able to link the struggle of Mexico to the struggle of the Civil War, so there were simultaneous fights for democracy."

Today, fittingly, it has evolved into a broader and equally noble cause: celebrating the ethnic diversity that makes this free country a rich and vibrant cultural mixing bowl.

May 6, 2004

Friends

After a ten-year run, the final episode of *Friends* aired on NBC to a national audience estimated at 52 million people. The show had debuted on September 22, 1994, and produced 236 episodes. Although the friends on *Friends* supposedly lived in Greenwich Village, it was filmed on a set in the Warner Bros. studios in Burbank.

The size of their apartment was more evocative of Southern California than New York City, and the six young pals (Joey, Ross, Rachel, Phoebe, Chandler, and Monica) didn't spend much time working—or worrying about jobs and money. So what was the show about? For the answer, consider that the long run of *Friends* on network television overlapped for several years with *Seinfeld*, another NBC sitcom that had its own great ride from 1989 to 1998.

In 2002, as *Friends* was nearing the end of its run, *TV Guide* proclaimed *Seinfeld* the greatest show in television history. This was a stretch, even more so because the common description of *Seinfeld* was that it was "a show about nothing." This became such a well-known cliché that it was incorporated into a *Seinfeld* episode, but it always struck the show's coproducers, Jerry Seinfeld and Larry David, as wildly off the mark.

It's true, Jerry Seinfeld noted, that "we never obsess over anything that isn't mundane." That doesn't mean the show was about nothing. Ostensibly, it was a show about how comedians get their material. But, like *Friends*, what made *Seinfeld* work was friendship.

Who cares that it wasn't about life-and-death situations? Wasn't there enough of that elsewhere on network television—and in the culture as a whole?

Consider what was happening in American civic life during the ten years of *Friends*. A president was impeached and later disbarred. A national election was held in which the winner of the most votes wasn't inaugurated. An act of war was launched against the United States, with frightful civilian casualties. The U.S. responded by going to war in two countries.

If Americans wanted to watch laugh-track-aided sitcoms about silly everyday social situations—and two sets of neurotic and oddball friends who cared for one another—well, why not? Those shows weren't about nothing; they were about friendship. They were about love. In an uncertain, violent, and frightening world, that was something to hold on to.

May 7, 1886

Paying the Costly Price

Chicago police on this date arrested—and inexplicably released—German immigrant Rudolph Schnaubelt on suspicion of murder. By the time they realized that Schnaubelt, who preached revolution while working as a machinist, was likely a deadly terrorist, he had fled the country, never to be seen again. But someone had to pay.

The Haymarket Riot began when workers at Chicago's McCormick Harvesting Machine plant went on strike over an eight-hour workday. They were locked out by management, who hired new workers. At a May 3 rally outside the plant, August Spies, editor of a radical German-language newspaper, directed vicious invective at the strikebreakers. Inflamed, workers rushed the gates of the plant at the end of the afternoon shift, attacking their replacements. Guards fired into the crowd, killing two strikers.

A protest rally led by anarchists was organized for the next day in Chicago's Haymarket Square. Around 10:30 p.m., as it began to rain, police officers moved in to disperse the crowd. Suddenly, a bomb was tossed in their path, killing one officer instantly and leaving six others mortally wounded. Gunfire erupted on both sides. Several other policemen were wounded, and four demonstrators lay dead.

It was over in four minutes. The Haymarket Square incident wasn't a "riot." It was a slaughter. August Spies and other anarchists were arrested. Spies was one of eight men—six them German—put on trial. There was scant evidence directly tying the defendants to the crime. Only two, Spies and Samuel Fielden, were even at Haymarket Square that night. So, the prosecutors put anarchy itself on trial. Convinced they wouldn't get a fair trial, the defendants bought into this logic—and put capitalism on trial. This tactic sealed their fate. Eight anarchists were convicted, with seven sentenced to die. One of the condemned men took his own life. Four others, including Spies, went to the gallows singing the "Marseillaise," labor's popular anthem.

"If you think that you can crush out these ideas...by sending us to the gallows, if death is the penalty for proclaiming the truth, then I will proudly and defiantly pay the costly price!" Spies declared at trial. "Call your hangman!"

Brave words, and honestly felt. But neither politicians nor union leaders wanted any part of radicals who countenanced the murder of police officers, and it took the labor movement years to recover its momentum.

May 8, 1950

Arkansas Empire

On this date, Samuel Moore Walton said his prayers and went to bed in his new home in Bentonville. The following morning, he'd open a new store in that town, which few people outside of Arkansas could find on a map. What Sam Walton was really on the verge of doing was redefining retail shopping. Was he nervous? In his autobiography, he doesn't say so. He sounded confident. The new outlet was part one of a genre then called "five and dime" stores. This one would be the first to carry his surname: "Walton 5-10" it said on the storefront.

Born in Oklahoma and raised in Missouri, Sam showed star quality early on—along with a bent for entrepreneurship. After milking cows in the morning as a boy, he bottled the excess milk and sold it on his paper route. On a dare in junior high, he became the youngest Eagle Scout in Missouri's history. In high school, he was student body president and quarterback of the state championship football team and was named his graduating class's "Most Versatile Boy." After college, he joined the Army, serving during World War II, and mustering out as a captain before embarking on his true calling. His retail empire was built on ideas that seem obvious today: keeping the shelves fully stocked, letting customers browse through the store themselves and pay at front cash registers, treating business partners like family and employees like partners.

When Walton opened his first Walmart in 1962 in Rogers, Arkansas, he was mocked for thinking large stores could thrive in small rural towns. When he died thirty years later, his empire had surpassed Sears, Roebuck to become the largest retailer in the country—with 1,735 stores in forty-two states. Yet, his corporate headquarters remained in a Bentonville warehouse and kept the same hours he always had—despite being one of the world's richest men.

"This is a man who was at work at 4:30 in the morning, had warmth and charm throughout the day, an interest in his customers, and who treated his associates as persons, not just as clerks and salespeople," Walter Loeb, a retailing consultant who'd known Walton since 1976, said when he died in 1992. Three weeks earlier, Sam received a visit from President George H. W. Bush, who presented him with the Presidential Medal of Freedom. Bush choked up while praising Sam Walton as "an American original" and a shining example of "America's success."

"I think it's important that all Americans understand that some things are going very, very well in the United States of America," Bush said. "And one of those things is Walmart."

Hello, Louis!

One hundred and fifty years after British troops burned Washington, D.C., the Beatles were torching the American music scene with hit after hit. In February, "I Want to Hold Your Hand" reached the number one spot in the Billboard Hot 100 rankings. This was followed by "She Loves You" and "Can't Buy Me Love," meaning that the lads from Liverpool held the top spot for three and a half months. At one point in mid-April the Fab Four held the top five slots.

Then came a song from Louis Armstrong.

By 1964, it seemed that Armstrong's best days were behind him. At sixty-two, "Satchmo" was still playing the jazz venues and nightclubs where he'd perfected his art, but he was doing so in an era in which the music industry's stars had begun filling open-air stadiums. The music had changed, too: Rock was supplanting nearly everything else. Then, in December 1963, Armstrong's manager acted on a hunch. On Broadway, the finishing touches were being put on "Hello, Dolly!" scored by thirty-two-year-old phenom Jerry Herman. Why not have Satchmo record it and release it as a single?

In the musical, the title song appears in Act Two, when Carol Channing, in the role of Dolly Levi, returns to her favorite New York restaurant, which she hadn't visited since the death of her husband. There, she runs into old friends, including her favorite waiters. One of them, as it happens, is named "Louie," which is how many of Armstrong's fans knew him and she sings the soon-to-be-famous number with the entire chorus.

It was a stroke of marketing genius to have Armstrong record this song. It gave valuable advance publicity to the musical, while reviving his career in a way that allowed him to reprise his own music—all while also being true to "Hello Dolly!" which is set in the Dixieland musical era. Near the beginning of Armstrong's version, he sings, "This is Louis, Dolly," which was perhaps the first watermark in the music industry. (Armstrong used the formal version of his name when he performed.)

If Satchmo had Americans going around humming the tune, the victory over the British invaders, if you can call it that, was fleeting. "Hello, Dolly!" lasted as the Billboard number one for only a week. By May 30, the Beatles topped the charts again with "Love Me Do."

May 10, 1908

Mothers' Day

In 1914, President Wilson signed a joint resolution of Congress encouraging Americans "to display the flag...on the second Sunday in May as a public expression of our love and reverence for the mothers of our country." Venerating motherhood predates Western civilization, but this idea of setting aside a specific day belonged to a Virginian named Ann Jarvis.

The Civil War split the Old Dominion in half, and when the government in Richmond seceded from the Union, Jarvis found herself living in a new state, West Virginia, in a community of divided loyalties. Before the war, she'd launched Mothers' Day Work Clubs to address local health needs. When the bloodshed started, Jarvis urged the clubs to stay neutral—and to provide medical care to both Union and Confederate soldiers and solace to mothers on each side. Jarvis knew the pain of losing a child: Eight of her twelve children never reached adulthood. In 1902, she was widowed and moved to Philadelphia. When she died, her daughter Anna vowed to keep her mother's tradition alive. On this date, Mother's Day ceremonies were held at the Wanamaker Store auditorium in Philly and the Andrews Methodist Church in Grafton, West Virginia. But Anna's tribute begs the question: What about those of us whose mothers are no longer living—what are we supposed to do with this day? Eighty years after Woodrow Wilson's declaration, another president addressed this question in a commencement address at Gallaudet University, a school for deaf students started by Abraham Lincoln.

"A few days ago, when we celebrated Mother's Day, it was my first Mother's Day without my mother," Bill Clinton told the students. "So, I have been thinking about what I should say to all of you, those of you who are lucky enough still to have your parents, and, perhaps, some of you who do not. On graduations, it is important for us to remember that none of us ever achieves anything alone. I daresay as difficult as your lives have been, you are here today not only because of your own courage and your own effort, but because someone loved you and believed in you and helped you along the way.

"I hope today that you will thank them and love them and, in so doing, remember that all across this country, perhaps our biggest problem is that there are too many children, most of who can hear just fine, who never hear the kind of love and support that every person needs," Clinton added. "And we must commit ourselves to giving that to those children."

May 11, 1934

Dust Bowl

The windstorm swept across the drought-stricken farmlands of the Great Plains, denuding them of topsoil, which it spewed eastward across the country. Millions of tons of dust and dirt blackened towns, sending people scurrying indoors as far away as Boston and Atlanta. Arriving as it did during the Great Depression, the whirlwind of dust seemed almost Biblical.

"Climate change" wasn't a buzz phrase in the 1930s, but human activity played a direct role in what was called the Dust Bowl. Not regarding the weather, but the condition of the land.

"The soil is the one indestructible, immutable asset that the nation possesses," stated a 1909 report by the U.S. Bureau of Soils. "It is the one resource that cannot be exhausted; that cannot be used up." This prediction was proven spectacularly wrong. By the early 1930s, the tall-grass prairie had been ploughed under for agriculture. Overplanting, particularly of wheat, followed the advent of the gasoline-powered tractor. A drought was the last factor needed to create a disaster. And the drought came. And stayed.

A dozen severe dust storms were recorded in 1932. The next year, that number was thirty-eight. By the end of 1934, an estimated 100 million acres of Great Plains farmland had been taken out of production because its topsoil was simply gone. The mass migration of the "Okies" described by John Steinbeck in *The Grapes of Wrath* to California, was already underway when the dry spring of 1935 revealed the full scope of the catastrophe.

For years, a young North Carolina soil surveyor named Hugh Hammond Bennett had warned about the dangers of topsoil depletion. After he was proven right, Franklin Roosevelt tapped him to head the newly created Soil Erosion Service. "Americans have been the greatest destroyers of land of any race or people, barbaric or civilized," Bennett announced while calling for reform of existing agricultural practices. His rhetoric raised hackles among farmers, but Bennett believed that unless Americans changed their ways, more Dust Bowls would occur.

In the East, Bennett was seen as an alarmist. That was when Mother Nature gave him an assist. When he testified to Congress, the remnants of a Midwestern dust storm hit Washington, D.C. The grit in the mouths of members and their staffs in the U.S. Capitol on this date was the best testimony. The seeds of the Soil Conservation Act of 1935 were sown. It was signed by President Roosevelt a year later, putting the nation on a path to preventing soil erosion.

May 12, 1949

Flying Angels of Mercy

The scheme, even for murderous Russian dictator Josef Stalin, was stunning in its maleficence: unite postwar Berlin under Soviet control by using starvation as a weapon. How could Berliners be saved? The few thousand Americans and British soldiers stationed in West Berlin in 1948 were surrounded by several hundred thousand Red Army troops blockading the city. The United States maintained air superiority in Europe, so Allied troops could be resupplied that way. But what about the two million German civilians in West Berlin? No one thought they could be fed and clothed solely through the air.

Well, one man did—and he was the one who counted.

"We stay in Berlin, period," Harry Truman told his military advisers. With that, the great Berlin Airlift was launched. Bunking in barns and muddy tents, allied crews flew over Soviet-occupied East Germany day and night, dodging sporadic antiaircraft fire, evading Russian fighter planes, and bringing in enough food, coal, and other essentials to provide for two million people for more than a year. In the end, these men would fly 277,569 missions into Berlin before the Soviets ended their blockade, delivering 2.3 million tons of essentials, mostly in C-47s and C-54s that traveled 92 million air miles. For 467 days in 1948 and 1949, they flew in good weather and bad, morning, noon, and night, costing 101 lives in the process, thirty-two of them Americans.

Stalin's aim had been to force the Allies to quit the city or abandon their idea of a free West Germany. Thanks to Truman's determination and those brave aviators, the Soviets achieved neither goal, and on this date Stalin was forced to concede. By then, West Germany was a functioning nation, and the NATO alliance had been forged. Although the Berlin Airlift faded from Americans' collective memories, without it, John F. Kennedy would have had no place to deliver his famous *"Ich bin ein Berliner"* speech. Nor would Ronald Reagan have been at the Brandenburg Gate a generation later daring Soviet leaders to tear down the Berlin Wall.

As for the pilots and crews who had scrambled to active duty in the middle of the night, often when a local policeman knocked on their door and handed them a telegram, they simply returned home again when it was over. Some of them, author Richard Reeves noted in his splendid 2010 book about the Berlin Airlift, had forgotten where they had parked their cars the night they answered the call.

May 13, 1864

National Cemetery

William Henry Christman, a twenty-year-old laborer from Lehigh County, Pennsylvania, was an infantryman of no particular distinction. He'd joined the U.S. Army only weeks before his death. He'd been paid $60 by his government for doing so, and was given a promissory note for $300 more. Military life agreed with him, he wrote in a letter to his parents a week after enlisting, but he contracted the measles in April and died a month later.

It was the fourth year of the Civil War, and the sheer number of dead soldiers was overwhelming authorities' ability to find space to bury them. William Christman, who'd died in a Washington hospital, was transported across the Potomac for burial on this date in a field on the plantation that had been home to Robert E. Lee and his wife, Mary Anna Custis Lee. The place was called Arlington. Two more men were buried that Friday, and several more on Saturday and Sunday—all of them in a field on the northern edge of the property about a half mile from the Lee home. By war's end, sixteen thousand bodies were interred on those grounds, their crosses and headstones serving—in the minds of the Union officers who had commandeered Lee's estate—as a permanent rebuke to the man who'd taken up arms against his government.

On April 22, 1861, Lee left for Richmond to accept command of Virginia's military forces. The previous night was the last he ever spent in Arlington House. Lee told his wife in a letter that war was "inevitable" and that its consequences would soon "burst around you." He advised her to move, quickly and quietly. As Lee feared, Virginia's secession resulted in federal troops occupying the grounds, and he understood what this meant. Early in the war, he penned Mary another letter: "It is better to make up our minds to a general loss. They cannot take away the remembrance of the spot, and the memories of those that to us rendered it sacred."

Commanders on the other side, most notably U.S. Army quartermaster general Montgomery C. Meigs, had a competing vision of what would sanctify that ground, and in 1864 they began implementing it.

By August, Meigs directed that Union dead be buried just outside the border of Mary Lee's rose garden, only a few yards from the mansion. Montgomery Meigs is not much better known today than William Henry Christman. He's certainly no rival to Robert E. Lee in fame or prominence. Yet it was General Meigs's vision that survived and made Arlington National Cemetery a synonym for sacrifice and honor and service to country.

May 14, 1918

Mensch in the Trench

After America entered World War I, Henry Johnson enlisted and was assigned to the all-black, U.S. Army 369th Infantry Regiment. The unit, nicknamed the Harlem Hellfighters, was loaned to the decimated French Fourth Army. On this night, in the Argonne Forest, fighting under the French flag, Johnson and another Hellfighter named Needham Roberts ran into a German unit probing the Allied lines. Hit by enemy fire, Roberts tossed grenades from a trench to Johnson, who threw them at the enemy. Shot in the side and head, Johnson kept fighting after running out of ammunition, using the butt of his rifle and bolo knife. He killed four of the enemy and wounded ten. The two Americans stopped the line from being breached.

General John J. Pershing wrote a battlefield report praising the two privates, who were awarded the Croix du Guerre, France's highest military honor, and a ticker-tape parade back home. But the paperwork in Johnson's discharge was botched; he received neither a Purple Heart nor a disability pension. He returned to his job as a railroad porter, but his injuries made work difficult. He took to drinking, was divorced by his wife, and died poor in 1929.

His story came to light during a Pentagon review of servicemen who'd been overlooked on account of prejudice when it came to awarding the nation's highest military award. In a June 2, 2015, White House ceremony, Henry Johnson finally received the Medal of Honor. Another man honored posthumously that day by President Obama was World War I veteran William Shemin.

As a nineteen-year-old sergeant, Shemin led his troops out of the trenches under heavy machine-gun fire to rescue members of his platoon. Wounded in the head by a German rifleman, he was hospitalized for three months and awarded a Purple Heart and Distinguished Cross, but the paperwork citing him for consideration for the Medal of Honor never went anywhere.

After the war, Shemin's family found out why. His twelve-year-old daughter, Elsie, was sitting on her front porch in the Bronx when a visitor arrived. He was James Pritchard, a Bayonne, New Jersey, policeman—and one of the men saved by William Shemin. Pritchard told Elsie that her father deserved the medal, but hadn't received it because he was Jewish.

Seventy-four years after that visit, Elsie proudly accepted it in a 2015 East Room ceremony. "The president called me and we had a lovely, lovely conversation," she recalled. "He's a mensch."

May 15, 1928

Empire Built on a Mouse

Walt Disney and his top illustrator, Ubbe Iwerks, were under contract to Universal Studios when they hit it big in 1927 with an animated character called Oswald the Lucky Rabbit. It turned out that Disney didn't own the rights to Oswald, which he learned when he went to New York to negotiate a contract extension with studio executive Charles B. Mintz. "But Walt had underestimated Mintz and overestimated Universal," wrote Disney biographer Neal Gabler.

Instead of signing a lucrative agreement, Disney learned that Mintz had hired away his animators, save for Iwerks, who wouldn't forsake Walt, and had cut his own deal with Universal. Angry and dispirited, Disney took a train from New York. His wife Lillian described her husband "a raging lion" on that train ride home. Yet it was a railroad trip that would become associated, in a legendary way, with an animal much smaller—but no less brave—than a lion.

Somewhere in his native Midwest, after leaving Chicago, but before arriving in Los Angeles, Walt Disney sketched out a story of a new animated character. "Mortimer" was the name Disney fancied, and he was a mouse. A fearless mouse, though. Inspired by Charles Lindbergh's solo flight over the Atlantic, the mouse would be cast in a silent animated film, *Plane Crazy*. The protagonist is trying to impress a female friend, who we now recognize as Minnie Mouse. The silent film's highlight was Minnie using her bloomers as a parachute when our hero wrecked his airplane. The test audience liked it well enough when it was screened for the first time on this date, but Disney and his brother Roy were unable to pick up a distributor, so the project was tabled. It turns out this stuff was funnier with sound effects, which Disney realized after seeing *The Jazz Singer*. Later that year, he released another episode, *Steamboat Willie*, with synchronized sound, to great acclaim. Walt Disney was off and running.

As for the name Mickey Mouse, that happened almost casually. Lillian Disney recoiled at the name Mortimer, thinking it too snooty. So, Walt asked, "How about Mickey?" An Irish name, an outsider's name. Lillian liked it. After *Steamboat Willie*, starring Mickey Mouse, became a hit, Disney rereleased *Plane Crazy*, with sound, in 1929. The rest of it—Mickey, Goofy, and Donald Duck; the Mickey Mouse Club with Annette Funicello; *Wonderful World of Disney*, Disneyland, Walt Disney World, Walt Disney Pictures—followed suit.

It's a small world, after all.

May 16, 1805

"Fortitude and Resolution"

Handpicked by Thomas Jefferson, Meriwether Lewis and William Clark were tasked with finding a navigable passage from what is now the American Midwest to the Pacific Ocean. This was how Jefferson presented the expedition to Congress, but in the president's mind the real purpose was scientific—and cultural. How was the geography and weather in the vast lands the United States had purchased from France? Who were the indigenous people there? What plants and animals existed in this wilderness?

At Jefferson's insistence, Lewis traveled throughout the Eastern seaboard learning the latest in botany, zoology, and paleontology before setting out on May 14, 1804. It was Jefferson who chose the official name of the expedition, *Corps of Discovery*, which conveys the excitement its patron experienced in anticipation of learning new things. Lewis and Clark were explorers; Monticello, to use a twentieth-century analogy, was Mission Control. But this Mission Control had no satellite pictures, no audio hookups, no computer feeds. The expedition differed from the Apollo missions, too. For one thing, the Corps of Discovery had a slave, not to mention a teenage wife and her baby. The African-American slave—whom Captain Clark refused to free even after his heroic service to his country—was named York. The teenage wife was Sacagawea. She was the Shoshone wife of Toussaint Charbonneau, a French-Canadian fur trader who served as an interpreter for the expedition. It was fortunate she was there.

One year into the trip, Sacagawea's husband was at the helm of their large canoe as they attempted to navigate a river that today lies under Fort Peck Reservoir in Montana. Charbonneau couldn't swim, a handicap that led him to panic when the boat got away from him. In Lewis's telling he was "perhaps the most timid waterman in the world."

This begs the question of why he was put at the helm in the first place. When a sudden squall inundated the boat and swept vital instruments and supplies overboard and Charbonneau was reduced to loudly appealing to the Lord for help, it was Sacagawea who silently and efficiently retrieved the precious cargo before it floated away.

"The Indian woman," Lewis wrote in his journal on this date, "to whom I ascribe equal fortitude and resolution with any person on board at the time of the accident, caught and preserved most of the light articles which were washed overboard." In other words, Sacagawea saved the day, and perhaps the expedition.

Geronimo's Way

He defied the U.S. government on this date by slipping out of the Apache reservation in Arizona. Although accompanied by only forty-two warriors and ninety-two women and children, Geronimo's reputation was so fearsome that the following summer he would be pursued by 5,000 U.S. Army regulars, as many as 3,000 Mexican soldiers, and an estimated 1,000 miners, settlers, posse members, and assorted vigilantes.

None of them would so much as set eyes on Geronimo.

He was born in the 1820s at the headwaters of the Gila River near the present-day Arizona–New Mexico border. Geronimo belonged to an Apache tribe known as Chiricahua, which regularly raided the Comanche, Ute, and Navajo—and Mexicans living in the area. Bounties were offered by the Mexican army for Apache scalps, igniting a bloody, decades-long war of attrition. It became Geronimo's fight when Mexican soldiers murdered his mother, wife, and small children in their settlement. He vowed revenge and took it against the very soldiers who had committed the atrocity. He didn't stop there.

In the 1850s and 1860s, Geronimo was unknown to Americans, but mere mention of his name caused Mexican settlers to shudder. When he first met the "white eyes," Geronimo believed he could live with them in harmony. That changed when gold and silver was discovered in the area, bringing in people with whom no Indian could peace-ably coexist. Atrocities on both sides brought calls for the U.S. Army to subdue the Apache. Years on the run took its toll on Geronimo's people, and he finally turned himself in. The tribe was scattered by the government to the four winds: to reservations in Florida, where many died; to schools in Pennsylvania, where their religion and language were forbidden; and finally to Fort Sill, Oklahoma.

When Geronimo arrived in Florida, local whites had jeered the hated captive. Eight years later, he received a different welcome at Fort Sill, where the crowd was respectful and nostalgic. By 1905, Theodore Roosevelt asked Geronimo to lead his inauguration parade. The great warrior complied, and was featured at Old West shows and allowed to attend fairs and expositions.

Regrets? He had a few—mostly for the scalps *not* taken. Geronimo died in 1909 in Oklahoma. "I should never have surrendered," he confided on his deathbed to his favorite nephew. "I should have fought until I was the last man alive."

May 18, 1926

Sister Act

Distraught followers of charismatic Pentecostal preacher Aimee Semple McPherson scoured the beaches of Los Angeles on this date, searching for their beloved pastor. "Aimee is with Jesus," they chanted. "Pray for her." Some did more than pray. One parishioner was so overcome she waded into the Pacific and drowned, an apparent suicide. As Coast Guard cutters searched the waters, one of the deep-sea divers lost his life. Yet Aimee's followers held out hope.

"God wouldn't let her die," one of them told a local newspaper reporter. This premonition proved prescient. Aimee surfaced five weeks later on the Mexican side of the border near Douglas, Arizona. She told a harrowing tale of being kidnapped after her morning swim, drugged and held for ransom, but escaping as her captors slept. Composed and wearing polished shoes, she didn't look like someone who'd walked thirteen hours across the Sonoran Desert, as she claimed. And what about sightings the L.A. cops kept hearing about from a seaside hamlet of an Aimee look-alike and a handsome man ensconced in a romantic cottage?

Aimee had first arrived in California after leaving Rhode Island and her second husband in a Packard touring car with the words "Jesus Is Coming Soon—Get Ready" painted on the side. She spoke at tent revivals and stray churches before ending up in Los Angeles, where she built Angelus Temple, which has a thriving ministry to this day. But Aimee was not a plaster saint—and her face was well-known. While she was missing, several witnesses reported seeing it in Carmel-by-the-Sea, 325 miles north of her Los Angeles home. A handsome fellow was said to be with her, in a rented cottage. He turned out to be a married man named Kenneth Ormiston, an engineer at her Christian radio station who went missing at the same time as Aimee.

Ormiston gave himself up for the team, so to speak, eventually confessing that he was having an affair with a married woman he would gallantly identify only as "Mrs. X." Pressed by authorities, Sister Aimee stuck to her story, well, religiously. Her testimony left doubt in the minds of grand jurors weighing fraud and perjury allegations and they declined to indict her. She resumed her ministry until the day she died, at fifty-three, of an accidental drug overdose.

Carmel residents were proud that the couple had chosen their hamlet for their rendezvous. In the summer of 1926, as the scandal played out in the newspapers, a civic-minded soul put a sign outside the cottage to assist curious tourists. AIMEE SLEPT HERE, it said. Another local wag, motivated by wit more than malice, altered the placard slightly to read, AIMEE SLIPPED HERE.

May 19, 1836

Twice Kidnapped

Araiding party of Kiowa, Caddo, and Comanche braves came riding down from the Canadian River country to the Parker Ranch, near the present-day Oklahoma-Texas border. They attacked the Parker family, butchering several men and kidnapping five women and children.

Among the captives taken on this date was Cynthia Ann Parker, whose sad saga would become a metaphor for two peoples not destined to live in harmony, but intertwined nonetheless. Ten years earlier, James Fenimore Cooper had written *The Last of the Mohicans*, a story set in the East. Unlike the two Munro sisters in Cooper's novel, Cynthia Ann Parker and her kidnapped kinsmen were real people. Their abduction played into an ancient fear among white settlers: the taking of Europeans as battle trophies, with all its attendant horrors, some sexual in nature. This wasn't a fictional concern. Seizing captives was a customary tactic of war among the indigenous peoples of North America. Adult males were routinely tortured to death. Female captives would sometimes be gang-raped and killed. Other times, they were unmolested. Children of either gender would often be raised as members of the new tribe. Some would marry of their own free will and literally go native, which was what happened with Cynthia Parker.

Although she became the focus of an obsessive manhunt by her relatives, white traders who encountered Cynthia found that she wouldn't speak with them. A Comanche warrior named Peta Nocona told the men he'd married Cynthia and that "she is unwilling to leave." This was the truth. In time, she would have three children including a son who would become a famous Comanche chief. His name was Quanah, and he would survive the Comanche wars, the intratribal intrigues of the southern plains Indians, and the wrath of his multiple wives.

Quanah emerged as a spokesman for his people and, like Geronimo, was invited by Theodore Roosevelt to the presidential inauguration. Quanah reciprocated by hosting Roosevelt at his Oklahoma home. As for Cynthia, she missed all that. In 1860, she was captured by Texas Rangers in a raid not unlike the one in which she had originally been abducted. Once again, she was taken against her will—Peta Nocona may have been killed in the skirmish—and sent along with her daughter, Prairie Flower, to live with white relatives in Texas. She tried to escape several times, and after Prairie Flower died of pneumonia, Cynthia stopped eating and died in 1870, ostensibly of influenza, but really of a broken heart. She never saw her son again.

May 20, 1998

Ireland's American Dimension

Bill Clinton made an unusual pitch on this date: He told people in Ireland how he wanted them to vote. "You can do nothing to erase the past," he said in support of a proposal to end Northern Ireland's sectarian bloodshed. "But you can do everything to build the future."

His appeal culminated a five-year push dating to the 1992 presidential primaries when Clinton and Jerry Brown tried to curry favor with Irish-American Democrats in New York. Really, it began much earlier. Gen. Ulysses S. Grant led thousands of Ireland-born troops in the Civil War; and following his tenure as president, Grant visited Ireland where he foreshadowed the future of Irish-American politics. "I am by birth," he told a Dublin crowd in 1879, "a citizen of a country where there are more Irishmen, either native born or the descendants of Irishmen, than there are in all of Ireland."

British prime minister William Gladstone had taken note of this fact in describing "an American dimension" to British-Irish frictions. In the 1880s, Home Secretary William Harcourt articulated England's vision of this dimension: "In former Irish rebellions, the Irish were in Ireland," he said. "We could reach their forces, cut off their resources in men and money—and then to subjugate them was comparatively easy. Now there is an Irish nation in the United States, equally hostile, with plenty of money, absolutely beyond our reach."

Irish nationalists were so cognizant of this truism that when John F. Kennedy made his 1963 visit to his ancestral homeland, Irish prime minister Eamon de Valera felt comfortable enough with it to tell JFK that getting the British to pay attention to Irish grievances "means letting them know that you are willing to throw an occasional bomb into one of their lorries."

Although American financial support to Irish Catholic paramilitaries had a long antecedent, by the time Bill Clinton took office, terrorism of this type was viewed with deep disdain in the United States. In that environment, a more benign vision of U.S. involvement in Irish politics took shape. This view was described poignantly by Irish author Tim Pat Coogan.

"Given American support, Ireland and England could be at peace," he wrote as Clinton began to address the violence in Northern Ireland that had claimed more than three thousand lives. "Ireland and England are both mother countries. There is a time in life when parents look to their children for support. That time is now."

May 21, 1881

Angel of the Battlefield

Clara Barton had asked two successive U.S. presidents for help, to no avail, so on this date she just decided to launch the American Red Cross on her own—in the parlor of her Washington, D.C., apartment on I Street.

Clarissa Harlowe Barton was born on Christmas Day, 1821, in the Massachusetts town of North Oxford. The youngest of five children, she was educated mostly by her siblings and was a teacher herself by the age of seventeen. She pursued a career as an educator for a while, but by the time Abraham Lincoln became president, Clara, as she preferred to be called, was working in the U.S. Patent Office in Washington, D.C. When the Civil War broke out, Clara Barton answered the call without being asked. At her own instigation, and eschewing a salary, she began nursing, cooking, counseling, and caring for the wounded fighters. It wasn't easy work.

"My business," she explained, "is staunching blood and feeding fainting men."

Union soldiers dubbed her the "Angel of the Battlefield," but she was more than that. Possessing an organizational genius and a can-do attitude that was the envy of most of Mr. Lincoln's generals, she eventually became the officially designated superintendent of Union nurses. Barton's true gift was perceiving a societal need—and rushing to fill it. In the waning days of the Civil War, for instance, she received President Lincoln's blessing to launch a letter-writing campaign to identify and find missing soldiers.

After the war, inspired during a trip abroad by the work of the Red Cross in Switzerland, she brought the same idea to the United States. President Rutherford B. Hayes shied away from a formal U.S. affiliation—he fretted over the question of foreign alliances. Barton had a more receptive audience in Hayes's successor, James A. Garfield, but before he could act Garfield was cut down by an assassin's bullet. So at sixty years of age, Clara Barton convened a meeting of like-minded exemplars to incorporate the American Red Cross without government help.

She led the organization for twenty-three years before passing away in her home, which is now a small and lovely little National Park located in the suburban Maryland hamlet of Glen Echo.

"It has long been said that women don't know anything about war," she once wrote. "I wish men didn't either. They have always known a great deal too much about it for the good of their kind."

May 22, 1948

Jimmy's Fund

Eleven-year-old Carl Einar Gustafson had never heard the word *lymphosarcoma* until he was diagnosed with it. He figured things were bad when his father, a stoic potato farmer from Maine, wept when told the news. Non-Hodgkin's lymphoma killed 70 percent of its childhood victims when the boy was put in the care of Dr. Sidney Farber. The Boston physician who founded the Children's Cancer Research Foundation bonded with him, and when he was approached by the producers for a radio show, *Truth or Consequences*, suggested Carl as a guest. Protective of his privacy, Farber insisted the announcers call the boy "Jimmy." So, popular radio personality Ralph Edwards, broadcasting from Children's Hospital on this date, asked him this question about the local National League team, the Boston Braves:

"Who's the catcher on the Braves, Jimmy?"

"Phil Masi," he replied.

"That's right. Have you ever met Phil Masi?"

"No," the boy said. But then listeners across the country heard a man's voice: "Hi, Jimmy! My name is Phil Masi."

Then, as if by magic, one Braves star after another walked into the hospital room, bringing hats, balls, and bats. "We play the Chicago Cubs tomorrow in a doubleheader at Braves Field," Boston skipper Billy Southworth told him. "We're calling it Jimmy's Day."

Edwards promised if the program reaped $20,000 in donations, "Jimmy" would receive a television set to watch Braves games in the hospital. Ten times that amount came in. "Jimmy" got his TV, and the Braves went to the World Series. It's a storybook ending that keeps repeating itself.

The Braves moved to Milwaukee and then Atlanta, but the Jimmy Fund stayed in New England, where it has raised $750 million for cancer research. As for Jimmy, New Englanders assumed he died in childhood. He didn't. He got better, went back home to Maine, grew up, became a truck driver, started a construction company, married, and switched his allegiance to the Red Sox after the Braves skipped town. Asked to throw out the first pitch at a 1998 Red Sox–Yankees game at Fenway Park, he complied, but not before putting it in perspective. Asked about the standing ovation he was certain to receive, Gustafson said, "I've had that before. They did that for me at the Braves game in '48, and I waved to the crowd."

Jackie Rests

In the hallowed ground of Arlington National Cemetery, Jacqueline Kennedy rejoined her husband. She was buried on a green hillside next to John F. Kennedy under the vigilance of the Eternal Flame, a symbol she had first proposed as a tribute to the fallen president. Jackie Kennedy was thirty-one years old when she became First Lady. She was sixty-four when lymphoma took her. Americans had believed in 1963 that Camelot had been buried under a dismal November sky. But what many realized on this date was that as long as the First Lady of Camelot was alive, an essential component of our memories survived as well.

Philip J. Hannan, the retired archbishop of New Orleans—and the priest who had eulogized President Kennedy three decades earlier—summed up Americans' feelings in six words: "So dearly beloved," he said of Jacqueline Kennedy. "So sorely missed."

Countless books have been written about the Kennedys, and Jackie's funeral is worth a book of its own. But one vignette captures her generous spirit. The services included Old Testament and New Testament verses read by her children, Caroline and John Jr., and several other readings, including a poignant Edna St. Vincent Millay poem about Cape Cod. It also included an a cappella singing of the "Navy Hymn" by thirteen members of the Navy Band Sea Chanters, the United States Navy's official chorus. The formal name of that song is "Eternal Father, Strong to Save," and its haunting strains evoked JFK's World War II naval service.

A month earlier, the naval chorus had sung the same tune out in California at the funeral for another old U.S. Navy enlistee, Richard Nixon, the Republican whom Jack Kennedy had defeated to win the presidency. Two years after his loss to JFK in the close 1960 presidential election, Nixon suffered another crushing political defeat, losing the 1962 California gubernatorial election in a landslide, a result that most people (Nixon included) believed had thwarted his planned comeback.

President Kennedy's assassination the following year put politics in perspective, which Nixon acknowledged in a warm letter of condolence to Jackie. In reply, she sent Nixon a touchingly personal letter. She encouraged him to persevere, gently reminding him of what was most important. "We never value life enough when we have it," she wrote, "if it does not work out as you have hoped for so long, please be consoled by what you already have—your life and your family."

May 24, 1844

Morse's Code

Inventor Samuel Morse was at one end of the line on Capitol Hill, while his collaborator, Alfred Vail, waited in a Baltimore railroad station at the other end of a newly installed telegraph wire. Morse typed out in the code that bears his name—the first public message transmitted over wire in human history. Choosing a line from the Bible, he tapped out the words: "What Hath God Wrought?"

Samuel Finley Breese Morse was born in Charlestown, Massachusetts, on April 27, 1791. He always had an eclectic mind, and among the subjects that fascinated him while attending Yale were painting, politics, and the emerging field of electricity. All three would play a role in the development of the telegraph.

After graduating in 1810, young Morse moved to England to further his art studies and soon became a respected portraitist. He returned to the United States in 1825 and settled in New York, where he helped found the National Academy of Design. While serving as the academy's first president, Morse found that he enjoyed being in charge. He sought to broaden his portfolio while pursuing executive authority. He ran twice for mayor of New York as an anti-immigration candidate—think Donald Trump without the charisma, but with a keen scientific mind—and finished dismally on each occasion. Afterward, he lost interest in elective politics.

Yet, the Nativist Party's loss was science's gain. Soon, Morse was off to Europe again. While sailing across the Atlantic he was privy to a technical discussion about electromagnetism. This chance conversation convinced Morse of the feasibility of the electric telegraph, an idea being studied by various engineers on both sides of the ocean.

Returning stateside, he labored with Alfred Vail and New York University professor Leonard Gale on the mechanics of the device, while working out the dot-and-dash system still called the Morse Code today. His dabbling in politics taught him that congressional support would be valuable, and Morse got Congress to appropriate $30,000 to construct the telegraph lines between Washington and Baltimore.

On this date, Samuel Morse showed Americans this was money well spent, while showing the world that his vision into the future was true. The invention worked, and human communications would never be the same. What hath God wrought, indeed?

May 25, 1915

Madam Marie

Born in Neptune City, New Jersey, on this date, Marie Castello became known to Asbury Park locals as "the gypsy queen of the boardwalk." For seven decades until her death in 2008, she told fortunes on the Jersey Shore, most of that time out of a small shack with an inviting sign that read: MADAM MARIE'S TEMPLE OF KNOWLEDGE.

Madam Marie certainly saw enough in her ninety-three years to learn how to read people. In the early 1930s, men and women strolled by in formal wear on their way to the dinner theaters or Asbury Park's Convention Hall. In the early 1970s, as the town's luster ebbed, the crowd got younger—and a bit rougher—and faded jeans and Army surplus jackets replaced the evening gowns and tuxedos of an earlier era. On one occasion, a long-haired seventeen-year-old musician, who often strummed his guitar on the railing opposite Madam Marie's, strolled in to her shop. He didn't have enough money, but she told his fortune anyway. Looking in her crystal ball, Marie foresaw a boy destined for fame and success. His name was Bruce Springsteen.

Ah, she probably told that to all the young people, Springsteen later allowed with a laugh. Bruce returned the favor anyway, including her in one of the best lines in one of his best songs, in one of rock 'n' roll's best canons. In the process, Springsteen made Madam Marie the most famous fortune-teller in the world. "Did you hear the cops finally busted Madam Marie," Springsteen wrote, "for tellin' fortunes better than they do."

Those were the iconic lines from a 1973 song called "4th of July, Asbury Park (Sandy)," and, from that time forward, Bruce and Madam Marie were forever linked. It was an association benefitting both parties, and probably helped Asbury Park, too, although town authorities were quick to say that the soothsayer was never really arrested. Springsteen took literary license to make a point about prejudice, and judging other people: about the expectations those in authority have about people who don't look or act the way their parents did.

Upon Madam Marie's death, New Jersey columnist and radio commentator Mike Kelly explained that he'd once asked Marie about her "tarnished town" and she'd replied that Asbury Park was doing just fine, thank you.

"To be a fortune-teller, you have to believe in the future, warts and all," he said. "Madam Marie believed, and she saw Asbury Park not just as a wonderful old shore town, but as a vibrant new shore town, rebuilding and reinventing itself."

May 26, 1864

The Treasure State

The president who talked of America as the "last, best hope of Earth" took a respite from his duties as commander in chief on this date to sign legislation creating the Montana Territory, which in 1988 was dubbed by writer William Kittredge—partly in homage to Lincoln—as "the Last, Best Place."

In one sense, Abraham Lincoln was taking a baton handed to him by Thomas Jefferson, who included the area in the vast expanse he commissioned Meriwether Lewis and William Clark to explore. The two captains' reports on their upper Missouri River adventures were among their most evocative writings. In another way, Montana was an old, familiar story: The lure of gold in the Northern Rockies had brought white miners and prospectors into the territory, meaning that the U.S. government drew lines on maps and plastered its own place names on land only a handful of people in Washington, D.C., had ever seen.

But how Montana got its lyrical name added a nice wrinkle to the story.

It seems that the name Montana City, with variations on the spelling, arose when a group of prospectors settled in Colorado. "It was a very pretty site, on the right bank of the Platte River, and thirty or forty feet above the level of the stream, commanding a magnificent view of the mountains," Montana historian Wilbur Edgerton Sanders wrote decades later.

He was describing the founding of Denver. One of the town's settlers, Josiah Hinman, had recently matriculated from Wisconsin's Beloit College, which had a Latin requirement. It was Hinman who proposed *Montana*, a Spanish derivative of the Latin word meaning "mountainous." Local politics interceded, as it often does in such cases. The men on the Platte, desiring favorable treatment for the only authority in that part of the country, decided to name their settlement after the Virginia-born, Ohio-raised governor of Kansas: James W. Denver.

It was James Denver, in turn, who suggested to Illinois senator Stephen Douglas that the huge territory to the north be called Montana. The name stuck, along with the mystique. "Big city turn me loose and set me free somewhere in the middle of Montana," sang Merle Haggard.

In *Travels with Charley*, California native John Steinbeck put it this way: "I'm in love with Montana. For other states I have admiration, respect, recognition, even some affection. But with Montana it is love. And it's difficult to analyze love when you're in it."

May 27, 1937

Golden Gate

The first people to cross the stunning new suspension bridge that opened on this date—the first two hundred thousand to cross it—were pedestrians, not drivers. Exemplifying the mood of a weeklong celebration, a few traversed the span on stilts, others on roller skates. Some San Franciscans walked backward; others ran. All of this was recorded by Bay Area newspapers, which covered the Golden Gate Bridge Fiesta in a spirit simultaneously civic-minded and competitive. There was much to cover: The official program ran to seventy-six pages.

Politicians spoke, bands played, enterprising food vendors set up hot dog stands at the entrance. Two U.S. Post Office letter carriers toted mail sacks across the bridge. A Golden Gate Fiesta queen was selected, though rival newspapers disagreed on which lovely lass was chosen. Florentine Calegari, a maintenance man at San Francisco's Palace Hotel, was the one who donned stilts. Two sisters, Carmen and Minnie Perez, were the first to cross on roller skates.

Construction on the iconic engineering and aesthetic marvel connecting San Francisco with Marin County began on January 5, 1933. It was famous even before it was built. The project had been planned for years, but ran into delays that are not unfamiliar today: political rivalries, environmental concerns and ensuing litigation, a dearth of funding owing to the outbreak of U.S. military intervention abroad—in this case, World War I.

Then came the Great Depression. Yet because San Francisco lies at the north end of a long peninsula, its civic leaders and business community knew that for the city to become an important urban center, those conduits just had to be built. "San Francisco needs the bridge," chief engineer Joseph Strauss urged Bank of America founder A. P. Giannini.

An innovative visionary, Giannini didn't need to be told twice. Born in nearby San Jose to immigrant parents, he'd founded the Bank of Italy in 1904 to cater to hard-working immigrants ignored by other banks. After San Francisco's 1906 earthquake, he personally carried the bank's deposits out of the smoldering building. By 1922, he'd renamed it the Bank of Italy and America. In 1928, it simply became Bank of America, and a financial force far beyond California's borders. When Joseph Strauss made his appeal for B of A to help underwrite the building of the Golden Gate Bridge, A. P. Giannini answered directly. "We will take the bonds," he said. Construction could then begin.

May 28, 1867

Alyeska

Seward's Folly" was only one of the derisive names applied to the proposal negotiated by Secretary of State William Seward for the United States to purchase Alaska from Russia for $7.2 million—less than two cents an acre. "Seward's Icebox" was another. "Andrew Johnson's Polar Bear Garden" was another favorite. What these critics of President Andrew Johnson were making fun of was one of the most beneficial real estate deals in U.S. history. Setting aside their misgivings about handing a political victory to an unpopular president, the Senate ratified the treaty with Russia on April 9, by a 39–2 vote. Johnson signed it on this date.

East Coast newspaper editors were another matter. That was where the "Seward's Folly" stuff took root. "Russia sold us a sucked orange," opined the *New York World* on April 1, 1867. "What remains of the Russian fur trade is not of sufficient importance to justify the expense of naval protection." Ten days later, the *New York Daily Tribune* added its addled two cents: "We simply obtain by the treaty the nominal possession of impassable deserts of snow, vast tracts of dwarf timbers, frozen rivers, inaccessible mountain ranges," the paper proclaimed. "We may make a treaty with Russia, but we cannot make a treaty with the North Wind or the Snow King."

The editorializing grew less clueless as one moved closer to the lands in question. The *Chicago Evening Journal*, noting that Alaska was eight times as large as Illinois, termed $7.2 million a "paltry sum" and predicted correctly that the commerce of the Pacific Ocean would someday surpass that of the Atlantic. Moving even further westward, the *Portland Daily Oregonian* called it "the most valuable acquisition of territory obtained by the United States since the [obtaining] of California."

It took a while for this wisdom to permeate the dense skulls of chroniclers in the East. Ten years after the purchase, the New York-based *Harper's Monthly Magazine* sent a writer to survey Seward's prize. Although impressed by the magnificence of the landscape, the magazine's correspondent still wasn't convinced Americans had gotten their money's worth. Less prophetic words were rarely written.

Today, some 25 percent of America's oil and over half the nation's seafood come from Alaska. The richness of that land was never doubted by the people who lived there. The place-name itself is derived from the Aleut word *Alyeska*, which simply means "great land."

May 29, 2012

Yes, We Can

When Barack Obama pinned a Presidential Medal of Freedom on an octogenarian grandmother, he was doing more than acknowledging her influential social activism to improve working conditions in the breadbaskets of this nation that writer Carey McWilliams called the "factories in the field." The president was also paying homage to an organizer who helped fuel his own march to the presidency. But first, Dolores Huerta, a single mother of seven, cofounded, along with Cesar Chavez, the United Farm Workers, a labor union that fought for decent wages, basic sanitation, fresh water, and workers' protection from pesticides in those field factories.

In the early 1960s, Chavez, Huerta, Gilbert Padilla, and other Mexican-American community activists worked to help poor field hands negotiate life's everyday problems. These ranged from filing taxes, studying English for citizenship exams, or enrolling their kids in public schools. All these issues were exacerbated by the itinerant nature of seasonal work in the fields, so Chavez and Huerta started a new organization focusing solely on agricultural workers. They didn't even call it a union—it was named the National Farmworkers Association.

But in 1965, a largely Filipino union affiliated with the AFL-CIO went on strike against the growers of table grapes in Delano, California. Within a week, Chavez, Huerta, and the other leaders of the NFWA agreed to join. Out of that action came a merger.

The new union, the UFW, headed by Chavez, would become famous for its distinctive flag (a stylized black eagle on a white circle in a red field), its long marches (Chavez led them 245 miles from Delano to the steps of the California State Capitol in Sacramento), its lengthy strikes (the grape boycott lasted five years), and its rhythmic chants of protest and solidarity. The most famous of these was, "*¡Viva La Huelga!*" ("Long live the strike!"). But in those early years, when things seemed darkest, Huerta coined another simple mantra: "*¡Si, se puede!*" Yes, we can!

In 2008, the Obama campaign appropriated this phrase, perhaps with insufficient attribution, which the president alluded to lightheartedly while presenting Huerta her medal at a White House ceremony on this date.

"Dolores was very gracious when I told her I had stolen her slogan," Obama said. "Knowing her, I'm pleased that she let me off easy—because Dolores does not play."

May 30, 1851

Nothing But the Truth

On this date, word started trickling out in the newspapers that something extraordinary had taken place on May 28 and May 29, 1851, in Akron, Ohio. The Woman's Rights Convention had been gaveled to order by Frances Dana Gage, an Ohio abolitionist, social reformer, temperance activist, wife, children's book author—and mother of eight. Mrs. Gage also possessed talent as a note taker. The notes in question preserved the words of an extemporaneous address by Sojourner Truth, a former slave who had electrified the convention.

Human bondage was a subtext of the suffrage movement in those pre–Civil War years, just as voting rights for women was the political issue around which battle lines were drawn. Slavery would be abolished on the battlefield, but women wouldn't win the vote for three more generations. Yet the minutes of the 1851 Akron convention, the speeches given there, the reports submitted by various delegates, and letters of support from around the country all reveal that mid-nineteenth-century feminists were tackling issues Americans still wrestle with today. Frances Gage set the tone in her opening speech by reminding the delegates that the original source of male domination over women was brute strength.

Elizabeth Cady Stanton sent a letter, read to the gathering, that envisions girls becoming more educated, playing sports without inhibition, walking boldly on the streets of this country unescorted by males, and thriving in the professional world. "The trades and professions are all open to us," she wrote. "As merchants, postmasters, silversmiths, teachers, preachers and physicians, woman has already proved herself fully competent." But much needed to be done, as the Akron convention's "Report on Labor" made clear. Male school teachers in Ashtabula were paid an average of $16.50 a month; female teachers less than half that amount. Male school principals in Cincinnati made $65 per month; female principals were paid $35.

So there it all was, in 1851: The battle lines were already drawn around issues that sound familiar in the twenty-first century: glass ceilings and Title IX; the "Take Back the Night" movement, and the enduring fight over equal pay for equal work. And it was all given moral authority by Sojourner Truth. "I have borne thirteen children, and seen 'em most all sold off to slavery," she thundered. "And when I cried out with my mother's grief, none but Jesus heard me! And ain't I a woman?"

May 31, 1876

Kellogg's Last Stand

Orphaned as a boy, Clement Lounsberry volunteered for a Michigan infantry unit at the outbreak of the Civil War and served with distinction from 1861 until the war ended in central Virginia four years later. He was wounded in battle and captured at the First Battle of Bull Run, spent a year in Confederate confinement, was exchanged for other prisoners, rejoined his unit, earned battlefield promotions, worked his way through the officer ranks, and was a colonel in command of two Michigan regiments when he received the Confederate surrender at Petersburg in 1865.

After the war, he moved West and opened a newspaper, the *Bismarck Tribune*. In its pages, he extolled the Indian-fighting exploits of George Armstrong Custer, whom he knew in the Army. Lounsberry was planning to accompany his pal into the field in June 1876, but Custer met one of Lounsberry's reporters, Marcus Kellogg, on a snowbound train and invited him instead—meaning that when the U.S. Army's Seventh Cavalry Regiment rode out from Fort Abraham Lincoln on this date, Kellogg, and not his old Army friend Lounsberry, was by Custer's side. Kellogg filed three dispatches from the field, the last from the Army's encampment along a stream called the Rosebud River, a tributary of the Little Big Horn.

"We leave the Rosebud tomorrow," Kellogg told his readers, "and by the time this reaches you we will have met and fought the red devils, with what result remains to be seen. I go with Custer and will be at the death." Marcus Kellogg wasn't predicting his own death—or Custer's. The phrase "at the death" comes from fox hunting, and meant "at the kill." It was prophetic nonetheless. Four days after Kellogg wrote those words, Custer and all those who rode with him—including his own brother and the jaunty newspaperman he'd met on a train—would be slain by the Sioux and Cheyenne warriors riding with Sitting Bull.

In its July 6, 1876, special edition on Custer's Last Stand, Clement Lounsberry's newspaper paid homage to its own. THE BISMARCK TRIBUNE'S SPECIAL CORRESPON-DENT SLAIN, read the headline over an article about Kellogg. "The body of Kellogg alone remained unstripped of its clothing," the paper reported, "and was not mutilated."

The *Tribune* speculated that this mercy may have been prompted by the Indians' "respect (for) this humble shover of the lead pencil." That seems a stretch, but it was one of the few contemporary reports that attributed humanity to those on both sides in the Battle of Little Bighorn.

164

June 1, 1980

Mouth of the South

The first story that aired from Cable News Network's studios at 6 p.m. Eastern time on this date was the wounding of National Urban League president Vernon E. Jordan Jr., in an assassination attempt in Indiana. No one in CNN's Atlanta studios realized it immediately, but it was a formula that would prove durable: a breaking story—often a shocking crime—with broader public policy implications. At the time, network coverage was dominated by the Big Three (NBC, CBS, and ABC), and CNN was available in only two million U.S. households. But even before it became profitable, CNN launched a revolution in how Americans received their news.

Robert Edward "Ted" Turner III made his money in an outdoor advertising business he inherited from his father. While expanding the billboard business, he acquired radio stations across the South, which he in turn flipped for struggling UHF television stations. Turner soon parlayed them into a singular enterprise: an Atlanta-based "superstation" he renamed in honor of himself: WTBS. To supplement the programming schedule of old movies, Turner bought the Atlanta Hawks and Atlanta Braves, and broadcast their games as well.

Along the way, he won America's Cup as a yachtsman, while offering his opinions on business, politics, and sports. His brashness earned him uncomplimentary nicknames— "Captain Outrageous," "Mouth of the South," and "Terrible Ted"—but the new media mogul didn't seem to mind.

The last moniker had origins in Turner's reputation as a difficult boss. But this was not a universal view. His baseball players recalled Turner's stint as team owner with fondness. He was unpretentious, for one thing, often showing up in the Braves' clubhouse in flip-flops and shorts. Mainly, his players respected Turner's competitive fire.

On May 11, 1977, after the Braves had lost sixteen consecutive games, Turner removed his manager and put himself in the dugout as skipper for a game. Years later, Braves infielder Darrel Chaney was discussing that game with ESPN when he remembered a long-forgotten incident that showed why his players appreciated their owner. It seems that Ted Turner and Philadelphia Phillies pitcher Tug McGraw made a friendly bet over who could push a baseball farthest up the baseline—with his nose. "It was really funny because Ted got down on all fours to start rolling the ball with his nose, and Tug never did do anything," Chaney recalled. "When Ted got up from rolling the ball he had blood from his forehead all the way down the top of his nose. Those kinds of things he wanted to win, even something like that. He was all out."

Youngest First Lady

Weddings are usually joyous occasions, but they can be fraught with family politics, even if the groom isn't president of the United States—and even if he isn't twenty-seven years older than the bride. Grover Cleveland had known Frances Clara Folsom all her life when he married her on this date in the White House. Her father had been Cleveland's law partner and close friend in Buffalo, New York. After Oscar Folsom was killed in an 1875 carriage accident when Frances was eleven, Cleveland became the executor of his former law partner's estate.

Cleveland was reintroduced to Frances, as it were, in a March 1885 meeting at the White House. The young lady, recently graduated from college, was brought to see the newly installed president by her mother, Emma, who seems to have had designs on the president. Cleveland was a bachelor, and one with a reputation: A former sheriff, mayor of Buffalo, and governor of New York, he had fathered a child out of wedlock before coming to Washington. (The baby was named Oscar Folsom Cleveland, after Frances's father). In any event, it must have been an awkward meeting in 1885 when Oscar Folsom's widow came with her daughter to the White House and the forty-eight-year-old president mentioned his desire for marriage—but to twenty-year-old Frances, not forty-four-year-old Emma.

Frances was taken to Europe for a year of "finishing," as it was then called, before being married a year later in a private East Room ceremony. The wedding was limited to close friends—and news correspondents and photographers—but curious crowds that gathered outside the executive mansion could hear the faint strains of the Marine Band, which on this day was led by John Philip Sousa. After the ceremony ended, church bells pealed throughout the city and boats on the Potomac River sounded their horns.

Replacing Cleveland's sister, who'd acted as First Lady for the initial fifteen months of his presidency, Frances Cleveland was an immediate sensation, becoming a national icon of beauty and fashion. She also became fodder for the media at a time when the "penny press" was still in its heyday. The tabloids, as we'd call them today, dubbed her Frankie (a foreshadowing of Jacqueline Kennedy's newspaper nickname), but even people who had no use for her husband conceded their admiration for Frankie. As one Grover Cleveland detractor quipped, "I detest him so much that I don't even think his wife is beautiful."

June 3, 1953

Bombshell

When Elvis Presley graduated from high school on this date, his Memphis classmates already knew he could sing: His performance at the school's annual talent show had proved that much. "To me," recalled classmate Dwight Malone, "that was when rock-and-roll was born." It would be three years before Elvis would play Las Vegas, but the day he graduated, the Sahara Hotel made news by attempting to worm out of a contract with another act it had booked.

The performer's name was Christine Jorgensen, who could be described as the un-Elvis: She could neither sing, nor dance, and was uncomfortable onstage. So why was she booked into Vegas's then-iconic venue? The answer to that question had arrived in the form of a December 1, 1952, New York *Daily News* headline: EX-G.I. BECOMES BLONDE BOMBSHELL.

Six decades before the tabloids chronicled Bruce Jenner's long journey on the transgender trail, Jorgensen was a household name. It must have been a lonely trek. As a child growing up in the Bronx, George Jorgensen Jr. was, in his words, a "frail, tow-headed, introverted" kid who "ran from fistfights and rough-and-tumble games." At five, he'd hoped for "a pretty doll with long gold hair" under the Christmas tree, but neither Santa nor his parents understood this boy. He got a red railroad train instead. Drafted into the Army as World War II was ending, he used words that sound familiar now, but weren't then: He felt like a woman trapped in a man's body.

After the war, he learned of physicians in Scandinavia who could help. After a two-year regimen that included castration, hormone therapy, and cosmetic surgery, George Jorgensen became Christine Jorgensen. As the Vegas nightclub scene was being reinvented, Sahara Hotel owner Milton Prell booked Jorgensen sight unseen. But Prell had second thoughts when she bombed onstage at her Los Angeles debut. Christine was nervous, lacked a singing voice, and hadn't perfected the patter that such venues require. To get out of the $25,000, two-week contract, Prell challenged Christine, whose genital reconstruction surgery was still incomplete, "to prove she's a woman."

Charlie Yates, her famed Hollywood press agent, sued the Sahara. Prell capitulated, and by November 1953 Christine Jorgensen was playing the Sahara to audiences who appreciated her for the person she had become. She died of cancer in 1989 in San Clemente, California. Before her passing, she told the *Los Angeles Times* that gender transition "wasn't news anymore."

June 4, 1919

Suffrage

Born in Newburyport, Massachusetts, in 1827, Aaron Augustus Sargent met his future wife as a teenager. The object of his affections—and they were always reciprocated—was a girl named Ellen Clark. They were Sunday school teachers at the Methodist church, abolitionists, and young people of modest means. Seeking to better his prospects, Sargent apprenticed as a printer in Philadelphia, worked as a newspaper reporter, and served as a congressional aide.

In 1849, with a borrowed stake of $125 from an uncle, he set sail for the California gold fields. He didn't strike it rich, but he became the editor and publisher of a California newspaper. He studied the law, passed the bar, and became active in the fledgling Republican Party. In early 1852, he returned to Newburyport, married Ellen, and brought her back out West. They raised a family and went into politics. Aaron was elected to Congress. Ellen became Northern California's most prominent suffragist. For five decades, this nineteenth-century power couple split their time between San Francisco and Washington, D.C. In Congress, Aaron Sargent was known for his backing of the transcontinental railroad, his support for women's rights, and his opposition to Asian immigration—apparently, his liberalism on race and gender went only so far.

His lasting contribution to U.S. history came with an assist from Susan B. Anthony, who accompanied the Sargent family on a wintertime trip to the East after Aaron was elected to the Senate. In those years, the suffrage movement was divided—as gay marriage advocates would be a century and a half later—over whether to pursue the vote on a federal basis or state by state.

Eventually, both strategies were pursued, but on that long train trip from California, aboard a railroad line Sargent helped bring into existence, Miss Anthony cemented an alliance. Aaron Sargent would serve only one term in the Senate, but in 1878, before he left, he authored an amendment to the U.S. Constitution proposed to him by the famed suffragist.

The measure didn't pass in that session of Congress or the next—or in the lifetimes of Susan B. Anthony, Elizabeth Cady Stanton, Ellen Clark Sargent, or her husband, Aaron. But it did pass Congress overwhelmingly on this date in 1919. It was sent to the states for ratification, which came the following year. That succinct measure, the Nineteenth Amendment, reads simply: "The right of citizens of the United States to vote shall not be denied or abridged by the United States or by any State on account of sex."

June 5, 1993

The Woman Who Talked to Horses

The mile-and-a-half long Belmont Stakes, jockey Jerry Bailey told ABC race caller Dave Johnson before post time, is the most difficult of the three legs of thoroughbred racing's Triple Crown. Why? Because its long distance gives a rider "more time to make mistakes."

Bailey, a Hall of Famer, was half-kidding, but his mount that day, Kentucky Derby winner Sea Hero, finished seventh. The winner on this date was 14–1 shot Colonial Affair, a horse piloted by Julie Krone, the first female rider to win a Triple Crown race. She rode flawlessly.

The weather in New York City that day was drizzly, foggy, and nearly dark at race time. The two Belmont Stakes favorites were Sea Hero and Prairie Bayou, the gelding who'd won the Preakness three weeks earlier. It would be a tragic day for Prairie Bayou. He would break down during the race, throwing jockey Mike Smith, and be euthanized.

For Julie Krone, the horse's death marred her historic victory. She was close friends with Smith, and had given him a photograph of him and Prairie Bayou taken at Saratoga. As she entered the stretch on Colonial Affair, she glanced around expecting to see the two horses in close quarters.

"Turning for home I was looking for Mike because I knew he'd be coming," she recalled. "He loved that horse. When I saw him after the race I could hardly say anything except 'I'm so sorry.' He was surrounded by reporters, crying."

In the winner's circle, however, there was a feeling of accomplishment. Julie Krone had broken a barrier, and done so in style: boldly directing a colt who made a stirring move in the stretch to win a classic horse race. Afterward, Colonial Affair's trainer, Flint "Scotty" Schulhofer, a racing lifer who had not initially cottoned to the idea of women riders, extolled Krone's gifts.

"She talks to the horses in body language," he said. "They respond to her. She's a very smart girl, with a great feel. I think she's got the finest sense of horses of anyone around."

June 6, 1944

D-Day, Part I

All of America looked nervously to Europe as the long-awaited invasion began. Back in New Castle, Pennsylvania, twenty-four-year-old Pauline Elliott wrote to her husband, Frank, who was serving with the 741st Tank Battalion. Frank M. Elliott had been a senior at Georgetown University when he enlisted in 1943. On this date, he was crossing the English Channel.

"Well…'D-Day' has finally arrived," his wife wrote. "The news brought a kind of relief and great concern. The first thought of all of us here at home was a prayer. I can't deny, darling, that anxiety for your well-being fills my heart. True, I don't *know* that you are taking part in this phase of the invasion but it is very probable that you are. And my thoughts are with you. Spiritually, I *am* with you."

"Polly" Elliott, as her family called her, then referred to a letter Frank had written her four weeks earlier, in which he discussed the impending invasion and his own mortality. "It is God's will darling, to which we must all bow, and His will be done is a daily admonition we make. I don't hold with the 'theory of the inevitable' school and so you may be sure that I won't invite disaster in any form. In prep school we had a quarterback who always qualified his pre-game prayers with the phrase, 'Not my will God, but Thine' and so it is sweetheart and so it must always be—we must trust our God unflinchingly, unquestioningly."

Pauline took solace in these words, and said so in her D-Day letter. "You are the one who is making all the sacrifices—and yet you are the one who could find the proper words to give us both strength," she wrote. "The letter in which you reminded me that the desire of both of us is that 'God's will be done' continues to be my favorite 'bedtime story,' darling—it's a masterpiece." She concluded by saying, "I am unable to tell you of the depth of my emotion on this day—but without my telling you I think you know and understand."

This letter, which Frank Elliott would never read, was signed "Polly and Dee"—the second name being the couple's three-year-old daughter, DeRonda. Her mother had said in a previous letter that she was thinking of taking the little girl to the cinema.

"I would certainly like to be on

hand when Dee goes to see her first movie," Frank replied. "Don't postpone her enjoyment until I come home, but let me know how she reacts to all the glamour of Hollywood's productions. Love, Frank."[1]

1. These letters were made available fifty years after D-Day to *American Heritage* by DeRonda Elliott, who wrote that she was doing so "for anyone who might not understand what war does to each life that it touches." They appeared in the May–June 1994 issue of the magazine (http://www.americanheritage.com/content/d-day-what-it-cost).

June 7, 1776

Lee's Resolution

It was a three-part resolution read aloud to the Second Continental Congress that made clear to the world the scope of Americans' intentions regarding Great Britain. The Declaration of Independence unveiled the following month by Thomas Jefferson would formalize this break, but the unambiguous language proclaimed in Philadelphia was one of history's great spoiler alerts. "Resolved," it stated on this date, "That these United Colonies are, and of right ought to be, free and independent States, that they are absolved from all allegiance to the British Crown, and that all political connection between them and the State of Great Britain is, and ought to be, totally dissolved."

The man given the honor of reading these words was Jefferson's fellow Virginian, Richard Henry Lee. An ally of firebrand Patrick Henry, Lee was an England-educated Virginia planter and statesman. He was known as a gifted orator, esteemed not only for the quality of his rhetoric but for his theatrical gifts. His voice was lyrical, and he had a habit while speaking of waving his arm, which was covered in black silk to hide the scars from a hunting accident.

By 1776, Lee would have seemed the logical choice for drafting the Declaration of Independence. At forty-four, he was ten years older than Jefferson, and his patriotic bona fides were undisputed. A decade earlier, Lee galvanized local opposition to the Stamp Act by rounding up his brothers—and four brothers of George Washington—and riding into Leedstown, a Rappahannock River trading center in his home county of Westmoreland, Virginia, where they raised a crowd of 115 men to confront the local tax collector. This organized act of defiance bound the Virginians in common purpose with their radical cousins in New England.

So why, eleven years later, wasn't Lee chosen by his fellow Philadelphia delegates to write the Declaration? Historians aren't certain. What is known is that Lee went back to Williamsburg to take a leading role in forming Virginia's government. Perhaps he believed that independence was a foregone conclusion and that the more important work was being done in the Commonwealth's old capital. It is also known that Lee's wife was seriously ill and he wanted to be closer to home. The mystery will never be answered fully, but we can still remember how Richard Henry Lee spread the seeds of revolution with that melodious voice and stirring words of rebellion, his silk-sleeved arm waving in the air like a flag.

June 8, 1968

Ultimate Sacrifice

Libraries have been filled with books on the Kennedys, many of them hagiographic, a few fiercely critical, and some of them even-handed. Whatever your politics, this much cannot be denied: The sons of Joseph and Rose Kennedy devoted their lives to public service. It began during World War II, when Joe, Jack, and Bobby Kennedy answered their nation's call to arms. Joe died flying combat missions in Europe, and Jack served heroically in the Pacific. Bobby was only sixteen when Pearl Harbor was attacked, but he enlisted in the U.S. Navy before his eighteenth birthday. Martyred while running for president, Robert F. Kennedy was laid to rest in a grassy gravesite a few yards from his older brother in Arlington National Cemetery.

While addressing the Irish parliament during a trip to his ancestral home, President Kennedy had charmed his hosts by saying, "This is an extraordinary country. George Bernard Shaw, speaking as an Irishman, summed up an approach to life: Other people, he said, see things and…say: 'Why?' But I dream things that never were—and I say: 'Why not?'"

It was a nice thought, although it's unclear that Shaw was really "speaking as an Irishman" when he wrote those lines. That said, Shaw's prescience was impressive: Three years before the killing of Austria's Archduke Ferdinand thrust Europe into war, Shaw wrote, "Assassination is the extreme form of censorship." The Kennedys did not let that happen. After JFK was slain, RFK turned his brother's Dublin throwaway line into a brief prose-poem that inspired a generation of men and women from Los Angeles to South Africa. And on this date, Edward M. Kennedy turned it into Bobby's epitaph while speaking in St. Patrick's Cathedral.

His voice cracking with emotion, Teddy ended his elegy this way:

My brother need not be idealized, or enlarged in death beyond what he was in life. [He should] be remembered simply as a good and decent man, who saw wrong and tried to right it, saw suffering and tried to heal it, saw war and tried to stop it.

Those of us who loved him and who take him to his rest today, pray that what he was to us and what he wished for others will someday come to pass for all the world. As he said many times, in many parts of this nation, to those he touched and who sought to touch him: "Some men see things as they are and say why. I dream things that never were and say why not."

Wilson's Wisdom

Southern born and bred, Woodrow Wilson went to Davidson College for a year before transferring to Princeton University, then called the College of New Jersey. He gravitated toward political science, and upon graduation—after briefly practicing law—Wilson earned a doctorate degree at Johns Hopkins and taught at Bryn Mawr and Wesleyan before returning to Princeton as a professor. It proved a popular hire.

As a member of the Princeton faculty, Wilson was that rare professor who was well liked by students and well regarded by his peers. Chosen to give a commemorative address at Princeton's 1896 sesquicentennial, he impressed the school's trustees with his eloquence and vision. The trustees had decided to rename the school Princeton University, and Wilson's speech, "Princeton in the Nation's Service," struck just the tone they were looking for. Six years later, on this date, he was named Princeton's president at age forty-five.

"I feel like a new prime minister," he confided to his wife before he made his inaugural address as a college president, "getting ready to address his constituents." The analogy was prescient: Ten years later, he'd become the twenty-eighth president of the United States. In that inaugural address as university president, Wilson charted an ambitious path. "We are not put into this world to sit still," he said. "We are put into it to act in a new age. We must lead the world."

At Princeton, however, Wilson's idealistic plans to revamp the students' educational experience ran up against the entrenched interests of others, including powerful faculty members. He derided the politics of the university as "minor statesmanship," but identifying the problem wasn't the same as overcoming the obstacle. It was Wilson who made the now-famous observation—invariably attributed to others—that the politics of academia were so cutthroat because the stakes were so trivial. The reasoning behind that clever bon mot is debatable and, in Woodrow Wilson's case, irrelevant. In 1910 he was elected governor of New Jersey as a reformer and in 1912 he won the White House in a three-way race.

On the international stage, the stakes were anything but trivial. A gruesome world war had demonstrated the costs of failing at statesmanship, so Wilson strove, unsuccessfully, to create an international organization he believed would forestall future wars. Along the way, President Wilson revealed that ushering in fundamental reform is just difficult, period.

June 10, 1752

Polarized

As early as 1747, Benjamin Franklin had postulated that particles in the atmosphere are charged positively and negatively. Soon, he was theorizing about how electricity might be stored in something he termed "an electric battery," while imagining how such a device could be harnessed to power electric motors. In a 1749 letter to British scientist John Mitchell, Franklin opined that during thunderstorms water particles become electrically charged by violent movement during heavy winds, and that lightning is the result of this pent-up energy in the clouds. (He also noted that if his theories were correct, the last thing someone caught in a thunderstorm should do is what they invariably do—seek shelter under a lone-standing tree.)

Three years later, he proved it all with a famous scientific experiment. On this date, Franklin is believed to have flown a kite during a thunderstorm with a metal key tied to the string. When he noticed loose strands of the cord standing erect, he touched his knuckle to the key, and received a jolt that reverberates to this day. In the ensuing decades, lightning rods inspired by Franklin's experiments saved thousands of ships and buildings from fire. But Ben Franklin was a student of human beings as well as natural phenomena, and he extrapolated the scientific quality of polarity—the tendency of similarly charged particles to repel one another to opposite poles—to politics. Franklin himself had been polarized, in the words of historian H. W. Brands, by "an unpleasant

storm" in the House of Commons in which he was the target. Years later, as the U.S. Constitution was being printed in his adopted hometown of Philadelphia, with Franklin's guidance, he wrote to his sister with the tone of a man whose fingers are crossed: "We have, however, done our best, and it must take its chance."

Franklin almost certainly did not utter the famous witticism attributed to him—the one about the signers of the Declaration of Independence all hanging together lest they all hang separately—but such fears were not misplaced: The Constitution polarized mercantilists in the cities who embraced it and farmers who felt disadvantaged by it. It was a Virginia planter who put aside his own misgivings for the big picture. "Since the bond of Union is now complete and we once more consider ourselves as one family," proclaimed George Washington, "we must drive far away the demon of party spirit and local reproach." More than two centuries later, Washington's words, and Ben Franklin's experiments, remain relevant in American life.

June 11, 1950

Man at Work

William Ben Hogan was born in 1912 in the central Texas town of Dublin within months of Sam Snead and Byron Nelson. This triumvirate would virtually rule golf for decades. In Hogan's case, success was hardly foreordained. His father's suicide when Ben was nine plunged the Hogans into poverty. Ben's exposure to golf came when he caddied to make money for his family. He took to the game, dropped out of high school to pursue it professionally, and found himself vying with Nelson, a fellow Texan, for junior championships.

Ben Hogan's classic swing is still studied by golf instructors, but its explosive power was acquired by hard work more than natural athleticism. He practiced until his hands were blistered, and he didn't win his first major tournament until he was twenty-eight. Then he didn't stop winning. In 1948, he finished first in ten tournaments. Then, in February 1949, on a foggy stretch of road in West Texas, he was driving with his wife Valerie when a Greyhound bus plowed into his car head-on. Hogan threw himself across his wife's lap in an effort to save her, a reaction that probably saved their lives. But the crash broke Hogan's collarbone, his ankle, and one of his ribs, and fractured his pelvis. Told he might never walk again, let alone play professionally, he handled that news the way he handled his father's suicide: with stoicism—and golf.

Baby steps in the hospital corridors led to gingerly performed practice swings at home. By January 1950, he was back on tour. Convinced he could compete at his former level, Hogan entered the U.S. Open that June, which was held in Merion Golf Club in Ardmore, Pennsylvania. Heading into the final round, Hogan trailed only 1946 U.S. Open champ Lloyd Mangrum. Golf fans who once found Hogan aloof were now with him—and rooting for a miracle. They were not disappointed. His legs wrapped in bandages in the blistering heat, Hogan arrived at the seventy-second hole needing par to tie for the lead, which would put him in a playoff with Mangrum and a hard-charging Philadelphia native named George Fazio. Hogan was up to the challenge. In the ensuing eighteen-hole playoff, held on this date, Hogan buried them both. A year after his win at Merion, a movie celebrating his comeback appeared, with Glenn Ford playing Hogan.

Acclaim didn't change him much because Hogan never forgot the secret of his success. "I always outworked everybody," he explained. "Work never bothered me like it bothers some people."

June 12, 1987

Walls—and Gates

Thirty-eight years after the Berlin Airlift and twenty-four years after President Kennedy's famous Berlin speech, Ronald Reagan arrived in the divided German capital when relations between Washington and Moscow were at a pivot point. Although he received little credit for it at the time, Reagan had been fixated on reducing the world's nuclear arsenals for many years. The hang-up had been the Kremlin's longstanding aversion to allowing inspectors inside the Soviet Union to verify implementation of arms reduction treaties. This reluctance convinced many Americans, Reagan included, that the Russians were not to be trusted.

In 1986, Soviet leader Mikhail Gorbachev altered this calculation. After NATO ministers called for elimination of intermediate and short-range nuclear missiles on a "global and effectively verifiable basis," Gorbachev announced that his government would comply if the United States would do the same. In so doing, he threw verification back onto the Americans' laps. This gambit achieved its purpose. Although U.S. intelligence services warned Reagan that mutual verification might work to the Soviets' advantage, he didn't care. This was the opening he'd been looking for, and he instructed Secretary of State George Shultz to begin negotiating a pact.

But the arms race—and the insane doctrine of "mutually assured destruction"—was only half the problem as far as Reagan was concerned. The other half was the Soviet Union's virtual enslavement of its own people and those of Eastern Europe. "Secretary General Gorbachev, if you seek peace," Reagan said when he arrived at the Brandenburg Gate on this date, "if you seek prosperity for the Soviet Union and Eastern Europe—if you seek liberalization: Come here, to this gate. Mr. Gorbachev, open this gate. Mr. Gorbachev, tear down this wall!"

In 1987, neither Shultz nor the White House National Security Council wanted Reagan to call for Gorbachev to tear down the Berlin Wall. They considered it too provocative and feared that Kremlin hard-liners would use it to undermine Gorbachev. The State Department speechwriters' preferred language? "Someday this ugly wall will disappear." Fortunately, the old Hollywood leading man ignored that edit.

Reagan's theatrics did not end the Cold War, but they did set the stage for his successful diplomacy with Gorbachev, as Shultz had no trouble admitting to *Time* magazine two decades later. "People were afraid of the consequences of what Reagan would say," he acknowledged. "But it turns out he was right."

June 13, 1971

Seeds of a Scandal

The Pentagon Papers originated in June 1967, when Secretary of Defense Robert McNamara commissioned a secret study of the history of the Vietnam War. McNamara had been one of the war's architects, but this project showed that he had second thoughts early in the game. In his memoirs, McNamara claimed his motivation was to help historians, and that it was not a big secret. But he never mentioned the project to President Johnson or Secretary of State Dean Rusk, and he went outside Pentagon channels to produce it, tapping into a vein of sympathetic scholars, many of them Harvard men. When it came to light, Johnson and Rusk figured McNamara's intention was to give it to Robert Kennedy for use against Johnson in the 1968 primaries. That race never materialized, but the seven-thousand-page report survived.

One of the Harvard scholars who worked on it was Daniel Ellsberg, who by 1971 had completed his metamorphosis from Department of Defense analyst to antiwar activist. Only fifteen copies of the report had been produced, but Ellsberg surreptitiously copied it and snuck it out of the offices of the RAND Corporation, which had custody of one of them. Ellsberg shopped the classified report around, including to eventual 1972 Democratic Party presidential nominee George McGovern, but he found no takers in government. Neil Sheehan, who covered defense for the *New York Times*, was another matter. Sheehan knew a good story when he saw one. So did his editors, and on this date the paper began publishing excerpts. Soon, the *Washington Post* would follow suit.

Among other things, the Pentagon Papers revealed that the Kennedy administration was behind the 1963 assassination of South Vietnamese president Ngo Dinh Diem. They also showed that even while deriding 1964 Republican nominee Barry Goldwater as a warmonger for advocating U.S. buildup in Vietnam, the Johnson administration was already deeply into planning for a vast escalation. President Nixon's initial instinct was to downplay the significance of the report, which mostly cast the spotlight on his predecessors' perfidy, not his own. But Henry Kissinger forcefully railed against "this wholesale theft and unauthorized disclosure."

Unfortunately for his legacy, Nixon allowed Kissinger's argument to prevail over his own gut feeling. The administration became obsessed with the leak and went to court to try and stop publication. When he lost in the Supreme Court, Nixon directed those around him to find extrajudicial ways to stop leaks. "The Plumbers" were born, along with the seeds of Watergate.

June 14, 1922

O Say Can You Hear?

The Continental Congress adopted the Stars and Stripes on June 14, 1777, and presidents ever since associated themselves to the date. Woodrow Wilson first proclaimed June 14 "Flag Day" in 1916. Harry Truman signed a law in 1949 making it official. But the Flag Day ceremony that most impacted the modern presidency occurred in Baltimore on this date.

In a speech unveiling a memorial to Francis Scott Key at Fort McHenry, Warren G. Harding became the first sitting U.S. president to have his voice broadcast over the radio. The publisher of an Ohio newspaper before he became a senator from the Buckeye State, Harding was fascinated with modern communications even though his own speaking style was epitomized by flowery, if sometimes empty, prose. Here's an example, taken from 1920, the year he was chosen as the Republican presidential nominee: "America's present need is not heroics, but healing; not nostrums, but normalcy; not revolution, but restoration; not agitation, but adjustment; not surgery, but serenity; not the dramatic, but the dispassionate; not experiment, but equipoise; not submergence in internationality, but sustainment in triumphant nationality."

His contemporaries were not sure what to make of language like this. Former treasury secretary William Gibbs McAdoo, who sought the Democratic presidential nomination that same year, derided Harding's speeches as "an army of pompous phrases moving across the landscape in search of an idea." But Warren Harding wasn't an obtuse man. He spoke in generalities as a way of avoiding alienating factions within his own party. And he was quick to see the political implications of modern technology. In February 1922, he had the first radio installed at the White House.

Prior to Harding's trip to Baltimore, the mayor's office worried that Fort McHenry would not be able to accommodate the crowd wanting to hear the president. Frederick R. Huber, the Baltimorean heading the planning committee, proposed building a separate broadcasting station, but the estimated cost of $30,000 was too steep. So they improvised: The president's voice was carried by telephone to a broadcasting station in the Anacostia area of Washington, D.C., and then relayed back to receiving stations in Baltimore. The world would little note nor long remember what Warren Harding had to say that day in Charm City, but it never forgot that a president's words could now be transmitted through the air.

June 15, 1859

Pigheaded

Lyman Cutlar awoke on this morning to the sound of a pig rooting around in his vegetable garden. He didn't like it a bit, and the incident almost started the third shooting war between the United States and Great Britain.

The pig belonged to the Hudson's Bay Company, a Canada-based outfit given a royal charter by the British crown in 1670. In 1859, it was operating commercial activities, including a lucrative sheep-grazing operation, in the San Juan Islands in Puget Sound, where Cutlar lived. The intruder in Lyman Cutlar's garden belonged to the company, which raised hogs to feed its employees, and he did what most red-blooded American males would do at that time—and many would do today: He got his rifle and shot the pig.

Charles Griffin, the Hudson's Bay farm manager, took offense. It was a time of tension on the island because both the United States and the United Kingdom claimed possession of the entire San Juan archipelago. It was a dispute that would not be settled until 1872, when Germany's Kaiser Wilhelm I headed up an international tribunal that ruled in America's favor. In June 1859, however, there were men in the Pacific who wanted to settle it there and then by force of arms. Cutlar offered ten dollars as recompense for the pig. Griffin found this offer insulting and demanded that local British authorities arrest Cutlar.

A dutiful local British military commander deployed three warships and one thousand troops to arrest Cutlar. The Americans on the island asked for U.S. troops to protect them. A company of U.S. Army regulars was dispatched from Oregon, commanded by an officer who would achieve notoriety in the Civil War. He was Captain George E. Pickett, a Virginian, who'd been dispatched to Bellingham Bay three years earlier with orders to build a fort to protect local whites from attacks by "northern Indians."

Pickett accomplished that task, but the only potential hostiles he encountered belonged to the Royal Navy. If all this saber rattling seems like dangerous overkill today, it seemed that way to U.S. Army officials at the time, too. Others might have finessed the dispute over pints with their British counterparts in a seaside saloon. Not George Pickett. He was always ready to fight.

Cooler heads prevailed, however. It turns out that neither nation wanted to go to war over a farm animal. The only casualty of the Pig War was…a pig.

June 16, 1858

"Simple" Language

Abraham Lincoln was a country lawyer who'd served as a backbencher for one term in the House of Representatives as the only Whig Party member in Illinois's congressional delegation. Although Lincoln had yet to begin his famous debate series with Stephen A. Douglas on the issue of slavery, he was emerging as the Republican Party's most forceful and charismatic orator on this question. On this date, he made history while accepting his new party's senatorial nomination at the state party convention in Springfield.

His speech consisted of a blistering deconstruction of the previous year's *Dred Scott* decision, in which the court ruled that Southern slave owners could take their slaves into western territories with them. Lincoln took direct aim at the court's reasoning and the Democratic Party's concerted manipulations surrounding that case. "A house divided against itself cannot stand," Lincoln said, invoking Jesus' admonition to his disciples. "I believe this government cannot endure, permanently, half slave and half free."

"I do not expect the Union to be dissolved," Lincoln told the one thousand delegates. "I do not expect the house to fall; but I do expect it will cease to be divided. It will become all one thing, or all the other. Either the opponents of slavery will arrest the further spread of it and place it where the public mind shall rest in the belief that it is in the course of ultimate extinction, or its advocates will push it forward till it shall become alike lawful in all the states, old as well as new, North as well as South."

Lincoln left no doubt which course he thought was the moral and wise one. What few in his audience suspected was that when the crisis he predicted arrived, Lincoln himself would be the main instrument guiding his nation on the course he was describing. Before delivering the speech, Lincoln read it to his law partner, William H. Herndon, who found the speech morally courageous but politically unpropitious. Lincoln wasn't really looking for a second opinion. "The proposition is indisputably true," he responded, "and I will deliver it as written."

The "house divided" language, which comes from all three Synoptic Gospels (Matthew, Mark, and Luke), was a studied literary device. "I want to use some universally known figure," Lincoln told Herndon in reference to Jesus, "expressed in simple language as universally known, that it may strike home to the minds of men in order to rouse them to the peril of the times."

June 17, 1775

A True Patriot

The Battle of Bunker Hill actually took place on an adjacent knoll, Breed's Hill, one of the many mistakes that took place in the fog of fighting on this bloody day when British regulars overran a force of local militiamen.

"Our three generals expected rather to punish a mob than fight with troops that would look them in the face," one British officer wrote. To them, this was civil war. To the colonists, it was a war for independence. Either way, after Bunker Hill, both sides knew they were in a deadly struggle. It had immediate consequences, too. The top British commander would be recalled to England; the Americans would put George Washington in charge of their forces.

The first celebrated martyr of the Revolutionary War was Joseph Warren Jr., a Harvard-trained physician who had been radicalized by the punitive laws directed at the colonies from London. He penned columns in protest in the *Boston Gazette* under the byline "A True Patriot." Although lacking military training, he was put in command of the Massachusetts forces days before Bunker Hill. Three times that day, the British marched in formation uphill across an open field. Twice, they were rebuffed by patriot musket fire. The slaughter was horrible. One British officer paraphrased Shakespeare: "They make us here but food for gunpowder."

More than one thousand redcoats were killed or wounded in the battle, half their force, a disproportionate number of them officers: The Americans deliberately aimed for them. The rebels' ammunition proved to be in short supply, however, and the British changed tactics before their third assault. Since the Battle of Culloden thirty years earlier, British officers had known that grapeshot could annihilate an enemy in an exposed position. So they shelled the patriots' position before their final charge. Decimated and out of ammo, the militiamen used bayonets and even rocks before abandoning the field. Joseph Warren was shot between the eyes, dying on the spot. Watching the battle through binoculars was John Trumbull, whose iconic painting, *The Death of General Warren*, would solidify the fallen physician's hero status. A widower who had just turned thirty-four, Joseph Warren left behind four orphaned children, a fiancée who'd been one of his patients, and a mistress he'd recently gotten pregnant. As for Gen. Thomas Gage, the British commander in charge of this debacle, when he sailed for England, his sentiments about Boston were expressed in writing: "I wish this Cursed place was *burned*!"

Ride, Sally Ride

It was an astronaut's name Charles Dickens would have loved, and Sally Ride was aboard the space shuttle *Challenger* as it undertook its second mission. Born in Los Angeles, Sally was fourteen years old when Mattel produced its first "Barbie Astronaut." She was a member of a generation less willing to typecast girls living in a state where boys and girls were especially receptive to the idea that they could grow up and realize their dreams.

As a kid, Sally was a nationally ranked tennis player and a math and science whiz. She attended a prestigious Southern California high school and Swarthmore College and UCLA before landing at Stanford University, where she earned a bachelor's degree, a master's, and a doctorate in astrophysics. When the *Challenger* lifted off at Cape Canaveral on this date in 1983, Dr. Ride was a thirty-two-year-old NASA mission specialist who operated the space shuttle's robot arm, a device she had helped design.

The Russians had sent a female cosmonaut, Valentina Tereshkova, into space twenty years earlier, but it wasn't until 1978 that the United States got with the program. By then, there was a pent-up demand, and Sally Ride was one of six women among an applicant pool of three thousand chosen as the first female astronauts in the U.S. space program. Inevitably, she became an instant inspiration to generations of American girls and women. It's not quite right to say she was a reluctant spokeswoman—she made hundreds of public appearances over the years, speaking encouragingly to audiences and greeting fans and well-wishers warmly.

Yet she was by nature a shy person, drawn more easily to science than politics. She was also very private. She married fellow astronaut Steven Hawley in 1982 and divorced him in 1987, never speaking of it publicly. Until she died of pancreatic cancer in 2012, few people even knew she was sick. Her death brought another revelation: her longtime relationship with a female partner named Tam O'Shaughnessy. After Sally Ride was gone, her brother described O'Shaughnessy as "a member of the family."

"The pancreatic cancer community is going to be absolutely thrilled that there's now this advocate that they didn't know about," he added. "And I hope the LGBT community feels the same. I hope it makes it easier for kids growing up gay that they know that another one of their heroes was like them."

June 19, 1885

Lady Liberty

Officially named "Liberty Enlightening the World," the Statue of Liberty was the brainchild of a Paris native named Edouard de Laboulaye. A leading French abolitionist, Laboulaye's original inspiration wasn't America's welcoming immigration policies; rather, it was the presidency of Abraham Lincoln, the Civil War, and the Thirteenth Amendment outlawing slavery. It was designed by French sculptor Frederic-Auguste Bartholdi, who personally chose the location where it should stand, and who was later given the keys to New York City by appreciative local officials.

First erected in Paris, Lady Liberty was presented to the U.S. ambassador to France in 1884. It was then dismantled, packed into 214 huge crates and shipped here the following year aboard the French frigate *Isere*. It arrived on this date, and was dedicated in an October 28, 1886, ceremony overseen by President Grover Cleveland.

The grand statue's official donor was the people of France, and it is truly the gift that keeps on giving. It has been depicted and described in thousands of books, movies, letters home, family albums, and the imaginings of a billion pilgrims. This includes those, such as the brave souls at Tiananmen Square whose intentions were never emigration, but, rather, the importation of freedom to their own lands. Whether or not those Chinese students were familiar with John Winthrop, let alone Ronald Reagan and the "shining city on the hill," they were responding to liberty's lure.

The famous words affixed to Lady Liberty's pedestal are American written, not French. They were penned by a New York poet named Emma Lazarus, who was inspired by the Jewish refugees she met while volunteering at Ellis Island.

> *Give me your tired, your poor,*
> *Your huddled masses yearning to breathe free,*
> *The wretched refuse of your teeming shore.*
> *Send these, the homeless, tempest-tossed to me,*
> *I lift my lamp beside the golden door!*

One Russian immigrant who made good on these shores set those stirring words to music in a 1949 Broadway musical called *Miss Liberty*. His name was Irving Berlin, and it is the only song he ever produced that employed someone else's words.

June 20, 1948

A Really Good Show

On this date, *Toast of the Town* debuted on CBS. Its host was a former sportswriter from New York City who had, in the old phrase, "a face like the map of Ireland." Actually, it was a face that revealed an amateur boxing past. Then again, the voice wasn't so great, either, and the accent lent itself easily to parody. He would promise audiences "a really good show," which came out "a really good shew." And it was.

His hour-long variety show ran from 1948 to 1971. In 1955, CBS officially changed the title to the name everyone in America already knew it by: *The Ed Sullivan Show*. The opening program had featured Dean Martin and Jerry Lewis, along with the composing duo of Richard Rodgers and Oscar Hammerstein II, who provided the audience with a sneak preview of their upcoming Broadway hit, *South Pacific*. It was a leisurely pace by today's standard—each act got about ten minutes of airtime—and Sullivan spent too much of it chatting. From the start, though, he revealed an intriguing aspect of the new medium: In television, you didn't have to be a performer to perform. Ed Sullivan would surround himself with talented musicians and comedians, offer up sneak previews of movie clips, and occasionally film the show from an exotic change of venue to spice things up. It's a formula still widely copied today.

Among his many legacies, two others distinguish the man. First, he was color-blind at a time when that was noteworthy in American public life. It was a sensitivity he came by honestly: His marriage to a Jewish woman was at the time called a mixed marriage. African-American performers on his show included Louis Armstrong, Duke Ellington, Dizzy Gillespie, the Jackson 5, Flip Wilson, and The Temptations. A favorite—they appeared repeatedly—was the Supremes, whom Sullivan affectionately called "The Girls." He shook hands with Nat King Cole and kissed Pearl Bailey on the cheek when those were rare gestures from a white man on television.

"The most important thing," Sullivan said in a 1958 interview while assessing the show's first decade on the air, "is that we've put on everything but bigotry."

"He moves like a sleepwalker," proclaimed *Time* magazine in 1955. "His smile is that of a man sucking a lemon; his speech is frequently lost in a thicket of syntax; his eyes pop from their sockets or sink so deep in their bags that they seem to be peering up at the camera from the bottom of twin wells. Yet, instead of frightening children, Ed Sullivan charms the whole family."

June 21, 1945

Attack, Attack, Attack

The U.S. Army's Thirty-Fourth Infantry Division was created in World War I, but never saw combat. It did acquire a nickname, the "Red Bull Division," and a flashy logo: a red bovine skull painted on a Mexican water flask. World War II was a different story. The division, made up of National Guard units from North Dakota, South Dakota, Iowa, and Minnesota was activated ten months before Pearl Harbor.

Gen. Charles de Gaulle presented France's Croix de Guerre to the entire division. At great cost, this valiant fighting force had rousted German troops from North Africa and later chased them out of Italy.

The Thirty-Fourth had arrived in Europe just five weeks after Pearl Harbor. Newspapers in the UK heralded the Yanks' arrival, to the point of identifying the first GI to alight in Belfast. His name was Milburn H. Henke, a private from Hutchinson, Minnesota. It could have been anybody. Henke was sitting on barracks bags with fifteen other men as his ship docked. A colonel came up the gangplank, turned to a lieutenant, and said, "I want a man from Company B." The lieutenant pointed at Henke, who walked off that boat and into the history books. He survived the war, living until he was eighty, but so many of his comrades did not.

In 517 days of combat in five major campaigns, the Thirty-Fourth sustained 3,737 deaths, with another 3,460 missing in action and 14,000 wounded. Eleven Red Bulls were awarded Medals of Honor along with ninety-eight Distinguished Service Crosses and 1,072 Silver Stars.

The division's motto was "Attack, attack, attack." It was a credo they did proud, while racking up many firsts: the first Americans into Algiers; the first, while fighting with Gen. Mark W. Clark's Fifth Army, into Monte Cassino; first on the beaches of Anzio. They were also the first division to incorporate a Japanese-American unit into their ranks. And Red Bulls helped form the first Army Ranger unit.

Although the Thirty-Fourth was instrumental in creating a third front against the Germans, D-Day overshadowed the Red Bulls and Mark Clark's entire corps. It was on this date that de Gaulle proclaimed the U.S. Army's Thirty-Fourth "a *division d'elite*," yet when it was decommissioned, no one held parades for them. These men—those who were left—returned to their farms in Minnesota and Iowa and the Dakotas and went back to their chores.

June 22, 1944

A "Well-Rounded" Program

The First World War had produced hardship for America's veterans, who were given little more than $60 and a train ticket home. A promised "bonus" never materialized, prompting a march on Washington that ended when federal troops dispersed them by force. No one wanted a repeat performance after World War II, and in a 1943 fireside chat Franklin D. Roosevelt outlined six principles for aiding returning veterans: generous mustering-out pay, unemployment insurance while veterans looked for work, federal aid for education or job training, government-paid medical care, and pensions for those wounded or disabled.

FDR found allies in both houses of Congress and in both political parties for the GI Bill (officially, the Servicemen's Readjustment Act). The primary sponsor was Democratic senator Ernest McFarland of Arizona. "Mac" McFarland had barely survived a bronchial infection contracted while serving in World War I. Army doctors operated on his lungs, saving his life, a debt he never forgot. In 1944, both houses of Congress passed the two provisions considered the heart of the GI Bill. One was low-interest loans to buy a home, farm, or business. The other was subsidies for tuition, books, and room and board for higher education.

Both were momentous. Once considered a province of the well-to-do, U.S. colleges and universities saw their enrollments explode. By 1947, nearly half of all college students were veterans. By 1950, some 500,000 Americans graduated from college, triple the number who had graduated in 1939. By the time the original GI Bill lapsed in 1956, 7.8 million veterans had availed themselves of education or job training benefits. As for the housing provision, it changed the very look of the country, sparking growth in suburbs and home ownership nationwide, particularly in California and other Sunbelt havens. The Veterans Administration backed 4.3 million home loans between 1944 and 1955. Among the returning vets who got help buying a house were Bob Dole, Gerald R. Ford, George H. W. Bush, and Harry Belafonte.

"With the signing of this bill, a well-rounded program of special veterans' benefits is nearly completed," Franklin D. Roosevelt said on this date. "It gives emphatic notice to the men and women in our armed forces that the American people do not intend to let them down."

With a stroke of his pen, FDR ensured that millions of veterans would go to college and buy houses—and that when the war ended, the Great Depression would really be over.

June 23, 1961

The Summer of Our Discontent

John Steinbeck, a native of Salinas, California, usually wrote about life on the West Coast. The book published by Viking Press on this date, *The Winter of Our Discontent*, was set on the Eastern seaboard, featuring a tortured protagonist with a patrician's pedigree, a Harvard education, and a World War II combat record. Those circumstances provide insufficient grounding for the lead character, Ethan Allen Hawley, who takes ethical shortcuts in his quest for the material gain that defined success in postwar America. Although Steinbeck would win the Nobel Prize for literature the following year, this would be his last novel. It's not his greatest work—that distinction almost certainly belongs to *The Grapes of Wrath*—but its themes are enduring, and more relevant to twenty-first-century American politics. *The Winter of Our Discontent*, as Steinbeck assumed his readers would know, is borrowed from Shakespeare. The line comes from the first scene in the first act of *Richard III*, and sets up the tension in the play.

> *Now is the winter of our discontent*
> *Made glorious summer by this son of York;*
> *And all the clouds that low'r'd upon our house*
> *In the deep bosom of the ocean buried.*

The lines are Richard's, and he's not lamenting the winter, or his own discontent. He is hailing an upturn in the House of York—his family—precipitated by the success of his brother Edward IV in wresting the crown from Henry VI. But what kind of king is Edward proving to be? In Richard's mind, Edward's decadence and love of wealth mars the national landscape. It was a metaphor easily understood by Americans in 1961. The United States had emerged as a military and political powerhouse after World War II, and had come roaring out of the Great Depression economically. What Americans were doing with their success, or more precisely, what rampant consumerism was doing to Americans' moral compasses, is what *The Winter of Our Discontent* is about. The story contains themes and plot twists that are current: A hardworking immigrant is mistreated by the government and people he thought were his friends. Political office is used to manipulate public policy in ways that make officeholders personally rich. Plagiarism is rewarded, not punished. The size of a man's bank portfolio is considered more important than his morality.

In other words, it's not only Donald Trump who should read this book. We all should.

June 24, 1947

UFO Sighting

After the end of the Second World War, Americans were attuned to the frightening power of technology. Hiroshima and Nagasaki had taught them that. And Orson Welles's 1938 *War of the Worlds* broadcast wasn't merely a metaphor for the destruction erupting around the globe; it was a frightening campfire story about threats from the heavens. In this milieu, amateur pilot Kenneth Arnold flew his small plane from Boise, Idaho, to an Oregon air show. Looking out his cockpit at 3 p.m. on this date, while flying near Mount Rainier, something caught his eye.

He saw a flash of a bright light with a bluish tinge, which he initially thought came from another plane. Then he saw a series of flashing lights, nine in succession, and a series of airborne objects he estimated stretched for five miles. Moving in unison, they weaved from side to side, he said, like "the tail of a Chinese kite." Attempting to calculate their speed, he clocked how long it took the mysterious fleet to travel between Mount Rainer and Mount Adams, and concluded they were traveling 1,700 miles an hour.

He mentioned all this at a refueling stop at a small airstrip in Yakima, Washington. In so doing, he launched a national obsession with UFOs. Arnold would be quoted as saying he saw "flying saucers," but it was his assessment of the objects' speed that convinced people he'd witnessed extraterrestrial avionics. That airspeed is more than twice the speed of sound, and Chuck Yeager wouldn't go supersonic for four more months.

Arnold most likely was looking at a flock of geese, and miscalculated their speed because he misjudged how far away they were. But his imagination was off and running, and by the time he arrived at the air show, his tale had preceded him. A local reporter interviewed him and the story went out on the wires, making newspapers all over the country. Arnold hadn't really called the objects "flying saucers." He said they flew like "a saucer being tossed across the water." CBS newsman Edward R. Murrow would call this a "historic misquote," but the fault lies with Arnold. Reports of "flying saucers" spiked, and when a military weather balloon crashed outside Roswell, New Mexico, two weeks later, witnesses thought immediately of UFOs and spacemen. Two days after that, Harry Truman was queried about this phenomenon at a White House news conference.

"Mr. President," he was asked, "have you seen any flying saucers?"

"Only in the newspapers," he replied with a laugh.

June 25, 1950

"Give 'Em Hell" Harry

Harry Truman tried to keep to his schedule. The president was back home in Independence, Missouri, hoping to spend a restful weekend overseeing fence building on his family farm, ordering a new roof for the barn, and attending Sunday services at his local church. Those plans were interrupted by a Saturday night phone call from Secretary of State Dean Acheson, who informed Truman of a crisis unfolding half a world away: North Korea had invaded South Korea.

First Lady Bess Truman and the president's daughter Margaret would attend Sunday services at Trinity Episcopal Church on this date, and Harry went ahead with his plans to visit his brother, J. Vivian Truman, and his sister, Mary Jane, but by then the president's mind was on fast-moving developments on the Korean peninsula—happenings his daughter would later write had sparked fears in her father that "this was the opening of World War III."

As he was shown his brother's modern milking machine as well as a new horse on the property, his siblings mentioned not a word about Korea. Although it was all over the newspapers that morning and the impending action at the UN Security Council was discussed on the radio, his family knew Harry needed a respite before returning to the cauldron of wartime Washington. So they engaged in small talk, discussed family business, and made sure the president said hello to all five of his brother's grandchildren. Saturday had been the last day of his presidency that Korea did not cast a shadow over. But now it was Sunday, and time to head back East.

Truman's plane—it was then called the *Independence*, not Air Force One—landed at the airstrip we now know as Ronald Reagan Washington National Airport at 7:15 Sunday evening. Acheson was there to meet him, along with Secretary of Defense Louis A. Johnson. Sensing the historic import of the moment, the White House photographers who were on hand snapped away and asked Truman for another shot.

"That's all," he said tersely. "We've got a job to do."

On the plane ride back to Washington, Truman had become angry thinking of the North Korean invasion. It reminded him of Japan's brutal occupation of Manchuria and Italy's invasion of Ethiopia in the 1930s, events he considered the precursors to World War II, in which militarily strong nations had overrun weaker nations.

"By God," Truman told his advisers once inside his car, "I am going to let them have it!"

June 26, 1952

Mile-High Hardball

The Brown Palace Hotel in Denver, Colorado, opened its doors in 1892 near the state capitol, which was being built on land donated by the hotel's owner. "The Brown," as locals call it, was named after its proprietor, a transplanted Ohio native named Henry Cordes Brown. Although he soon became a Denver newspaper publisher and local tycoon, Brown's passion was architecture and carpentry, and he personally supervised the building of his fine old hotel.

Among other distinctions, the hotel's in-house historian says that every U.S. president in the last century save Calvin Coolidge visited the Brown. Marilyn Monroe, Oprah Winfrey, and the Beatles, too. Republican presidential candidate Dwight D. Eisenhower set up shop on the second floor of the Brown Palace while on a long, primary-season train trip. His ultimate destination was Chicago, where he hoped to wrest the Republican presidential nomination from Robert A. Taft and the Republican Party's would-be kingmakers. It was here that Ike signaled just how serious he was about trouncing Taft. Ensconced at the Brown, Eisenhower began receiving delegations from pivotal Midwestern state party bosses who were taking the measure of the candidate. These pols, many of whom were also military veterans, knew Eisenhower as the five-star general who'd led the Allies to victory in Europe. Now they were looking at him in a different light: Was he the man to extricate the United States from Korea?

Dwight Eisenhower did not disappoint. He publicly took issue with the policies of the two previous Democratic administrations. Ike denounced the accommodations made at the Yalta conference by Franklin D. Roosevelt (without mentioning FDR by name) and took direct aim at the Truman administration. "If we had been less soft and weak," Eisenhower said in a speech at the Denver Coliseum on this date, "there would probably have been no war in Korea!"

As president, Eisenhower returned to the Brown when visiting Colorado. The rooms he occupied in a 1955 visit are now called the "Eisenhower Suite." According to hotel lore, a chip on the mantel was caused by Ike practicing his golf swing. It's a charming story, probably apocryphal, but Eisenhower was an athlete—a baseball and football star at West Point. He knew how to play hardball, and when to lower his shoulder and steamroll an opponent.

Although Harry Truman's reputation was collateral damage, it was in these rooms at the Brown Palace where Ike bulldozed Bill Taft and the GOP's conservative establishment.

June 27, 1968

Return of the King

In 1968, Elvis Presley awoke from a decade of dabbling in B-list movies to find that rock 'n' roll, a genre he'd helped invent, had left him behind. But Elvis wasn't finished just yet. He and his wife Priscilla had a baby, and after vacationing in Hawaii, Elvis showed up at NBC's Burbank studios looking tanned and relaxed—and as svelte as he'd been since mustering out of the U.S. Army. Tom Parker, Elvis's primary handler, had notions of an Andy Williams–type Christmas special, but NBC's executives had higher ambitions. They placed the show in the hands of a demanding and talented young producer named Steve Binder in hopes Elvis would respond to Binder's creativity and rebellious nature. They knew their man—both of them. When Presley asked Binder to evaluate the state of his career, Binder replied, "I think it's in the toilet."

Appreciative of the candor, Presley bought into Binder's vision, which was nothing less than reintroducing the king to a generation of rock 'n' roll fans who had no idea how great a musician Elvis Presley could be. The taping, which began on this date, showed Elvis performing in black leather in front of a live audience, bantering with Priscilla, and jamming with other musicians. The dazzling result was acclaimed by critics and mass audiences. "He sang with the kind of power people no longer expect of rock 'n' roll singers," wrote Jon Landau. "There is something magical about watching a man who has lost himself find his way back home."

The hour-long show, now known as "the '68 Comeback Special," aired on December 3, 1968. It attracted a 42 percent share for NBC—numbers network suits can only dream of anymore—and prompted a comeback tour, a *Rolling Stone* cover, several new hits, and a 1969 album that rock critic Dave Marsh pronounced "a masterpiece in which Presley immediately catches up with pop music trends that had seemed to pass him by during the movie years."

His 1969 sessions produced several evocative songs that have stood the test of time: "Kentucky Rain," "In the Ghetto," "Don't Cry, Daddy," and "Suspicious Minds." But Elvis's life reminds us that the narcotics your doctor prescribes can be as lethal as those peddled by a drug pusher. Within five years of the comeback, Elvis was divorced, in the throes of addiction, and battling weight and health issues.

"We're caught in a trap," the man sang, and it surely applied to his own life. But for millions of people, Presley had the opposite effect: he was a liberating force. Hearing Elvis sing, recalled a young Bob Dylan, was like "busting out of jail."

June 28, 1787

Franklin's Prayer

As he listened to the partisan bickering and high-stakes wrangling threatening to derail the Constitutional Convention in Philadelphia, Benjamin Franklin—the most esteemed patriot present except for George Washington—had an inspiration. The delegates, he proposed, should seek guidance from a higher authority. Denis Diderot, a Frenchman and Franklin's fellow traveler in the Enlightenment movement, had once quipped that a Deist is someone who hasn't lived long enough to become an atheist. But by the time of the Constitutional Convention, Franklin was eighty-one and had not lost his faith. It was apparently stronger than ever.

Franklin's father was a Puritan who'd hoped his son would become a pastor. That didn't happen, and in his long faith journey from Calvinism to Deism, Franklin tried—and rejected—the doctrine of predestination, and found he disliked even sitting in church listening to sermons. Yet a constancy ran through his life. "I believe," he wrote at twenty-two, "there is one Supreme, most perfect being." Sixty-two years later, he wrote that although he harbored "some doubts" as to Jesus' divinity, he believed "in one God, the creator of the universe... [who] governs by his Providence." Franklin amplified on this creed: "That He ought to be worshipped. That the most acceptable service we render to Him is doing good to his other children. That the soul of man is immortal, and will be treated with justice in another life respecting its conduct in this."

"Doctor" Franklin, as he was known affectionately, didn't go into all that on this date in Philadelphia. To his fellow patriots, he used arguments he thought would cut more ice. In words written down by James Madison, Franklin noted that he believed Providence had played a hand in the American fight for liberation from Great Britain. Addressing the presiding officer, he said, "Our prayers were heard, sir, and they were graciously answered." Franklin thought a little supplication was in order now. He added: "How has it happened, sir, that we have not hitherto once thought of humbly applying to the Father of Lights to illuminate our understandings?"

Franklin's precise proposal was to appropriate money to retain local Philadelphia clergymen to open each session with a prayer. His motion was seconded, mainly out of respect for the old man, and then amended, and, ultimately tabled. The good doctor wasn't fooled, and made a written note of astonishment in his own hand at the bottom of his speech: "The convention, except three or four persons, thought prayers unnecessary!"

June 29, 1972

Judicial Fiat

As the long-awaited Supreme Court decision on a challenge to the constitutionality of capital punishment reached the White House, President Nixon got hold of White House counsel John Dean. "Send it over to me," Nixon said. "There are nine opinions," Dean informed his boss.

"Now I try to read fast, but I couldn't get through all nine opinions," the president told reporters at a prime time East Room press conference on this date. "But I did get through the chief justice's. As I understand it, the holding of the court must not be taken at this time to rule out capital punishment in all kinds of crimes."

He was right, but confusion over *Furman v. Georgia* was understandable. The court had consolidated three unrelated criminal cases, each with different constitutional questions at stake. One was the death sentence given a Georgia burglar, William Henry Furman, who broke into a Savannah home, killing William Joseph Micke Jr., a married father of five. The two other cases involved capital convictions for rape, one in Texas, the other in Georgia. In all three, the convicts were black, their victims white. Guilt or innocence was not at issue in the litigation.

Five justices ruled that the death penalty, as practiced in the United States, violated the Eighth Amendment's prohibition on cruel and unusual punishment. But they did not agree on why. William O. Douglas invoked the disproportionate number of death sentences given to racial minorities. Justices Thurgood Marshall and William J. Brennan were ready to rule capital punishment unconstitutional, period. Potter Stewart and Byron White seemed to be saying state death penalty laws were too strictly drawn—or maybe capriciously enforced. In response, some states passed laws making the death penalty automatic for specific crimes. Others bifurcated their murder trials into guilt or innocence phases and a punishment phase. Rape, it was clear, was no longer a capital crime in the United States, but first-degree murder could be—but only in aggravated circumstances. All this would play out in the courts, Congress, and state legislatures in ensuing years. One point made on this date is worth remembering. It came from a man who would resign from office under an impeachment cloud, but who on this occasion was clear-eyed about a president's responsibilities:

"I have expressed my views." Richard Nixon said. "And I will also say, of course, that we will carry out whatever the court finally determines to be the law of the land."

June 30, 1864

Yosemite

June had been a busy month for Abraham Lincoln in 1864. He was nominated to seek a second term at the GOP convention; called for a constitutional amendment abolishing slavery; accepted the resignation of Treasury Secretary Salmon P. Chase; and watched in dismay as Ulysses Grant crossed the James River in defeat after gruesome Union losses at Cold Harbor. On the last day of the month, Lincoln signed legislation that didn't seem particularly momentous. California lawmakers wanted a tract of land set aside for tourism rather than mining. The bill Lincoln signed on this date was the Yosemite Valley Grant Act. That was how the creation of America's "crown jewels"—our national parks—got started.

The statute laid claim, on behalf of the state of California, to the grand terrain we know as Yosemite National Park, upon the condition that it "be held for public use, resort, and recreation." In the latter part of the decade, John Muir would thrill Americans with written descriptions of the place. Later, Muir, Theodore Roosevelt, and conservation-minded Republicans would use Yosemite as a poster child that helped launch the Sierra Club, the national park system, and a national consensus about the value of setting aside wilderness areas.

Yosemite first entered Americans' collective consciousness in the decade before Lincoln took office. England-born entrepreneur James Mason Hutchings migrated to California, made and lost a mining fortune, and became a magazine publisher. His periodicals, graced by pictures drawn by artist Thomas Ayres, introduced Easterners to Yosemite's many wonders: giant sequoia groves, Half Dome, El Capitan, and the Tuolumne Valley. This was a place, in other words, worth saving. The effort to do so would succeed, mostly (Tuolumne would be flooded by a dam), and today Yosemite holds court in the High Sierra in all its glory.

Upon seeing it for the first time, modern visitors have the same reaction that Galen Clark, the first guardian of Yosemite, had a century and a half ago. Clark wrote of being "spell-bound and dumb with awe" when he encountered its "unspeakable, stupendous grandeur." John Muir himself said simply that no man-made temple could ever compare to it. Theodore Roosevelt, after camping his first night in Yosemite, used the same metaphor.

"It was like lying in a great solemn cathedral," Teddy Roosevelt wrote, "far vaster and more beautiful than any built by the hand of man."

July 1, 1898

Rough Riders

Theodore Roosevelt was, in the memorable description of his daughter Alice, someone who "never attended a wedding without wishing he was the bride or a funeral without wishing he was the corpse." This raises an obvious question: Was the acclamation for TR and the "Rough Riders" he led in the Spanish-American War deserved?

The answer is, yes, but with at least one important caveat.

The First U.S. Army Volunteer Cavalry was an amalgamation of Western cowboys and Eastern bluebloods, and on this date they led the U.S. Army to victory, helping to conquer San Juan Hill and occupying the strategic highlands above Santiago—thereby assuring that Spain would be driven from Cuba. Lt. Col. Roosevelt rode the publicity over this feat into the White House, and in 2001 was posthumously awarded the Medal of Honor by President Clinton.

When war broke out, Roosevelt resigned as assistant secretary of the Navy to enlist. Although this created an appetite among newspaper readers about his exploits, he left nothing to chance. Taking a page from George Custer, TR brought along a favorite newspaperman and penned his own memoirs of the action, an account so self-reverential that Mr. Dooley, the creation of humorist Finley Peter Dunne, quipped that it should have been called *Alone in Cuba*.

Neither Roosevelt nor the Rough Riders were alone in Cuba, of course. Besides the First Cav, the U.S. force included two dozen other regiments, most of them made up of professional soldiers. All told, 15,000 U.S. troops participated in the campaign; more than half saw action at San Juan Hill. About 2,000 of those soldiers were black, and of the 200 Americans killed in action, thirty came from the four black Army units—the famed Buffalo Soldiers.

Although they'd distinguished themselves in the Comanche wars, that action occurred out of the limelight. In 1898, they were very much in the news, and their heroism and skill were celebrated in Northern newspapers and the black press everywhere. TR praised them profusely.

So did John J. Pershing, then an Army lieutenant. "I never saw braver men anywhere," he wrote. "They fought their way into the hearts of the American people." Historian Rayford Logan noted that a generation of African-Americans hung prints on their walls of the famous charge up San Juan Hill—pictures depicting black soldiers, not Teddy Roosevelt. "They were," he wrote, "our Ralph Bunche, Marian Anderson, Joe Louis, and Jackie Robinson."

July 2, 1863

The Guns of July

Anyone who happened to wander into the civilian cemetery just south of Gettysburg, Pennsylvania, on the evening of this date would have seen a wooden sign at the gatepost. It warned visitors that the town would impose a $5 fine on anyone discharging a firearm on the cemetery grounds. But the peace and quiet cherished by local residents had been broken the day before. In the two days of fighting just concluded the sound had been unbearable.

> *They say the noise was incessant as the sound*
> *Of all wolves howling, when that attack came on.*
> *They say, when the guns all spoke, that the solid ground*
> *Of the rocky ridges trembled like a sick child.*

Those lines were penned by Stephen Vincent Benet, a writer born in Pennsylvania in 1898, in "John Brown's Body," an epic historical poem covering abolition and the Civil War. Forgotten now, it was a sensation when published in 1928.

Allen C. Guelzo, a current American scholar who teaches history at Gettysburg College, set the scene this way: "Two great armies, bound for the greatest and most violent collision the North American continent had ever seen." The forces were arrayed opposite each other in two long and parallel arcs roughly a mile apart. The Confederates were spread on a line across a place called Seminary Ridge. The Yankee lines ran along a curved line that formed the shape of a fishhook, ending at Cemetery Ridge—150,000 American fighting men and supporting troops were amassed at Gettysburg, encamped in the fields, hills, and forests surrounding the little town.

Despite the vast carnage on the field, the second day's fighting had been inconclusive. Robert E. Lee had asked Gen. James Longstreet to attack the Union's southern flank, but Longstreet was a little late getting there, and the Yankees who had finally occupied Little Round Top and Big Round Top had repelled him.

Confederate cavalryman J. E. B. Stuart had not shown up in time to really help Longstreet, and rebel generals A. P. Hill and Richard Ewell had not attacked the northern flank of the Union lines with their customary gusto. And so, as the Union officers gazed down on the vast meadow and saw the Confederate campfires burning like so many fireflies, they came to the same conclusion as their adversary: The third day of battle would decide it all.

July 3, 1863

Gettysburg

Two great armies amassed for the third day of battle outside a Pennsylvania town that would be forever stamped into America's consciousness. The heat and humidity were stifling. The aura of death was worse. As dawn broke, the soldiers on the scene knew they were part of something profound. Some had premonitions they wouldn't survive the day. Many were right.

"General, shall I advance?" one Southern division officer asked corps commander James Longstreet. The man doing the asking was a well-connected thirty-eight-year-old Virginian, George Edward Pickett. General Longstreet believed an impending charge was folly, and had conveyed his misgivings to Robert E. Lee. Instead of a frontal assault, Longstreet urged Lee to leave the field and circle around the federals, positioning the Confederates between the road to Washington and the Union Army, forcing the Northern commanders' hand. But Lee was tired of chasing Yankees, and he ordered the attack on well-fortified Union troops on Cemetery Ridge.

"Pickett's Charge" is the name given to the fateful engagement at the Battle of Gettysburg, but it's something of a misnomer. For one thing, Maj. Gen. Pickett was one of three Confederate leaders ordered to take Cemetery Ridge. Also, it wasn't really a charge. It was a slow advance, by infantry, across a mile-wide meadow that sloped upward—into withering rifle fire and artillery bombardment. It was a slaughter, and it broke the Confederacy's back.

In Longstreet's memoir, the tortured corps commander recalled his response when Pickett asked, "General, shall I advance?" Longstreet's foreboding was so profound that he literally could not find his voice. "The effort to speak the order failed," he wrote, "and I could only indicate it by an affirmative bow."

President Lincoln would mark Gettysburg as the second beginning of the American nation, "a new birth of freedom." Pickett's Charge stamped itself on the South's collective memory, too, but in a different way. In *Intruder in the Dust*, William Faulkner put it this way:

> For every Southern boy fourteen years old, not once but whenever he wants it, there is the instant when it's still not yet two o'clock on that

July afternoon in 1863, the brigades are in position behind the rail fence, the guns are laid and ready in the woods and the furled flags are already loosened to break out and Pickett himself with his long oiled ringlets and his hat in one hand probably and his sword in the other looking up the hill waiting for Longstreet to give the word and it's all in the balance, it hasn't happened yet, it hasn't even begun yet, it not only hasn't begun yet but there is still time for it not to begin against that position and those circumstances.

July 4

Independence Day

Calvin Coolidge was born on July 4, as was Malia Obama. There are only 365 days in a typical year, and in a nation as big as ours, famous people will share notable anniversaries. Still, when Thomas Jefferson and John Adams died on July 4, 1826, Americans sensed a higher power at work. Also fitting: On July 4, 1788, eighty-two-year-old Benjamin Franklin was too ill to participate in festivities, but the parade that passed under his window included clergymen of different Christian denominations, and Jewish rabbis, walking arm in arm. Franklin himself had led the fund-raising efforts for a hall in Philadelphia designated, in Franklin's words, "expressly for the use of any preacher of any religious persuasion who might desire to say something."

And Franklin meant *any* preacher: "Even if the Mufti of Constantinople were to send a missionary to preach Mohammedanism to us," he proclaimed, "he would find a pulpit at his service." As Franklin biographer Walter Isaacson noted in a 2003 *Time* magazine essay: "And when he was carried to his grave two years later, his casket was accompanied by all the clergymen of the city, every one of them, of every faith."

That was one signpost. There were others. In 1854, William Lloyd Garrison, the fiery and influential abolitionist, commemorated the Fourth of July by burning a copy of the Constitution at a rally in Framingham, Massachusetts. The document codifying slavery into the fabric of America's creation was a symbol of original sin, Garrison preached. Specifically, he called it "a covenant with death and an agreement with Hell."

Two years earlier, Frederick Douglass delivered a more nuanced, but equally passionate speech, "What to the Slave Is the Fourth of July?" Douglass offered a more charitable view of the patriots of 1776 than Garrison. They were heroes, he said, brave souls who had indeed risked their lives, fortunes, and sacred honor to challenge the divine right of kings and the British empire. The compromise they forged was the best that could be achieved at the time, Douglass told his audience. His tone changed quickly when he turned his focus on freedom's inert heirs.

"You have no right to wear out and waste the hard-earned fame of your fathers to cover your indolence," he told them. He challenged his listeners to look away from the Constitution to an earlier founding document, the Declaration of Independence. He described the remarkable language in the Preamble as "the ringbolt to the chain of your nation's destiny."

Finally, Douglass predicted that if America did not embrace the universal freedom so clearly called for in the Declaration, it would pay an awful price. In that 1852 speech, he suggested that it was perhaps already too late. "It is not light that is needed, but fire," he said. "It is not the gentle shower, but thunder. We need the storm, the whirlwind, and the earthquake."

Would it have surprised the Founders venerated by Frederick Douglass that the storm, the whirlwind, and the earthquake he predicted would be heralded by artillery fire at Fort Sumter and last four long years? Not George Washington. In his farewell address as president, Washington implored Americans not to succumb to partisan passions and regional rivalries.

But what would the slave-owning Washington make of Christopher Jackson, the African-American performer who played him in the Broadway musical *Hamilton* and who sang on the National Mall on Independence Day in 2016? What would John Adams, the first White House occupant, make of the fact that 190 years after he and Thomas Jefferson passed away, the First Family was African-American? My own view is that most of the Founders would be pleased by such developments, and find them a logical extension of the cause for which they labored. (I'm less sure what they'd make of the Washington Nationals' "Racing Presidents" mascots). Yet a theme flows through Independence Day ceremonies, and if you listen it's almost audible: the strains of the fife and drum that accompany the troops who have marched off to fight for liberty whenever they were asked. And the songs and chants of Americans marching in our streets for causes they believe will create "a more perfect union."

On July 4, 2016, Barack Obama paid homage to these complementary traditions. "Fourth of July—we enjoy the hotdogs, we enjoy the burgers, we enjoy the barbecue… we enjoy the fireworks," the president said. "But it's important to remember what a miracle this country is. How incredibly lucky we are that people, generations ago, were willing to take up arms and fight for our freedom. And then, people *inside* this country understanding that there were imperfections in our Union and were willing to keep on fighting on behalf of extending that freedom to all people and not just some."

The president ended on a personal note. "Just because it's a job of a father to embarrass his daughters," he said, as the audience laughed along with him, "I've got one last job. It just so happens that we celebrate our country's birthday on the same day that we celebrate my oldest daughter's birthday. So just a quick happy birthday for Malia."

Barack Hussein Obama then led the singing of "Happy Birthday." When it was over, he said, "Thank you, everybody. God bless you. God bless America."

July 5, 1810

The Greatest Show on Earth

In a small Connecticut hamlet, Philo and Irena Barnum welcomed a son into the world on this date. Christened Phineas Taylor, we know him as P. T. Barnum. The famed showman got his start by exhibiting a former slave named Joice Heth, who claimed to be 161 years old and a onetime nurse to George Washington. Both assertions were fanciful, but Barnum's career was launched. He soon opened the Barnum American Museum, a menagerie of entertainments including a rooftop garden, hot-air balloon rides, magicians, jugglers, fake mermaids, and exotic human beings ranging, in the parlance of the day, from albinos and midgets to circus fat men and bearded women.

Life magazine called Barnum "the patron saint of promoters." He showed Tom Thumb to Queen Victoria, showcased a giant man called "Jumbo," and brought soprano Jenny Lind to the United States, billing her as "the Swedish Nightingale." He eventually opened a traveling carnival he named "the Greatest Show on Earth." His powers of salesmanship were no exaggeration. This was a man who convinced the *New York Sun* to run his obituary while he was alive. The act billed as "General Tom Thumb"? He was not a general; he was a kid with dwarfism named Charles Stratton. Nor was he British, as Barnum claimed—and eleven years younger than advertised. Barnum taught him an English accent and paraded him around the world. But the little man didn't feel exploited. He made good money, and his fame helped him find a wife. (Barnum sold tickets to the wedding reception and the diminutive newlyweds were hosted at the White House by towering Abe Lincoln.) Spectacularly politically incorrect by modern lights, Barnum was unerring on the great moral question of his age. "A human soul that God has created and Christ died for is not to be trifled with," he said in support of the Thirteenth Amendment. "It may tenant the body of a Chinaman, a Turk, an Arab or a Hottentot—it is still an immortal spirit."

The most famous line ever attributed to P. T. Barnum—"There's a sucker born every minute"—was first uttered by others, and probably never by Barnum. Asked about it late in life, he replied that he doubted he ever said it, though he admitted to possibly having said, "The people like to be humbugged." Barnum also quipped, "There's a silver lining in every crowd," which gets closer to his true temperament, which was mostly optimistic.

One rarely remembered Barnum quote has a positively Reaganesque quality to it: "The public," he observed, "is wiser than many imagine."

July 6, 1945

Gerda's Lieutenant

It took courage for Gerda Weissmann to write to a young American officer she'd met two months earlier when his unit liberated her and more than one hundred other women along the Germany-Czechoslovakia border. If the fighting had lasted even another day, this emaciated young woman—she weighed less than seventy pounds—would have perished. But Gerda survived the war, the only member of her family to do so. Then she thrived, first in a converted U.S. Army hospital in Volary, Czechoslovakia, and later in upstate New York, which became her home. Gerda knew nothing of this future as she wrote a letter in German to the soldier the other girls in the ward teasingly called "Gerda's lieutenant." His name was Kurt Klein, and he was an intelligence officer with the Second Regiment of the U.S. Army's Fifth Infantry Division.

Lieutenant Klein, who had turned twenty-five the day before, left Gerda a single rose before his unit was ordered into Bavaria. In her letter written on this day, Gerda told Kurt that as part of her physical rehabilitation she had tried her hand at jewelry making. Her first effort as an artisan, she wrote, was "a tiny star meant for you."

Of the millions of senseless cruelties that epitomized the Second World War, the forced marches of prisoners from concentration camps in Poland in the war's waning days were among the most depraved. As the Red Army closed in on them from the east, SS units and labor camp commandants fled toward the German interior. Inexplicably, they forced their half-starving, barely clad prisoners to go with them. So it was that Gerda Weissmann, who had been hauled away to the camps in 1939 at age fifteen for the crime of being Jewish, found herself five and a half years later among 1,350 women and girls on a forced march to nowhere, in the middle of winter, in what became known as the Volary Death March. The sadistic commander ignored orders from Heinrich Himmler to stop killing the prisoners, and took to back roads to avoid Czech townspeople who wanted to feed the girls and American military units fanning through the countryside. Finally, in the first week of May, as U.S. pilots began strafing any uniformed Germans still marching under arms, the Nazi guards melted away into the forest, leaving Gerda and the other surviving prisoners locked inside a shack at an abandoned bicycle factory.

When the Fifth Army arrived in Volary on May 5, 1945, townspeople told them about the prisoners. Of the original 1,350 girls and women, only 116 were alive when the American soldiers found them. White-haired and skeletal, they looked to the Americans to be elderly. Most of them were very young. Gerda Weissmann was two days shy of her twenty-first birthday. Kurt Klein and another soldier were among the first two Americans to approach the prisoners. Kurt asked Gerda a question in both English and in German. Knowing no English, she responded in German. So he spoke to her in that language, but with a tone she hadn't heard in many years.

"Don't cry, my child," he told her. "It is all over now."

Gerda struggled to absorb a seeming miracle: that these brave, able, confident, well-fed, and well-armed—and kindhearted—Americans had crossed the ocean and a continent to fight for her freedom. The young lieutenant asked her another question: "May I see the other ladies?"

After six years of being demeaned and brutalized, the word *ladies* took her by surprise.

"We are Jews," she said in a small voice.

"So am I," replied Kurt Klein.

The young lieutenant was wearing sunglasses, so Gerda couldn't see whether he had tears in his eyes when he made this statement, but she thought she heard a catch in his voice. She was right about that: Kurt Klein and his older sister and brother were born in Germany and sent to the United States to live with relatives after Kristallnacht convinced their parents that it was time to escape. But Klein's parents didn't make it out in time and were killed in the death camps, as were Gerda's parents and brother. Klein was thinking of his own family as he attended to these abused, resilient refugees. There would be time for Gerda and Kurt to discuss all that later, just as there would be time for Kurt to come courting in the hospital and give Gerda a first kiss and propose marriage and take her back to Buffalo and raise their children together.

All that, and much more, would unfold in the fullness of time in the life of Gerda Weissmann Klein. In a 2011 ceremony, Barack Obama would drape the Presidential Medal of Freedom around her neck and praise her for reminding us all that "it is often in our most hopeless moments that we discover the extent of our strength and the depth of our love."

But on a beautiful spring morning in 1945, there was only time to be admitted into the German military hospital that the Americans had converted into a medical facility to treat death march survivors.

"Won't you come with me?" Kurt asked as he opened the door for Gerda. Although she was almost too weak and overcome by her ordeal to walk another step, that gallant gesture of holding the door helped Gerda summon her courage and her hope—and do just that.

July 7, 1981

Sandra Day O'Connor

The idea of naming a woman to the Supreme Court arose in October 1980, when Ronald Reagan's internal campaign polls showed solidifying support for the Republican nominee, with one glitch: an emerging gender gap. Longtime Reagan adviser Stuart K. Spencer suggested breaking the all-male bastion of the high court, advice Reagan promptly embraced: He announced that "one of the first" Supreme Court justices of his administration would be a woman. Reagan's gambit attracted little notice, but five months after his inauguration, Justice Potter Stewart announced he would retire when the high court's term ended that June.

In a White House meeting to discuss a replacement, Reagan mentioned his campaign promise. Reminded by an aide of his "*one* of the first" hedge, Reagan replied that Jimmy Carter had filled no Supreme Court vacancies, adding that this one might be his only chance. This message was received. Attorney General William French Smith had compiled a list of twenty candidates, including eight men, which he never sent to Reagan. Instead, Smith narrowed the list to four women, one of them an Arizona appeals court judge named Sandra Day O'Connor.

Reagan met with O'Connor, was charmed by her, and canceled the other meetings. On this date, he went to the White House briefing room to tell the press. "She is truly a person for all seasons, possessing those unique qualities of temperament, fairness, intellectual capacity, and devotion to the public good which have characterized the 101 brethren who have preceded her," Reagan said. "I commend her to you, and I urge the Senate's swift bipartisan confirmation so that as soon as possible she may take her seat on the court and her place in history."

Instead of focusing on the historical element, the press corps focused on the immediate: namely, conservatives' questions about O'Connor's views on abortion. Reagan tried to deflect those queries until he gave a one-word answer ("Yes") to the question of whether he was satisfied with her "right-to-life position." Although O'Connor would vote to uphold *Roe v. Wade*, to the chagrin of social conservatives, Reagan never wavered in his support for her. Near the end of his presidency, he revealed how warmly he regarded his first Supreme Court pick.

It came in a 1988 diary entry that nicely captured Reagan's approach to life: "Wouldn't you know—the sun was shining and it was a beautiful day," it began. "Nancy & I called Sandra Day O'Connor in the hospital. She's just had a mastectomy. Nancy was most helpful to her."

July 8, 1891

The Duchess

Warren G. Harding, a Marion, Ohio, newspaper publisher, was a handsome young man on the rise when he came courting Florence Mabel Kling DeWolfe. She was a plain, divorced, thirty-year-old single mother with an overbearing father—a German-American banker who opposed the relationship because he considered Harding a social climber. Harding's motives were complicated, which is often the case when matters of the heart are intertwined with professional ambition. Either way, whether by instinct or calculation, Warren Harding married Florence on this date. Whatever his reasons, he had paired off with a woman who could help him go further in politics than his talents otherwise would have allowed.

He called her the Duchess, and she sublimated any aspirations of her own to advance her mate's political career. She was up front about it, saying she had "only one real hobby—my husband." Yet, Florence was a feminist, albeit within the confines of the 1920s. She hosted an all-women's tennis tournament at the White House, promoted the Girl Scouts, and exercised her right to vote—the first time any woman had pulled the lever for her husband in a U.S. presidential election. A member of the League of Women Voters and the National Women's Party, she encouraged other women to vote as well. In Ohio, the Duchess had propelled Harding into the state's Republican political circles and she had arrived in Washington with a vision of what a First Lady could be—and she managed an impressive number of "firsts" for a First Lady. She preapproved his speeches, weighed in on cabinet appointments, and pushed the president to appoint women to government posts. Florence also adopted the welfare of World War I veterans as her signature issue, helping launch an East Wing tradition that exists to this day.

She was so strong a personality that when her husband died unexpectedly in office, rumors abounded that she had poisoned him. She didn't, though she had her reasons, but she may have inadvertently contributed to his death by choosing as a White House physician a homeopath who misdiagnosed her husband's 1923 heart attack as food poisoning. Florence burned thousands of his papers and letters after he died, explaining they might be "misconstrued." The Teapot Dome scandal was brewing by then, so that made sense. There were other reasons to get rid of his papers, too, particularly the steamy letters from various women that didn't surface for nearly a century. Perhaps a better way of saying it is that the letters might have been "construed."

July 9, 1850

Rough and Ready

Independence Day fell on a very hot day. Hot enough to help kill a president. Zachary Taylor was the second general who essentially went from the military to the presidency without holding other political office. (In the years to come, Ulysses Grant and Dwight Eisenhower would follow suit.) Taylor had been in office for sixteen months on July 4, 1850, a time without air-conditioning or refrigeration. To keep cool while attending festivities at the site of the proposed Washington Monument, the sixty-five-year-old president consumed quantities of iced milk and fresh cherries. Returning to the White House, he drank copious amounts of water. Was it cholera that killed him on this date? Heat stroke? Food poisoning? Gastroenteritis? Foul play?

No one knows for certain, although the water supply and the sewer system in the fetid capital were sketchy in those days. Zachary Taylor also had enemies. Elected as a Whig in 1848, he was a military lifer, an Army general, and a hero of the Mexican-American War. He was popular, too. His nickname was "Old Rough and Ready," and one of the things he had been readying for as president was quashing any Southern rebellion. Although born in Virginia and raised in Kentucky (and the owner of a Mississippi cotton plantation with slaves), Taylor's four decades in the Army made him an ardent nationalist with no sympathy for Southern sectionalism. Mere talk of secession offended him mightily. At a meeting with Southern politicians, Taylor warned them against trying to leave the Union, hinting that he'd personally lead the federal armies against them. He also vowed matter-of-factly to execute those who took up arms against the United States with less reluctance than he had hanged deserters and spies in the war with Mexico.

In the twentieth century, conspiracy theories arose that Taylor was murdered over these views, as Vice President Millard Fillmore was more pliant. An exhumation determined no evidence of arsenic or any other toxins, leaving the blame for his death where it had always been: on the capital city's poor sanitation and the backward medical care Taylor received after he took ill. But the question of what influence Taylor might have exerted if he'd lived remains. President Trump once mused aloud whether things would have been different had Andrew Jackson been in the White House during the run-up to the Civil War. That was whimsical—Old Hickory was born in 1767—but the question could be asked of Taylor. He was the last Whig elected president, his party giving way to the antislavery Republicans, and the Civil War he feared did indeed come. If it had come on the same schedule, Old Rough and Ready would have been a seventy-year-old former president in 1861, and probably much too old to lead troops in the field. Probably.

July 10, 1925

Monkey Trial

A small-town Tennessee courthouse was an early battlefield in the "culture wars." At issue in the famous Scopes Trial was whether a science and math teacher had committed a misdemeanor by teaching evolution from a textbook adjudged by the state legislature to be hostile to the Christian religion. The trial, which opened on this date, featured historical heavyweights: Clarence Darrow for the defense; three-time Democratic Party presidential nominee William Jennings Bryan for the prosecution. It was chronicled by H. L. Mencken, the caustic Baltimore columnist whose newspaper subsidized Scopes' defense team.

The drama still captivates intellectuals, mostly because of a brilliant 1955 dramatization by Jerome Lawrence and Robert Edwin Lee titled *Inherit the Wind*. Their play was made into a 1960 movie starring Spencer Tracy as the character inspired by Darrow and Fredric March as "Matthew Harrison Brady"—William Jennings Bryan. Gene Kelly played Mencken in the thinly disguised allegory comparing the supposed zealotry of 1920s Bible thumpers to the persecutors of suspected Communists in the McCarthy Era. (The film was reprised on college campuses after 9/11 as a warning against overreacting to Islam-inspired terrorism.) In the play and the film, Darrow is the voice of rationality; Bryan is a bigot, if not a village idiot. In real life, it wasn't that clear-cut. One of the reasons Bryan aligned himself against Darwin was that he was part of a progressive, but faith-based, tradition that feared the teaching of evolution would encourage "social Darwinism," that is, a move toward eugenics and marginalizing the poor and handicapped. In other words, this was not only a fight between modernity and traditional religion. It was also an intramural battle among Democrats. In addition, Bryan was a pacifist for whom World War I had confirmed his deepest fears about modern science and technology.

In a closing argument he prepared for the Scopes Trial, but was never allowed to deliver, the thrice-nominated "Boy Orator of the Plains" explained what frightened him. Not science per se, and certainly not monkeys, or even the idea that man originally came from apes. Bryan feared what mankind, unfettered by biblical teachings, could do to itself.

"Science has taught him to go down into the water and shoot up from below and to go up into the clouds and shoot down from above, thus making the battlefield three times as bloody as before," wrote William Jennings Bryan. "But science does not teach brotherly love."

Duelists

The two antagonists, famous politicians whose former friendship had long since curdled into mutual loathing, met on a quiet bluff at seven in the morning. Minutes later, one of them was mortally wounded, and a young country learned how it wanted presidential candidates to behave—win or lose. The lethal confrontation between Alexander Hamilton and Aaron Burr took place on the cliffs above the Hudson on the New Jersey side of the river. On this date, Hamilton lay dying from a bullet in his stomach. He would succumb the following day. Although Burr didn't immediately realize it, his political future died there, too.

Four years earlier, Thomas Jefferson had defeated John Adams in the Electoral College, but an anomaly in the Constitution threw the result into doubt. Each elector was supposed to write down two names. The candidate with the most votes would be president, the one with the second highest number would be vice president. But Jefferson and his running mate, Aaron Burr, each received seventy-three electoral votes. Breaking the tie was put to the House for what was expected to be pro forma approval of Jefferson as president and Burr as vice president. But machinations among the Federalists produced a tie in the House for thirty-five nerve-wracking roll-call votes. Finally, with Hamilton leading the way, the logjam was broken, and Jefferson was made the nation's third president. So, Burr already nursed a grudge before 1804, when Jefferson withdrew his support for a second Burr term—and Hamilton blocked Burr's plans to become governor of New York. It was then that the vice president's frustrations turned murderous. He used a social slight as a pretext to issue a challenge he knew Hamilton would have to accept.

Weehawken, the location for the duel, was known to both men. During the Revolutionary War, Burr was dispatched to the heights by George Washington to observe British ship movements. Hamilton knew the field as the place where his nineteen-year-old son, Philip, had been shot to death two and a half years earlier while defending his father's honor. Dueling had been outlawed in New

York, which was why Hamilton and Burr were in New Jersey, and the killing of such a prominent patriot made Aaron Burr a pariah even before his subsequent acts of treason. Yet the ghosts of Weehawken are soothed every four years when Americans peacefully hand over power even to people and political parties they despise. With rare exceptions, it's a tradition we honor—a quadrennial reminder that Alexander Hamilton did not die in vain.

July 12, 1984

Glass Ceilings

Upending Ronald Reagan's reelection bid was not going to be easy, as Walter Mondale and his campaign team knew. Attempting to jostle the status quo—and under pressure from prominent female Democrats—Mondale announced that he would ask the party's convention delegates in San Francisco to nominate a little-known congresswoman from Queens to be his running mate. In modern politics, such a "request" is automatically ratified, meaning that on this date, it became clear that Rep. Geraldine Ferraro of New York would be the first woman on the presidential ticket of a major political party.

"I know what it takes to be a good vice president—I was once one myself," Mondale said, in a rare bout of immodesty. "I looked for the best vice president, and I found her in Geri Ferraro."

"America is not just for some of us," Mondale added. "Our Founders said in the Constitution: 'We the People.' Not just the rich, or men, or white, but all of us. Our message is that America is for everyone who works hard and contributes to our blessed country."

Seven days later, standing on stage before the delegates and a huge television audience, the Democrats' vice presidential nominee amplified on this theme. "My name is Geraldine Ferraro," she declared to thunderous applause. "I stand before you to proclaim tonight: America is the land where dreams can come true for all of us."

The July dreams of the San Francisco delegates would evaporate in November. The "gender gap" Democrats had counted on never materialized—Reagan even won 56 percent of the women's vote—and the Mondale-Ferraro ticket carried only Mondale's native Minnesota and the District of Columbia. Ferraro couldn't even deliver her own congressional district.

In fairness, she wasn't the problem. Nor could the Democrats' landslide loss be blamed on Fritz Mondale. No one was going to defeat Ronald Reagan that year. The country was doing well economically, and Reagan ran a positive campaign that perfectly captured the prevailing national mood. Neither Ferraro nor Sarah Palin, who tried in 2008, would win national office. Nor would Hillary Clinton, who ran in 2008 and 2016 for the top job. Nonetheless, a glass ceiling was broken on this date. Although the barrier remains, it will be broken one day, too. As Geri Ferraro proclaimed twenty-eight years ago: "If we can do this, we can do anything."

July 13, 1978

Tall in the Saddle

Ron Turcotte's moment had come at Belmont Park five years earlier when he'd piloted the great Secretariat through the final leg of thoroughbred racing's Triple Crown. "Big Red," as the horse was known, won by thirty-one lengths, leading to track announcer Chic Anderson's iconic description, the most famous racing call in history: "They're on the turn, and Secretariat is blazing along!" Anderson blared over the din of the crowd. "Secretariat is widening now. He is moving like a tremendous machine!"

Watching the race, even decades later, can give track aficionados a chill. But race-horses aren't machines. They are animals, large and unpredictable, as the Belmont crowd was reminded on this date when Turcotte went into the starting gate aboard a horse named Flag of Leyte Gulf. Jockeys guide thousand-pound animals cushioned by only a tiny saddle, while traveling at speeds of more than thirty-five miles per hour in heavy traffic. It requires a combination of skill, conditioning, balance, and split-second decision making.

In a much-hyped list of the supposed one hundred best athletes of the twentieth century, ESPN ranked no jockey in the top fifty, although Secretariat checked in at thirty-five. The diminutive stature of jockeys is mostly likely to blame for this oversight. Legendary sportswriter Red Smith put it this way: "If Bill Shoemaker were six feet tall and weighed 200 pounds, he could beat anybody in any sport. Pound-for-pound he is the greatest living athlete."

In the 1980s, pioneering California sports medicine doctor Robert Kerlan and researcher Jack Wilmore performed a series of studies that bolstered this view. Each race a jockey rode, they found, was the equivalent of an eight-hundred-meter footrace. Jockeys had the lowest body fat of any athletes. Eighty percent of them could bench-press more than their body weight. Their powers of recuperation were legendary. These are, they concluded, the most finely conditioned athletes in the world.

None of that measures their most impressive attribute. Ronnie Turcotte was just out of the starting gate, when a horse named Small Raja, ridden by Jeff Fell, began drifting toward him. Turcotte reined his mount, and screamed, "Jeff!" but not in time. Flag of Leyte Gulf went down, taking his rider with him. In his midthirties, Ron Turcotte became a paraplegic.

To all those jockey attributes Dr. Kerlan and Jack Wilmore documented, add one more: tremendous physical and mental courage.

July 14, 1918
A President's Son Falls from the Sky

We know from Quentin Roosevelt's letters to his betrothed, preserved by his brother Kermit, how a young man's thoughts can turn from love to war. The precipitating act, as it was for his father, was the sinking of the British cruise liner *Lusitania* by a German submarine.

"We are a pretty sordid lot, aren't we to want to sit looking on while England and France fight our battles and pan gold into our pockets?" Quentin wrote from Harvard, where he was a student. "I wondered, as I sat by my fire, whether there are any dreams in our land anymore."

The recipient of this missive was Flora Payne Whitney, an heiress whom Quentin met at a Rhode Island ball. Initial attraction blossomed into mutual adoration. Yet Quentin did not "sit looking on" for long. After the United States entered the Great War in 1917, all five Roosevelt men volunteered for duty. At fifty-eight, Theodore Roosevelt proposed himself as the commander of a volunteer division, an offer President Wilson declined. But all four of his sons—Ted, Archie, Kermit, and Quentin—mustered into service. After a year of training, Quentin was made a flight commander in the Ninety-Fifth Aero Squadron. At twenty, he became an admired comrade. First, because he never traded on his famous name; and second, because of his conspicuous bravery. Those traits would cost his family dearly. Quentin was shot out of the sky by a German pilot after he broke off a formation to protect his men against a larger enemy squadron.

His loss was considered a national tragedy in America. It came on this

date, Bastille Day, while defending France, which one historian said would have been akin to Lafayette dying at Yorktown on July 4. But to "Quent," as he signed his name, France was worth fighting for. In a letter home, he described life in "the City of Lights" while the French endured that horrible war.

"It is not the Paris that we used to love, the Paris of five years past," he wrote. "There are no more young men in the crowds unless in uniform. Everywhere you see women in black, and there is no more cheerful shouting and laughing. Many, many of the women have a haunted look in their eyes, as if they had seen something too terrible for forgetfulness."

American ace Eddie Rickenbacker reported that the Germans buried Quent with full military honors. "No honors, however, could have compensated our group for the loss of that boy," he added. Quent was reburied at the American cemetery atop the bluffs at Normandy next to his oldest brother, Ted, who won the Medal of Honor on D-Day and died a month later.

July 15, 1954

Selling Airplanes

Boeing wasn't the first aeronautics company to envision, or even manufacture, a jet-propelled airplane designed for passengers. The British firm founded by pioneering aviator Geoffrey de Havilland had been making a passenger jet named "the Comet" since 1949. It was a fast plane, all right, but it kept crashing.

Into the breach flew Boeing, which had been building jet-powered bombers for the Pentagon since 1947. By 1952, Boeing engineers were busy on a prototype aircraft with a dual purpose: It could be refueled in midair for long-distance Air Force flights and also used as a nonmilitary plane capable of ferrying passengers at twice the speed of state-of-the-art propeller planes such as the popular Douglas DC-6.

Boeing called its innovation the Dash 80, although we know it as the Boeing 707. It is the aircraft that made jet travel pervasive. "Boeing was not the first company to produce a jet-powered airliner," noted *Wired* magazine aviation writer Jason Paur. "But just as Ford's Model T popularized the automobile despite being a latecomer in the car world, the Boeing 707 would be the airplane to popularize jet travel."

At the start, nothing was certain. Boeing had been developing and testing the plane without any assurances from the airlines that they would buy it. Was the new plane safe? Was it even stable?

Those questions were answered on this date in the skies above Seattle's Lake Washington, where Boeing invited dignitaries and air industry executives to see famed World War II military test pilot Alvin M. "Tex" Johnston fly the thing. Johnston was from Kansas, not Texas, but he cultivated his sobriquet by wearing cowboy boots and a Stetson—and it was easy to see how his personality fit the nickname. He loved the design of this new airplane, which he said would "reduce the size of the world by a factor of two, as measured by flight time," and he wanted to show everyone what it could do. So, as he brought it on approach toward the crowd, Johnston executed a low-speed, low-altitude barrel roll. The crowd gasped, and many cheered. Boeing's executives, who had not been forewarned, nearly had a collective heart attack

"What were you doing up there?" a chagrined company official demanded afterward.

"I was selling airplanes," replied the unrepentant Tex Johnston. And so he was. The orders came flooding in after that, and they have never stopped.

July 16, 1935

Pay Me Now or Pay Me Later

As automobiles replaced horses in this country, a new problem arose. Horses needed lots of care: barns, feed, water troughs, cleanup crews to pick up after the horses, to name a few. But cars were high maintenance, too, and one problem presented itself early in the game: finding adequate and appropriate parking spaces. There was a civic cost involved in solving this issue—and a revenue opportunity as well. The solution made its appearance in the heartland metropolis of Oklahoma City: the parking meter.

This maddening contraption was the brainchild of an educator turned lawyer turned newspaperman named Carlton Cole "Carl" Magee, one of the more versatile personages to ever inhabit an American newsroom. Controversy followed the man wherever he went. Or, to look at it another way, Carl Magee made news as well as covered it. Born and educated in Iowa in 1873, Magee earned two master's degrees and became an Iowa teacher and school superintendent. After studying law, he moved to Tulsa, Oklahoma, in 1901, where he became one of the city's most prominent lawyers. He also did some legal work in the oil business and became vice president of Black Hawk Petroleum, dabbled in the development of natural gas, helped build an electric light plant, and bought Tulsa's first privately owned automobile.

The idea of a parking meter came to him during his second stint in Oklahoma—he had a dramatic eight-year hiatus in New Mexico that is another story entirely and involves gunplay—after he was entrusted with an Oklahoma City Chamber of Commerce traffic committee. Some five hundred thousand cars were registered in Oklahoma City and the surrounding county, up from only three thousand two decades earlier. Downtown businesses were suffering because commuters left their vehicles all day on the streets, leaving potential customers nowhere to park while they shopped.

Magee hit on the solution, and a professor and former engineering student at Oklahoma State University helped him invent the contraption to implement it: They called it the Park-O-Meter, and on this date, 175 meters were installed in downtown Oklahoma City. Parking was affordable by today's standards—five cents an hour—but the tickets were steep: twenty bucks.

In one fell swoop Magee's traffic committee solved several problems: addressing the parking woes that had hurt merchants; supplying revenue for the city during the Depression; and increasing downtown property values, thus boosting building and construction projects.

July 17, 1955

Uncle Walt's Place

Walt Disney began sketching out his idea for a Southern California theme park after being disappointed by the dearth of imagination at the local amusement parks where he took his two daughters. He had a grander dream, one with a dual mission of providing education and entertainment. He envisioned an eleven-acre park across the road from his Burbank studios. But Burbank's city planners shocked Disney by refusing to approve the zoning. Undaunted, he drove south where he discovered a place that reminded him of his native Midwest.

The post–World War II migration to California was bursting Los Angeles at the seams, but only twenty-five miles south of Los Angeles's congestion, he found the Orange County hamlet of Anaheim. Now California's tenth largest city, Anaheim was then the same sleepy agricultural town it had been for a century. Founded by German farmers, its name was derived from a combination of the local river, the Santa Ana, and the German word *heim*, which means "home." This home by the river had fewer than fifteen thousand souls when Walt Disney bought 160 acres of farmland and orange groves. Disney rather quickly wished he'd purchased even more land, a mistake he did not repeat a decade later in central Florida.

On this date, though, magic happened. Disneyland opened its doors for the first time.

Things did not go smoothly. "Uncle Walt" and his crew were hardly prepared for the thirty-three thousand guests, many with forged tickets, who arrived at what was supposed to be an invitation-only soft launch. One woman's high-heeled shoe got caught in Main Street's still-solidifying asphalt. A gas leak in Fantasyland meant all attractions in that portion of the park had to be closed. Other rides simply broke down. So many patrons boarded Mark Twain's steamboat that it nearly capsized. The park's concession stands ran out of food and drink. Visitors on that terrifically hot day looked in vain for drinking fountains, which had yet to be installed.

Local news accounts documented all these glitches, and a dismayed Walt Disney would refer to the debut for years afterward as "Black Sunday." But the public knew better. By mid-September, one million visitors had gone through Disneyland's turnstiles. They've never stopped coming: to the original Disneyland, to Walt Disney World, and to other parks in Paris, Tokyo, and Hong Kong—and Disney cruise ships that sail the sea. "We are not trying to entertain the critics," Walt Disney once explained. "I'll take my chances with the public."

July 18, 1968

Moore's Law

Two U.S. scientists from different Midwestern towns, working in different labs, were in one of the great races in the history of technology. Each man was trying to produce the integrated circuit—to place transistors, resistors, and capacitors on a single "chip" of semiconductor material so they could work in rapid sequence. The competing researchers were Jack Kilby, an electrical engineer at Texas Instruments, and Robert Noyce of Fairchild Semiconductor, a firm he cofounded in Santa Clara County, which was then called by the local Chamber of Commerce "the Valley of the Heart's Delight." The name was derived from the sheer beauty of a place known for its fruit orchards, flower groves, and mild weather. It would become known as Silicon Valley, after the substance used in tiny devices that would change the world.

Although Noyce and Kilby more or less simultaneously invented the microchip, Noyce emerged as first among equals, because Kilby used the element germanium in his circuits, while Noyce settled on silicon, which would prove easier to mass-produce. This was more than a lucky guess. In the Massachusetts Institute of Technology physics department, young Noyce's intellect was so obvious that other students called him "Rapid Robert." He knew how to pick business partners, too. When he left to form the Intel Corporation on this date he took a half-dozen Fairchild brainiacs with him, including Gordon E. Moore.

It was the San Francisco-born Moore who gave his name to a postulate that altered the very concept of human connectivity. Six years after the invention of the microchip, Moore noted in a 1965 *Electronics* magazine article that the capacity of integrated circuits was doubling every year. He predicted that this trend would continue for ten years. In 1975, Moore revised his theory to a doubling every two years. Was he right? Yes, and more than he realized.

Splitting the difference between his two predictions gives us the correct answer—the amount of information a computer chip can hold doubles about every eighteen months. Caltech professor Carver Mead would dub this cycle "Moore's Law." It may or may not prove to be an actual law of science, but it represents something more profound. Moore's Law is not merely a guideline to help chip makers anticipate a future market for their products. It is an assumption of technology that raises an intriguing question, one with profound implications: If the information on a computer chip doubles every year and a half, does human knowledge itself expand at the same rate?

July 19, 1946

Hello, Norma Jeane

When a twenty-year-old blonde showed up at the studios of 20th Century Fox for a screen test on this date, the odds were stacked against her. The young woman had no previous acting experience, a hard-to-pronounce surname, and little clue of the culture she was attempting to join. For starters, dying her hair blonde for the audition was a miscalculation: studio head Darryl F. Zanuck preferred brunettes. She also told studio makeup artist Allan "Whitey" Snyder to paint her face heavily as though she were going onstage, causing casting director Leon Shamroy to explode.

The commotion upset Norma Jeane Dougherty, who began to sweat and stammer. Her face flushed, leaving red blotches. Assured that the screen test required no talking, however, she went through with it. Clad in a floor-length gown, Miss Dougherty was instructed to walk back and forth, sit on a stool, light a cigarette, and gaze out a stage window.

The change was immediate, the effect electric. Her hands stopped shaking, and she walked steadily, and confidently. "I got a cold chill," Shamroy recalled later. "Her natural beauty, plus her inferiority complex gave her a look of mystery. This is the first girl who looked like one of those lush stars of the silent era. Every frame of the test radiated sex."

Ben Lyon, the studio's top talent scout, reacted similarly to the Friday test. Both executives communicated their enthusiasm to Zanuck. By Tuesday, she was under contract in Lyon's office. Not the kind of man to take advantage of a vulnerable woman, Lyon gently asked about her career goals.

"I want to be a film star," she replied simply.

Lyon believed she could attain that aim. First, though, there was that last name, which audiences would stumble over. Was there another one she liked? The young woman thought of her grandmother, one of the few adults who'd been kind to her growing up. What was *her* name?, he asked. "Monroe," she answered. For a first name, Lyon told Norma Jeane that she reminded him of a "lovely actress" he knew before the war named Marilyn Miller.

What Lyon didn't reveal was that he'd broken off his wedding engagement to Miller, who'd also endured an abusive childhood, that she went on to have three unhappy marriages, that poor health would stall Miller's film career, and that she died at age thirty-seven. As he gazed upon the newly minted Marilyn Monroe, Ben Lyon felt he was almost seeing the reincarnation of Marilyn Miller. He had no idea how prescient his premonition would prove to be.

July 20, 1969

A Big Step for Man

O n their fourth day in space, Apollo 11 astronauts Neil Armstrong, Edwin "Buzz" Aldrin, and Michael Collins made final preparations toward accomplishing the goal President Kennedy had set eight years earlier—and that human beings had dreamed of for many millennia. At 4:18 p.m., Eastern Daylight Time, the landing vehicle known as *Eagle*, with Armstrong and Aldrin aboard, separated from the command module and began its historic descent to a place on the moon's surface named the Sea of Tranquility.

As this cosmic event unfolded, Armstrong radioed back to Mission Control in Houston a simple four-word message that became an iconic expression in the American language: "The *Eagle* has landed." But the line Neil Armstrong had hoped would inspire the world fell a little flat owing to a minor lapse. "That's one small step for man," he said as he stepped onto the moon, "one giant leap for mankind." Only later did Armstrong realize that he'd inadvertently omitted the article *a* in front of *man*—a one-letter word that gave the sentiment its cosmic meaning.

A meticulous U.S. Navy combat aviator, test pilot, and scrupulously thorough astronaut, Armstrong could hardly believe when he returned to Earth that he'd made such a significant, if tiny, omission. But his slip served as a reminder that those were human beings up there, and that despite their fallibilities, Americans met John F. Kennedy's 1961 challenge of sending astronauts to the moon and returning them safely by the end of the decade. The lunar landing underscored other truths as well: that despite budgetary limitations, exploration is in Americans' DNA. Also, that history is unpredictable, as JFK had been gone for five years by then. His successor signed civil rights legislation as part of a larger social movement that caused many people to question the expense of space exploration when so much still needed doing on Earth.

For their part, after taking that "one small step for man, one giant leap for mankind" on this date, more immediate concerns occupied Neil Armstrong's and Buzz Aldrin's attention. They explored the moon's surface, planted a U.S. flag, performed a few rudimentary scientific experiments, left a plaque saying that earthlings had come in peace, and spent the night on the moon's surface, the first human beings to do so.

The next morning, they headed back to Apollo 11 and the long ride home to their capsule's July 24, 1969, splashdown in the Pacific Ocean.

July 21, 1899

Ernest Abides

In the Chicago suburb of Oak Park, physician Clarence Hemingway went to the front porch of his house on this date and blew merrily on his cornet. Thus did Dr. Hemingway announce to the world—or at least to his neighborhood—the arrival of his second child, a boy, whom was named Ernest Miller Hemingway.

Later, Hemingway would call the predominately Protestant and upper-middle-class place of his birth a town of "wide lawns and narrow minds." Yet he learned to love reading and writing there, and his father taught him to fish and hunt and think for himself at their cabin in Northern Michigan. Eschewing college, he landed a writing job on the *Kansas City Star*, tried to enlist when the United States entered World War I, and when poor eyesight kept him out of the Army, he volunteered to drive Red Cross ambulances at the front. Weeks later, he was wounded by a mortar round while handing out supplies in the trenches. An Italian soldier beside him was killed, another's legs were blown off. Hemingway was riddled with shrapnel and knocked out.

In 1932, when he was the most famous novelist in the world, Hemingway wrote a nonfiction book, *Death in the Afternoon*. Ostensibly, it was a defense of bullfighting, but it was also a defense of his own spare literary style. "If a writer of prose knows enough about what he is writing about he may omit things that he knows and the reader, if the writer is writing truly enough, will have a feeling of those things as strongly as though the writer had stated them," he explained. Hemingway was open about where he got those ideas—from working in a newsroom. The *Kansas City Star* was known for insisting that its reporters write short sentences in brief, compact paragraphs, with active verbs that conveyed immediacy, clarity, and authenticity.

"Those were the best rules I ever learned for the business of writing," he'd explain later. "I've never forgotten them." In Paris after the war, he would join ranks with rebellious postwar cohorts, including Ezra Pound, James Joyce, F. Scott Fitzgerald, and Gertrude Stein.

In *The Sun Also Rises*, his first novel, Hemingway popularized Stein's phrase "the lost generation." But the author had a less apocalyptic view of the times he lived in. In a letter to Max Perkins, his editor in those early days, Hemingway said he thought the novel's characters were "battered" by life perhaps but not "lost." The very point of *The Sun Also Rises*, he added, wasn't that world war had left a lost generation, but rather that "the earth abideth forever."

July 22, 1947

The Black Buzz Aldrin

The story of how baseball's color line was broken is usually told as the courageous action of two men, Branch Rickey and Jackie Robinson. They were stellar, but they were not alone. Integrating baseball was a crusade pursued by many people, and off the diamond. In postwar America, it became a touchstone of the civil rights movement.

When Jackie Robinson debuted for the Brooklyn Dodgers in 1947, no big city in America had a black mayor. Only two African-Americans served in Congress. Baseball was a symbol, not a bastion. In 1945, New York City councilman Ben Davis, a former college football star, distributed pamphlets with pictures of two African-Americans. One was a dead U.S. soldier, the other a baseball player in uniform. "Good enough to die for his country," the leaflet said, "but not good enough for organized baseball."

The same year, Boston councilman Isadore Muchnick used direct leverage. Massachusetts still had "blue laws" precluding certain commerce on Sundays. Baseball was included, but local option allowed Boston to waive the law. Muchnick proposed denying the Red Sox that waiver unless they opened their roster to blacks. Several Boston sportswriters got behind this effort, which the black press had been covering for years. The so-called Negro League had many ballplayers of Jackie Robinson's caliber. One of them was Hank Thompson. At seventeen, he played for the Kansas City Monarchs before being drafted into the Army. A machine gunner with the combat engineers, he saw action at the Battle of the Bulge. On this date, he became the first black player to appear in an official game at Yankee Stadium. Thompson's trail, in turn, was blazed by Larry Doby, another military veteran—and the first black player in the American League.

"He was kind of like Buzz Aldrin, the second man on the moon, because he was the second African-American player in the majors behind Jackie Robinson," Cleveland Indians teammate Bob Feller said later. "He was just as good of a ballplayer, an exciting player, and a very good teammate." It was a nice thought, but Buzz Aldrin wasn't called the names Doby was, or forced to stay at different hotels than other astronauts, or taunted or threatened. Larry Doby endured all of Jackie Robinson's challenges with little of the support system. Acclaim came late, but it finally came. Doby was put in baseball's Hall of Fame, and in July 2015, the Cleveland Indians unveiled a statue of him at their ballpark. It was long overdue.

July 23, 1904

We All Scream for Ice Cream

Charles E. Menches, a turn-of-the century foodie, insisted until his dying day that on this date he conceived the most all-American of confections. Charles and his brother Frank were operating an ice cream stand at the St. Louis World's Fair when he noticed girls placing ice cream in the holes of small cakes. Inspired, he leaped from his chair and ran to a confectioner's booth. "The result," proclaimed his 1931 obituary, "was a revolution."

Did it really happen that way? The booth Menches raided for the pastry that became the first ice cream cone belonged to Syrian immigrant Ernest A. Hamwi. In Hamwi's telling, the Menches brothers ran out of dishes they were using to serve ice cream, so he helped them by improvising. He fashioned a thin Persian pastry into a conical shape to accommodate ice cream. So Ernest Hamwi was the true inventor of the ice cream cone? He certainly capitalized on it. After the 1904 fair, Hamwi became manager of the Cornucopia Waffle Company in St. Louis and later started the Missouri Cone Company. In 1928, he told his story to an industry publication called *Ice Cream Trade Journal*, which credited his claim.

Hold on there, say the descendants of another immigrant. His name was Italo Marchiony. If Menches and Hamwi created the first ice cream cone in St. Louis in 1904, why was Marchiony, who arrived at Ellis Island from Italy, selling ice cream cones on the streets of New York in 1896? Evidence for his claim comes in the form of a patent for a type of waffle cone issued to Marchiony by the U.S. Patent Office in mid-December 1903, months before the St. Louis World's Fair began. It sounds like a strong case. But others have traced the innovation to an earlier time, and across the Atlantic. In *Mrs. A.B. Marshall's Cookery Book*, the author (an Englishwoman) describes a recipe for a "coronet with cream." That was in 1888. Charles Ranhofer, the iconic chef at Delmonico's, includes specific recipes for such cones in his 1893 best-selling cookbook, *The Epicurean*.

What isn't in dispute is that whoever went first in St. Louis in 1904, by late summer dozens of booths were offering ice cream cones at the World's Fair. History's verdict seems to be that the invention evolved gradually, on at least two continents, by chefs and confectioners operating independently of one another—but that once it was popularized in St. Louis, it caught on everywhere. As for Charles and Frank Menches, there is evidence they understood the tenuous nature of their claim: They hedged their historical bets by also claiming credit for inventing the hamburger sandwich.

July 24, 1984

Exoneration

Former U.S. Marine Kirk Bloodsworth worked a twelve-hour shift unloading freight at a furniture import business in Baltimore County on this date. He then met his wife for drinks at 10:30 p.m. at a nearby saloon. They bickered, so she spent the night at her mother's house. Bloodsworth went home and slept until 10 a.m., hanging around the house until the afternoon when he saw a tragedy unfold on the local news. Nine-year-old Dawn Venice Hamilton had wandered away from the family's apartment complex in an unincorporated area of Baltimore County called Rosedale. Hours later, her lifeless body was found in the nearby woods. She had been battered and sexually violated. Two boys fishing in a local pond told police they'd seen a tall man lead her into the woods. A sketch was drawn up and publicized. An anonymous caller told police it looked like someone named Kirk, which is how Bloodsworth was arrested, put on trial, convicted, and sentenced to death. Except that he hadn't set foot in Rosedale that day.

Although he never encountered Dawn Hamilton in his life, Bloodsworth did meet her killer. In prison, he lifted weights with inmate Kimberly Shay Ruffner, a sexual predator with a long record—who never said a word about the case. Bloodsworth owed his conviction to junk social science, dubious lawyering, a prosecution that hid exculpatory evidence, and two gullible juries. No physical evidence linked him to this crime. His alibi witnesses were disregarded in favor of "eyewitnesses" who didn't come forward until they saw Bloodsworth on television. The first conviction was overturned, but the second trial ended with the same verdict: guilty.

Bloodsworth spent his time in prison studying extensively in hopes of finding some way to prove his innocence. In 1992, after reading an article about how a DNA test had cleared a double-murder suspect in England, he ran through the cellblock screaming for joy. Initially, Maryland authorities claimed the DNA evidence taken from Dawn Hamilton's body had been destroyed. This was as false as the rest of the prosecution's case, and Bloodsworth was freed on June 28, 1993. He'd served nine years in prison, two of them on Death Row, for a crime he hadn't committed. Even then, Maryland was uninterested in finding the real killer. Nine years later, a Baltimore County forensic biologist found stains that had not been analyzed and ran the DNA through a sex offender database. The name it kicked back was Kimberly Ruffner. Reached on the phone by a journalist, Kirk Bloodsworth wept. "It's finally over," he said.

July 25, 1941

Lofty Goals

Henry Ford's politics were complex and controversial and did not lend themselves to the usual liberal-conservative template of American politics—then or now. Yet, when the founder of the Ford Motor Company sat at his desk on this date, the fan letter he wrote was something of a surprise, even to the missive's recipient, Mahatma Mohandas Gandhi.

"Dear Mr. Gandhi," it opened without fanfare. "I want to take this opportunity of sending you a message through Mr. T. A. Raman, to tell you how deeply I admire your life and message. You are one of the greatest men the world has ever known. May God help and guide your lofty work. Sincerely yours, Henry Ford."

Ford was a committed capitalist, but one who raised the pay for workers in his factories to the then-generous sum of $5 a day. He was far less discerning about global politics. For one thing, he was a prolific anti-Semite who blamed everything from World War I to U.S. labor strikes on "the Jew." His ravings appeared in public speeches he made and a newspaper he published, the *Dearborn Independent*. Adolf Hitler was among those who took note. In 1938, the Third Reich gave Ford an award, the Grand Cross of the German Eagle.

Yet, this was a misreading of Henry Ford, too. His pre–World War II isolationism didn't flow out of admiration for Nazism as much as from his pacifist and nonimperialist views. Ford's desire that the United States stay out of Europe's war put him in the mainstream of American political thought. When the Roosevelt administration pressured Detroit to convert to a wartime footing, Ford agreed only reluctantly to build B-24 bombers at his Willow Run plant.

Gandhi's efforts to push the British out of India peacefully struck a chord with Ford. He thought this a better solution than building FDR's "arsenal for democracy"—even though providing that arsenal would profit Ford personally. He hoped that Gandhi's nonviolent revolution would show the world that political change can be accomplished without bombs falling. In an ironic twist, Ford's hopeful letter didn't find its way into the Mahatma's possession for four and a half months. The date it arrived was December 8, 1941, the day after the bombs had fallen at Pearl Harbor.

July 26, 1948

The Do-Something Congress and the Do-Something President

Harry Truman would win the presidency in his own right in a highly partisan 1948 campaign based on a singularly dubious bogeyman: the supposedly "do nothing" Congress. Besides revamping the entire national security apparatus, the Eightieth Congress passed Taft-Hartley, the Presidential Succession Act, the Twenty-Second Amendment— and funded every element of the Truman Doctrine, including the Marshall Plan. If they'd done only the Marshall Plan, it would have been an impressively effective body. "It's astounding the things that Congress accomplished," congressional scholar Michael Robinson once observed. "It's a complete crock to call it a 'Do-Nothing' Congress. And Truman knew it."

Truman also knew that reorganizing the nation's defense apparatus left in place a festering injustice. He and most Americans had been appalled by reports of racially motivated beatings and killings of black World War II veterans in the South, most notably a shocking mass lynching in Georgia. The victims in that horrific quadruple murder orchestrated by the Ku Klux Klan included George W. Dorsey, a veteran of the war in the Pacific, murdered along with his pregnant wife. Truman ordered the FBI to investigate and backed anti-lynching legislation that was killed by Southern Democrats. What this episode made clear was that by 1948, the Democratic Party could no longer gloss over its differences on race.

"The time is now arrived in America," thundered Minnesota firebrand Hubert Humphrey at the party's Philadelphia convention, "for the Democratic Party to get out of the shadow of states' rights and walk forthrightly into the bright sunshine of human rights!"

Half the delegates from Alabama and the entire all-white Mississippi delegation walked out of the convention hall on the last day while delegates from across the South threw their support to Georgia senator Richard Russell in protest. Harry Truman's response came less than two weeks later, on this date, when he issued a simple, 405-word executive order ending segregation in the U.S. armed forces. This was the final straw for the Dixiecrats. They formed the States Rights Party and ran South Carolina's Strom Thurmond for president.

Thurmond did not cost Democrats the White House, which Truman managed to keep against great odds. In the end, the president once dismissed as "Little Harry" managed something even the sainted Franklin Roosevelt hadn't been willing to try.

July 27, 2004

Rookie of the Year

Barack Obama was only an Illinois state legislator when he was tapped by presidential nominee John Kerry and Democratic Party kingmakers to deliver the keynote address at the 2004 convention in Boston. To say he made the best of his opportunity is a historic understatement. The forty-two-year-old lawmaker from Illinois wasn't an unlikely selection solely because he was the son of a white woman from Kansas and a black man from Kenya—a true African-American—or even because of his unorthodox-sounding full name: Barack Hussein Obama. The most unlikely factor was that he had accomplished so little in politics.

He'd lost his only race for Congress, and was a U.S. Senate candidate when given the honor of speaking for his political party. He'd not been a governor, either, or a member of the U.S. military. He'd never run a company, or even been a mayor. But the Kerry campaign found him exceedingly charismatic, liked his personal story, and thought he had an important message to impart. They weren't wrong.

Whatever one thinks of race relations in this country now—or however one assesses his presidency—State Sen. Barack Obama struck a chord in the American psyche that night, and not only with loyal Democrats. "Even as we speak, there are those who are preparing to divide us, the spin masters and negative ad peddlers who embrace the politics of anything goes," he told the delegates, and a huge national television audience. "Well, I say to them tonight, there's not a liberal America and a conservative America; there's the United States of America."

He continued: "There's not a black America and white America and Latino America and Asian America; there's the United States of America. The pundits like to slice and dice our country into red states and blue states: red states for Republicans, blue states for Democrats. But I've got news for them, too. We worship an awesome God in the blue states, and we don't like federal agents poking around our libraries in the red states.

"We coach Little League in the blue states and, yes, we've got some gay friends in the red states. There are patriots who opposed the war in Iraq, and there are patriots who supported the war in Iraq. We are one people, all of us pledging allegiance to the Stars and Stripes, all of us defending the United States of America."

July 28, 1945

Secret Mission

Veteran naval officer Charles Butler McVay III stood on the bridge of the USS *Indianapolis* as it eased out of the harbor in Guam on this date and headed east into the vast, open water of the Pacific Ocean. McVay's ship was a 610-foot Portland-class heavy cruiser weighing 9,800 tons. Commissioned at Philadelphia Navy Yard in 1932, the *Indianapolis* was a favorite of Franklin D. Roosevelt. The president had chosen it as his "ship of state"—a kind of prewar version of Air Force One—on several trips.

In 1941, the *Indianapolis* was moved, along with much of the U.S. Fleet, to Pearl Harbor. But when the Japanese attacked Pearl on December 7, the "*Indy*" had just arrived at Johnson Island, seven hundred miles southwest of Hawaii, for exercises. When word reached the ship of the attack, all extraneous weight was burned or thrown overboard so the *Indy* could race back to Honolulu. Among the ballast jettisoned that day was President Roosevelt's ornate bedroom suite. In the next four years, the ship and its crew saw action in some of the Pacific theater's most decisive battles. At Okinawa, she took a hit from a kamikaze. Nine sailors were killed and twenty-six wounded, but the ship steamed back to California under its own power for repairs.

It was there, in July 1945, that Captain McVay was informed that he had ninety-six hours to get his crew together for a top-secret assignment. Initially, he wasn't even told where they were going, or why. The "where" turned out to be, after a refueling stop in Hawaii, the U.S. Army's B-29 base at Tinian Island in the Marianas. This was a distance of 5,300 nautical miles, and the *Indy* was asked to cover it in ten days. She was one of the fastest ships in the U.S. Navy, and under McVay's guidance, she and the crew of 1,196 made it in time. The "why" turned out to be the cargo loaded amid great secrecy. It included a fifteen-foot-long crate and two small, heavy lead-lined containers. Painted black, the containers were only eighteen inches by eighteen inches but weighed more than two hundred pounds. The crate contained a firing mechanism for a secret bomb code-named "Little Boy." The black containers held the uranium-235 that made "Little Boy" the most devastating weapon the world had ever seen.

The combination of those components would produce a cataclysmic explosion over Hiroshima that would bring World War II to an end. Although that event was only three weeks in the future, few of the men aboard the USS *Indianapolis* would live to see it.

July 29, 1945

Indy Maru

Leaving the Marianas on a course for Leyte Gulf in the Philippines, the USS *Indianapolis* was scheduled to rendezvous with the USS *Idaho*. Capt. Charles B. McVay III was informed that he would be traveling 1,300 miles without the destroyer escort he requested. A heavy cruiser, the *"Indy Maru"*—as her crew called her, per Japanese custom—was not equipped with sonar and didn't carry depth charges. This was the job of the destroyer crews—submarine hunters—who would drop fifty-five-gallon drums loaded with explosives overboard when they spotted subs. At Guam, Lt. Joseph Waldron, the routing officer, inquired when the next convoy was heading to Leyte. No ships were available, he was told: the *Indy* would make the trip unescorted. McVay took this news in stride, which was his way.

A movie-star-handsome Naval Academy grad and the son of a revered admiral, he trusted the U.S. Navy to give him the best equipment, men, and information at its disposal.

"We are going to Leyte," he told his officers, "to prepare for the invasion of Kyushu."

Kyushu was one of the Japanese home islands. What their captain was telling them was that the *Indy Maru* was still in the thick of the fight. This was truer than anyone aboard that ship could know. Setting course for the Philippine Sea, they were making seventeen knots through seas with swells that ranged from four to six feet high. The sailors did chores and pulled their duty. When not working, they played cards, read magazines, talked to the ship's chaplain, and wrote letters home. The sun set very late, and before midnight on this date there was a shift change. One sailor, Edgar Harrell, later described his last moments aboard the *Indy Maru*.

"Her large engines, combined with the sound of her wake, droned a familiar lullaby," he recalled. "Tired and homesick, and missing my little brunette back home, I wrapped my blanket around me and curled up on the steel deck hoping for a few hours of rest. After thanking the Lord for His provision and protection thus far, I asked him to watch over my loved ones back in Kentucky. Then, using the arch of my shoe for a pillow, I drifted off to sleep."

At that moment, just after midnight, a Japanese submarine captain, aided by a moon that emerged from the clouds, had the USS *Indianapolis* in his sights. The big ship had literally wandered into his path. Capt. Mochitsura Hashimoto ordered that six torpedoes be loaded into their tubes. The *Indy Maru*, he would testify later, was an easy target.

July 30, 1945

"Abandon Ship!"

The first Japanese torpedo that struck the USS *Indianapolis* hit the starboard bow just below the waterline; the second penetrated the hull closer to midship—each with devastating effect. The first detonated the ship's powder magazine, which had been replenished at Guam. The second one ignited 3,500 gallons of aviation fuel. The ship's diesel gasoline tanks ruptured, sending oil onto the decks. It caught fire, too. Power was instantly lost, leaving Capt. Charles McVay III unable to communicate with the engine room. A hurried distress signal was broadcast, but could not be followed up. Men with their clothes in flames rushed above decks. Some of those below were trapped in a fiery furnace when sailors trying to prevent the ship from sinking began sealing hatches.

There was no saving the storied ship that had been one of Franklin D. Roosevelt's favorite cruisers in the U.S. Navy. But what about the crew? When the USS *Indianapolis* sank twelve minutes after being torpedoed, one-fourth of the sailors and U.S. Marines aboard were already dead or dying. This still left some nine hundred men alive in the water.

"Suddenly the ship was gone and it was very quiet," Dr. Lewis Haynes, the ship's chief medical officer, recalled later. "We started to gather together. Being in the water wasn't an unpleasant experience except that the black fuel oil got in your nose and eyes. Soon everyone had swallowed fuel oil and gotten sick."

The heat that day had been stifling, but the ocean, they discovered, was cold. The sea was also choppy on this night, and many men had been dumped into the water without life jackets. The macabre task of removing life vests from the dead and giving them to the living began. It was only five hours until dawn, though, and the men figured they could hang on until the Navy sent ships and planes to rescue them.

What the survivors did not know was that the appalling series of miscommunications that had put them in harm's way in the first place was about to be reprised: Nine hundred American fighting men had been thrown into the water to fight off dehydration, hypothermia, drowning, starvation, and feeding sharks—and no one was even looking for them.

July 31, 1945

Jaws

Filmmaking has changed since 1975. The absurdly large and mechanical-looking great white shark in the movie *Jaws* now looks campy instead of terrifying. But one scene remains as chilling as when it was filmed. It comes when Quint, the salty captain played by Robert Shaw, recounts being thrown overboard from the USS *Indianapolis* in 1945 and contending with predatory sharks for the better part of five days.

It is not known how many of the sailors and U.S. Marines from the *Indianapolis* were eaten by sharks. On this date, many had already died from drowning, exposure, thirst, or saltwater poisoning, while others were starting to go mad. Some were drowned by their own water-logged life vests. Yet the first rescuer on the scene, Lt. Adrian Marks, arrived in a sea plane, and saw men being attacked by sharks, probably an aggressive species known as oceanic whitetips. Marks deemed the situation so dire that he disregarded standing orders and landed his seaplane on the open ocean. He rescued fifty-six men, strapping some of them to his wings, and alerted a nearby destroyer, the USS *Cecil J. Doyle*, which was captained by future Amtrak president W. Graham Claytor. When the *Doyle* arrived hours later, it shined a beacon into the darkness to aid survivors. Other ships and planes converged on the spot by morning.

Help was only on the scene at all because another pilot, Lt. Wilbur Gwinn, was testing a new antenna in his twin-engine Ventura patrol bomber. Flying at three thousand feet, the new piece of equipment came loose, and Gwinn crawled back in the plane to tighten it. Looking down through the tail-gunner's window, he saw an oil slick below. Crawling back to the cockpit, Gwinn took his plane down to nine hundred feet. The slick was twenty-five miles long, so it wasn't new. Men were bobbing in the waves. He didn't think they were Japanese, but his preflight briefing mentioned nothing about a missing U.S. Navy vessel. Taking his plane even lower, he counted thirty men in the water, and radioed to the closest base at Palau Island. At Palau they were skeptical, telling him no ships had been reported lost. By then, however, the pilot could see that the men were Americans. He dropped rafts and life jackets and radioed the position.

Of the original crew of 1,196 souls aboard when the *Indy* was attacked, only 318 men would be pulled from the ocean. One of them was its captain, Charles Butler McVay III, who was about to discover that sharks come in various forms.

August 1, 1945

Scapegoat

The USS *Indianapolis* never arrived for its rendezvous with the USS *Idaho*. It seems inexplicable that a Navy ship of war with 1,200 men aboard could go missing for five days and no one would wonder why. But on this date the "Big Spud," as the *Idaho* was called, performed its training exercises alone. When they learned that the Navy had ignored an intercept message from a Japanese sub reporting the sinking of a large vessel, its crew wondered why no one in the Navy had checked on either of the two ships that fit the sub commander's description.

But someone had to pay for a disaster of this magnitude, and on December 3, 1945, Capt. Charles McVay went on trial on charges of failing to give an order to abandon ship and failure to zigzag as a maneuver to avoid enemy torpedoes. Legendary admiral Chester Nimitz scoffed at the idea of court-martialing a captain on those grounds, but he was overruled by Navy Secretary James Forrestal and Chief of Naval Operations Ernest King. McVay was informed of the charges after proceedings had started, was denied his choice of attorney, and was given a lawyer who lacked trial experience. Even then, the evidence didn't support a conviction. A U.S. submarine captain testified that he could easily sink a zigzagging ship. Mochitsura Hashimoto, the Japanese submariner who sank the *Indianapolis*, gave similar testimony. McVay was convicted anyway.

Nimitz later set aside the sentence and promoted McVay to rear admiral upon his retirement. But why was his career ruined at all? In World War II, 350 U.S. Navy ships sank. McVay was the only skipper court-martialed. One theory is that the officers who engineered the court-martial were covering up their own mistakes. McVay had asked for, and been denied, a destroyer escort. He was told of a low probability of running into a Japanese submarine even though the Navy knew an enemy sub was in the area because the Japanese code had been broken. But this was a closely held secret. Too closely, for the good of the *Indianapolis* and its crew.

Moreover, the *Indy*'s entire mission had been so top secret that normal protocols were not followed. There were breakdowns after she was torpedoed, too. The *Indy* managed to send out a distress signal before it sank, but this SOS had been inexplicably ignored by three other U.S. vessels. There was plenty of basis for pointing fingers of blame—just not at Capt. McVay.

Yet every Christmas from 1945 until the end of his life, McVay would receive hate mail from a small group of relatives of men who hadn't survived the *Indy*'s sinking. They subscribed to the mythology that a captain who doesn't go down with his ship is a coward. As William J. Toti, the captain of a U.S. submarine named after the *Indianapolis* later noted, this is absurd. A skipper who goes down with his ship after he's done all he can do to secure it or help others is committing suicide, not following protocol.

The *Indy*'s survivors certainly understood this. For years, however, they didn't talk about what they'd been through, even to their families. This began to change in 1958 with the publication of a book titled *Abandon Ship!* The *Indy*'s crew began talking about what they'd endured, and a reunion was organized in 1960. Urged by his wife to attend, McVay showed up and was asked to speak. He told the surviving crewmen he would always consider himself "Captain McVay of the *Indianapolis*." A former crewman, Joe Kiselica of Hartford, Connecticut, approached him. "Skipper, if the war had continued, all of us would have been proud to serve under you again," he said. "Not one of us ever blamed you for a second."

But this was not a story that could have a happy ending. Eight years later, dressed in his Navy uniform, clutching the tiny toy sailor given to him by his father that he always carried for good luck—and had carried the night his ship went down—Charles McVay took his own life.

His men never stopped trying to clear their captain's name. Years later, they found an unlikely advocate in twelve-year-old Hunter Scott of Pensacola, Florida. Watching Quint's famous soliloquy in the movie *Jaws* inspired him to learn about the disaster. What began as a sixth grader's class project evolved into a crusade to clear McVay's name. The boy found allies among the surviving crew and a local congressman named Joe Scarborough. Almost everyone in Congress who looked at the case came to the same conclusion as the *Indy*'s biographers: that McVay was railroaded. McVay's supporters included his old foe, submarine captain Hashimoto, who sent a letter to Senate Armed Forces Chairman John Warner.

"Our peoples have forgiven each other for that terrible war," Hashimoto wrote. "Perhaps it is time your people forgave Captain McVay for the humiliation of his unjust conviction."

A resolution doing just that was passed by Congress and signed by President Clinton in October 2000. For his part, Hunter Scott was so impressed by the *Indianapolis* survivors he interviewed that he enlisted after college, becoming a Navy pilot. By then, he'd carried Charles McVay's dog tags as a talisman, as he explained while testifying to Congress.

"I carry this dog tag," said young Mr. Scott, "to remind me that only in the United States can one person make a difference no matter what the age."

Change of Heart

Michigan Democratic representative John Conyers and the Congressional Black Caucus hoped to mark the fifteenth anniversary of Martin Luther King's assassination by passing legislation Conyers had faithfully introduced in each session of Congress since 1968: creating a federal holiday on King's birthday. But congressional Republicans in the era of Ronald Reagan wanted to shrink government, and giving federal workers another vacation day didn't feel right.

House Democrats were dismayed, in particular, by the resistance of Republicans they expected to see the bigger picture. These included Jack Kemp, who loathed racism and who spoke against it in public and private; Dan Lungren, a California conservative who fully understood the symbolism of honoring the most revered civil rights activist since Frederick Douglass; and Newt Gingrich, who wanted to expand his party's demographic reach.

After voting against Conyers's bill, Lungren told his wife he felt he'd made a mistake. She advised him to rectify it. Lungren shared these feelings with Kemp, who was having misgivings of his own. Kemp had played professional football for a dozen years and formed friendships with African-American teammates that superseded politics. Kemp heard from these pals, who were dismayed by his opposition. Both men confided in Gingrich, who suggested they all go see Conyers. They asked the Michigan Democrat how they could help him pass his bill. Conyers's advice was basic: Speak in favor of it on the House floor. On this date, they did.

"I have changed my position on this vote," Kemp said flatly. Both Kemp and Lungren told their colleagues that King hadn't just liberated black Americans, he'd liberated *all* Americans. Whites, because of the binding nature of their thinking, had been liberated most of all. The tide was turned. House Speaker Tip O'Neill personally called for the yeas and nays, and Conyers's legislation sailed through on a vote of 338–90. In the Senate, a majority of Republicans joined a solid bloc of Democrats, and the bill went to the White House, where President Reagan signed it into law on November 2, 1983.

"Dr. King had awakened something strong and true, a sense that true justice must be color-blind," Reagan said at the signing ceremony. The president quoted King, who, when speaking about white Americans, had said, "Their destiny is tied up with our destiny, and their freedom is inextricably bound to our freedom. We cannot walk alone."

August 3, 1914

The Road to Public Life

For two days, the U.S. embassy in London found itself swamped with frightened American expats. World War I had erupted two days earlier, plunging Europe into war, and the U.S. ambassador and his staff were utterly overwhelmed. For help, they turned to an American mining executive with proven organizational skills.

The ambassador was a North Carolina–born and Duke University–educated former newspaperman and New York publishing executive named Walter Page. The businessman was Stanford-trained mining engineer Herbert Hoover. Ambassador Page inquired whether Hoover would help him get these people home safely. This simple request would change world history.

When "the Guns of August" erupted on August 1, 1914, Herbert Hoover was nine days away from his fortieth birthday and living in England. Hoover had started a worldwide mining concern with offices in London, the city where his wife, Lou, bore two sons whom she "registered," in the nomenclature of the day, as American citizens.

When Ambassador Page asked for his help, Hoover reacted in a way that would become the pattern of his life. It was how he'd respond when Democratic president Woodrow Wilson asked him to coordinate famine relief in the middle of World War I, when the Republican Party asked him to run for president in 1928, when Harry Truman asked him to reprise his relief-czar duties in the aftermath of World War II. Each time, he answered his country's call.

It's tempting to contemplate what Hoover's reputation would be today if he'd never acceded to this middle request—if he and Lou had never lived in the White House. But this much is a matter of historical record: Forty thousand Americans were stranded in Great Britain in 1914. Many of them had fled the Continent, lacking lodging and even luggage, let alone a way to get home.

In response, Hoover tapped nine of his business partners. Morphing instantly from titans of industry to Good Samaritans, these ten gentlemen pooled their resources and assembled some five hundred volunteers at London's Savoy Hotel. There, they dispensed everything from clothing and cash to tickets aboard steamships bound for New York, receiving vouchers in return—promises of future payment.

"I did not realize it at the moment, but on August 3, 1914, my engineering career was forever over," Hoover wrote later. "I was on the slippery road of public life."

August 4, 1905

Attorney Grant

Eddie Leslie Grant made his Major League debut on this date, collecting three hits, causing the Cleveland Indians to believe they had a gem. They were right about that, although when Eddie struck out four times the next day, he was released. Back in the majors by 1907, he played four seasons in Philadelphia and three in Cincinnati before going to the New York Giants, managed by the legendary John McGraw. Although Eddie Grant wasn't a great player, he was a selfless one who helped his team win in myriad ways. This was a harbinger. He was also smart.

While his teammates spent their nights on the road in saloons, Eddie attended the opera. They played poker on the train; he smoked a pipe and read books. Some of those volumes were law books. In the 1908–1909 off-season, he was admitted to the Massachusetts bar. Sportswriters at the time, most of whom hadn't gone to college themselves, gave him nicknames such as "Harvard Eddie" or "Attorney Grant."

He retired after the 1915 season and was practicing law in Boston when the United States entered World War I. Eddie enlisted, and was commissioned as a captain in the 307th Infantry Regiment, Seventy-Seventh Division. A year later, Eddie's unit was in France fighting in the Meuse-Argonne Offensive. There, nine companies in Eddie's division advanced too far, and found themselves cut off and surrounded. As it happened, the famed "Lost Battalion" was commanded by Maj. Charles Whittlesey, a friend and law school classmate of Eddie's. But as everyone who knew him noted at the time, Eddie would have gone after the missing Americans no matter who was leading them. He was killed by a German artillery shell on October 5, 1918, two days before what was left of the Lost Battalion was rescued. "When that shell burst and killed that boy," said Whittlesey, "America lost one of the finest types of manhood I have ever known."

This time the sportswriters weren't patronizing. "Eddie Grant has played his last game of baseball," *Baseball Magazine* announced. "But the memory of a brave man and a gallant gentleman will adorn the annals of sport long after the wooden cross has crumbled beneath the winds and ruins of that France he died to save."

Grantland Rice wrote a poem in Captain Grant's memory. In 1921, the Giants erected a monument to him in center field at the Polo Grounds. It can be seen in some of the photographs of Willie Mays's famous catch in the 1954 World Series.

August 5, 1887

Butch and Sundance

It was a minor criminal case against a youthful offender in Crook County, Wyoming. Indicted on three counts of larceny for stealing a saddle, a pistol, and a horse from local ranch hands, nineteen-year-old Harry Longabaugh was sentenced on this date to eighteen months in the local jail. The case was reported in the local newspapers, which dubbed him "Kid Longabaugh."

The Kid emerged from jail as a decidedly unrehabilitated twenty-one-year-old convict who promptly resumed his chosen vocation, which was robbing trains and banks. Soon he joined forces with a lapsed Mormon named Robert Leroy Parker, who called himself Butch Cassidy and who led a criminal band based in a remote mountainous redoubt in the Big Horn Mountains called Hole-in-the-Wall. To complete his transition, the young man needed a new name. "The Kid" part was okay, but Longabaugh was a mouthful. Besides, he now had a criminal record. The solution was obvious: The jail where he'd served time was in a small town called Sundance.

The Hole-in-the-Wall Gang became infamous in the West in the 1890s for their daring train heists and a certain je ne sais quoi. Even as they rode around the West on horseback stealing money at gunpoint—and sometimes blowing up train cars to access the safe—a romantic mythology attached itself to the gang. It was said that Butch and Sundance never killed anyone, which might have been right (but it certainly wasn't true of gang member Harvey Logan, a deadly pistolero who was especially lethal to lawmen trying to arrest him).

By 1969, the gang was forgotten except to Old West historians. That year, Hollywood director George Roy Hill, armed with an inspired script from William Goldman, brought them back to life in a classic western, *Butch Cassidy and the Sundance Kid*, featuring Robert Redford and Paul Newman. Its pacing and cinematography is masterful; the repartee between the two bandits priceless. The story is also fairly accurate, a rarity in Hollywood. This is true even of the scene that seems most hokey—Butch riding a bicycle while "Raindrops Keep Falling on My Head" plays in the background. Apparently, Butch became enamored of the new contraption in Fort Worth, which was where an iconic photo of the Hole-in-the-Wall Gang was taken. As for Sundance, Wyoming, its civic leaders want visitors to know that their village—and not the Utah ski resort / film mecca created by Robert Redford—is the original article. They have a statue of the Kid outside the courthouse, a bronze testament to a teenage horse thief who did his time and rode off into history.

August 6, 1944

D-Day, Part II: Casualties of War

When we count up [those] who perished," Aleksandr Solzhenitsyn once noted, "we forget to multiply them by two, by three." The great Russian writer was talking about the Soviet labor camps, but the principle also applies to those lost on the battlefields of war.

Pauline Elliott of New Castle, Pennsylvania, kept writing to her husband, Frank, after the Normandy invasion fearing—but not knowing—that she was writing to one of the fallen. She wrote for two months, until she received a telegram on this date from the War Department informing her that he'd been killed in action on D-Day. No explanation was offered for the delay. And though Pauline got back the letters she mailed between June 6 and August 6, none of the letters he received, nor any of his personal effects were ever returned.

For the rest of her life, she kept the correspondence in a trunk, occasionally encouraging her daughter, DeRonda, who was three years old when her daddy was killed, to read it. DeRonda couldn't bring herself to do it until 1993, three years after her mother died. When she did, she was overwhelmed, and shared them with others. The letters tell a love story so poignant and a loss so deep that *American Heritage* magazine included them in a fiftieth anniversary piece of the invasion at Normandy. President Clinton read aloud a portion of two of the letters between Frank and Polly during the June 6, 1994, ceremonies at the Norman American Cemetery and Memorial at Colleville-sur-Mer.

DeRonda herself wrote an epilogue to the saga. It confirms Solzhenitsyn's wisdom, while offering a cautionary tale for political leaders who would commit troops to combat before exhausting all other possibilities.

"My mother never remarried, although she had several opportunities to do so," it began. "Heartache and sadness, hard work and worry, punctuated by a few moments of humor in the company of friends and family, characterized the rest of her life. She made the best of her life, but she never could forget her first and lasting love."

"I didn't marry the only man I ever loved, fearing that he, too, would somehow die and leave me and I would go through the same pain my mother did," DeRonda Elliott continued. "I later experienced two unsuccessful marriages. Having never known the affirmation of my father's or any man's love for a sustained period of time as a child, I have always found it difficult to believe that any man could love me.

"We were, all three, casualties of war."

Fighting for Pie

The first major military offensive launched by the United States in the Pacific theater came in the Solomon Islands at a place called Guadalcanal. Occupying it meant rooting out an entrenched and determined foe from a ninety-mile-long island. The First U.S. Marine Division landed on the beaches on this date, with two Army divisions reinforcing them. By the time the enemy evacuated the last of their surviving troops in February, the Americans had suffered 1,592 killed in action, with 4,183 wounded and thousands of other troops disabled for a time by disease. Japanese losses were stunning—fifteen times that many dead.

A buoyed Franklin Roosevelt, speaking to the White House Correspondents' Association, extolled the bravery and skill of the American fighting man, whom he said would tell anyone who asked that they were "fighting for freedom." FDR was the twentieth century's most eloquent U.S. president. But the Marines on Guadalcanal were even more so. Embedded *Life* magazine correspondent John Hersey was accompanying a detachment of Marines gathered in a jungle clearing, when he put the very question FDR had referenced to them: What are you fighting for?

After a long silence, one of them muttered, "Jesus, what I'd give for a piece of blueberry pie." Hersey initially believed the man was changing the subject—or making fun of him.

"But of course he was not," Hersey wrote in a brilliant little book, *Into the Valley: Marines at Guadalcanal*. "He was answering my question very specifically." A second Marine quietly added, "Personally, I prefer mince." A third whispered, "Make mine apple with a few raisins in it and lots of cinnamon—you know, Southern-style." Hersey later filled in the scene:

Fighting for pie... is not exactly what they meant. Here, in a place where they had lived for several weeks mostly on captured Japanese rice, then finally had gone on to such delicacies as canned corned beef and Navy beans, where they were usually hungry and never given a treat—here pie was their symbol of home....

For certain men, books are the thing; for others, music; for others, movies. But for all of them, these things are just badges of home. When they say they are fighting for these things, they mean that they are fighting for home—"to get the goddam thing over and get home." Perhaps this sounds selfish....But home seems to most Marines a pretty good thing to be fighting for. Home is where the good things are—the generosity, the good pay, the comforts, the democracy, the pie.

Spies

The men, eight in all, landed by sea, the first team off the coast of Long Island, the second near Jacksonville, Florida. They were the vanguard of Operation Pastorius, personally approved by Hitler, to infiltrate American society and blow up power plants, munitions factories, canals—and even Jewish-owned department stores.

One team leader was thirty-nine-year-old George John Dasch, a veteran of the German Army in World War I who'd emigrated to the United States in 1923 and worked as a waiter. When war broke out in 1939, he returned to Germany because of his mother's entreaties, and regretted it immediately. Dasch had no intention of carrying out the mission, which he confided to Ernest Burger, another member of his team, over dinner in Manhattan. Burger, who'd also lived previously in the United States, replied that he, too, was planning to defect. The pair went to the FBI, which was already looking for them because Dasch had identified himself to a Coast Guard sentry who'd run to get help. After phoning the FBI from a New York telephone booth, Dasch took a train to Washington and checked into the Mayflower Hotel. The two other members of his team were rounded up, as was the second team, which landed in Florida on June 18.

At least two members of that team had also expressed second thoughts. Herbert Haupt, twenty-two years old, the youngest would-be saboteur, had grown up in the United States and had returned to Germany impulsively. He went to his parents' house in Chicago, confessed everything to them, used his sabotage money to buy a new car, and proposed to his girlfriend. He then went to the local FBI office hoping to clear up his draft problems. Another member of the Jacksonville team, Hermann Neubauer, confided the plans to friends of his wife—people he hardly knew—and left the money in their care while frittering away his time at Chicago movie theaters. He was arrested upon returning to his hotel after watching a Saturday night film.

Wanting neither publicity nor the risk of leniency in a civilian court, President Roosevelt convened a special military tribunal behind closed doors. The verdicts were pronounced ten days later. Dasch was sentenced to thirty years in prison and Burger got life. The others, including the hapless young Herbert Haupt, were sentenced to death. There were no appeals. On this date, the six condemned men were strapped to electric chairs in Washington, D.C., executed and buried in a potters' field in Anacostia.

Human Race

The 1936 Olympic Games in Berlin were envisioned in Hitler's twisted mind as a venue to showcase the superiority of the "master race." With the largest contingent of athletes, Germany did win the most medals, but in the glamour events of track and field, the U.S. team led by African-American Jesse Owens refuted the Nazis' sinister racial theories. On this date, Owens led the U.S. 4-by-100 relay team to a victory—Owens's fourth gold medal of the Berlin games.

The only question leading up to the relay was which Americans would race. The U.S. had brought seven sprinters to Berlin, six of whom were world-class. They could have fielded two sprint relay teams and won gold and silver. But politics is not entirely absent from athletics, and in 1930s Germany this meant racial politics. Two of the best U.S. sprinters were Jews. Would U.S. officials allow them to take the track—or kowtow to their hosts?

At the U.S. trials, the top six sprinters were Owens, Ralph Metcalfe, Frank Wykoff, Foy Draper, Sam Stoller, and Marty Glickman, an eighteen-year-old phenom from New York City who played football at Syracuse. Owens and Metcalfe were black, the other four white. Stoller and Glickman were Jewish. Just before the trial heats in Berlin, the U.S. coaches, with only a cursory explanation, sidelined Glickman and Stoller. The coaches said only that they wanted the fastest runners, which was widely disbelieved because Stoller and Glickman were both faster than Drapes.

Nonetheless, the Americans won gold while setting an Olympic record that would last twenty years. (The Germans got bronze.) It would have been nice to have Glickman there, but the result was hard to argue. Besides, the events of the ensuing years would put athletics in perspective. Jesse Owens retired and struggled in business before finding his niche as a kind of unofficial goodwill ambassador for track and field. He tried, unsuccessfully, to persuade Jimmy Carter not to boycott the 1980 Olympic Games. Ralph Metcalfe earned a master's degree at the University of Southern California, served in World War II, went into Chicago politics, was elected to Congress, and cofounded the Congressional Black Caucus. Frank Wykoff also earned a master's degree and became an educator. Stoller returned to the University of Michigan to run track. No longer in Jesse Owens's shadow, he won the collegiate championship in 1937. Although only a teenager, Glickman would never get to run in the Olympics. The 1940 games, scheduled for Tokyo, and the London games of 1944 were canceled. He remained bitter about Berlin a long time, but after Syracuse, he had careers in both professional football and basketball, and went on to become a Hall of Fame sports broadcaster in New York. He lived to be eighty-three, dying in 2001. Three years earlier, the U.S. Olympic Committee tried to atone by awarding the USOC's first General Douglas MacArthur Award to Glickman and, posthumously, to Stoller. "We regret this injustice," said USOC Chairman William Hybl.

The greater injustice was meted out to Foy Draper. On January 4, 1943, the former Olympian, now a captain in the U.S. Army Air Force, was piloting his bomber over North Africa when his plane went down, presumably by enemy fire. He was only thirty-two. There was one more track athlete in this drama, and he didn't survive the war, either. No sprinter was going to defeat Jesse Owens in Berlin, but one athlete had a chance of upending the American in the long jump. He was a German named Carl Ludwig Long, known throughout Europe as Luz Long.

A twenty-three-year-old lawyer from Hamburg, Long fit the ideal of the early amateur athlete of the twentieth century. Tall, blond, and handsome, he also fit the Aryan stereotype peddled by the Nazis. But in a story often told by Owens himself, it was Long who gave his American challenger invaluable counsel. In the preliminary rounds of the long jump, Owens fouled on his first two attempts. With one jump remaining, Long suggested that Owens aim for a takeoff point several inches before the board. Trusting in his talent, Owens followed the advice and qualified for the final round, where he won the gold, relegating Long to silver.

"It took a lot of courage for him to befriend me in front of Hitler," Owens said later.

Although Owens told the story for years, including to Luz's son Kai Long, doubts arose over time about the details. Grantland Rice trained his binoculars on Owens during qualifying and never saw him speak to Long. When historian Tom Ecker asked Owens in 1965 about the discrepancy, Owens conceded that he didn't meet Long until the competition ended. But if the sequence in Owens's story wasn't right, Long's bravery was not apocryphal. After the long jump finals, he embraced Owens in front of Hitler, which took courage. And they did become friends, the kind who exchange letters for years, even after one of them joins the army and goes to war. The kind of friend who finds your son after you are killed to tell him what a good man you were. Luz Long died in Sicily while wearing the uniform of his country.

In his final letter to Owens, Luz Long anticipated that he might not return from the front, and made a request of his American friend. "Someday find my son," he wrote, and "tell him about how things can be between men on this Earth."

August 10, 1846
Diffusion of Knowledge

By birth, James Smithson was officially French, having come into this world in 1765, in Paris, with the Franco-sounding handle of Jacques-Louis Macie. This was a bit of a ruse, as his parents were British. Naturally, there was a story there: His mother, Elizabeth Hungerford Keate Macie, was not married to his father, Hugh Smithson, the first Duke of Northumberland. It seems that when Miss Macie became "in the family way," she was sent away to avoid scandal.

The young man and his mother would arrive at other ideas, however. By the time he was ten years old, the boy was officially registered as a British citizen. And by the time his father died, when he was nineteen, the lad was using the name James Smithson. By then, he was enrolled at Pembroke College, Oxford, where he concentrated on the natural sciences, including the burgeoning field of chemistry. He must have been an impressive scholar: London's prestigious scientific academy, the Royal Society, accepted him as a member in 1787, only a year after he graduated from college.

Orphaned at a young age, Smithson came into an impressive inheritance: $20 million in today's dollars. He never married or had children of his own—or, interestingly, as events panned out—ever set foot on American soil. In 1826, when Smithson drew up his will, he left his entire fortune to a nephew: Henry James Hungerford. One caveat was attached to this bequest: If young Mr. Hungerford also died without a direct heir, all of Smithson's money was to go to "the United States of America, to found at Washington, under the name of the Smithsonian Institution, an establishment for the increase and diffusion of knowledge."

Three years later, while in Genoa, Italy, James Smithson died at age sixty-four. Six years later, his nephew died, fortuitously without having married or having had children. Smithson's fortune came to the United States, most of it in the form of gold, albeit not without some high-level legal wrangling between lawyers on both sides of the Atlantic. That's how it happened that, on this date, President James K. Polk signed the Smithsonian Institution Act into law.

The Duke

Katie Ledecky became so athletically dominant in the pool during the early twenty-first century that the only meaningful yardstick was historical comparisons—to famous male swimmers. In a story titled "Somebody Get Katie Ledecky a Time Machine," Benjamin Morris of FiveThirtyEight noted that at thirteen, Ledecky swam the 100-meter faster than Hawaiian legend Duke Kahanamoku when he set a world-record time in 1920 at age thirty. This is true, but it hardly does justice to the person who may be the most impressive waterborne human being in history. For starters, Duke also set a world record on this date, when he was twenty, in Honolulu Harbor—in a time so fast that mainland swimming organizations wouldn't recognize it for years.

Kahanamoku didn't care. He'd won gold and silver medals at the 1912 Olympics in Stockholm and was internationally famous. World War I canceled the 1912 Games, when Kahanamoku was at his peak, but he came back in the 1920 Olympics, again winning gold in the 100-meter freestyle and anchoring the gold-winning U.S. 800-meter relay team. Four years later, while in his midthirties, he finished second in a storied U.S. sweep in the 100-meter freestyle at the 1924 games. Johnny Weissmuller won gold, Duke won silver, and his younger brother, Samuel Kahanamoku, won bronze. Duke's Olympic career ended in the 1932 Los Angeles games as a forty-two-year-old alternate on the U.S. water polo team.

During those years, he reintroduced the world to an ancient sport. Surfing—or "wave sliding"—had been the provenance of Hawaiian royalty. Riding a sixteen-foot longboard that weighed one hundred pounds, Duke showed the world that the big waves were accessible to anyone with the guts and skill to ride them. Known as "the father of surfing," he was the first person inducted into both the International Swimming Hall of Fame and the Surfers' Hall of Fame.

In 1925, as he and two pals eyed the surf break at Newport Beach, a sudden storm capsized a forty-foot yacht with seventeen people aboard. Braving

huge waves on his twelve-foot mahogany board, Kahanamoku rescued eight of them in three trips, while his companions saved four. The five men they were unable to reach all drowned. Duke made several movies in Hollywood, usually playing a Polynesian chief, before returning to Hawaii where he was elected to several terms as sheriff in Honolulu, first as a Democrat and later as a Republican. In 1966, as the "Ambassador of Aloha," he taught Elizabeth, Queen Mother of England, how to do the hula. Katie Ledecky, call your agent.

August 12, 1939

Munchkins

For decades, it was Hollywood practice to prescreen high-budget motion pictures in small markets to see how Middle America responded to films that were in any way unorthodox. With its flying monkeys, melting witches, talking scarecrows, and other marvels, *The Wizard of Oz* certainly fit that description.

As early as 1902, L. Frank Baum's story had been made into a Broadway musical, but bringing it to the big screen cost MGM a cool $2 million—a fortune in 1939—and the studio executives were nervous. Sneak previews were held on August 11, 1939, in three locations and, on this date, it premiered at the Strand Theater in Oconomowoc, Wisconsin.

As luck would have it, Oconomowoc is only a twenty-mile drive down Wisconsin State Route 16 from Watertown, the home town of Meinhardt Raabe. In 1939, Raabe was a diminutive twenty-three-year-old pitchman for Oscar Mayer. Although he kept growing until he was in his thirties, he never surpassed four foot seven, and in 1939 he was something less than that.

He always knew he was small, with no idea why. Growing up in Watertown, he wrote later, he never so much as heard the words *dwarf* or *midget* and assumed there was no one else in the world like him. At eighteen, though, Raabe attended the Chicago World's Fair, where he encountered "Midget Village"—and an entire tableau of little people of all ages.

He took a job as a barker there the next summer, received a bachelor's degree from the University of Wisconsin, got his pilot license, and began scaling any barrier put in his way. Two years after graduating, he heard Hollywood was casting a slew of little people in a new film. He got a leave of absence from his job and hopped on a train to Los Angeles, where he landed a role in the picture playing the part of the Munchkins' coroner in *The Wizard of Oz.*

Meinhardt Raabe would live a long life and do many things, including marry, serve as a wartime aviator in the Civil Air Patrol, and go on tour as Oscar Mayer's "World's Smallest Chef." But it was thirteen seconds of uncredited airtime that made him a star, as he sang a memorable verse of "Ding Dong, the Witch Is Dead," the Munchkins' iconic number:

As coroner, I must aver
I thoroughly examined her.
And she's not only merely dead,
She's really most sincerely dead.

August 13, 1974

Follow the Dialogue

William Goldman was drafted into the U.S. Army after graduating from Oberlin College in 1952. He wanted to be a writer, so he learned to type. Because he could type, the Army made him a clerk instead of an infantryman. It wasn't Goldman's idea to pair Paul Newman and Robert Redford in *Butch Cassidy and the Sundance Kid*, but it was his script that contained one memorable line after another, including Paul Newman asking, "Who *are* those guys?"

Few people think about who wrote the script (or the novel it's based on) while quoting such lines—or when reciting dialogue from *Butch Cassidy and the Sundance Kid* or *The Princess Bride*, which Goldman also wrote, or any of their favorite movies. They think of the star, not the writer, as Goldman acknowledged himself.

"Nobody cares about who the screenwriter is," he once said. "That's one of the things you have to deal with if you write a screenplay. Nobody has the least knowledge of what's going to work, and everybody wants Tom Cruise."

This theme informs a nonfiction book Goldman wrote about Hollywood, *Adventures in the Screen Trade*, in which he famously said, "Nobody knows anything." This is truer than Goldman intended. When Bob Woodward's mysterious Watergate-era source was finally identified in 2005, much of the media reported that "Deep Throat"—former FBI official Mark Felt—had coined the Watergate-era mantra "Follow the money."

Deep Throat actually said no such thing and neither Woodward nor Carl Bernstein ever quoted him to that effect in the *Washington Post* or in *All the President's Men*, their best-selling account of the Watergate saga.

"Follow the money" appeared for the first time in the movie version of *All the President's Men*. The line was uttered by Hal Holbrook, who plays Deep Throat—but it was crafted by the screenwriter, William Goldman, who submitted the first draft of his script to Warner Brothers on this date.

August 14, 1834

Dana's Point

On this warm New England summer day, a bored Bostonian named Richard Henry Dana left home and hearth to sail the seas. Life aboard the eighty-six-foot brig *Pilgrim* was unlike anything this nineteen-year-old upper-class Brahmin had ever experienced. If you failed an exam at Harvard, where Dana had been studying before he followed his whim, you would not be flogged by a sadistic professor. The captain of the *Pilgrim* meted out this punishment, and others, to crewmen regularly, even to those who'd done nothing wrong. It was enough to send young Dana back to school. He returned to Cambridge in 1836 and reenrolled at Harvard, where he earned a law degree. But he never forgot his adventures on the high seas.

The result was his best-selling book and an American classic, *Two Years Before the Mast*.

After becoming an attorney, Richard Dana gravitated to the specialty that he knew firsthand: maritime law. He defended sailors in court and wrote another acclaimed book, *The Seaman's Friend*, which detailed the rights and responsibilities of ships' captains and crewmen. Later, he became an activist in the abolition movement. During the Civil War, Dana issued a legal opinion stating that it was legal for Union forces to blockade Southern ports, a proposition he argued successfully all the way to the Supreme Court. Before the war, Richard Dana was treated in the East as a California expert. To modern ears, his observations sound, let us say, patronizing.

"The Californians are an idle, thriftless people, and can make nothing for themselves," he wrote. "The country abounds in grapes, yet they buy bad wines made in Boston and brought round by us, at an immense price, and retail it among themselves by the small wine-glass."

As a futurist, Dana was no Thomas Jefferson. He didn't foresee the wine country of Napa or Sonoma, let alone the Silicon Valley hub of invention that has become the world's economic engine. He was at his best, however, when describing California's physical beauty. Here is his 1835 description of a scenic beach located in present-day Orange County:

There was a grandeur in everything around, which gave almost a solemnity to the scene: a silence and solitariness which affected everything! Not a human being but ourselves for miles; and no sound heard but the pulsations of the great Pacific!

He called that place "the cliffs of San Juan." It is now, fittingly, named Dana Point.

August 15, 1935

American Sage

Will Rogers helped Americans cope with the Great Depression when suddenly, in the midst of it, he was gone. On this date, Rogers and famous test pilot Wiley Post died in a plane crash in Alaska. Both houses of Congress suspended deliberations, notwithstanding the fact that Congress was a perennial target of Rogers's celebrated wit.

William Penn Adair Rogers was born in 1879 on an Oklahoma ranch. The youngest of eight children, he was part Cherokee and all cowboy. (Regarding his Native American roots, he liked to say, "My ancestors didn't come over on the *Mayflower*, but they met the boat.")

A rodeo rider and trick roper, he performed in "Wild West" shows that eventually led him to Hollywood—and into the hearts of his countrymen. It's hard today to overstate the following he had, particularly among working-class Americans. Although openly a Democrat, Rogers was the kind of man who was friendly with both Calvin Coolidge and Franklin Roosevelt. His most famous line was true to this spirit: he quipped that his tombstone should read, "I joked about every prominent man in my lifetime, but I never met one I didn't like."

Beginning in 1926, Will Rogers's "daily telegrams" were published in newspapers, under the headline WILL ROGERS SAYS. They were short and pithy, more like a blog post than a full-blown column, laconic observations invariably informed by a bedrock optimism. In his last missive, dispatched from Alaska on August 15, 1935, Rogers expressed gentle skepticism of a dubious government effort to have agricultural workers grow vegetables near the Arctic Circle. "You know," Rogers wrote, "there is a lot of difference in pioneering for gold and pioneering for spinach." He had hardly given up on the New Deal, but he knew a boondoggle when he saw it.

"The newspapers say: 'Congress is deadlocked and can't act,'" he once said. "I think that is the greatest blessing that could befall this country." Another time he quipped that Americans had come to the point where they "feel the same when Congress is in session as when the baby gets hold of a hammer." Here are three other timeless Will Rogers–isms:

- *"The income tax has made more liars out of the American people than golf has."*
- *"There's no trick to being a humorist when you have the whole government working for you."*
- *"The man with the best job in the country is the vice president. All he has to do is get up every morning and say, 'How's the president?'"*

August 16, 1896

They Built a Fire

The Panic of 1893 had subsided, as had the economic Depression that followed, but the presidential campaign between Republican William McKinley and Democrat William Jennings Bryan turned on esoteric, if passionately held, views on whether U.S. currency should be based on silver or gold. Mother Nature occasionally has a way of winking at human folly. While Bryan preached against gold all over the country, and McKinley tried to seem statesmanlike by sticking close to his Ohio home, three fishing buddies and part-time prospectors noticed something shiny in a place called Rabbit Creek, a tributary of the Klondike River. (For those who take stock in omens, they found gold, not silver, and the gold-standard Republicans did win in November.)

The leader of the Yukon trio was George Washington Carmack, who subscribed to *Scientific American* magazine, stocked his cabin with literature, and played classical music on an organ he'd picked up in his travels. In his downtime, he penned poetry. The California-born Carmack had an affinity for the Tagish people indigenous to the Yukon, marrying into the tribe, and adopting its ways. On his fateful trip, he was accompanied by a brother-in-law, whose birth name was Keish, which means "lone wolf," but who went by Skookum Jim Mason. The third man was Skookum Jim's nephew, rendered to history as Dawson Charlie.

It's unclear which man saw the first nugget or even whether it happened on this date or the next day. But when they staked their claim in the closest mining town, it started a stampede. The following July, when steamers pulled into the harbors in San Francisco and Seattle laden with tons of gold, the fever took hold. Some fifty thousand fortune seekers set out for Alaska. Although the gold wouldn't play out for a hundred years, most of these dreamers found the best claims were taken by early birds or mining companies. Yet, it wasn't a bust even for those who never panned a single nugget from an Alaskan stream. Americans feared entering a new century on a sour note, and the Klondike Gold Rush reminded Americans of their birthright: the possibility of discovery. This often took the form of self-discovery.

Here, George Carmack's literary bent was another omen. In July 1897, San Francisco native Jack London set sail for the Alaska fields. He didn't find gold, but he found his voice, and the Klondike inspired his wildly popular novels, *Call of the Wild* and *White Fang*, and a short story, "To Build a Fire," which became an American classic.

August 17, 1790

To Bigotry, No Sanction

As he began the process of creating an institution—the presidency in a democratic country—George Washington thought it important that he be seen by the people. "George Washington slept here" wasn't a punch line in eighteenth-century America. It was a point of civic pride for communities and innkeepers—and it was often true. In his first year or two in office, President Washington also made it a point of writing back to religious congregations that sent him letters of congratulations. Of necessity, this was an ecumenical exercise: An Episcopalian himself, Washington wrote to Catholic parishes, Methodist churches, and on at least two occasions to Jewish congregations. As civic leaders in Newport, Rhode Island, readied for a presidential visit, the Hebrew Congregation there sent a letter to Washington on this date.

The letter, written by Moses Seixas on behalf of "the children of the stock of Abraham," welcomed the president to the city. It also alluded to past persecutions of Jews around the world and trumpets the new nation's commitment to religious liberty. Seixas was a first-generation American whose parents had emigrated from Portugal. He had risen to prominence in Rhode Island as warden of Newport's Touro Synagogue of Congregation Jeshuat Israel. He was cofounder of the largest bank in Rhode Island, which had recently ratified the U.S. Constitution, the last former British colony to do so.

By way of reply, President Washington echoed Moses Seixas's words, while adding some of his own, a gesture still remembered in the Jewish communities of this country, and by all those who cherish religious liberty.

"It is now no more that toleration is spoken of as if it was the indulgence of one class of people that another enjoyed the exercise of their inherent natural rights," Washington wrote. "For happily, the government of the United States, which gives to bigotry no sanction, to persecution no assistance, requires only that they who live under its protection should [comport] themselves as good citizens."

The two letters were published side by side in Jewish bulletins in the summer of 1790, and in several secular newspapers as well. Reinforced by George Washington, Seixas's original formulation, "To bigotry...no sanction, to persecution no assistance," became the credo—imperfectly implemented, then as now—of a new nation.

August 18, 1980

Noble Causes

Ronald Reagan defended the Vietnam War long after most politicians stopped doing so, both as governor and as a presidential candidate. "There are those who say that Vietnam was a war without heroes because the conflict became a controversy," Reagan said as his governorship and the U.S. effort in Southeast Asia were winding down. "I do not accept that," he added. "They were all heroes, especially those we're honoring today."

Many listeners heard this as boilerplate rhetoric not meant to be taken literally. But Reagan, who had been meeting freed American prisoners of war, chose his words carefully. He was championing the Americans who had gone to fight in Asia's jungles, not the politicians who'd sent them there. As he ran for president in 1976, he fashioned that sentiment into a dependable applause line. "Let us tell those who fought in that war," Reagan would say, "that we will never again ask young men to fight and possibly die in a war our government is afraid to win."

After losing the 1976 GOP nomination to Gerald R. Ford, Reagan was back campaigning four years later. He reprised the line about wars the U.S. was "afraid to win," but, on this date, in a speech to the Veterans of Foreign Wars, Reagan veered from his prepared text when discussing Vietnam. "It is time we recognized that ours, in truth, was a noble cause," he said.

This was not a Reagan ad-lib. The candidate wrote it into his speech in his own hand. It was a formulation with a rich provenance. George Washington used the phrase in a 1776 field order ("It is a noble Cause we are engaged in...") and the vets gave Reagan a standing ovation for it. The phrase had ripple effects, too. It helped get Reagan elected, and restored a measure of pride to many Vietnam veterans. According to author Robert Timberg, it galvanized a generation of grateful Vietnam veterans who'd entered public service and were looking to translate Reagan's words into deeds. Some of those vets, as Timberg noted in his acclaimed book *The Nightingale's Song*, were motivated too highly, resulting in the Iran-contra scandal.

As for Reagan's insistence that the United States shouldn't fight wars it could not or would not win, that was widely embraced, too. In his campaign-trail manifesto, *A Charge to Keep*, Texas governor George W. Bush proclaimed, "We must not go into a conflict unless we go in committed to win." But as Bush learned in the White House—as had presidents before him—that is an easier charge to assert than to keep.

August 19, 1914
Seeking Neutrality

Ellen Wilson, First Lady of the United States, lay dying of kidney failure. And as her grief-stricken husband kept watch by her bedside, Europe descended into madness. Great Britain declared war on Germany. Like chess pieces controlled by demonic forces, the great powers of Europe moved inexorably toward a terrible fate none could foresee. In late June, Archduke Franz Ferdinand, heir to the Austro-Hungarian throne, had been assassinated in the Balkans by Serb nationalists. They killed his wife, too. The world was truly at war. But not the United States. On August 4, 1914, President Wilson issued a statement proclaiming U.S. neutrality. The next day, he issued two executive orders, one of them written from Ellen's room. The first prohibited U.S. radio stations "from transmitting or receiving for delivery messages of an un-neutral nature, and from in any way rendering to any one of the belligerents any un-neutral service, during the continuance of hostilities." In an address on this date, Wilson went further, urging Americans to refrain from speaking, or even thinking, in non-neutral terms about Europe.

"The United States must be neutral in fact as well as in name during these days that are to try men's souls," Wilson implored, invoking Thomas Paine. "We must be impartial in thought as well as in action, must put a curb upon our sentiments as well as upon every transaction that might be construed as a preference of one party to the struggle before another."

This, too, was easier said than done. The *New York Times*' coverage underscored one facet of human nature: True neutrality is difficult. Under a sub-headline, ENGLAND COOL IN GREAT CRISIS, the paper's London correspondent left little doubt about his own sympathies. "England is facing this, the greatest crisis in her history, with calmness and courage," he wrote. "All parties and all classes present a united front.... The peace-at-any price advocates are submerged beneath the huge majority who would have welcomed peace with honor but prefer war to dishonor."

The piece quoted approvingly from the *Westminster Gazette*, a liberal newspaper, which proclaimed, "Here we stand, and we can do no other."

"The Germans will recognize that famous phrase," the *Gazette* added, "and understand that it expresses the feelings of the vast majority of the British people." The historic allusion was to Martin Luther, who is said to have uttered those defiant words when questioned by Charles V about his break from Catholicism. But what both the editors of the *Westminster Gazette* and the *New York Times* had forgotten is what Martin Luther said next, which was "God help me."

Horace Greeley's Pen Pal

An early supporter of Abraham Lincoln, newspaper publisher Horace Greeley launched the *New York Tribune* in 1841 to advance his many causes, including abolition. But on this date, he published a blistering editorial in the form of a letter urging Lincoln to free the slaves in the Confederacy and Border States. Although he'd corresponded privately with Lincoln before, Greeley could not have expected Lincoln to answer his attack, especially considering its condescending and tendentious tone. But Lincoln still maintained his ability to surprise. He penned a reply as concise as Greeley's had been verbose, judicious where Greeley had been intemperate, calculating where Greeley had been emotional. Lincoln opened by saying that he would not respond to the erroneous assertions in Greeley's editorial. Lincoln also acknowledged Greeley's "dictatorial" tone, a transgression the president said he'd "waive" in deference to an old friend "whose heart I have always supposed to be right."

Then Lincoln got to the heart of his argument: The Constitution didn't allow him to eradicate slavery with the stroke of a pen. In an oft-quoted passage used to impugn him a century later by critics with advanced degrees but little common sense, Lincoln said that his "paramount object" was to save the Union—and neither to save nor to destroy slavery. He added his personal desire for people everywhere to "be free." This last sentiment was more than a throwaway line.

Lincoln had already drafted the Emancipation Proclamation and was awaiting a Union battlefield victory before announcing it. In the meantime, he sought to reassure his supporters without driving the Border States into the Confederacy. Lincoln was sending a signal his supporters would understand. They knew, for one thing, that many slaves had gained their freedom by presenting themselves at the gates of U.S. Army forts and encampments.

"The letter was, in effect, a presidential address hidden within a response to an attack, an address that the president could not have made directly, for political reasons," Lincoln scholar Paul Finkelman has written. "Lincoln made clear that emancipation would be his policy."

The whole country was now on notice that Lincoln was saying slavery might have to be destroyed to "save the Union." This was a tactical position, not a moral argument. Nonetheless, it placed the Lincoln administration, the federal government, and the blue-clad Northern fighting men on the same sort of secure high ground that would be seized by Union troops at Gettysburg.

August 21, 1959

Aloha, Senator

Hawaii's inclusion as the fiftieth star on the American flag was a political victory for Dwight Eisenhower, who'd campaigned for Alaska and Hawaii statehood when he ran for president. Alaska, rich in natural resources and a strategic chess piece against the Soviet Union, was an easy sell. Hawaii was tougher, with opposition rooted among Southern senators who feared a dilution of their power. But Hawaii held a special place in the hearts of military men like Ike—and in the hearts of most Americans. It was glamorous and exotic, its people friendly and welcoming. If the Japanese attack on Pearl Harbor was an attack on the United States—as Franklin Roosevelt and everyone else viewed it to be—what was the counterargument to statehood?

At the White House signing ceremony on this date, Ike was his usual understated self. He said only a few words, pronouncing the proceedings "a truly historic occasion," while expressing good wishes for the Aloha State. Many of those present, however, found their eyes wandering from the president to one of the guests, a young man named Daniel K. Inouye, who'd fought in Eisenhower's army in World War II and lost his right arm in battle. Inouye was the representative-elect from the new state, and although he didn't have a speaking part, his presence was a reminder of what the country had been through—and why it had prevailed.

Dan Inouye was a seventeen-year-old high school senior in Honolulu heading to church with his family on the Sunday morning when the Japanese planes, with their famous Rising Sun insignias, came zooming in over his hometown. Because he knew first aid, Inouye was called to the local Red Cross station. He rode his bike there, and didn't leave for five days. It's not too much to say that he spent the next seven decades in service to his country. When the U.S. Army dropped its ban on Japanese-Americans in 1943, Inouye left college and joined the famed all-Nisei 442nd Regimental Combat Team. Later, he recalled his father's reaction:

"My father just looked straight ahead, and I looked straight ahead, and then he cleared his throat and said, 'America has been good to us. It has given me two jobs. It has given you and your sisters and brothers education. We all love this country. Whatever you do, do not dishonor your country. Remember: Never dishonor your family. And if you must give your life, do so with honor.' I knew exactly what he meant. I said, 'Yes, sir. Good-bye.'"

He died on December 17, 2012, as Hawaii's senior senator. His last word was "Aloha."

Hiroshima

Leslie Nakashima was born in the Hawaiian Islands, meaning that he was an American citizen. Like Barack Obama, who went by "Barry" as a boy, Nakashima took an Anglicized name as a kid. His Japanese name of Satoru Nakashima became "Leslie" Nakashima in his byline after he became a newspaper reporter. Friends from both countries simply called him Les.

His family moved back to Japan, and Les followed them. He was working in the Tokyo bureau of United Press when Japan attacked Pearl Harbor. Like many other Americans of Japanese descent, he was stuck there for the remainder of the war. It was known that the bombs dropped on Hiroshima and Nagasaki ended the war, but until Japan surrendered, details of the destruction were not known. Nakashima entered what was left of Hiroshima on this date, sixteen days after the bombing. He had a personal reason to go: He was looking for his mother. Miraculously, he found her. He also filed the first news accounts to a Western audience from the city.

"Alighting from the train I found that Hiroshima Station, which was one of the largest in western Japan, had gone out of existence," he wrote. "I was dumbfounded with the destruction before me. The center of the city immediately to the south and west of the station had been razed to the ground and there was a sweeping view to the foot of the mountains to the southeast and north of the city. In other words, what had been a city of 300,000 population had vanished."

Les Nakashima kept a reporter's composure when describing how he found his mother alive. "She said she was weeding grass in a relative's vegetable field about two miles to the southeast of the city on the morning of August 6, when she saw the flash. She immediately threw herself face down on the ground. She said she heard a terrific explosion and getting up, she saw columns of white smoke rising from all parts of the city high into the sky. She said she then started running to her home as fast as she could because she didn't know what was coming next."

Les Nakashima went back to work at his Tokyo bureau after the war, but he was never allowed to return to the United States, and he remained in Japan until his death in 1990. He gravitated toward sports reporting, with one exception: Every year, he would file a story on the anniversary of Hiroshima. On the fortieth anniversary of the bombing, he ended his piece from the city this way: "Their appeal is simple and sincere: Abolish nuclear weapons. Their slogan reflects that sentiment: 'No more Hiroshimas.'"

Sierra Club

John Muir was a Scottish immigrant and self-taught naturalist who had turned thirty-one the spring he decided to escort a flock of sheep belonging to a man named Patrick Delaney from the foothills of California's Mother Lode country into the High Sierra for the summer. It was Muir's first extended trip into the high country. He took with him a writing journal and a dog, a St. Bernard named Carlo who belonged to a neighbor. Muir was faithful to the dog and to his journal. His notes formed the basis of many magazine articles and was published in book form in 1911. By then, Muir was internationally known for his efforts to preserve Yosemite, which led him to cofound the Sierra Club. The book, *My First Summer in the Sierra*, was dedicated to "The Sierra Club of California, Faithful Defender of the People's Playgrounds."

The passage Muir wrote that opens chapter 10 begins this way:

August 22: Clouds none, cool west wind, slight hoarfrost on the meadows. Carlo is missing; have been seeking him all day. In the thick woods between camp and the river, among tall grass and fallen pines, I discovered a baby fawn. At first it seemed inclined to come to me; but when I tried to catch it...it turned and walked softly away, choosing its steps like a cautious, stealthy, hunting cat.

"I am distressed about Carlo," he continued. "There are several other camps and dogs not many miles from here, and I still hope to find him. He never left me before. Panthers are very rare here, and I don't think any of these cats would dare touch him. He knows bears too well to be caught by them, and as for Indians, they don't want him."

Alarmed readers who feared for Carlo's fate were not kept in suspense long. Here is John Muir's entry for the following day, August 23, 1869:

Cool, bright day, hinting Indian summer. Mr. Delaney has gone to the Smith Ranch, on the Tuolumne below Hetch-Hetchy Valley, thirty-five or forty miles from here, so I'll be alone for a week or more—not really alone, for Carlo has come back. He was at a camp a few miles to the northwestward. He looked sheepish and ashamed when I asked him where he had been and why he had gone away without leave. He is now trying to get me to caress him and show signs of forgiveness. A wondrous wise dog. A great load is off my mind. I could not have left the mountains without him. He seems very glad to get back to me.

Dolley Madison

After helping themselves to the larder, British troops occupying Washington torched the White House on this date. Everything in the mansion, including personal effects belonging to President James Madison and First Lady Dolley Madison, were burned. But not the huge Gilbert Stuart painting of George Washington. That was rescued at the last minute by Mrs. Madison.

The daughter of Quakers who emancipated their slaves, Dolley, a widow in her mid-twenties, had been introduced by family friend Aaron Burr to a diminutive but brilliant and popular Virginia congressman in his forties. "The 'great little Madison' has asked to be brought to see me this evening," she wrote to a friend in anticipation. For his part, James Madison was smitten instantly. Four months later, they would marry, a union that lasted four decades. Dolley is responsible for starting the tradition of the inaugural ball—and she was the first in a long line of First Ladies considered (by the opposition party) to be overly involved in politics.

"I was beaten by Mr. and Mrs. Madison," Charles Pinckney complained after losing the 1808 presidential election. "I might have had a better chance had I faced Mr. Madison alone."

But Dolley Madison *never* let James Madison face his troubles alone. On August 22, 1814, Madison ventured from the White House to confer with his generals as the invading British enveloped the capital city. Before departing, he asked his wife to be prepared to evacuate on a moment's notice, and to take important papers with her if it came to that. It did come to that, and what White House artifact could be more important than the full-length portrait of George Washington painted by Gilbert Stuart? None that she could see. The portrait was a copy, which Dolley knew, but she abhorred the thought of the British parading it through the streets of London as a trophy of war. She ordered the huge frame broken and the canvas rolled up. Her instincts about George Washington's place in the American identity were

proven right that very week. As the city burned, Washington residents looked upon the English troops with a defiant rage that foreshadowed ultimate victory and recalled a burning pride in an American general turned president who had defeated the British a generation earlier.

"If George Washington had been alive, you would not have gotten into this city so easily," one American shouted at British admiral George Cockburn, commander of the invading forces.

"No, sir," Cockburn conceded. "If General Washington had been president, we should never have thought of coming here."

August 25, 1875

Comanche

Famously resisting entreaties to run for political office, William Tecumseh Sherman continued his military career after the Civil War, and a decade later was bivouacked in the Texas Hill Country when a "respectable-looking woman," as described by one of his men, approached their encampment. Sherman was the most feared man in the South, but this German immigrant named Augusta Lehmann viewed him as a potential savior. A year earlier, her two sons had been plucked out of a field by raiding Indians, strapped to horses, and carried off. The younger boy, eight-year-old Willie, had been rescued, but eleven-year-old Herman was still out there. Please, she beseeched Sherman in her accented English, can the Army find him? Sherman listened attentively, probing for details, starting with the most basic: Which Indians took him?

Herman Lehmann was taken by Apache warriors but ended up with the Comanches. As he grew into manhood, Herman learned their ways, forgetting the German and English languages—and even his own name. Herman raided with Comanches, married into their band, and became a formidable warrior. He was nearly shot on this date by Texas Rangers and Army regulars trying to rescue him. While it's not accurate to say that the anger fueled by the abductions of children like Herman Lehmann and Cynthia Ann Parker was manufactured, it is true that whites' obsession with rescuing or avenging these hostages was a convenient way of rationalizing the grim truth: Whites were overrunning and killing Indians at every corner of this continent. One man who saw that clearly was Lehmann.

"I have always found the Comanches to be my most devoted friends," he told an interviewer in 1906. "Don't you believe that the Comanche is a bad man. You hate him . . . but the Comanches don't keep books and their side of history has never been written."

Lehmann, who was eventually reunited with his people, attempted to do just that.

"It will be remembered that Texas had refused to make a treaty with the Comanches, but by force had driven them from the land of their inheritance," he wrote. "For this cause many hundreds of white families, men, women and children, had come to a horrible death, while on the other hand many a brave Comanche with his wife and children had gone to the happy hunting ground."

He continued: "What would have been the outcome if instead of doing evil to the Indian the white man had done good, we can only conjecture."

August 26, 1964

Hurricanes Hubert and Barry

Running for office nine months after assuming the presidency amid tragedy, Lyndon B. Johnson put his stamp on his party's Atlantic City nominating convention, revealing that the Democrats' ticket in November would include Hubert H. Humphrey, a popular liberal senator from Minnesota.

"Nothing has given me greater support in the past nine months than my knowledge of President Kennedy's confidence that I could continue the task that he began," Johnson said. "I have found a man that I can trust in the same way. This confidence and this recommendation are not mine alone. They represent the enthusiastic conviction of the great majority of the Democratic Party in the United States."

Left unsaid was that this moment represented the one facet of the passing of the torch JFK had alluded to: A president from Texas was choosing as his running mate the human dynamo most identified with the Democrats' break from their slave-holding and segregationist roots. In years to come, political professionals would marvel at the rapid sea change in public opinion that made gay marriage the law of the land—how much faster change had come when compared to the struggle for racial equality. But progress did come. On this date in history, a Democratic president born in a segregated bastion of the Old Confederacy, chose as a running mate a passionate civil rights advocate who'd ignited a firestorm at his party's nominating convention sixteen years earlier.

At the same time, the Republican presidential nomination had gone to conservative Arizona senator Barry Goldwater, a man so committed to shrinking the scope of federal authority that two months earlier, he'd voted against the Civil Rights Act of 1964. Another contrast: instead of allying himself with a giant of his party, as Johnson did, Goldwater chose as his running mate an obscure congressman from western New York with a name, William Edward Miller, as ordinary as Hubert Horatio Humphrey was memorable. Bill Miller tried to compensate for his forgettable name and record with blistering rhetoric on the campaign trial, some of it quite clever. (He dismissed JFK as "the foundering father of the New Frontier.")

But in November 1964, voters simply were not inclined to choose their third U.S. president in less than a year, and the Johnson-Humphrey ticket won in a landslide. Not that Goldwater ran a flawless campaign. In a May 24, 1964, appearance on ABC News's *Issues and Answers*, moderator Howard K. Smith asked him about the escalating war in Vietnam.

"There have been several suggestions made," Goldwater replied. "I don't think we would use any of them, but defoliation of the forests by low-yield atomic weapons could well be done. When you remove the foliage, you remove the cover."

He rambled on for a while, casually discussing the deployment of tactical nukes. This gave the Johnson campaign the opening it was looking for. Its now-infamous "Daisy Girl" ad aired only briefly in early September, and it neither quoted Goldwater nor mentioned him by name. It merely showed a little girl counting as she picked wildflowers. A male voice picks up the count, but this is a countdown—to Armageddon. The picture changes to a thermonuclear explosion, as President Johnson's words are heard: "We must love each other—or die."

The implication that the GOP presidential nominee preferred death to love was a harsh one, and Republicans responded furiously. Sen. Thruston B. Morton of Kentucky called the ads and accompanying Democratic talking points "despicable, distasteful acts of cowardice." Morton wasn't alone in his revulsion, and the Daisy ad was quickly pulled. As Johnson aide Jack Valenti later noted, this was a tactical retreat. For one thing, the ad—and the news coverage it generated—had already made its point. Secondly, pulling it "showed a certain gallantry."

Being gallant wasn't what Johnson and his advisers cared about, anyway. "Look, campaigns are jungles," Valenti said in a 1981 oral history. "And everybody who fights in a campaign understands that you go for the jugular and you do what you think will most persuade the American people to your point of view." In that sense, the 1964 contest wasn't any different from the 2016 campaign. Then, as now, however, the image makers can only do so much. The rest is up to the candidates, for better or for worse. In Goldwater's case, his inelegant response to Howard K. Smith was not an isolated example.

A year earlier, he was quoted in *Newsweek* as saying he'd nuke "Chinese supply lines" into North Vietnam, "or maybe shell 'em with the Seventh Fleet." Three weeks before his *Issues and Answers* appearance, Goldwater was asked what he thought of JFK's plan to put a rocket ship on the moon by the end of the decade. "I don't want to hit the moon," he quipped. "I want to lob one into the men's room of the Kremlin."

No wonder Dwight Eisenhower once said to him, "Barry, you speak too quick and too loud." It was a trait that Goldwater, a true American original, was quick to concede. "There are words of mine floating around in the air," he once said, "that I would like to reach up and eat."

August 27, 2005

Hurricane Katrina

Initially called Tropical Depression 12, the weather system that formed in the Atlantic Ocean north of Puerto Rico and east of the Bahamas was upgraded to tropical storm status and given a name on this date. The next day, Hurricane Katrina sliced across Florida before heading into the Gulf of Mexico, where she gathered frightening force. By 10:11 a.m. Sunday, the National Weather Service warned that the storm appeared to be a hurricane of "unprecedented strength"—and might leave "most of the area uninhabitable for weeks, perhaps longer."

That prediction proved a great understatement. While President Bush adhered to a schedule that had him visiting a Veteran's Administration hospital in San Diego, Katrina made landfall at 6:10 a.m. Monday, in Plaquemines Parish. Land usually weakens hurricanes, but this one treated Mississippi's Gulf Coast cities and Louisiana bayou towns as speed bumps. It tossed barges around like toy boats, upended oil rigs, washed away bridges and interstate highways, then took aim at New Orleans. The storm surge, rainwater, and breaches in the levees bordering Lake Pontchartrain inundated the Crescent City. When it was over, 1,460 Louisianans were dead, most by drowning, along with some two hundred Mississippians. It was, George W. Bush told the nation, "a cruel and wasteful storm."

Although Bush's empathy was obviously sincere, it was also tardy. Bush cut short his California trip as New Orleans filled with water, only to return to his ranch in Texas for two nights and a day. His aides said the president didn't want to interfere with first responders or detract from the region's security needs. Yet on Wednesday, August 31, when Bush headed back to Washington—directing Air Force One to fly over the flooded area en route—it solidified the image of an out-of-touch chief executive. When Bush finally went to the stricken area Friday, he literally hugged dazed local residents. But he undermined himself when he tried to buck up beleaguered FEMA director Michael Brown by saying, "Brownie, you're doing a heckuva job!" This discordant ad-lib alienated locals on another level: As Louisiana senator Mary Landrieu noted, it was the federal infrastructure that failed. "This was a flood," she said, "not a hurricane."

Actually, it was both, and the response represented a failure of government at all levels, while underscoring the humbling capriciousness of Mother Nature. As Sen. John Cornyn of Texas ruefully noted, "When it rains, it pours—figuratively and literally."

August 28, 1854

The Immigrants

Johannes Remeeus, a Dutchman, departed from Antwerp with his family to a new land. He kept a diary, which is how we know what he was thinking on this date, and nearly every day that summer on a trip that took up all the family's money, depended on the goodwill of strangers, and required good luck and fortitude as they sailed the sea and traversed overland to his planned destination in Wisconsin. The "Hollanders," as Remeeus called himself and his countrymen, sailed aboard the *Robert C. Winthrop*, a sturdy New England vessel with a proud Massachusetts name. They were paired on ship with an equal number of Germans. The language barrier between the two groups—and the ship's crew—was an issue, which might be why the Dutch passengers thought they were heading to New York, instead of Boston, their actual destination.

Remeeus's diary, written for his descendants, eventually made its way into the Wisconsin public library. Here are three entries, including the last in which he's already calling himself "John" Remeeus. Gone from Europe less than ninety days, he is practically an American already.

June 23: Fair weather, the ship was steady. In the evening the Germans fittingly celebrated Saint John's Day, which also was the 25th birthday of one of their group. This man was escorted to the aft deck where his sister presented him with a bottle of wine, of which they had a plentiful supply....After having given him our congratulations, we all drank his health with many bottles of beer which the captain had in store. We also proposed a toast to the captain, the officers of the ship, and in fact everybody and everything. That evening we learned how the Germans surpassed all other peoples at singing.

July 4: Declaration of Independence, which is celebrated by every American. So did we. Early in the morning flags were run up....One man who had been a dealer in fireworks got permission to open a box of guns. Everybody who had a liking for shooting could do as much of it as he wished....Saw many fish, also a ship. We had a fresh breeze; the evening was fair but cold. The captain gave the Hollanders permission to sing psalms. The captain sang the last psalm with us. We were approaching the Newfoundland Banks.

August 28: I began to work for an English-speaking man, earning $1.25½ a day. Soon I became a citizen of Milwaukee, a youthful and beautiful city, ideally situated for commerce.

Your Father, JOHN REMEEUS

They Had a Dream

Millions of words have been written about the 1963 march and speeches that took place on the National Mall, especially Martin Luther King's electrifying benediction that brought the events of this day to a close. His "I Have a Dream" speech is remembered for its soaring and optimistic language, with its rich religiosity, that formed a crescendo at the speech's climax. But there were darker allusions in King's speech, and in the remarks of the other speakers as well.

These references were to the police brutality, lynching, intimidation, beatings, and murders underpinning the American form of apartheid known as "Jim Crow," and which were not limited to the Deep South. This was why John Lewis, leader of the Student Nonviolent Coordinating Committee, wanted to deliver a more militant speech on this date; it was why Malcolm X was so dismissive of the marchers; and it was why King twice mentioned "police brutality" in his speech, along with other degradations and attacks against African-Americans, while issuing a blunt warning to Jim Crow and Washington lawmakers alike.

At the very hour King spoke, two women in their early twenties were stabbed to death inside the apartment they shared in Manhattan. Seven months later, George Whitmore Jr. of Wildwood, New Jersey, an African-American drifter with a limited IQ, was picked out of a photo lineup by an assault victim. It turned out to be a misidentification, but before the case unraveled, Brooklyn police beat Whitmore, interrogated him for hours, fed him details about the Manhattan murders, and finally extracted a false confession to the killings. The defendant immediately recanted, but he was convicted and put on Death Row.

Eventually, the facts were sorted out, and the real killer imprisoned. The case played a role in the Supreme Court *Miranda v. Arizona* ruling and in New York's abandonment of capital punishment, and spawned the *Kojak* television series—but not before Whitmore spent nine years in prison. Even then, it happened only because dedicated journalist Selwyn Raab didn't accept the official version. The doubts Raab's reporting cast on the conviction hinged on Whitmore's alibi—and the fact that a dozen witnesses could back it up.

They remembered Whitmore being in Wildwood on the day in question because it was the date of Martin Luther King's great speech. It was all anybody in their circle was talking about that day, they recalled. They had the dream, too.

Gentleman Gene

John L. Sullivan had a nickname (the "Boston Strong Boy"), an aptitude for boxing, and the desire to be a champion. What he lacked was a venue where he could legally fight. When a promoter in Cincinnati, Ohio, arranged a bout, local authorities tried to stop it. They were unsuccessful, however, so on this date, Sullivan defeated challenger Dominick McCaffrey in a seven-round match—the first in this country contested under the Marquis of Queensberry rules.

Until then, fights were mostly bare-knuckled affairs with uncertain weight classes and even more uncertain rules and refereeing. John L. Sullivan fought all comers at county fairs and seedy saloons, and was known for walking into barrooms and announcing, "I can lick any man in the house." Usually, this gambit resulted in Sullivan getting free drinks, although sometimes a local tough guy had to be knocked on his backside first. By 1882, Sullivan was recognized in boxing circles—especially its Irish precincts—as the heavyweight champion of the world.

Although the evolution of the "sweet science" was hardly linear, in 1882 boxing had arrived as a sport. So had the fighter who would take Sullivan's title away from him. The usurper was a handsome and well-spoken San Franciscan who'd graduated from the city's respected Sacred Heart High School. His name was James John Corbett, and he'd learned his trade from a boxing coach while sporting a nickname, "Gentleman Jim," that bespoke loftier pretensions.

Corbett has been called the father of modern prize fighting, but the crossover artist who became boxing's first superstar was Jack Dempsey. He was a throwback, a willing brawler who emulated John L. Sullivan, not Gentleman Jim. As a teenager he'd stroll into the toughest mining camps in Colorado and announce, "I can lick any man in the house." Often, he couldn't, but Dempsey learned to fight, and the American public became enthralled.

Like his idol, Jack Dempsey would also run up against an Irish-American fighter of scientific bent. His name was Gene Tunney, and after knocking Dempsey out in the infamous 1927 "long count" fight at Soldier Field in Chicago, Tunney retired undefeated. His lineage would prove to be in politics, not in boxing. Tunney married a wealthy socialite and settled in Connecticut. His son John Tunney became a U.S. senator from California, and the inspiration behind an ahead-of-its-time film critique of modern politics, *The Candidate*. Thus did actor, director, and political activist Robert Redford descend, in a way, from John L. Sullivan.

Mother Knows Best

It was a minor election—replacing an alderman in Hannibal, Missouri. With an eye on history, however, Marie Ruoff Byrum and her friend Nita Harrison had a friendly competition to see who could cast the first vote. So Byrum and her husband decided on this date to be first in line when the polls opened the following morning at 7 a.m. They walked to the polling station before dawn and had already voted by the time Mrs. Harrison arrived, via car, at 7:10 a.m.—giving Marie Byrum the honor of being the first woman to vote after passage of the Nineteenth Amendment.

Two weeks earlier, Tennessee became the thirty-sixth state to ratify the constitutional amendment granting women the vote. Impassioned Tennesseans on both sides of the issue gathered in the state capital for the dramatic denouement. Arriving at the Nashville train station, members of the General Assembly were met by supporters and opponents, who gave them flowers to wear on their lapels. A yellow rose signified a pro-suffrage lawmaker; red roses were given to opponents. Harry T. Burn of McMinn County took a red rose. At twenty-four, he was the youngest member of the legislature. But young men are known to change their minds, especially when a woman is involved. The state senate had already ratified the amendment, leaving its fate in the hands of the lower chamber. Voter counters on both sides considered the tally too close to call.

Carrie Chapman Catt, the most prominent suffrage leader in the country, took up residence (as did anti-suffrage leader Josephine Pearson) in the Hermitage Hotel, across the street from the capitol. The night before the vote, Catt and her supporters had done all they could think of. Asked by her lieutenants what else they could do, she replied, "We can pray."

The next day those prayers were answered. Harry Burn, it seems, had been petitioned by a pro-suffrage farm wife from his district, in a letter. "I have been watching to see how you stood, but have not noticed anything yet," the missive began. "Don't forget to be a good boy and help Mrs. Catt put the 'rat' in ratification."

This letter would do the trick. Its author was Phoebe Burn, Harry's mother. Although he'd worn a red rose in opposition, forever after this vote he would wear the mantle of history.

"I believe in full suffrage as a right," he explained. "I believe we had a moral and legal right to ratify. I know a mother's advice is always safest for her boy to follow, and my mother wanted me to vote for ratification."

August 31, 2009

Always Faithful

A regional reporter in the bureau of Newhouse Newspapers, William John Cahir felt strongly after the September 11, 2001, attack on our nation that he needed to do more than just write about it. So, despite being in his early thirties, with a physique appropriate to a man his age who had sat for years behind a desk, Bill worked his way into terrific physical shape—and enlisted in the United States Marine Corps.

He survived basic training at Parris Island and by August 2004 was serving his first of two tours in Iraq. U.S. Marines march to the fighting, and Bill's first stint in combat was in Ramadi; the second, in 2006–2007, was in Fallujah. Afterward, he returned to the U.S., married a lovely lawyer named René E. Browne, and ran for Congress as a Democrat in a Pennsylvania district that includes his native town of State College, Pennsylvania.

Bill finished second in that primary, despite the airing of "Cahir Cares," one of the most positive and charming television campaign ads in political history. Afterward, he landed a job as a business consultant, and he and René moved back to the Washington, D.C., area. They were preparing for the impending birth of twin girls when Bill, still a reservist, got the call to return to active duty. He was deployed to Afghanistan as part of the Selected Reserve Marines assigned to Fourth Civil Affairs Group, Marine Expeditionary Brigade.

The unit was dispatched to wrest control of the town of Dananeh from the Taliban in Helmand Province. The goal was to make the place safe enough for local residents to vote in the August 20, 2009, Afghan presidential elections. If you don't know this story, you have probably guessed by now how it ends: On August 13, 2009, Staff Sgt. William Cahir was among the Marines entering the town in a predawn action when they came under enemy fire. He was shot in the neck and killed.

Bill Cahir was buried on this date at Arlington Cemetery, at age forty, never living long enough to see the birth of his daughters. Hardened men wept at the news. His brave widow asked those who knew Bill to write letters to her twin girls about their father, to be shared with them when they are older.

Semper Fi, Bill.

September 1, 1939

Gipper in the Air

Raymond L. Schrock turned in his screenplay to Warner Bros. for a science fiction-themed spy thriller titled *Murder in the Air* the same day Nazi Germany invaded Poland. The fourth in a series produced by the studio's "B" picture unit, it showcased the heroics of a Department of Treasury agent named Brass Bancroft, played by Ronald Reagan.

As the Wehrmacht raced through Eastern Europe, Schrock made changes in the script, mindful that Hollywood censors enforcing the "Hays code" had forced the studio to tone down previous plot lines about enemy spies. Harry Warner, particularly, was obsessed with this threat, and made little distinction between fascists or communists—or between would-be infiltrators from Italy, Germany, or the Soviet Union. In 1939, however, the United States wasn't at war with any of those nations, and the Hays Office didn't want Hollywood to start one. As for Reagan, he was ready to perform. Arriving on the set for the second Brass Bancroft film, *Code of the Secret Service*, he shook hands with director Noel Smith, and quipped, "When do I fight—and whom?"

Ironically, however, much of the action in the Secret Service series takes place in the air, Reagan hadn't flown much at that time, and the little flying he'd done convinced him that he didn't like it. It was a fear he wouldn't conquer until he ran for president.

More like an original cable television series than something that would appear in a movie theater today, *Murder in the Air*, released in 1940, ran less than an hour and took only twelve days to shoot. It had no romantic subplot, and featured decidedly unambitious special effects for the ray gun and other science fiction scenes. Yet that ray gun in *Murder in the Air* was an interesting angle. Called "The Inertia Projector," it predates the "Death Star" in the original *Star Wars* movie by four decades—except that Raymond Schrock's version was for defensive purposes. In this sense, it also anticipated Reagan's 1983 Strategic Defense Initiative, an undeveloped technology to shoot down Soviet missiles before they enter U.S. airspace.

In any event, although *Murder in the Air* was the last of the Secret Service pictures, Reagan was still under contract to Warner Bros. Rewarding his loyalty and professionalism, the studio cast him the same year as doomed Notre Dame football quarterback George Gipp in *Knute Rockne All American*. This was an "A" picture that solidified Reagan's place as a bona fide movie star and gave him the nickname his fans use to this day.

September 2, 1944

No Place to Land

The air battle in the Pacific was so routine it had no name. It certainly had historical consequences. The action involved a squadron of U.S. Navy Avenger bombers launched from the USS *San Jacinto*. Their target was the Japanese radio towers on Chichi Jima. That island is largely forgotten now because the Marines never landed on it, as they did on nearby Iwo Jima, and because the U.S. government never wanted to talk about what happened there.

Chichi Jima was strategically important for its communications facilities, which kept intercepting U.S. Navy radio transmissions. The pilot of one Avenger was twenty-year-old George Bush, two years removed from Phillips Academy at Andover where the 1942 commencement speaker, Secretary of War Henry Stimson, had urged the graduates not to rush into military service. It's going to be a long war, Stimson said, and we'll need you in three or four years—as officers. As he and his family filed out of Cochran Chapel on June 12, 1942, Prescott Bush asked his second son whether he'd taken Stimson's words to heart.

"No, sir," the young man replied. "I'm joining up."

Twenty-six months later, on this date, he was flying a combat mission over Chichi Jima when his squadron encountered antiaircraft fire. Engine aflame, the cockpit filling with smoke, Bush managed to release his bombs, get clear of the island, and head back toward the carrier before bailing out. One man, probably radioman John Delaney, bailed out, too, but his chute didn't open. The third crewman, intelligence officer William White, went down with the plane. The young pilot was in the ocean, clinging to a rubber raft, with a Japanese gunboat speeding toward him. One of the fighter planes escorting the Avengers strafed the Japanese boat and circled Bush while radioing for help. A U.S. submarine rescued him. The horrors awaiting young George Bush on that island would not be known for sixty years, and then only due to the efforts of military historian James Bradley, who detailed the fate of eight American aviators downed on Chichi Jima. The tale includes bravery, cannibalism, beheadings, and secret war crimes trials.

"On English maps the chain is called the Bonin Islands," Bradley wrote. "The name Bonin is a French cartographer's corruption of the old Japanese word *munin*, which means 'no man.' These islands were uninhabited for most of Japan's existence. They literally contained 'no peoples' or 'no mans.' So Bonin translates loosely into English as No Mans Land."

September 3, 1919

Madam President

Like many presidents before and after him, including Barack Obama, Woodrow Wilson grew frustrated at the intransigence of the United States Senate. It wasn't an election year, but Wilson took to the campaign trail trying to convince the American people to pressure their home state senators to embrace the League of Nations.

Even before President Wilson departed Washington, his grueling schedule worried his wife and physicians. He'd spent months in Europe negotiating an end to World War I—and trying to set up the League, a forerunner of the United Nations, in hopes of avoiding future wars. "I do not want to do anything foolhardy, but the League of Nations is now in its crisis, and if it fails, I hate to think what will happen to the world," Wilson told his doctor, Navy admiral Cary Grayson. "I cannot put my personal safety, my health, in the balance against my duty—I must go."

Wilson left Washington by train on this date, and began his arduous task. He'd give a speech in the back of the train, and move on to the next town. He logged eight thousand miles in three weeks, but by the time the presidential party reached Montana, he was experiencing severe headaches and asthma attacks. It was becoming clear that Dr. Grayson's fears were being realized. The president collapsed on September 25 while giving a speech in Pueblo, Colorado. The train headed back to Washington to provide Wilson some rest. It was already too late.

On October 2, he suffered a massive stroke in the White House that left him paralyzed on one side and unable to speak. The First Lady and Dr. Grayson collaborated in keeping the president's condition from the American people. Someday, a woman will hold the highest office in this country, but she will not be the first to exert the powers of the presidency. That dubious distinction belongs to Edith Galt Wilson, who for the ensuing seventeen months functioned as her husband's proxy. I say "dubious" because in her zeal to protect Wilson's legacy, Edith undermined any chance of getting the League of Nations through Congress.

Obtaining the requisite two-thirds approval in the Senate required the backing of influential senator Henry Cabot Lodge, and getting that support would have entailed making concessions to the Massachusetts Republican. It never happened. Edith Wilson was hamstrung by the dual handicaps of secrecy and love. Moreover, she was disinclined to compromise with men she blamed for her husband's failed health.

September 4, 1888

Point and Give

George Eastman, a Rochester bank clerk, was planning a trip to Santo Domingo with his mother when a coworker suggested he take a camera to document the Caribbean sights. If that seems like obvious advice now, it wasn't in 1878, when civilian photography was in its infancy. The camera he subsequently purchased was expensive and weighed as much as a microwave oven does today. The necessary accoutrements included a tent, a weighty tripod, heavy glass plates, a metal holder for those plates, chemical solutions, and aquarium-like glass tanks.

It cost $5 to get a lesson on how to use it all, which twenty-four-year-old George Eastman paid. He never did make the trip to the Dominican Republic, but he became convinced that photography could be much simpler. Learning his craft by reading technical journals and working in rented office space at night, he figured out how to make film that was much lighter than the glass-backed plates then in use. He experimented with dry plates instead of wet ones, developed a machine to mass-produce them, and came up with lighter, paper-backed film.

His goal was "to make the camera as convenient as the pencil." This audacious aim was all but realized on this date when the U.S. Department of Commerce issued patent number 388,850—the point-and-shoot camera. That same year, Eastman registered the trade name Kodak and coined the company's memorable advertising slogan, "You press the button, we do the rest."

He wasn't kidding. By the end of the year, the first box cameras were on the market. They cost $25 and came with one hundred exposures. Kodak would develop the film and return the camera to the user, loaded and ready to go. This device changed the way human beings viewed their natural world and made Eastman a wealthy man. He built a mansion and went on safari, but mostly he bestowed his money on others. He poured much of Kodak's profits back into his company and its employees, pioneering the concept of profit sharing, and generously supported institutions of higher learning. He gave Massachusetts Institute of Technology $20 million, most of it anonymously under the name "Mr. Smith." He was the biggest giver to the Rochester Institute of Technology, financed dental clinics across Europe, and donated to several historically black colleges. On one day in 1924 alone, George Eastman wrote checks totaling some $30 million to the University of Rochester, MIT, Tuskegee Institute, and Hampton Institute.

He then laid down his pen and said, "Now I feel better."

September 5, 1975

Jerry Ford's Near Misses

Fittingly, considering what came next, the topic that President Gerald R. Ford was discussing with lawmakers in Sacramento was how government could best combat violent crime. Then, as now, Jerry Brown was governor of California, and both men had spoken at a Chamber of Commerce breakfast that morning before heading to the state capitol.

Suddenly, while Ford was walking across the capitol grounds on this date, a diminutive woman in the crowd raised a .45-caliber pistol and aimed it at the president. Onlookers heard the ominous click of the hammer dropping. So did the Secret Service agents in the president's protective detail, who pounced, wrestling the woman to the ground. As the agents pried the weapon from her hands, she shouted, "Don't get excited! It didn't go off!"

The would-be assassin turned out to be a follower of notorious mass murderer Charles Manson named Lynette "Squeaky" Fromme. The reason her gun didn't discharge was that although she had four rounds in the pistol's magazine, the chamber was empty. Immediately after the assassination attempt, the president held a brief session with the traveling members of the press for the express purpose of thanking the Secret Service.

"Let me add, with great emphasis," Ford said, "this incident under no circumstances will prevent me or preclude me from contacting the American people as I travel from one state to another and from one community to another."

That resolve would be tested only seventeen days later, when another unhinged California woman fired a shot at Ford outside San Francisco's St. Francis Hotel. Although Sara Jane Moore was involved in the city's left-wing politics, she grew up in West Virginia and was proficient with a pistol. She came within six inches of hitting Ford, missing because the sighting on the gun she bought that morning was faulty—and she hadn't had time to test it.

Upon returning to the White House, the president met with the media again, and uttered a sentiment rare for a president—relief at the sight of the White House press corps. The exchange began this way:

REPORTER: Mr. Ford, could you speak to us for just a moment please and tell us how you feel?
THE PRESIDENT: Can I have just a minute to look at all of you?

Looking to America

Jane Addams, the first woman to win the Nobel Peace Prize, was nominated ninety-one times between 1916 and 1931, the year she finally won. Halvdan Koht, who served on the Norwegian Nobel Committee for most of that time, noted that with the 1931 prize (Addams shared it with Columbia University president Nicholas Murray Butler), the United States now ranked first among peace prize winners. This was fitting, as Koht saw it. The United States he asserted, had risen to the point where it wielded more influence over war and peace than any nation on earth.

"All who yearn for a lasting peace," he said, "look to America for help."

In the 1930s, a "lasting peace" was what the world longed for, but not what it would get. This wasn't Addams's fault. She risked her life for peace—and devoted her career to the poor.

Laura Jane Addams was born in Cedarville, Illinois on this date. Her father, Robert H. Addams, was a banker and state legislator, a charter member of the Republican Party—and a confidant of the first Republican president. The eighth of Robert Addams's nine children cofounded America's first "settlement house," as havens for the underprivileged were known. This was in Chicago and the place was called Hull House. Inspired by Toynbee Hall in London's East End, which Addams visited in the 1880s, Hull House spawned many other such houses, and eventually altered this country's sensibilities about feeding and educating the needy.

Jane lived in Hull House herself, and she used Chicago as a base of operations for investigations that led to reforms in areas as disparate as the milk supply, child labor, unemployment insurance, and sanitary conditions. She was a proponent of women's suffrage and a vocal opponent of U.S. involvement in the First World War. A cofounder of the Women's Peace Party, she braved German U-boats to sail across the Atlantic in 1915 to a women's international peace congress. After the United States entered World War I, Addams's reputation suffered at home when public opinion rallied around the commander in chief and America's troops, as happens in wartime. Afterward, when disillusionment set in, she enjoyed a kind of rehabilitation. In his introductory speech, Halvdan Koht noted that Addams was only the second woman to win the Peace Prize—adding that she certainly wouldn't be the last.

"In honoring Jane Addams," he said, "we also pay tribute to the work which women can do for peace and fraternity among nations."

September 7, 1608

Dateline—New World

Capt. John Smith arrived on this date back in Jamestown, where he was promptly named "president" of the settlement's council. Could Smith be considered the first American president? That's a stretch, but his fellow colonists were certainly happy to see him in office: Smith was a human good-luck charm: He fought in Austria, battled Ottomans in Turkey, was taken prisoner and sold as a slave, then was shipped to Crimea, where he escaped before returning to England. He sailed for the New World where he was captured while exploring the Chickahominy River—and marked for death by an Algonquian chief the colonists called Powhatan.

In Smith's telling, he and two English companions were ambushed by Algonquian braves. The other two men were slain, but Smith was taken to Chief Powhatan, who decided to have the white interloper killed by being ritualistically clubbed to death as part of a tribal ceremony. The chief changed his mind, Smith wrote (referring to himself in the third person), only when his daughter Pocahontas, who was probably twelve years old at the time, interjected herself between the captive and his would-be executioners.

When spring came the following year, the real life John Smith didn't settle down in animated picture-land Indian princess bliss. Instead, he took to his ship and explored a vast stretch of the Chesapeake basin, returning to Jamestown as the pre-autumn breezes began to nip the air. We know all this because Smith wrote it down. Was he telling the truth? Well, one wonders about the details of the Pocahontas rescue story for the simple reason that he told a similar tale about a Turkish princess helping him escape death at the hands of the Ottomans.

Yes, the vainglorious Smith embroidered his tales to make himself look heroic. Yet he was dependable on the big stuff. While his cohorts were spinning wild tales of gold in the New World, John Smith painted a more realistic, if overly optimistic, picture for would-be European emigrants in the land across the sea. "Here every man may be master and owner of his owne labour and land," wrote the man who would later explore—and name—New England. "If he have nothing but his hands, he may...by industrie quickly grow rich."

So, yes, it's a stretch to call Capt. John Smith the first president of the New World. But you can say that he was the first foreign correspondent to prowl these shores, even that he was America's first writer.

September 8, 1966
To Boldly Go

The starship *Enterprise* fulfilled its creator's mission of boldly going where no network series had gone before. On this date, it sailed into Americans' living rooms. NBC executives were lukewarm about Gene Roddenberry's project, television critics missed its point, and even Isaac Asimov quibbled with the science. (Taking aim at *Star Trek* and *Lost in Space* in *TV Guide*, the great science writer complained, "Nobody seems to know what a galaxy is.")

Although *Star Trek* developed a devoted following, it was a ratings disappointment and was canceled after three seasons. But it was that rare show that was perfect for its time and also timeless. *Star Trek* reruns have delighted insomniacs for decades, spinoffs were churned out, and feature films reprising original cast members have grossed some $2 billion. The series was always a work in progress. Viewers didn't hear the iconic opening narration by Capt. James T. Kirk, played by William Shatner, until a November episode: ("Space, the final frontier. These are the voyages of the starship *Enterprise*. Its five-year mission: to explore strange new worlds, to seek out new life and new civilizations, to boldly go where no man has gone before.")

"To boldly go" entered the American lexicon. So did other phrases, some profound, such as "prime directive," and others more whimsical, like "Beam me up, Scotty." By themselves, such catchphrases are mainly evidence the show was well written. But they also became cultural touchstones. Why? For starters, its debut came halfway between President Kennedy's death and the lunar landing he'd foreseen. From 1966 to 1969, Americans' hearts and heads were in the heavens. The show also anticipated the future, and viewers sensed it. Those flip-up handheld communication devices? They predated flip-up cell phones by decades. *Star Trek* also anticipated social progress. The demographically diverse crew on the bridge of the *Enterprise* put Gene Roddenberry light years ahead of NASA in this regard.

Finally, the show reflected Gene Roddenberry's own irrepressible optimism about the future. This isn't uniquely American, but it is very American, and *Star Trek* depicted it as a universal trait that human beings would take with them into the galaxy (sorry, Isaac Asimov) as they interacted—and even intermarried—with other species.

Asimov himself came to see this pretty quickly. In 1967, he gave an interview to *Time* magazine and was asked to name his favorite television show. "*Star Trek*," he replied.

September 9, 1965

Rabbi Koufax

A high school star in Brooklyn, Sanford Koufax signed a professional baseball contract with his hometown team in 1955 after an Ebbets Field tryout. "There are two times in my life the hair on my arms has stood up," Dodger general manager Al Campanis recalled. "The first time I saw the ceiling of the Sistine Chapel and the first time I saw Sandy Koufax throw a fastball."

Campanis was Catholic, Koufax Jewish, but the pitcher's talent was not a question of faith. By 1961, he was the best in baseball. In 1962, he threw the first of four career no-hitters, culminating in a 1–0 perfect game on this date against the Chicago Cubs. The drama was captured by another Hall of Famer, Dodger announcer Vin Scully. ("There are twenty-nine thousand people in the ballpark," Scully intoned at the top of the ninth, "and a million butterflies.") Koufax fanned the last six Cubs he faced, entering the history books and the nether regions of our imaginations.

This was particularly true for Jews, not all of them boys—and not all of them kids. Koufax had signed with the Dodgers only ten years after the liberation of Auschwitz. And after leading his team into the World Series, he declined to pitch Game 1 because it fell on Yom Kippur. He threw a complete game shutout in Game 5, though, and came back on two days' rest to dominate the Minnesota Twins in Game 7, earning the Most Valuable Player award for the Series and *Sports Illustrated* Sportsman of the Year honor.

Graying but still handsome, he was invited to the White House forty-five years later for Jewish American Heritage Month. Spotting Koufax in the front row, President Obama briefly channeled a Borscht Belt comedian. "Sandy and I actually have something in common," the president deadpanned. "We are both lefties. He can't pitch on Yom Kippur; I can't pitch."

For Koufax, though, the more evocative moment came after the ceremony ended when he was approached by prominent rabbi and author Brad Hirschfield, who asked Koufax what it felt like to be a Hall of Famer and "one of the most important rabbis of the twentieth century."

"Believe me," Koufax replied, "I'm no rabbi."

Hirschfield explained to Koufax that the All-Star pitcher had empowered a generation of American Jews to claim their Jewishness with "pride, confidence, and joy," adding that if that didn't constitute being a great rabbi, he didn't know what did. Koufax, as gracious as he was so many autumns earlier, replied, "Thank you, Rabbi, for putting me in your club."

September 10, 2001

Eve of Destruction

George W. Bush was in Florida highlighting his plan to bolster more effective methods of teaching in the nation's public schools. "It's time to wage war on illiteracy for the young, and to whip this problem," Bush said while appearing with his younger brother, Florida governor Jeb Bush, at the Justina Road Elementary School in a working-class Jacksonville neighborhood. Both Bushes emphasized that quality education should not be a partisan issue.

"Getting every child to read in America is an American issue, and it ought to be an American goal," the president said. "There are great teachers who have got wonderful hearts who don't know how to teach reading."

Jeb Bush, who had helped White House officials select Justina Road Elementary as the backdrop because of its rising test scores, concurred. "I agree with you," he said, "and you agree with our mother—that reading is maybe the most important thing we can do to ensure there is rising student achievement."

The president would spend the night in Longboat Key, before heading to Sarasota for a similar school event on September 11. The next day's event was at Sarasota's Emma T. Booker Elementary. There, Bush planned to read aloud to children from a book titled *The Pet Goat*. The event promised to be a feel-good session, but one with a serious underlying message.

The purpose of George W. Bush's two Florida education events was drumming up public support for his administration's education initiative, the No Child Left Behind Act. In Washington, education wasn't yet strictly a partisan issue, but the Senate and House had passed differing versions of the bill, which meant the legislation was languishing in a conference committee. Among his influential allies was Democratic senator Edward M. Kennedy. The iconic Massachusetts liberal had scheduled hearings the following day, and among the invited witnesses was First Lady Laura Bush, who planned to tell the Senate Education Committee chaired by Kennedy about the results of a summit on early childhood cognition she had hosted earlier that summer at Georgetown University.

Ted Kennedy had attended some of those July sessions and he had personally invited Mrs. Bush to testify before his committee. On the eve of the hearings, his staff checked with the First Lady's office to make sure things were on track for Tuesday, September 11. They were told that Mrs. Bush was looking forward to it, that all was fine. That was what almost everyone thought.

September 11, 2001
This Changes Everything

On a humid Florida morning, President Bush went for a four-and-a-half-mile run on a Longboat Key golf course. At the Pentagon, Secretary of Defense Donald Rumsfeld hosted a breakfast for members of Congress, while on Capitol Hill Edward M. Kennedy prepared to welcome Laura Bush to his office. In downtown Washington, veteran campaign operatives Bob Shrum, Stanley Greenberg, and James Carville were headlining a *Christian Science Monitor* breakfast, called "Sperling Breakfasts" in honor of the founder of the feast, eighty-five-year-old *Monitor* bureau chief, Godfrey "Budge" Sperling Jr. His guests, all Democrats, arrived that morning with Greenberg's polling data and talking points designed to show that George W. Bush already was looking like a one-term president. "He's not formidable, politically," Greenberg told the reporters.

Shrum offered the caveat that President Reagan had also seemed vulnerable in 1982, but the old Kennedy aide did this mainly as a way of suggesting that Bush 43 was no Ronald Reagan. Colorful as always, Carville chimed in with his premeditated sound bite. "My line is: We're busted at home and distrusted around the world," he said. To win in 2002 and 2004, Carville added sarcastically, Republicans would have to run on "their successful foreign policy."

About this time cell phones started going off around the table, despite Sperling's usual admonition. One of those phones belonged to Shrum, who saw it was from his office and answered it nervously because he'd left explicit instructions not to be interrupted except in the case of an emergency. Shrum was so shocked at what he'd heard that he repeated it aloud to the room word for word: "A plane has just crashed into the World Trade Center."

Minutes later, Greenberg received a call: A second plane had hit the World Trade Center. Reporters were being told the same thing by their editors. The mood in the room changed instantly. Carville, who had been the most caustic, was suddenly the most concerned. His wife, Mary Matalin, worked in the White House. She was at that moment running in her stocking feet at the urging of Secret Service agents to a secure location. Perhaps because of his

worries for Mary—or maybe because of his preternatural political instincts—Carville was the first in that room to instantly comprehend the seismic political shift that had just occurred. As everyone hurriedly gathered up their personal effects before rushing to work, Carville told the journalists, "Disregard everything we just said! This changes everything!"

September 12, 1963

Bombingham

Black students seeking to integrate their Birmingham high school had been attacked for three straight days when the Rev. Fred Shuttlesworth sent a telegram to President Kennedy. "Please take immediate steps," he implored, "to insure adequate escort protection so that these children will be safe and the nation spared another embarrassment or possible tragedy." Tragedy was just what was brewing in Alabama. How could it be otherwise in a place nicknamed "Bombingham"?

In 1957, Shuttlesworth and four fellow African-American pastors founded the Southern Christian Leadership Conference. A sharecropper's son with little formal education, he took the Bible literally and applied the same uncompromising passion to civil rights, leading voting drives, boycotts, school integration efforts, and every other manner of challenge to Jim Crow. Such activism was perilous, as Shuttlesworth knew firsthand. He expressed a fatalistic determination "to kill segregation or be killed by it." It turned out that Fred Shuttlesworth was a hard person to kill.

On Christmas night in 1956, the Bethel Baptist Church parsonage—that is to say, Shuttlesworth's home—was dynamited while he and his family slept inside. "The wall and the floor were blown out," Pulitzer Prize–winning author Diane McWhorter wrote, "and the mattress heaved into the air, supporting Shuttlesworth like a magic carpet." He viewed it as a sign from the heavens, of course, and when a white policeman responding to the bombing told him it would be safer to leave town, Shuttlesworth replied that he hadn't been saved by Jesus to run away.

The next year, when Shuttlesworth tried to enroll his kids in an all-white school he was attacked by a Klan-led mob wielding bicycle chains and brass knuckles. At the hospital, the attending physician searched in vain for evidence that Shuttlesworth had suffered a concussion. "Doctor," he replied, "the Lord knew I lived in a hard town, so he gave me a hard head."

His style, not to mention theological outlook, placed him in contrast with other civil rights leaders, notably the erudite Martin Luther King. Shuttlesworth biographer Andrew M. Manis wrote that when King suggested in a private rap session that after the crucifixion, Christ's disciples had imagined seeing Jesus—or perhaps seen an apparition—Shuttlesworth objected so vehemently that King never felt comfortable discussing theology with him again. A similar tension existed between the two men about politics. If Shuttlesworth was more theologically conservative than King, he was more radical politically—and more confrontational. Yet the two pastors complimented each other. While King skillfully employed Gandhi-inspired passive resistance in his letter from the Birmingham jail, Shuttlesworth continued his long war of wills on the streets with Birmingham public safety commissioner Eugene "Bull" Connor. The expectation was that the city's whites would reveal themselves via their typical response, epitomized by the fire department's hosing of demonstrators and the unleashing of Bull Connor's police dogs.

It unfolded this way, too, and when Shuttlesworth was among those injured when the high-pressure fire hoses were turned on the crowd, Connor snarled of Shuttlesworth: "I'm sorry I missed it. I wish they'd carried him away in a hearse."

By September, the worst seemed to be over. Bull Connor had been removed from office, and some of the city's largest merchants had agreed to integrate. But the white establishment had unleashed forces so malevolent they could not be controlled. A middle-class black neighborhood in Birmingham was named "Dynamite Hill" after the frequent attacks there against civil rights activists. On this date, Kennedy held a press conference in which he praised the majority of Southerners for not letting emotion overrule their respect for the rule of law. "The courage and the responsibility of those community leaders in those places," JFK said, "provide a meaningful lesson, not only for the children in those cities but children all over the country."

The lesson that children "all over the country"—and adults, too—would soon be subjected to, however, proved to be so horrific that it would undermine the foundations of segregation. Down in Birmingham, a Ku Klux Klansman known as "Dynamite Bob" Chambliss was conspiring with four confederates to send a message of their own. The target they fixated on was the 16th Street Baptist Church.

If segregation, and the white violence that had undergirded it, killed four little girls at their church, segregation did not kill Fred Shuttlesworth. It was the other way around. When he went to his reward in October 2011, the governor ordered flags lowered to halfstaff. By then, the old hate had mostly faded away. Shuttlesworth outlived Bull Connor by nearly four decades and preached until he was eighty-four. He lived another five years after that, surviving long enough to see an African-American hold the job that John F. Kennedy had when the pastor sent him that telegram on this date.

In July 2008, Fred Shuttlesworth's old town renamed its transportation hub. It is now the Birmingham-Shuttlesworth International Airport.

September 13, 1949

Another Babe

On this date, the first president of the Ladies Professional Golf Association was chosen. Patty Berg was the pride of Minnesota golf—and of the U.S. Marine Corps, for which she served as a World War II procurement officer. Among the LPGA charter members was another star who outshone all the others: Mildred Didrikson Zaharias, long known to an adoring public as "Babe."

All these years later, the only question about Babe Didrikson is whether she was the greatest female athlete in U.S. history—or just the greatest athlete, period?

Born in 1911 to Norwegian parents who settled in Port Arthur, Texas, Babe was a tomboy and all-around jock who claimed that her nickname came from all the home runs she hit. This provenance is doubtful, but Babe Didrikson certainly excelled at baseball—and every other sport she ever tried, including track and field, basketball, tennis, swimming, diving, boxing, volleyball, handball, bowling, billiards, skating, and cycling. And, of course, golf. Asked if there was anything she didn't play, she quipped, "Yeah, dolls."

"My goal," she said when asked about her youthful ambition, "was to be the greatest athlete who ever lived." Many of her contemporaries thought she succeeded. "She is beyond all belief until you see her perform," wrote Grantland Rice. "Then you finally understand that you are looking at the most flawless section of muscle harmony, of complete mental and physical coordination, the world of sport has ever seen."

At the 1932 U.S. Olympic trials, Didrikson (she would change her name after marrying in 1938) entered eight of the ten events, winning six of them. Female Olympians were limited to three events at the time, so Babe threw the javelin at the Los Angeles Olympics that year (winning easily), ran the 80-meter hurdles (setting a world's record), and competed in the high jump (she tied for first place, but was given a silver instead of her third gold because of her unorthodox jumping style—one now used by all jumpers, male and female).

Afterward, she barnstormed as a professional basketball star, bowler, and tennis player. Golf eventually afforded her a way to make a steady living, but she did more than that. She opened a nation's eyes to the true possibilities of female athletes.

Asked once how she managed to rip off drives that carried some 250 yards despite not even weighing 150 pounds, she replied, "You've got to loosen your girdle and let it rip."

Music of 9/11

The day after the attacks, Democrats and Republicans joined hands on the steps of the U.S. Capitol and sang "God Bless America," a song that became a staple in the cathedrals of Major League Baseball. That was only the beginning. At services on this date at a real church, Washington's National Cathedral, the audience belted out "The Battle Hymn of the Republic."

In the Civil War, each side sung hundreds of ditties as they marched into battle. And despite Abe Lincoln's fondness for "Dixie," there was nothing like "John's Brown's Body" to rally the Union troops. One Confederate major told his Union counterparts days after Appomattox, "Gentlemen, if we'd had your songs, we'd have licked you out of your boots."

After 9/11, America's most famous singers and songwriters repurposed other old anthems: Bruce Springsteen's "My City of Ruins" was given a new context, as were Stevie Wonder's "Love's in Need of Love Today," Paul Simon's "Bridge over Troubled Water," and Bob Marley's "Redemption Song," reprised by Wyclef Jean. Many artists penned original compositions. Springsteen, not surprisingly, was the most ambitious. Like other residents of northern New Jersey, Springsteen could hardly go about his daily life without passing funerals at local churches. One day, a passing motorist rolled down his window and exhorted Bruce: "We need you now!" Springsteen accepted this mantle, and did more than write songs from his gut: he spoke with widows and other 9/11 survivors to better capture their feelings and voices for the tracks he wrote for a stunning album called *The Rising*.

Other musicians rose to the occasion, often in surprising ways. Three decades earlier, Canadian-born rocker Neil Young wrote a song after the Kent State shootings called "Ohio" that became an iconic anthem of the antiwar movement. After 9/11, he recorded "Let's Roll," in homage to Todd Beamer and the other heroes of doomed United Airlines Flight 93. Similar themes were heard in country music. Earlier in 2001, Toby Keith's father, a U.S. Army veteran, died in a car accident; after 9/11 Keith wrote a tribute to his dad and other veterans in an aggressively patriotic tune, "Courtesy of the Red, White and Blue (The Angry American)." The song delivers on its subtitle: "We'll put a boot in your ass," goes the chorus, "it's the American way." At first, he didn't record the song, preferring to sing it on U.S. military bases where it was cheered wildly. Eventually, he embraced the song completely, singing it not just on military bases but as a warm-up act for George W. Bush's appearances on those installations—and, later, on the steps of the Lincoln Memorial the night before Donald J. Trump's inauguration.

In time, America's equilibrium returned, not always to unifying effect. By the time of the 2003–2004 election cycle Toby Keith was warming up military crowds for campaign-style rallies by the commander in chief, who was running for reelection. And although *The Rising* comprised a remarkably nuanced and thoughtful set of songs, by 2004 Springsteen was stumping for John Kerry and saying intemperate things about George W. Bush. (Gravity also exerted its inexorable effects on Neil Young, who eventually composed another tune he titled, "Let's Impeach the President.") The most notable exception to this return to default partisanship was country singer Alan Jackson. A Georgian with a strong, but soothing voice who still wears a cowboy hat and writes unabashedly about family and faith, Jackson was an unlikely crossover artist—until he wrote "Where Were You (When the World Stopped Turning)."

The idea of this poignant ballad is that the world didn't really stop turning—it was up to us how we responded to the horror of the attack. "Did you weep for the children who lost their dear loved ones and pray for the ones who don't know?" Jackson's song asks. "Did you rejoice for the people who walked from the rubble and sob for the ones left below?" Each verse presents a series of choices, but with a gentle nudge toward love over hate: "Did you lay down at night and think of tomorrow—or go out and buy you a gun? Did you turn off that violent old movie you're watching, and turn on *I Love Lucy* reruns?"

Alan Jackson was on his morning walk when the first plane hit. He saw the second plane strike the World Trade Center on a television in his kitchen. A few weeks later he awoke with a tune going through his head. The words came to him as he sang them into a tape recorder, and he completed the song while his wife took their children to Sunday school.

Unsure about releasing a song that capitalized on a national tragedy, Jackson played it for his wife and manager, both of whom found it moving, so he recorded it a few days later and played it for a group of executives at his record label.

"We just kind of looked at one another," RCA Label Group chairman Joe Galante recalled. "Nobody spoke for a full minute."

September 15, 1963

Thunder

Can I go march?" eleven-year-old Denise McNair asked her parents.

"No, you're too little," she was told.

"Well," the girl responded, "*you're* not too little."

By this date, Birmingham's 16th Street Baptist Church, where the Rev. John H. Cross was pastor, had emerged as the civil rights movement's nerve center in that highly volatile and segregated city. College students, then high school students, and finally middle school students had been joining the marches. In some cases, schoolkids had been jailed.

If the intent in locking up young black people was to intimidate them, it had the opposite effect. This was a struggle in which Birmingham's entire African-American community was engaged. White racists, too, not all of them peacefully. Yet, there had to be limits—didn't there? Twenty times in the past eight years, bombs had gone off in Birmingham; some of them to send a message, some designed to maim or kill civil rights leaders. But to dynamite a black church filled with families during a Sunday morning worship service? Even to those who lived through Birmingham's worst days, this was unthinkable. And yet it happened.

When the blast went off, Denise McNair's relatives believed it was a thunderstorm. The wife of pastor John Cross thought of the Russians. Others assumed it was an explosion at one of the city's aging foundries. Actually the rumbling they heard at 10:22 a.m. that Sunday was the sound of hate. As the 16th Street Baptist Church shook, several girls were caught in the basement rubble. Four of them—Denise McNair, and fourteen-year-olds Cynthia Morris Wesley, Carole Robertson, and Addie Mae Collins—were killed instantly. A fifth, Addie Mae's younger sister Sarah, was gravely injured, losing an eye and suffering lasting psychic wounds.

Ambulance and police sirens filled the air, mixing with the anguished cries of parents. "They are killing our children!" a mother cried out. As the church emptied, numbness turned to anger. Police officers, themselves stunned by what they were seeing, struggled to hold back the crowd. The Reverend Cross found a megaphone and struggled to recite the famous psalm. "The Lord is our shepherd," he said between sobs. "We shall not want..."

As he spoke this prayer aloud, some congregants noticed that only a single stained glass window in the church remained. It depicted Christ leading a group of little children—but Jesus' face was blown out.

September 16, 1920

Ground Zero

The sky was that same "unbelievable blue" in New York City, to use Springsteen's phrase, as it would be eight decades later on 9/11. Almost instantly, the air was black with smoke, the street red with blood. A horse-drawn wagon with a covered cargo pulled up in front of the J. P. Morgan building at 23 Wall Street, near the corner of Wall and Broad streets, a place known simply as the Corner.

The House of Morgan, as historian Ron Chernow would write, "spoke to foreign governments as the voice of the American capital markets." It stood, in the same way the Twin Towers did, as a symbol of American economic might. Precisely at noon on this date—witnesses were certain of the time because they could still hear the echoes of the twelve o'clock bells at Trinity Church—the driver of the wagon dropped the reins and bolted. Seconds later, the dynamite in the wagon exploded with a fury.

The bombing was almost certainly the work of Italian anarchists; yet the blood that ran down Wall Street belonged mostly to working-class people: messenger boys, clerks, lower-rung stockbrokers, and unsuspecting passersby. The scene was barbaric and gruesome.

"As I gazed horror-struck at the sight, one of these forms, half-naked and seared with burns, started to rise," wrote George Weston, an Associated Press reporter who witnessed the bombing. "It struggled, then toppled and fell lifeless to the gutter."

Thirty-eight people perished, hundreds were wounded. The attack, wrote the *Washington Post*, in a pre-echo of 9/11, was "an act of war." But except for the garrison of the Twenty-Second U.S. Army Infantry, rushed to the scene of the crime from their barracks on Governor's Island along with 1,700 New York policemen, no troops were ever dispatched. The Wall Street bombing did not lead to a shooting war. Trading was halted on the floor of the stock exchange, but only for the rest of that day. The bodies and debris were cleaned up so fast investigators worried that evidence had been lost. The crime was never solved. Wall Street was up and running the very next morning. Trading was high, not out of greed, but out of a sense of defiance.

"Destructive as it was, the 1920 bomb that exploded in Wall Street's heart did not halt the rise of our new financial capital," economic writer Daniel Gross noted. He added that it backfired in the most literal way: The bombing, Gross wrote, "helped to humanize Wall Street."

September 17, 1960

Remember the Alamo

The last presidential candidate to campaign in eastern North Carolina was William Jennings Bryan, in 1896, during an election he lost to William McKinley. But on this date John F. Kennedy, Massachusetts's junior senator and the Democratic Party's 1960 nominee, showed up. The Democrats' old guard cautioned the Kennedy camp that they might not find the area receptive to a Roman Catholic. Terry Sanford, a 1960 North Carolina gubernatorial candidate the same age (forty-three) as Kennedy, was warned in a caustic letter by the senior clergyman at Greenville's oldest Methodist Church that a Catholic president would "surely cut America's head off."

But Sanford and Kennedy represented a new generation of postwar Democrats who didn't frighten easily. (Sanford was a U.S. Army paratrooper who fought at the Battle of the Bulge. Kennedy still suffered the physical effects of his heroics in the Pacific after his PT boat was sunk.) In any event, Kennedy was met by large, young, and enthusiastic crowds in North Carolina where he could see that his decision to address the Catholic issue head-on was paying dividends.

Although Kennedy's faith was a source of great pride to Catholic voters, particularly Democrats and most particularly Irish-Americans, a 1959 Gallup Poll showed 25 percent of voters were disinclined to support a Catholic for president. Antipathy was strongest in the Bible Belt, which presented a problem: A successful Electoral College strategy for a Democratic presidential candidate necessitated running well in the South. It was why Kennedy was in North Carolina on this date, why he had picked Texas senator Lyndon Johnson as his running mate, and why he had ventured five days earlier—on his seventh wedding anniversary—into the inner sanctum of anti-Catholicism when he spoke to the Greater Houston Ministerial Association.

"I am not the Catholic candidate for president," Kennedy told the Protestant pastors. "I am the Democratic Party's candidate for president who happens also to be a Catholic. I do not speak for my church on public matters, and the church does not speak for me."

Earlier that day, Kennedy had visited the Alamo. In preparation, he'd attempted to find out how many Catholics had fought there. The best his aides could do was a list of Irish names among the dead, resulting in one of the most evocative sentences of the campaign: "Side by side with Bowie and Crockett died McCafferty and Bailey and Carey," Kennedy said. "But no one knows whether they were Catholics or not, for there was no religious test at the Alamo."

September 18, 1793

A Capitol Idea

Moving America's capital city to the middle of the country had obvious political logic, as did naming it after George Washington. But the new site consisted mainly of a waterfront along the Potomac where present-day Georgetown sits. The rest of it was mostly uninhabited forests and fields. Pierre Charles L'Enfant, tapped by Washington to design the city, opted to house Congress on high ground. His plans called for "Congress House" to be built on a place he (but no one else) called "Jenkins Hill," after a man who owned the land but had never lived on it.

Reviewing L'Enfant's work, Jefferson crossed out the words "Congress House," replacing them with the words "Capitol" throughout the document. This simple edit, noted author Guy Gugliotta, had the effect of "endowing the building with the primacy it would never relinquish."

Meanwhile, George Washington commenced a contest, $500 going to the winner, for a design. Seeing nothing he particularly liked, Washington extended the deadline into 1793, eventually choosing the plans drawn up by an amateur architect named William Thornton. One of the also-rans, Stephen Hallet, the only formally trained architect of the bunch, was given a $500 consolation prize and asked to critique Thornton's work. Naturally, he found it wanting.

This led to bickering, recriminations, special pleadings, backroom dealings, and, well, politics. If it never quite resulted in gridlock, that bane of twenty-first-century governance, that was due to the personal interest shown by George Washington, who essentially operated as the general contractor.

"Anyone who ran afoul of the boss could expect to be quickly sacked," Gugliotta noted. "L'Enfant needed only five months to fall out of favor. Hallet, never Washington's first choice, lasted nine months." Somehow it got built, just as somehow it has survived. When Washington personally laid the cornerstone on this date, bands played and a crowd followed behind, some flying flags and cheering. The event devolved into a barbeque and picnic—think tailgating outside a football stadium—as newly minted Americans reveled in the idea of a building for representatives elected by the people, not chosen by a king or a far-off power.

By 1850, it was clear that a growing country needed a larger capitol building, and an appropriation was duly shepherded through Congress by a Southern senator named Jefferson Davis. After Davis's subsequent plans to halve the size of the nation were thwarted, the United States kept growing—the Capitol complex along with it.

September 19, 1982
Hello, Smiley

The campus of Carnegie Mellon University was in a state of near panic about rumors of a mercury spill. It was a false alarm, stemming from an obscure joke that was misconstrued in the thread of a multiway conversation on an electronic message board in the school's computer science department. Scott Fahlman, a research professor in that department, noticed that such misunderstandings had happened before.

"Given the nature of the community, a good many of the posts were humorous, or at least attempted humor," he'd recall later. "The problem was that if someone made a sarcastic remark, a few readers would fail to get the joke and each of them would post a lengthy diatribe in response." Seeking to avoid future confusions, Fahlman proposed that e-mailers include a modest qualifier to signal humorous intent.

"I propose," he wrote on this date, "the following character sequence for joke markers." Then he typed the now-famous characters that form an online smile. :-)

This solution took root and spread to other campuses and online communities. The "smiley," later called an "emoticon" to accommodate the markers for other feelings, was born.

This was an old idea. As author Keith Houston revealed in his book *Shady Characters: The Secret Life of Punctuation, Symbols, and Other Typographical Marks*, using punctuation to signal humor, or irony, was an impulse of writers long before computers.

As early as 1887, Ambrose Bierce penned an essay, "For Brevity and Clarity," in which he sarcastically proposed rendering clichés such as "much esteemed by all who knew him" as a single word ("mestewed") and a new punctuation mark to help the reading audience know when it should laugh. This new symbol was a horizontal line with the ends turned up. "It represents, as nearly as may be, a smiling mouth," Bierce deadpanned. His innovation did not catch on because it wasn't supposed to. But the same idea kept cropping up, apparently because it fit a need.

A *Baltimore Sun* columnist, Ralph Reppert, wrote about an aunt who used punctuation to "write a facial expression." Vladimir Nabokov had the same idea. A difficult interview who insisted questions be submitted in advance, the Russian émigré was once asked where he ranked himself among writers of his generation.

"I often think there should exist a special typographical sign for a smile—some sort of concave mark, a supine round bracket," he said, "which I would now like to trace in reply to your question."

September 20, 1739

American Cato

The slaves who had gathered at a South Carolina bridge had freedom on their minds. Born in a Portuguese-controlled and Catholic part of Africa, they were brought in bondage to a land controlled by British Protestants. The rebel leader was called Jemmy by whites, although his followers called him Cato. He probably came from Angola or the Congo and spoke some Portuguese. He certainly knew that Spanish authorities in Florida had promised freedom to New World slaves who managed to make it that far south. On September 9, 1739, Cato's band met at Stono River, and armed themselves by looting a store and killed two white shopkeepers.

They marched on the road, their numbers swelling with other slaves, beating drums, chanting "Liberty!"—and murdering white men, women, and children at a succession of plantations. By the time they stopped to camp for the night in a large field near the Edisto River, their force had quadrupled. They lit fires and danced in celebration of what seemed like a victorious day. Around dusk, however, a force of armed white militiamen on horseback attacked. Three dozen rebels were cut down on the spot. Many of the others ran into the woods, to be hunted down in the days and weeks ahead, shot or hanged or returned to their plantations. By this date, order was restored and the Stono River Slave Rebellion was over.

The history of this bloody episode was recorded by whites, which is where the information above comes from. Yet, one wonders. Whites believe the name "Cato" is a corruption of "Carter" or "Cater," and that they must have been Jemmy's owners. Perhaps. But South Carolina's blacks recorded their history orally and their version of his name evokes the eloquent and tenacious Roman senator who opposed Julius Caesar. That might be a stretch. But this much is true: During the Depression, Cato's great-great-grandson was asked for his family's version of the rebellion. The two accounts are strikingly similar except when it came to the underlying cause of the rebellion. On this part of the story, Cato's white contemporaries sound clueless. Not Jemmy's great-great-grandson. He understood it clearly, as he related in the 1930s:

"When the militia come in sight of them . . . Commander Cato speak for the crowd. He say, 'We don't like slavery. We start to join the Spanish in Florida. We surrender but we not whipped yet and we is not converted.' The other forty-three men say, 'Amen.'

"They was taken, unarmed, and hanged by the militia," he added. "He die, but he die for doing right, as he see it."

September 21, 1776

Only One Life to Give

George Washington had dispatched a brave, twenty-one-year-old Continental Army captain on a dangerous mission behind enemy lines. The young officer's name was Nathan Hale, and he was sent out to ascertain British troop movements on Long Island. Hale did not succeed and he paid for his failure—and General Washington's desperate gambit—with his own life.

In 1775, when the yearnings for independence spilled into a shooting war between British troops and their restive colonials, Nathan Hale enlisted and was commissioned as a lieutenant; in six months' time he was made a captain. Like many officers in George Washington's citizen army, Hale was not a professional soldier, let alone a properly trained spy. He was a schoolteacher.

Born in 1755 in Coventry, Connecticut, he graduated with honors from Yale College in 1773 and was teaching in New London when the shots fired in Lexington and heard 'round the world inspired him to enlist in the Continental Army. Washington was impressed by the young man, and as British general William Howe amassed troops outside New York City in September 1776, Washington tasked him with the fatal mission of going behind enemy lines and ascertaining the strength of the redcoats and the colonial Tories still loyal to the crown.

Little is known about what Hale discovered when he landed on Long Island on September 10, 1776, with whom he met, or where he went. What is known is that he was captured on this date and hanged by orders of General Howe the following day. It is also known, thanks to meticulous research by James H. Hutson, chief of the Manuscript Division at the Library of Congress, that Hale may have been betrayed by a cousin, Samuel Hale, a Tory who fought with Howe.

Legend holds that as he was led to the gallows, Hale told Howe aide-de-camp John Montresor, "I only regret that I have but one life to lose for my country."

Did he really say it? The historical evidence is scant, and if he did, he was cribbing a famous line from *Cato*, a popular eighteenth-century play by Joseph Addison. The line certainly belongs to Nathan Hale now, however, which is fair considering the price he paid for it.

September 22, 1875

A Good Cigar and a Good Yarn

A Wisconsin newspaper, the *Oshkosh Daily Northwestern*, published an item in the winter of 1914 that would become a staple of political humor. An unnamed U.S. senator had just given a speech "telling exactly what this country needs," the paper reported. Afterward, the senator saw Vice President Thomas R. Marshall in the senator's private lobby, lighting a cigar.

"You overlooked the chief need of the country," Marshall told the senator.

"What's that?" the other man replied.

"The thing that seems to be needed most of all," declared Marshall as he puffed away, "is a really good five-cent cigar."

Thomas Riley Marshall was a popular Indiana Democrat elected governor in 1908 and placed on the 1912 ticket with Woodrow Wilson. Although Wilson seems to have had little regard for his vice president, Marshall had a winning personality, which his biographer, Charles M. Thomas, attributed to his not being overly rigid in his personal habits or political views.

Marshall was known for an ever-present cigar or a pipe in his mouth. Franklin D. Roosevelt told a story dating to when he was assistant secretary of the U.S. Navy and Marshall boarded a naval vessel sporting a cane, wearing a silk hat, and smoking a cigar. When the band struck up "The Star-Spangled Banner," Marshall "realized his predicament," Roosevelt recalled. Shifting the cane from right hand to left, he took the cigar out of his mouth, doffed the hat, and managed a salute. When the first gun went off, "the whole works went two feet into the air."

As for that cigar quote, Marshall said it—he just didn't say it first. Historian John E. Brown traced the quotation back to an early twentieth-century Indiana newspaper cartoonist name Kin Hubbard, author of a comic strip called *Abe Martin of Brown County*. Hubbard had put the cigar gag in the mouth of his fictional lead character. "As a fan of the cartoon strip," noted Senate historian Mark O. Hatfield, "Marshall simply picked up the phrase, repeated it, and became its surrogate father." Fred R. Shapiro, editor of the *Yale Book of Quotations*, has traced it back further. Four decades before Midwestern newspapers began attributing the cigar quip to Marshall, a Connecticut daily, the *Hartford Courant*, printed this item in an unsigned "News and Notions" column on this date. "What this country really needs is a good five cent cigar."

Even then it wasn't original. The gem was attributed to another paper, the *New York Mail*. "Indiana homespun humor," wrote Shapiro with a trace of regional pride, "was preceded by the more sophisticated wit of the Big Apple."

September 23, 1779

Fighting Words

Scottish-born John Paul Jones was the skipper of the large and lumbering *Bonhomme Richard*, a ship given to him by the French upon the request of Benjamin Franklin, America's man in Paris. "I intend to go in harm's way," Jones told the French, and he did exactly that, pillaging and pirating up and down the British coast. The Royal Navy captain entrusted with stopping him was Richard Pearson, who headed a small fleet sent to intercept Jones.

Pearson's smaller, faster, and better-armed ship, the *Serapis*, led the British convoy. In the ensuing engagement on this date, Jones' ship collided with *Serapis*. Jones ordered his men to lash the two together, leading to a deadly scene in which the two crews fired at each other point-blank for hours. As darkness overtook the battle, the Americans' situation was desperate. A full moon and the fire from the *Bonhomme Richard*'s burning masts revealed a scene of carnage; meanwhile, seawater poured through holes in the ship's hull. Two of Jones's officers, thinking him dead, tried to surrender. This enraged Jones, who was very much not dead. Above the din, Pearson appeared on the rail of his ship and asked Jones if he wished to strike his colors.

"I have not yet begun to fight!" Jones replied famously. Or did he?

Nobody knows for sure, except that everyone present reported that Jones refused to surrender, and did so with aplomb. "I answered him in the most determined negative," Jones wrote to Franklin days later. A contemporaneous account in British newspapers quotes Jones as replying, "I may sink, but I'm damned if I'll strike." A *London Evening Post* account goes further, reporting that Jones said that he wouldn't dream of surrendering, but was intent on making Pearson strike his own colors. The words we recall today were furnished by Captain Pearson himself, who qualified his account (at his own court-martial) by saying he didn't hear it personally, but that one of his midshipmen relayed it: "It was to the effect that he was just beginning to fight."

"History," noted naval scholar Rick Beyer, "had its quotable quote."

As for the famous battle's outcome, the *Bonhomme Richard* eventually sank beneath the waves, but not before Jones captured the *Serapis*, which he sailed to the Netherlands for repairs. More significant, the feisty captain's never-say-die spirit helped convince the French to support the colonists' quest for independence—and embedded itself in the American psyche.

September 24, 1881

Garfield for President

The funeral train carrying President James A. Garfield pulled into Cleveland, Ohio, at 1:21 p.m. on this date. Over the next two days, 250,000 mourners came to pay their respects—at a time when Cleveland's total population was 150,000. On the overnight rail trip from Washington, untold thousands had gathered along the tracks, some lighting bonfires in his honor.

A decorated officer in the Union Army, and Republican member of Congress for eighteen years, Garfield had been president for only four months when he was shot by a deranged gunman in Washington, D.C. He lingered until September 19, 1881, before dying of his wounds—and the incompetent medical care he was given. The year before, he'd been the Republican Party's surprise choice to run against another popular Civil War general, Winfield Scott Hancock. Garfield had gone to the Chicago convention that year to push for fellow Ohioan John Sherman, the brother of William Tecumseh Sherman. But after Garfield gave a thoughtful and eloquent speech in support of Sherman, the delegates turned to a compromise candidate.

"And now, gentlemen of the convention," Garfield asked at the end of his oration, "what do we want?" From the suddenly silent convention hall came a shout: "We want Garfield!"

The stampede had begun. Garfield did the best he could to quell it. He told supporters to vote for Sherman and said publicly and privately he didn't want the nomination. This reluctance only further convinced his newfound supporters that they'd found their man. By the thirty-sixth ballot, the tide had become clear. From Washington, Sherman telegraphed the Ohio delegates to get behind Garfield. He tried to refuse the nomination, but was ruled out of order. Garfield attempted to leave the hall early, but was told that was impossible. To a delegate from Maine who congratulated him, he muttered, "I am very sorry that this has become necessary."

He served only a fleeting time. But his presidency and his painful, lingering death helped unite the country. Upon his passing, grief-stricken Americans—North and South, Republican and Democrat—felt that they had lost *their* president. Garfield was the first leader since the Civil War who engendered such universal feelings. He left too soon, and is too little remembered.

Yet there is much to admire in this man, including a quote that sums up his natural inclination for conciliation, and his steely resolve—all in one sentence. "Of course I deprecate war," he wrote, "but if it is brought to my door, the bringer will find me at home."

September 25, 1867

A Feisty Gentleman

Oliver Loving and Charles Goodnight first met sixty miles west of Fort Worth in a Texas town called Black Springs (present-day Oran) and forged a fateful partnership with a handshake. Their association would result in a historic trail that bears their name, an initial cattle drive that netted the men $12,000 in gold coins, Loving's fatal encounter with a Comanche war party, and the inspiration for Larry McMurtry's *Lonesome Dove* novel and television miniseries.

In real life, Oliver Loving succumbed to gangrene at Fort Sumner, New Mexico, after being pierced in the side and the arm with arrows. He might have survived if his arm had been amputated, but the doctor at the fort had no experience removing limbs, and shied away from the procedure. In *Lonesome Dove*, the two trailblazing cattlemen are named Augustus McCrae (played by Robert Duvall) and Woodrow F. Call (Tommy Lee Jones). As one might imagine, Gus McCrae's fictional death is more romantic than Oliver Loving's actual passing, which occurred on this date. McCrae, also wounded by Indians, has one leg removed because of infection, but balks at losing the other—pulling his pistol to keep the doctor at bay.

Nor is there any indication that Oliver Loving's last words were as poetic as Gus McCrae's: "By God, Woodrow," Gus exclaims, "it's been one hell of a party." But there is evidence in the historic record of Oliver Loving expressing sadness at the prospect of being buried "in a foreign country." So Charles Goodnight—as Woodrow Call would do on screen 122 years later—promised to take his partner's body back to Texas. In the movie, Woodrow's quest ends with Gus buried in a pecan grove beside a creek where he often picnicked with his beloved Clara.

In real life, Charles Goodnight, along with Oliver Loving's son Joseph, honored a dying man's wish by bringing his body six hundred miles from Fort Sumner to Weatherford, Texas. There, Loving is buried, alongside his wife, in Greenwood Cemetery. But his descendants, and all of us, can appreciate the folk wisdom of Gus McCrae, as epitomized by his advice to a young friend named Lorena who is thinking her problems will all be solved if she can get herself to California.

"Lorie darlin,' life in San Francisco, you see, is still just life," Gus tells her. "If you want any one thing too badly, it's likely to turn out to be a disappointment. The only healthy way to live life is to learn to like all the little everyday things, like a sip of good whiskey in the evening, a soft bed, a glass of buttermilk, or a feisty gentleman like myself."

September 26, 1957

Parting Is Such Sweet Sorrow

The inspiration for *West Side Story* was *Romeo and Juliet*, but where did Shakespeare get his idea? And what, exactly, was the beef between the houses of Montague and Capulet? The answers are that Shakespeare borrowed his idea, characters, plot line—even the title—from a poem published in 1562 by a British playwright named Arthur Brooke. Unlike Shakespeare's version, Brooke's poem, with its anti-Catholic undertones, is a cautionary tale about how lust leads young people to ignore their elders and pursue love outside their religious caste.

Four centuries later, the great dance choreographer Jerome Robbins (née Rabinowitz) endeavored to explore that theme in a musical and dance production. He tentatively called his idea "East Side Story" and planned to stage the action in the spring when Passover and Easter expose the underlying tensions between the families of a Jewish girl (Juliet) and her Catholic boyfriend (Romeo). In 1949, he began collaborating with two other towering talents, playwright Arthur Laurents and famous composer and conductor Leonard Bernstein. While in Hollywood on a film project, Bernstein and Laurents were brainstorming around the pool at the Beverly Hills Hotel. Los Angeles's newspapers were full of stories about ethnic-based gangs so Laurents and Bernstein decided that Robbins's (and Arthur Brooke's) religious tensions would give way to a more primal turf fight between a Puerto Rican street gang and a self-described "American" crew.

The two men added a fourth virtuoso to their creative group, a young writer named Stephen Sondheim. What ensued was magic. *West Side Story* opened on Broadway on this date and would run for 732 performances before going on tour. By that time, a film project was in the works, aided by the infusion of even more talent, including director Robert Wise and actress Natalie Wood. The 1961 film was a commercial and critical success: the top grossing movie of the year, and winner of ten Academy Awards, including Best Picture.

Is it time for a remake? A contemporary version could draw on the original play, perhaps with feuding Muslim and Christian (or Jewish) families. Or even better: What if one of the doomed lovers was a Republican and the other a Democrat? Would Independents still be caught in the middle, as was Mercutio—neither a Montague nor a Capulet—in the Shakespeare original?

"A plague o' both your houses!" Mercutio proclaims after being stabbed by one of the factions. "They have made worms' meat of me!"

September 27, 1869

Law and Order

The tradeoff between safe streets and heavy-handed law enforcement, an issue which burst on the American political scene during Barack Obama's second term in the White House and roiled the 2016 presidential campaign, is not a new topic in this country. The good townspeople of Hays, Kansas, saw both sides of this issue in 1869.

Tired of being brutalized by itinerant cowboys and local roughnecks who liquored up in the saloons in the county seat of Hays City, voters in Ellis County turned to an outsider in a special election on August 23, 1869. The results were disputed—"rigged" elections are not a new subject either—but ultimately Wild Bill Hickok was installed as sheriff.

It didn't take long for people to notice. Just a few days after Hickok assumed office, a bad hombre from Missouri named Bill Mulvey showed up in town. Mulvey's reputation as a mean drunk preceded him, and the journey to Hays hadn't mellowed him. When informed that Wild Bill was the new lawman in town, Mulvey registered his displeasure by shooting the mirrors in the saloon where he was drinking while using bad language and issuing threats.

These were not veiled threats, either. Mulvey went so far as to boast that he'd come to Kansas to kill Bill Hickok. This may have just been whiskey talk, but as events unfolded it happened the other way around. According to an eyewitness account, Mulvey rode up the street on his gray horse, rifle at the ready. Wild Bill strode out to meet him and called out to an imaginary gunman behind Mulvey.

"Don't shoot him in the back," Hickok shouted. "He is drunk."

When Mulvey turned around, Hickok drew his pistol and shot him in the head.

A few weeks later, on this date, Hickok and his deputy came upon a gang of cowboys tearing the hell out of John Bitter's Beer Saloon. When Hickok ordered them to desist, one of the men, Samuel Strawhun, turned as if to rush the sheriff. Hickok quickly shot and killed him, quelling the melee.

The city fathers of Hays were left to contemplate that after only five weeks in office Wild Bill Hickok had killed two men in the name of law and order. Voters mulled it over, too, and in the regular November election that year, Hickok was voted out of office in favor of his deputy.

September 28, 1941

Teddy Ballgame

Ted Williams had a decision to make: to play or not to play? The Boston Red Sox were in Philadelphia for a doubleheader against the Athletics—the last two games of the season. Neither team was in pennant contention, and Williams's mind must have at least partially been on events in Europe and Japan that were drawing the United States into war.

"The Kid" was leading the league in hitting. His average, to the last decimal point, was .3995. Rounded off, it came to .400—a hallowed mark now, a milestone then—and the dilemma was whether Williams should risk it by playing in two meaningless games. He decided to play, and went six for eight in the two games on this date, with a double and a home run, raising his average to .406, a standard never equaled since.

Williams did go off to war in 1942. A U.S. Marine combat pilot, he answered the call in Korea, too, and by the time his career ended, he'd missed nearly five seasons to military service, while managing to make a strong case in support of his stated ambition to be considered "the greatest hitter who ever lived." As fate would have it, it was also September 28—in 1960—that the Fenway faithful caught their last glimpse of Williams. In 1959, with his back hurting, the "Splendid Splinter"—one of Williams's many nicknames—had put up the numbers of a journeyman. He was a "kid" no longer, but determined not to go out that way, he'd returned for the 1960 season, at forty-two years of age, for a curtain call. It lasted all season.

He hit .316 that year, with twenty-nine home runs. The only one of the twenty-nine that anyone remembers now was clubbed off Jack Fisher of the Baltimore Orioles. Williams, who'd had an uneven relationship with the fans and a toxic one with Boston's sportswriters, circled the bases with his head down, not acknowledging the meager crowd, which stood and cheered for his last at-bat.

The day was memorialized by John Updike in a classic 1960 *New Yorker* piece, "Hub Fans Bid Kid Adieu," which has held up through the years, and not just for its marvelous prose.

The line in that story best recalled today takes place after Williams homers and the crowd begs him to come out for a curtain call. These faithful, these ten thousand, were Williams partisans. But the hurts of previous years were too deep, the stubbornness that made Williams who he was, too profound. "Gods do not answer letters" was how John Updike put it.

September 29, 1954

A Great Catch

The score was tied in the eighth inning in Game 1 of the World Series when Cleveland Indians first basemen Vic Wertz sent a towering 425-foot shot to center field in the Polo Grounds. But Willie Mays was playing centerfield for the New York Giants, and Willie Mays's glove, in the immortal words of a Dodgers executive, was "where triples go to die."

"I don't know how Willie did it," New York–based announcer Russ Hodges enthused on NBC, "but he's been doing it all year!"

In baseball circles, Mays's defensive gem was simply called "the Catch." It set the tone for the Series, which the Giants swept over the shell-shocked Indians—a demonstrably better team during the regular season—in four straight games. Yet fascination with the Catch, and with Mays, transcended baseball. Only twenty-three, the Giants' center fielder was in the vanguard of a generation of black players too young to have been barred by baseball's color barrier. And Mays, this blend of power and speed, who played with unfettered elan and high baseball IQ, had come to New York from Alabama and stolen hearts as well as bases. Actress Tallulah Bankhead, a Southern white woman—but racial liberal—reportedly quipped in her trademark husky voice, "Genius? Dahling, there are only two geniuses, Willie Shakespeare and Willie Mays."

The Giants and Dodgers decamped to the West Coast as California was starting to eclipse New York as a cultural and political power. But San Francisco wasn't yet the cosmopolitan burg it aspired to be. There were neighborhoods in "the City" where the color of Mays's skin made him an unwelcome homeowner. Baseball fans of a certain age compared Mays to their city's hometown hero: Joe DiMaggio and his brothers were from San Francisco. Joe didn't strike out as much, the old-timers groused. He made tough chances in center field look easy, while Mays showboated.

Young Bay Area fans were enthralled with how Mays tore around the diamond, however, and we cheered happily when his cap flew off as he slid into base. That squad was heavily black and Latino, but the Giants were our team. "Black is beautiful" seemed less a statement of liberation than an observation of the world as it really was. The "brown-eyed handsome man" heading for home in the song "Centerfield" by John Fogarty (the pride of El Cerrito High School in the East Bay)—that man was Jackie Robinson, Willie Mays, and a whole generation of black stars.

Yes, the times, they were a-changin'.

September 30, 1952

Little Mo

What do you give a girl who has everything? Or, at least, a girl who wins the U.S. Open at sixteen and then Wimbledon and the U.S. Open the following year—but who has no father in her life? If it's the early 1950s and you're the mayor of San Diego, you throw a parade for home girl and have the city give her a horse. The tennis star's name was Maureen Connally, although a San Diego sportswriter had already dubbed her "Little Mo"—"Big Mo" being, in that Navy town, a familiar reference to a famous battleship, the USS *Missouri*. The horse was a Tennessee Walker named Colonel Merryboy, and on this date she was getting to know him.

Little Mo had learned tennis on San Diego public courts while other prodigies had private tutoring at cloistered country clubs. As Maureen took the Southern California junior tournaments by storm, she signed on with famed Beverly Hills tennis coach Eleanor Tennant, who helped round out Connolly's game while stoking her competitiveness and insecurity into a white-hot fury—*hate* was the word Maureen later used—for her opponents. Maureen would quickly become the world's best female tennis player.

On September 17, 1951, her seventeenth birthday, *Time* magazine proclaimed her the "new hope" for women's tennis. She won the U.S. Open again the next year, but when Tennant had wanted her to withdraw because of an injury at Wimbledon, Little Mo fired her on the spot—and won the tournament. Her third and final coach was Australian legend Harry Hopman, who taught her that she didn't need to hate her opponents to beat them: She just had to play her game, because her game was the best in the world.

She won tennis's Grand Slam in 1953 at nineteen and would have been great for a decade, but while riding Colonel Merryboy in 1954, a cement truck spooked the horse. Connolly's leg was crushed and her career cut short. Yet, this mishap had a nice ending. Her father, who she hadn't seen since she was four, and who she thought dead, showed up in the hospital to tell her he loved her. They resumed their relationship. Maureen also resolved while recuperating to marry her on-again, off-again boyfriend, Norman Brinker, an Olympic equestrian who had also been injured while riding. They moved to Dallas, and started a family of their own. Norman became a successful businessman; Maureen raised two kids, wrote a sports column, launched a foundation, and died of ovarian cancer at thirty-four.

She was a comet.

October 1, 1962
"Heeeere's Johnny"

The Tonight Show was already successful when Johnny Carson took over hosting from Jack Paar on this date. At 11:30 p.m., from 1962 to 1992, sidekick Ed McMahon would announce "Heeeere's Johnny," and Carson would spend the next ninety minutes (later reduced to sixty minutes) bantering with band leader Doc Severinsen, donning his goofy "Carnac the Magnificent" turban, and interviewing movie stars, celebrities, politicians— all prefaced by an opening monologue that would make fun of various figures, especially the current resident of the White House.

Richard Nixon, Carson deadpanned, was the first president whose official portrait was painted by a police sketch artist. After Republicans flirted with the idea of pairing Ronald Reagan and Gerald Ford as their presidential and vice presidential nominees, Carson quipped: "That would have been a great ticket, Reagan and Ford—an actor and a stuntman."

Born in Iowa, and raised in Nebraska, Carson lived almost his entire adult life on the two coasts, and it showed in the biting humor of New York, which he leavened with a smile that evinced the supposedly easygoing ethos of Southern California. Tough to work for, and apparently even harder to live with (he was married four times), Carson kept his liberal politics well hidden, while making salary demands that would make a movie star blush. It was also asserted, by no less a guardian of Eastern prerogative than the *New York Times*, that when Carson moved the show to Burbank ten years into his run, it "meant a realignment of American pop culture from East Coast to West Coast, from Broadway to Hollywood."

Perhaps, but *The Tonight Show* had originated as a 1951 Los Angeles radio show.

Part of Carson's appeal was that he helped us laugh at ourselves as well as our politicians. In the 1970s, when a gasoline crisis coincided with an outbreak of UFO sightings, Carson quipped: "The bad news is that aliens have landed. The good news is that they pee gasoline."

"Johnny was reliable when life was brutal," is how Raymond Siller put it. As Carson's head writer, he thought a lot about how Americans liked to be entertained, and why Carson was their favorite late-night guy. "You drove through a hurricane, got fired, your wife left you, a coyote ate your cat...and he was there, a witness through America's rites of passage who pointed to our fads and warts, heroes and scoundrels, booms and busts," Siller said. "He defanged the snakes, told light jokes about heavy matters, and coaxed us not to take ourselves too seriously."

October 2, 1950

Charlie Brown

A new comic strip, which debuted on this date, made its maiden appearance in the *Washington Post*, the *Boston Globe*, the *Chicago Tribune*, the *Denver Post*, and five other U.S. newspapers.

Its author and illustrator was a twenty-seven-year-old Minnesota native named Charles Schulz. The new syndicated strip was called *Peanuts*. By the time Schulz died fifty years later—a millionaire with books and TV specials to his credit, his name etched in the annals of mass culture—his drawings and commentary were considered by some newspaper editors to be corny and tame, and tragically unhip. Millions of readers, particularly those of a certain age, still found them profound. One thing is sure: At its inception, *Peanuts* was edgy for its time. The initial 1950 strip featured two unnamed kids whom readers would come to know as Shermy and Patty, sitting on a sidewalk. A third kid, who says nothing, passes by.

"Well, here comes ol' Charlie Brown," observes Shermy.

In two successive frames, the boy uses the expression "good ol' Charlie Brown," until the innocent object of this discussion is out of the picture—and out of earshot. That's when Shermy delivers the punch line: "How I hate him!"

October 3, 2012

Happy Anniversary, Michelle!

Barack Obama wanted to be somewhere else. It wasn't Mitt Romney, exactly, who was bothering him, or the hordes of media—or even the debate stage. It certainly wasn't the city of Denver, Colorado, where he'd accepted the presidential nomination four years earlier. It was just that this day was his wedding anniversary. Any romantic inclinations of the First Couple were deferred, which helps explain why he was widely adjudged to have flubbed the debate so badly.

Was his mind elsewhere? The president said as much. Instead of forgetting his anniversary, as Jack Kennedy had done on the day he went to the Alamo in 1960, Obama prefaced his first debate answer with a personal aside.

"There are a lot of points I want to make tonight, but the most important one is that twenty years ago, I became the luckiest man on Earth because Michelle Obama agreed to marry me," the president said. Turning from debate moderator Jim Lehrer to his wife, he added: "And so I just want to wish, sweetie, you a happy anniversary and let you know that a year from now we will not be celebrating it in front of forty million people."

October 4, 1957

Space Race

Four years to the day after the first Obama-Romney debate, the two major parties' vice presidential candidates squared off at Longwood University in Farmville, Virginia. That week, the latest flare-up in the 2016 presidential race concerned a private comment Hillary Clinton made about WikiLeaks founder Julian Assange. "Can't we just drone this guy?" she said, presumably in jest. Clinton's crack was an interesting example of twenty-first-century gallows humor: she employed the word *drone* as a verb, a usage presupposing that space technology is now harnessed for purposes of war. This was a long-standing concern, although Americans worried about being on the receiving end of such attacks. On this date, those fears were stoked by a *beep, beep, beep* sound that came unexpectedly over the radio. Those blips were the signal emitted by a 184-pound Soviet satellite orbiting the Earth.

"Listen now," an NBC radio announcer told his audience, "for the sound that forevermore separates the old from the new."

When they had awakened that morning, Americans took their nation's technological superiority for granted. Innovations ranging from the telephone to the atomic bomb had fostered confidence that the United States would always be first in the frontier of applied science. Sputnik indicated otherwise, and it was a shock to the national psyche.

"Never before," wrote historian Daniel J. Boorstin, "had so small and so harmless an object created such consternation."

The day after the launch, President Dwight D. Eisenhower demanded answers from his science advisers. How could such a thing happen? Why was the U.S. government caught so completely unaware? A grilling by Ike was never a pleasant experience. More recriminations were coming: Senate Majority Leader Lyndon Johnson convened hearings before the Armed Services Committee. The *New York Times* published a three-part series extolling the supposed superiority of Russia's educational system. A young senator from Massachusetts began formulating an angle for his expected 1960 presidential run.

John Kennedy's hook was the so-called "missile gap" between the United States and the Soviet Union. This was fiction, but trailing Russia in the space race was fact—and in Washington, Democrats and Republicans joined forces to address it. By the following July, Eisenhower had signed the National Aeronautics and Space Act. "The enactment of this legislation," Eisenhower said in a written statement, "is an historic step, further equipping the United States for leadership in the space age."

Eisenhower's successor invoked Sputnik in his exhortation to his fellow Americans committing the U.S. to reaching the moon. President Kennedy would not be alive when that happened; his successor, Lyndon Johnson, would also be out of office. But four consecutive U.S. presidents stayed the course, and on July 20, 1969, a shared national goal was attained. It all started on October 4, 1959. That night, Johnson, then Senate majority leader, was hosting a barbeque at his ranch in Texas. After learning of Sputnik's launch, he took some of his guests to the banks of the Pedernales River, with its impressive nighttime view of the stars.

"In the open West, you learn to live with the sky," he wrote in his 1972 memoir. "It is a part of your life. But now, somehow, in some new way, the sky seemed almost alien."

Publicly, Johnson gave voice to his deepest fears, warning Americans of the grim possibility that nuclear-armed Soviet satellites would "be dropping bombs on us from space like kids dropping rocks onto cars from freeway overpasses." *Newsweek* sounded a similar alarm, while Montana senator Mike Mansfield warned: "What is at stake is nothing less than our survival."

But Eisenhower and his countrymen had seen enough during World War II and its aftermath to instill confidence in America's ability to produce the scientists necessary to win the space race. This faith would prove well-placed. The same night Lyndon Johnson pondered the cosmos and Ike demanded answers from his staff, fourteen-year-old Homer H. Hickam Jr. gazed skyward from his West Virginia mining hamlet and imagined space travel.

"I saw the bright little ball, moving majestically across the narrow star field between the ridgelines," Hickam recalled later. "I stared at it with no less rapt attention than if it had been God Himself in a golden chariot riding overhead. It soared with what seemed to me inexorable and dangerous purpose, as if there were no power in the universe that could stop it. All my life, everything important that had ever happened had always happened somewhere else. But Sputnik was right there in front of my eyes in my backyard in Coalwood, McDowell County, West Virginia, U.S.A. I couldn't believe it."

In that way, a threat became a challenge, answered by thousands of young dreamers such as Homer Hickam, who went on to become a top NASA engineer and the protagonist of an unlikely best-selling memoir titled *Rocket Boys*.

October 5, 1947

Guns, Then Butter

To address a looming human catastrophe taking shape across the ocean, a U.S. president employed a new technology—the first televised address from the White House. Speaking into the camera, Harry Truman used that format to urge his fellow Americans to eat less meat and poultry so that grain being fed to U.S. livestock could be exported across the Atlantic to help alleviate the threat of mass starvation in postwar Europe.

"The situation in Europe is grim and forbidding as winter approaches," Truman said on this date. "They cannot get through the coming winter and spring without help—generous help—from the United States and from other countries which have food to spare."

The program had already been outlined by administration officials, including Secretary of State George C. Marshall, which was fitting because the food conservation program was the precursor to the huge U.S. aid package that would bear Marshall's name. Besides appealing to Americans' altruism, Marshall and Truman framed the issue in national security terms: The United States and its allies had prevailed in a costly world war, and now faced a new adversary in the form of the Soviet Union.

"An essential requirement of lasting peace is the restoration of the countries of Western Europe as free self-supporting democracies," Truman said in his televised speech. "If the peace should be lost because we failed to share our food with hungry people there would be no more tragic example in all history of a peace needlessly lost."

His ensuing pitch seems quaint now, even discounting for the casual sexism of the day. Like a Great Plains elementary school teacher from an earlier time, Truman supplied the lesson:

"Learn it, memorize it, keep it always in mind," he said. "Here it is: One: Use no meat on Tuesdays. Two: Use no poultry or eggs on Thursdays. Three: Save a slice of bread every day. Four: Public eating places will serve bread and butter only on request."

"I realize that many millions of American housewives have already begun strict conservation measures," Truman added. "I say to those housewives, 'Keep up the good work,' and save even more when and where you can." The president didn't directly discuss Americans' waistlines, which were narrower than today, but he concluded with a sentiment that would be embraced by a First Lady six decades in the future:

"Our self-denial," he said, "will serve us well in the years to come."

October 6, 1877

They Will Fight No More Forever

U.S. Army colonel Nelson A. Miles was in his field tent in Montana when he penned a letter to his superiors about the progress of his military campaign against the Nez Perce, which in their language means the "real people." This kind of ethnocentrism was common in the language of the Indian societies encountered by whites in their westward push across this continent. But in the case of the Nez Perce it seems an apt description: This was a tribe that won the admiration of whites from the beginning, mainly because of their fair and charitable dealings, beginning with their virtual rescue of the Lewis and Clark expedition.

Although it's still painful to think about even all these years later, this honorable treatment was not reciprocated. Their land was taken, promises were broken, and treaties violated until finally the Nez Perce could take no more. Their great chief in the mid-nineteenth century was a Christian convert who swore his allegiance to the U.S. Constitution and negotiated the contours of a reservation that included much of the historic Nez Perce land running from what is now eastern Oregon into the Idaho mountains. This chief took a western name: Chief Joseph or Joseph the Elder. In a depressingly familiar tale, however, gold was later discovered on their land. Whites rushed in; agreements were ignored or unilaterally altered. When the government wouldn't help him, Joseph burned his American flag, along with his Bible, and took a stand in his native Wallowa Valley.

Joseph the Elder died in 1871, leaving his people in a state of roiling agitation. The Nez Perce didn't have a single commander in chief, like a U.S. president, but one of the chiefs was Joseph's eldest son, Hin-mah-too-yah-lat-kekt, which means "thunder rolling down the mountain." Out of respect for his father, he was usually called Joseph the Younger. The U.S. Army simply referred to him as Chief Joseph, the name we know him by today.

Under threat from cavalry commanded by Gen. Oliver O. Howard, the Nez Perce began leaving their homes for a reservation one-tenth its original size in Idaho. A breakaway faction of twenty militant warriors went on the warpath, raiding and killing whites. Suddenly, Chief Joseph's main band of seven hundred Indians, most of them women and children, found themselves being pursued by U.S. Army units accompanied by heavily armed and violent Montana militias intent on exterminating them.

What ensued next was what the Army and the newspapers called the Nez Perce War. But it was really a brave and brilliant tactical retreat toward Canada, where "the real people" believed they would be safe. Chief Joseph seems to have been the domestic leader, keeping the people together, keeping them fed, keeping them on the move. Other war

310

chiefs, including Looking Glass and Joseph's younger brother, Olikut, led the skirmishes against the Army. For three months, a band of Indians with fewer than two hundred warriors led two thousand mounted and seasoned U.S. Army troops on a 1,400-mile chase before the Indians were surrounded.

The letter Colonel Miles wrote to his superiors on this date explains the denouement: how the Indians had suffered many casualties as they fought unsuccessfully the day before trying break out of the trap, and how Chief Joseph had finally surrendered. Miles's report is dry and soulless even for a military dispatch. It is also vintage Nelson Miles: He gives little credit to the enemy and even less to his fellow officers, including longtime rival General Howard.

William Tecumseh Sherman, the Army chief of staff on the receiving end of Miles's reports, had no such qualms. The Nez Perce, he noted later, "fought with almost scientific skill, using advance and rear guards, skirmish lines, and field fortifications."

Chief Joseph was brilliant in defeat, too. His eloquent surrender speech helped turn the tide of American public opinion in the Nez Perce's favor. This got him an audience with President Rutherford B. Hayes, and eventually some of his people's land back.

"I am tired of fighting," he proclaimed.

"Our chiefs are killed," Chief Joseph continued. "Looking Glass is dead. Too-hoolhoolzote is dead. The old men are all dead. It is the young men who say, 'Yes' or 'No.' He who led the young men [Olikut] is dead. It is cold, and we have no blankets. The little children are freezing to death. My people, some of them, have run away to the hills, and have no blankets, no food. No one knows where they are—perhaps freezing to death. I want to have time to look for my children, and see how many of them I can find. Maybe I shall find them among the dead. Hear me, my chiefs! I am tired. My heart is sick and sad. From where the sun now stands I will fight no more forever."

October 7, 1849

In a Kingdom by the Sea

Contrary to popular perception, Edgar Allan Poe's personal life was not in turmoil when he died in Baltimore. He had just become reengaged to Sarah Elmira Royster. When Poe left for college, the Virginia beauty jilted him for another man. After she became a widow in her thirties, she and Poe found each other again. The writer left Richmond for a business trip to Philadelphia, but he only made it as far as Baltimore. He was discovered in a gutter by an acquaintance in a half-conscious state, wearing unfamiliar clothes with no recollection of what had happened to him. He was taken to a local hospital, where he died on this date.

The notion that Poe drank himself to death was planted in a nasty obituary penned by Rufus Wilmot Griswold, a professional rival. It's true that when Poe was taken to the hospital he was placed in a tower where those with alcohol poisoning were housed to avoid disrupting other patients. But it's also true that the attending physician, future Falls Church, Virginia, mayor John J. Moran, concluded that Poe was not intoxicated at all. Dr. Moran surmised, judging by Poe's shabby clothes and lack of recollection, that he'd been robbed and struck a blow on the head that cost him his memory. Other theories: that Miss Royster's brothers had Poe attacked; that Poe contracted rabies; that he was felled by the flu. It's a mystery unlikely ever to be solved, which seems apt for a writer who pioneered the detective story.

If Griswold did a disservice to Poe's reputation, however, he also is the one who gave a copy of the as-yet-unpublished "Annabel Lee" to the *New York Daily Tribune*, which printed it two days after his death. Various women came forward over the years to say they were the girl in the poem, but most Poe biographers agree that "Annabel Lee" was Poe's cousin and first wife, Virginia, whom he married when he was twenty-seven and she was not quite fourteen. She died of tuberculosis six years later. It is not a relationship that would pass muster today, any more than the famous Vladimir Nabokov story it inspired. But the opening stanza of that haunting love poem reverberated many decades into the future, and does so still:

It was many and many a year ago,
In a kingdom by the sea
That a maiden there lived whom you may know
By the name of Annabel Lee
And this maiden she lived with no other thought
Than to love and be loved by me.

October 8, 1871

Hot Time in the Old Town Tonight

It was another dry day in Chicago, and a warm one. The weather was that way all across the Midwest, and had been for most of the summer and early autumn. Fire had been a constant worry, and sometimes more than a worry. Chicago's Burlington Warehouse had burned to the ground a week earlier. Smaller fires had sapped the Chicago Fire Department's energy, while revealing the city as a kind of tinder box. A fire at a mill on Canal Street spread quickly, encompassing four blocks before firemen got it under control.

Everyone kept saying it, and it was true: They needed rain. In the previous one hundred days, the cumulative rainfall was about an inch. A steady wind was blowing from the southwest. "The absence of rain for three weeks [has] left everything in so flammable a condition that a spark might set a fire which would seep from end to end of the city," warned the *Chicago Tribune*.

Weather was not on the mind of the owner of Crosby's Opera House. Albert Crosby had raised $80,000 to refurbish his palace, hoping to restore it to its former glory. The Crosby had hosted the 1868 Republican National Convention that nominated Ulysses S. Grant. For its reopening, Albert Crosby had booked Theodore Thomas, famed conductor of Chicago's classical music orchestra. That show would not take place.

Shortly after 9 p.m. on this date, a fire began in or near a barn behind a house owned by Patrick and Catherine O'Leary on DeKoven Street on Chicago's southwest side. What happened next was tragedy, and legend. The Great Chicago Fire, as it is called, took eighteen thousand homes and commercial buildings, including the opera house, which never reopened.

The conflagration left one-third of Chicagoans homeless, and took 250 lives. Considering how fast the inferno spread, the death toll could have been much higher. A swath of the city three-fourths of a mile wide and four miles long was rendered a moonscape—if the face of the moon could be littered with smoldering wreckage and charred remnants of American life.

Mrs. O'Leary's cow took the blame, at least in a famous ditty, for supposedly kicking over a lamp in that barn. It was a story that couldn't be verified, and was quite possibly invented by the press. Chicago's city council officially exonerated Mrs. O'Leary a century after she died. Her barn is long gone—it was gone that night—and on the site now is the Chicago Fire Department training academy.

October 9, 1871

Towering Inferno

The Great Chicago Fire was a devastating event, but it wasn't even the deadliest fire in that region that night. That grim distinction belongs to the Peshtigo Fire, named after the Wisconsin lumber village it obliterated, along with half the town's population. It ignited in the remote Wisconsin woodlands and claimed eight or nine times as many victims as Chicago—eight hundred people in Peshtigo alone. The exact place it ignited isn't known, but the underlying cause was always known: a year-long drought in northern Wisconsin. It had snowed little the winter before, spring hadn't produced the promised wet season, and the summer was exceedingly dry. A heavy rainfall came on July 8, but it didn't last, and the parched land soaked it up immediately. It didn't rain again until September 5, and then only lightly.

Everyone was on edge. Towns such as Sugar Bush and Peshtigo were nestled among billions of trees—giant candlesticks waiting to be lit. The swamps had dried up, and drinking water was an issue. Smaller fires were being put out every day. The residents knew they needed rain. Instead they got wind, and fire and then an apocalyptic combination of the two. Everyone who lived through it, and those who came later to write about it, expressed awe at the physical forces of the wind, exacerbated by a cold front that moved in, producing a fire tornado.

"A firestorm is called nature's nuclear explosion," wrote Denise Gess and William Lutz, authors of a book on the Peshtigo Fire. "Here's a wall of flame, a mile high, five miles wide, traveling 90 to 100 miles per hour, hotter than a crematorium, turning sand to glass."

The town of Sugar Bush was simply obliterated, with no survivors. By 10 p.m., residents in Peshtigo couldn't breathe the air. Trees exploded, while homes, horses, and people caught fire. One group of residents found safety in the only remaining marshy piece of ground on the east side of the Peshtigo River. Those who made it through the night remembered later how eerily quiet it was the next morning. Peshtigo and several other towns were destroyed, lumber camps in a swath of forest ten miles wide and forty miles long were incinerated, the names of their inhabitants forever lost to history. Because the only telegraph office in the region had burned up, news of the disaster took days to filter out of Wisconsin. By then, the world was transfixed by the Chicago fire. It wasn't just a few small forest towns or hundreds of itinerant lumberjacks and their families whose stories disappeared into the haze of history, it was the Peshtigo Fire itself.

October 10, 1957

Say It Loud

Two well-dressed black men walked into a Howard Johnson's in Delaware on this date and ordered a glass of orange juice, thirty cents apiece. But the beverages came in paper cups and a bag, along with instructions from a waitress to take it outside.

"Colored people are not allowed to eat in here," she explained. The men asked for the manager. One of them showed him an identification, which revealed his name, Komla Agbeli Gbedemah, and his position—finance minister of the new African nation of Ghana. The other man was his American secretary. The rules are the rules, the manager replied. The would-be customers paid for their juice, left it on the counter, and departed—but not before telling the proprietor that he'd not heard the end of it.

Gbedemah, known popularly in his country as Afro Gbede, was one of the architects of Ghanaian independence. He'd hosted Richard Nixon for dinner in his own home seven months earlier to celebrate Ghana's founding. "If the vice president of the U.S. can have a meal in my house when he is in Ghana," he told reporters, "then I cannot understand why I must receive this treatment at a roadside restaurant in America."

Among those moved by this logic were Howard Johnson's corporate managers, who reversed their policies (at least in Delaware), and the U.S. State Department, which issued a swift apology. Nixon's boss, President Dwight Eisenhower, went a step further. Ike invited Gbede for breakfast at the White House, where he explained that "little bits like that happen all over the place and you never know when they'll blow up or where." Eisenhower knew better, but the civil rights movement was fueled in the 1950s by such incremental victories. Ike was curious about something, though, and asked Gbede directly: "What brings you to my country?"

Gbede was ready for this question. Ghana needed industry, he said, and what he had in mind was an aluminum smelter. Ghana had the requisite elements, namely bauxite, but the project required energy sources the country did not possess.

He wanted to construct a large dam to generate hydroelectric power. Out of that conversation flowed World Bank loans, U.S. investment, and a high dam on the Volta River. This was not the last time Afro Gbede used his knowledge of American culture to advance his agenda. Later, when running for office, he employed the slogan "Say it loud: I am black and proud," which he borrowed from a James Brown song.

October 11, 1884

Eleanor the Good

New York socialites Elliott Bulloch Roosevelt and his wife, Anna Hall Roosevelt, welcomed a baby girl into their home on this date. Christened Anna Eleanor, she always used her middle name. Her mother called her "Granny," ostensibly because young Eleanor displayed such seriousness of purpose, but it must have seemed to a tall and plain girl that her pretty mother found something lacking in her. If Eleanor had a somber side, who could blame her? Her mother also suffered chronic headaches and bouts of depression. Her father was an alcoholic.

When Eleanor was a toddler, her family was aboard an ocean liner that was rammed in the Atlantic. The Roosevelts were safely evacuated to lifeboats, but a dozen people died. It was a harbinger. Eleanor's mother didn't live to be thirty, dying in December 1892. Six months later, Eleanor's three-year-old brother died of scarlet fever. Her father, Theodore Roosevelt's brother, died in the summer of 1894, a victim of incessant binge drinking. Before her tenth birthday, Eleanor Roosevelt was an orphan. But she was an orphan with determination, and the conviction that quality of character could take you far in life. She grew from a shy, awkward orphan into a prominent social worker, humanitarian, political activist, and wartime First Lady who saw four sons go into military service during World War II.

She was also a newspaper columnist, a published author, a UN delegate, and, at the time of her death in 1962, a beloved international icon. The secret to her success? A bedrock conviction that inner beauty counted for a great deal. At fourteen, she wrote this: "No matter how plain a woman may be, if truth & loyalty are stamped upon her face all will be attracted to her."

After she was widowed, Eleanor was appointed by Harry Truman as U.S. envoy to the United Nations. Delegates from around the world rose to applaud when she strode into the great hall. We know that her marriage to Franklin Roosevelt was a troubled one. Certainly, many Americans sensed it at the time. "Nor did President Roosevelt always confide in his wife where matters of state were concerned," the *New York Times* noted gingerly in its 1962 obituary.

There were other things FDR didn't tell his wife, matters of the heart. She kept similar secrets from him as well. Nonetheless, theirs was an alliance that worked, and as the *Times* summarized in its obit: "During her 12 years in the White House she was sometimes laughed at and sometimes bitterly resented. But during her last years she became the object of almost universal respect."

October 12, 1945

With Magnificent Fortitude

Desmond T. Doss didn't care for the term "conscientious objector," calling himself a "conscientious cooperator" instead. A Seventh-Day Adventist from Lynchburg, Virginia, he'd enlisted in the U.S. Army at twenty-three. After Pearl Harbor was attacked, he felt pulled in two directions by his country and his faith. The tenets of his religion precluded him from killing an enemy combatant or even carrying a firearm. But America had been attacked and Doss wanted to answer Uncle Sam's call. He did that—and then some—and on this date, President Truman awarded him the Medal of Honor.

Even in a group receiving an award designed for those who "distinguished themselves by their gallantry in action," Desmond Doss stood out. He could have stayed stateside and worked in a shipyard. But as he explained in 1998, he believed he could serve both God and his country by volunteering for a medical unit. "I didn't want to be known as a draft dodger," he explained. "But I sure didn't know what I was getting into."

What he was getting into was the bloodiest fighting in the Pacific theater. Assigned to the U.S. Army's Seventy-Seventh Infantry Division, Doss wound up on Okinawa in a battle in which a contingent of GIs gained a summit, only to be pinned down by Japanese artillery and machine-gun fire. Seventy-five Americans were left wounded or dying on the cliffs. But not for long.

Under withering fire, Private Doss carried all seventy-five casualties, one by one, to the edge of the escarpment and lowered them on a rope-supported litter to safety. For the next three weeks, Doss repeated similar feats. On May 21, 1945, in a night attack, he himself was seriously injured by an enemy grenade. "Rather than call another aid man from cover, he cared for his own injuries and waited five hours before litter bearers reached him and started carrying him to cover," his Medal of Honor citation says. "With magnificent fortitude, he bound a rifle stock to his shattered arm as a splint and then crawled 300 yards over rough terrain to the aid station."

His bravery is the subject of a 1982 biography and the 2016 feature film *Hacksaw Ridge*. I commend both, but the most eloquent explication of his deeds came from this steadfast man himself. "I wasn't trying to be a hero," he explained in 1987. "I was thinking about it from this standpoint: In a house on fire and a mother has a child in that house, what prompts her to go in and get that child?

"Love," he said, answering his own question. I loved my men, and they loved me....I just couldn't give them up, just like a mother couldn't give up the child."

October 13, 1792

Bless This House

It would take eight years to build, and the work crews included enslaved people—a rather stark incongruity for an executive mansion built for a new nation formed around the idea of liberty—but the cornerstone was laid on this date in the wetlands of a new capital city named after the first American president.

The logic behind moving the capital from Philadelphia to Washington was that Philly fans kept booing their own cricket team, leading to poor civic morale. Well, no, I was just seeing if you were paying attention. The real rationale was a desire to place the capital city closer to the geographical and political center of the new nation. John Adams would be the first president to occupy the house on the site selected by George Washington himself. It was destined to be called—at first unofficially and later by fiat—the "White House," and in the ensuing years, it would be torched by the British, and remodeled and improved numerous times. But the iconic manse at 1600 Pennsylvania Avenue would survive.

President John Adams moved into the White House on November 1, 1800. On the verge of losing his reelection bid to Thomas Jefferson, Adams wasn't in a frame of mind to appreciate the place. How could he? Not only was the drafty dwelling barely furnished, the construction itself wasn't even completed. Putting the best face on things, Adams dutifully wrote his wife, Abigail, who was still at their home in Massachusetts, a letter beneath the dateline: "Presidents house, Washington City."

"My dearest friend," Adams's letter began, "we arrived here last night, or rather yesterday, at one o Clock and here we dined and Slept. The Building is in a State to be habitable. And now we wish for your Company." The nation's second president concluded his brief missive with another poignant sentiment, this one for the ages:

"Before I end my Letter I pray Heaven to bestow the best of Blessings on this House and all that shall hereafter inhabit it," John Adams wrote. "May none but honest and wise Men ever rule under this roof." It is a prayer, to paraphrase a later president, that has not been answered fully. But we, the voters, generally do our best, as do the families who occupy that house.

October 14, 1781

Lafayette, You Were Here

This devil Cornwallis is much wiser than the other generals with whom I have dealt. He inspires me with a sincere fear, and his name has greatly troubled my sleep." So wrote the Marquis de Lafayette, in a July 9, 1781, letter to a friend. Three months later, on this date, with help from France, George Washington and the men under his command—including Lafayette—set a trap for the feared British general that would bring the Revolutionary War to an end.

As battle lines formed at Yorktown, a French fleet sailed from Haiti to the Chesapeake Bay, meaning that even as he fortified Yorktown, Lord Charles Cornwallis and his army were being surrounded by a joint Franco-American force twice their size. The British still had twenty-six thousand troops in the colonies, but Cornwallis's mystique was broken—as was the will of the British public.

This debt was not forgotten. Gen. John J. Pershing and his "doughboys" marched through Paris on July 4, 1917, regimental bands playing and crowds cheering. *"Lafayette, nous voilà!"* proclaimed Charles E. Stanton, one of Pershing's staff officers. ("Lafayette, we are here!")

October is also the birthday of Dwight Eisenhower, who liberated France a generation later. In a 2002 memorial service at the American cemetery in Normandy, George W. Bush told of a Frenchwoman who met some of the U.S. paratroopers dropped by Ike behind enemy lines the night before D-Day. Stumbling upon the waiting soldiers, she implored them tearfully to stay. "We're not leaving," one of the Americans reassured her. "If necessary, this is the place we die."

On an October day 159 years earlier, Thomas Jefferson also encountered a Frenchwoman in the countryside. Jefferson was visiting Fontainebleau, where the king of France hunted each autumn. On his way out of town on a morning hike, Jefferson met a female day laborer, who looked impoverished. As he explained in a letter to James Madison, Jefferson inquired "into her vocation, condition, and circumstance." He was told that times were tough, that she had two children and no real way of earning enough to feed them. Jefferson gave her money and an additional gift: He told her it was not charity, but payment for her services as his "guide" on his walk. Overcome by his generosity, she burst into tears and was unable to speak.

In her silence, Jefferson formulated a theory about the inequity of land ownership and wealth in French society, ideas he naturally shared with Madison, his pen pal and co-conspirator in building a different kind of nation across the ocean.

October 15, 1860

Mr. Lincoln's Whiskers

Abraham Lincoln had no illusions about his physical appearance. Once, when accused of being "two-faced" during a debate with Stephen Douglas, Lincoln quipped, "If I really had two faces, do you think I'd hide behind this one?" But his rugged and honest mug appealed to his fellow Americans. This was true of women (who could not vote in 1860) no less than men. A century later, Marilyn Monroe adjudged Lincoln "the sexiest man in American history," adding that she'd married playwright Arthur Miller because of his Lincolnesque countenance.

Grace Bedell of Westfield, New York, was only eleven when she saw Lincoln's photo. Inspired, she penned him a letter advising that growing a beard would improve his election prospects. "You would look a great deal better," she wrote on this date, "for your face is so thin.

"All the ladies like whiskers and they would tease their husbands to vote for you and then you would be President," she added. Lincoln's delight at receiving this missive was evident in his reply, sent from Springfield, Illinois, four days later. "My dear little Miss," it began, "Your very agreeable letter of the 15th is received." He told Grace of his "regret" at having no daughters of his own, mentioning his three sons, then addressed the subject of her letter. "As to the whiskers, having never worn any, do you not think people would call it a piece of silly affection if I were to begin it now?" He signed it, "Your very sincere well-wisher, A. Lincoln."

The campaign continued for another three weeks, absent public discussion of beards, and Lincoln won. But the letter made an impression. After being elected, he began growing his now-famous facial hair, and when his train passed through Grace's upstate New York town in February en route to his inauguration, Lincoln mentioned her from his speaking platform, saying if she was in the audience, he'd like to meet her.

"There was a momentary commotion, in the midst of which an old man, struggling through the crowd, approached, leading his daughter...whom he introduced to Mr. Lincoln as his Westfield correspondent," reported the *New York World*. "Mr. Lincoln stooped down and kissed the child, and talked with her for some minutes. Her advice had not been thrown away upon the rugged chieftain. A beard of several months' growth adorns the lower part of his face. The young girl's peachy cheek must have been tickled with a stiff whisker, for the growth of which she was herself responsible."

October 16, 1773

John Brown's Body

The *Pennsylvania Gazette* published the first public opposition to the Tea Act, which was enacted by Parliament to bolster the beleaguered British East India Company. The "Philadelphia Resolutions" printed in the *Gazette* on this date denounced the tax as amounting to "arbitrary government and slavery" upon the Americans living in the colonies.

This was incendiary language, which was intentional, but unintentionally ironic as well, when one considers that actual slavery was practiced on these shores. October 16 is one of those recurring dates in U.S. history in which Americans tackle similar themes, but with varied perspectives as time marches by. Eighty-one years later to the day, for instance, an obscure congressional candidate from Springfield, Illinois, discussed slavery in a speech in Peoria that resurrected his own flagging political career—and changed the course of history.

Ostensibly, Abraham Lincoln was denouncing the Missouri Compromise, and the possibility that slavery would be extended westward into the Kansas and Nebraska territories. But on the evening of October 16, 1854, he went further, attacking the underpinnings of the institution of slavery as contradictory with the United States' founding principles—and immoral on its face. The question, he said, ultimately was a simple one: Are blacks human?

"When the white man governs himself that is self-government," Lincoln explained. "But when he governs himself, and also governs *another* man, that is *more* than self-government—that is despotism. If the Negro is a *man*, why then my ancient faith teaches me that 'all men are created equal,' and that there can be no moral right in connection with one man's making a slave of another."

Five years later to the day, John Brown and his ragtag followers—including three of his sons and five freed blacks—attacked the armory at Harper's Ferry. The men were quickly surrounded by a military detachment led by Colonel Robert E. Lee and Lieutenant J. E. B. Stuart. Brown's men were captured or killed, and their leader was led to the gallows two months later.

Before he was executed, Brown handed his guard an unrepentant note proclaiming his certainty that "the crimes of this guilty land will never be purged away but with blood." Not only did this grim prophesy come true, but less than two years later Union troops in "Mr. Lincoln's Army" were marching into battle against Lee and Stuart singing the "John Brown hymn."

October 17, 1989

Loma Prieta

At 5:04 p.m., Pacific Coast time, twelve miles beneath a densely forested, mountainous state park six miles inland from the beach town of Aptos, California, two immense tectonic plates slipped, generating a fantastic release of energy. Aboveground, the earth ruptured along a twenty-five-mile line during the fifteen-second temblor. At the epicenter inside the Forest of Nisene Marks State Park, the quake strewed huge redwood trees like matchsticks while the quake reverberated toward populous locales—one, in particular.

In San Francisco, as Candlestick Park was preparing to host a nationally televised World Series game that would never take place, Giants pitcher Don Robinson raced through the clubhouse hollering, "Earthquake! Earthquake!"

Sixty-three people died in the Loma Prieta earthquake, which toppled the Cypress Street Viaduct in Oakland, killing dozens, and taking out a section of the Bay Bridge, where one motorist plunged to her death. In San Francisco's Marina District, a ruptured natural gas main burst into flames that could be seen across the city, claiming four more lives. Inside Candlestick, the scene was surreal. Giants first baseman Will Clark thought it sounded like an F-15 roaring overhead. But the noise was coming from the earth itself. He was running in the outfield when he saw the grass ripple "like a wave." Clark added: "The damn thing nearly knocked me down."

There was another noise, too, and it came from the stands. Hardly anyone panicked, and most fans stood and let out a roar as the amped-up crowd realized that the old maligned ballpark had proved to be a safe shelter. "It was supposed to be a rotting whorehouse of a ballpark," *San Francisco Chronicle* baseball writer Ray Ratto recalled afterward, "but it took this huge beating from the Earth's crust like it was nothing."

"I'll never forget the noise," added Giants pitcher Mike LaCoss. "After I opened the door to the dugout, sixty thousand people were standing on their feet." The crowd took up a spontaneous chant usually heard at football games: "WE WILL, WE WILL, ROCK YOU!" One Giants' fan held a makeshift sign: "If you think that's something, wait until the Giants come to bat."

Alas, no more baseball was to be played that night, and as the public address announcer informed the crowd that the Bay Bridge had collapsed, the fans became instantly somber as they made their way to the exits, their thoughts turning from baseball to the fate of friends and loved ones.

October 18, 1944

Duck Soup

Groucho Marx was working on a new book, *Variety* reported on this date, a book about the Wild West to be titled "*Homicide on the Range*." In Hollywood, journalistic scoops are nice, and *Variety* always prided itself on being in the know, but you wonder how people kept falling for such Groucho gags, which they did all his life.

He was born on October 2, 1890, the third of five sons and named Julius by his parents Minnie and Simon Marx. We know him as Groucho—just as we remember his four brothers (Leonard, Arthur, Milton, and Herbert) by their stage names: Chico, Harpo, Gummo, and Zeppo.

The Marx Brothers began as a musical act, sometimes joined by their mother and an aunt. They became a musical act with comedy until finally morphing fully into a comedy act. The family members all recalled how this evolution began, just not where. One evening in 1912, perhaps at the Nacogdoches, Texas, opera house, their performance was interrupted by shouts from the street about a mule on the loose. The crowd rushed out to see the commotion.

When they returned to their seats, an irritated Groucho made snide comments at their expense, such as "The jackass is the flower of Tex-ass." Instead of taking offense, the audience roared. In his autobiography, Harpo Marx placed the runaway mule incident in Ada, Oklahoma; other sources say it was Marshall, Texas. It doesn't matter. What matters is that thanks to Groucho's spontaneous wit, they'd learned that insults could be funny if they were clever, and as long as they weren't perceived as mean-spirited.

"I never forget a face," Groucho often quipped, "but I'm going to make an exception in your case." Or how about this one: "I bet your father spent the first year of your life throwing rocks at the stork." That's a Groucho line in the 1939 film *At the Circus*. Perhaps the most famous Marx Brothers one-liner—appropriated over the years by many others—is, "Well, who you gonna believe, me or your own eyes?" That's Chico Marx in *Duck Soup*.

In *A Day at the Races*, Groucho plays a "Dr. Hackenbush," a quack who checks the pulse of a man found lying in the street. "Either he's dead," says the good doctor, "or my watch has stopped." Groucho Marx's watch stopped in 1977, meaning he didn't live to see cable news.

It's a medium he'd have had fun with. "I must say, I find television very educational," he once said. "The minute somebody turns it on, I go into the library and read a good book."

October 19, 1814

O Say Can You See?

After sacking Washington and burning the White House, the invaders turned north, to Baltimore. The British ground forces were led by General Robert Ross; its ships commanded by decorated Admiral George Cockburn. But Ross was killed by a sharpshooter, and two days later, Cockburn's naval force was stymied in Baltimore Harbor by the big guns of Fort McHenry.

Watching the momentous battle aboard a truce ship was Maryland lawyer Francis Scott Key. What he observed "by the dawn's early light" on September 14, 1814, was that the Stars and Stripes still flew above the American fort.

Deeply moved, he began scribbling verses on the back of a letter, the only stationery on his person. After his release, he took a room at Baltimore's downtown Indian Queen Hotel, and finished the poem, which he initially titled "The Defence of Fort McHenry." Key always intended that the verses be sung aloud, and the melody he had in mind was "To Anacreon in Heaven," a bawdy London drinking tune.

According to the Smithsonian Institution, the first documented public performance of Key's work took place on this date at the Holliday Street Theatre in Baltimore. A local music store subsequently published the score as "The Star-Spangled Banner."

The theater, which eventually became known as Old Drury, no longer exists. It was razed to make room for City Hall Plaza. The Indian Queen Hotel is gone, too. It stood at the corner of Hanover and Baltimore Streets, just a few blocks from Camden Yards, where Francis Scott Key's song is belted out every night that the hometown team takes the field.

Baltimore Orioles fans jar first-time visitors to their ballpark by shouting "O!" (for "Orioles") at the beginning of the penultimate line of "The Star-Spangled Banner." Not everyone appreciates that local custom, but Baltimoreans—the descendants of Fort McHenry's defenders—long ago earned the right to punctuate that song with a demonstration of civic pride.

> *And the rocket's red glare, the bombs bursting in air,*
> *Gave proof through the night that our flag was still there,*
> *O say does that star-spangled banner yet wave*
> *O'er the land of the free and the home of the brave?*

October 20, 1945

"We Shall Overcome"

The song began as a Negro spiritual, became a gospel hymn, then a ballad used by organized labor before it was appropriated by civil rights activists in the South, and ultimately became a protest song against injustice anywhere in the world. So where does an anthem that potent even come from? The answer is many places, with help from lots of people, but it starts with Baltimore native Charles Albert Tindley. Born in 1851 to a father who was enslaved and a mother who was free, the "Prince of Preachers," as he came to be known, married at seventeen, moved to Philadelphia, taught himself Greek and Hebrew, and became a scholar of the Bible and an ordained minister in the American Methodist Episcopal Church.

A gifted preacher who was named head pastor in the same Wilmington AME congregation where he'd worked as a janitor in his teens, Tindley was also a turn-of-the-century civil rights leader. His career would still be worth celebrating if he'd never written a single song, but his reputation has been overshadowed by his many musical compositions. The man helped invent American gospel music. He's a crossover artist, too. Five of Tindley's songs are in the United Methodist Hymnal, while his classic, "Stand by Me," has been covered a thousand times, including by Elvis Presley and Tennessee Ernie Ford. One song, published in 1901, was destined for even greater glory. It was called, "I'll Overcome Someday." It opens like this:

This world is one great battlefield
With forces all arrayed,
If in my heart I do not yield
I'll overcome some day

The tune became a staple in black churches in the twentieth century and it was a favorite of a Charleston, South Carolina, tobacco factory worker named Lucille Simmons, who learned on this date, a Saturday, that her union was going out on strike on Monday morning. That winter, as the predominately female African-American workforce manned their picket lines, Simmons fanned out into the neighborhood drumming up support for the strike, singing her song, which she altered from "I'll Overcome" to "We'll Overcome," while ad-libbing some new verses. ("We will overcome…and win our rights one day.") By 1947, Simmons's version of Charles Tindley's old song was adapted by Zilphia Horton, musical director of Highlander Folk School, a progressive retreat in Tennessee formed during the Depression to aid and instruct labor organizers. At some point under Horton's care, "We'll Overcome" became "We Will Overcome." She altered the tempo, added new verses ("We will walk hand in hand"), and taught it to folk singer Pete Seeger. A progressive activist in his own right, Seeger tinkered some more, changed "We Will" to "We Shall," mainly to make it easier to sing. By the late 1940s and early 1950s, it became one of the refrains in the American labor movement's canon.

Horton died in 1956, but the torch she lit at Highlander was passed along. Rosa Parks visited Highlander before her historic act of civil disobedience aboard a Montgomery bus; Martin Luther King came in 1957. In October 1959, Highlander hosted a retreat attended by students at Fisk University, a historically black college in Nashville. One of those students, future civil rights icon John Lewis, said it was the first time he'd seen blacks and whites not only dining together, but cleaning the kitchen together after mealtime. By then, Zilphia Horton's old job as music director belonged to a Southern California transplant named Guy Carawan. With help from Frank Hamilton of the Weavers, Carawan reworked the song a bit more. Its byline now included Charles Albert Tindley, Lucille Simmons, Zilphia Horton, Pete Seeger, Frank Hamilton, and Guy Carawan. And it wasn't finished evolving yet.

In the autumn of 1959, Carawan taught visiting students various protest songs, including the latest version of "We Shall Overcome." The following April, he did the same thing publicly, to a student delegation at Shaw University in North Carolina at the formation of the Student Nonviolent Coordinating Committee. The first evening, Carawan was invited to lead the two hundred delegates in song. He stood, holding his guitar and strummed the chords while singing, "We Shall Overcome. We Shall Overcome. We Shall Overcome, someday..."

Soon, the students were standing, linking arms, swaying to the music, and joining him in song. By the weekend, it was SNCC's unofficial anthem. Carawan later recalled what happened next: "At a certain point, those young singers, who knew a lot of a capella styles, they said, 'Lay that guitar down, boy. We can do this song better.' And they put that sort of triplet to it and sang it a capella with all those harmonies."

By 1963, the *New York Times* labeled "We Shall Overcome" the "Marseillaise of the integration movement." It was more than that. It was sung during the crusade to end apartheid in South Africa; it was sung as the Berlin Wall came down; it was sung by protesters at Tiananmen Square. As civil rights leader Julian Bond once said, "People tell me that you can go anywhere in the world today and there's somebody singing this song."

October 21, 1867

Big Medicine

It was billed as a negotiation, this parley along Medicine Lodge Creek, and the white men at least had the decency to hold it outdoors instead of in a fort. The U.S. government was represented by John B. Henderson, chairman of the Senate committee on Indian Affairs, and Gen. William Tecumseh Sherman, who brought five hundred armed cavalrymen with him, along with several artillery pieces, just in case.

The other side were Kiowa, Arapaho, Cheyenne, Kiowa Apache, and Comanche chiefs. Although no longer on the warpath, they'd brought four thousand mounted braves, none of them Sioux. In the words of writer S. C. Gwynne, the meeting that took place on this date "was the last great gathering of free Indians in the American West."

Each side did its best to impress the other. Sherman had his mounted soldiers in their dress blue uniforms and those field howitzers, but the general also brought wagon upon wagon stuffed with sugar, bread, tobacco, and coffee. The Indians outdid them. A dispatch from Alfred A. Taylor, future Tennessee governor and one of nine newspaper correspondents in attendance, set the stage by describing how the thousands of mounted warriors entered the field, "forming themselves into a wedge-shaped mass... [in] a feat of horsemanship which for dexterity, perfection of plan, skill and precision in execution, I dare say has never been equaled in all the history of military maneuvers, by any race of men.

"When within a mile of the head of our procession, the wedge, without a hitch or break, quickly threw itself into the shape of a huge ring or wheel without hub or spokes, whose rim consisted of five distinct lines of these wild, untutored, yet inimitable horsemen," he wrote. "This ring winding around and around with the regularity of fresh oiled machinery nearer and nearer to us with every revolution. Reaching within a hundred yards of us at breakneck speed, the giant wheel or ring ceased to turn and suddenly came to a standstill."

The idea, at least the idea of those who ran the federal government, was that such brilliant horsemanship should henceforth be relegated to Western traveling shows—and not deployed during bloody raids on white settlers. The Army didn't sugarcoat the terms: The Plains Indians' hunting days were over. The tribes were to live on reservations, much smaller than the lands they had previously been promised, and less agreeable land to boot. Whites would not be able to hunt on those lands, the government said, though this was never put in writing. It wouldn't have mattered. The chiefs couldn't read, and the government officials had no intention of enforcing the ban against white hunters anyway.

In a sense, the whole thing was for show. All that really mattered was what General

Sherman told them: "You can no more stop this than you can stop the sun or the moon," he told the chiefs. "You must submit, and do the best you can."

The Indians knew they were being told to surrender; they just didn't know how to stop it.

"I have heard that you intend to settle us on a reservation near the mountains," Kiowa chief Santana told the commissioners bitterly. "I don't want to settle there. I love to roam over the wide prairie and when I do I feel free and happy."

Ten Bears, a Comanche chief who had been to Washington and met the president—for all the good that did him and his people—gave a speech that astonished his hosts for its eloquence and melancholy prescience. "My people have never first drawn a bow or fired a gun against the whites," he said. "There has been trouble between us. My young men have danced the war dance. But it was not begun by us. It was you who sent the first soldier." He continued:

You have said that you want to put us on a reservation, to build us houses and to make us medicine lodges. I do not want them. I was born under the prairie, where the wind blew free and there was nothing to break the light of the sun. I was born where there were no walls and everything drew free breath. I want to die there, not within walls. I know every stream and every wood between the Rio Grande and the Arkansas River. I have hunted and lived all over that country. I live like my fathers before me and like them I live happily.

When I was in Washington the Great Father told me that all the Comanche land was ours and that no one should hinder us from living on it. So why do you ask us to leave the rivers and the sun and the wind and live in houses? Do not tell us to give up the buffalo for the sheep. . . . If the Texans had kept out of my country, there might have been peace. But that which you say we must now live in is too small. The Texans have taken away the places where the grass grew thickest and the timber was best. Had we kept that, we might have done as you ask. But it is too late. The whites took the country which we loved, and we wish only to wander the prairie till we die.

October 22, 1965

American Beauty

Lady Bird Johnson didn't ask for a lot from her husband, but she asked this time, so the great dealmaker muscled it through Congress. At 2:15 p.m. on this date, President Lyndon Baines Johnson strode into the East Room of the White House to sign it.

Officially, the legislation was the Highway Beautification Act, Public Law 89-285, but everybody in the White House and on Capitol Hill simply called it "Lady Bird's Bill." It built on the Federal Highway Act of 1958, which promised federal money for the states to voluntarily control billboards and other outdoor advertising along America's roads and byways.

Regulating billboards was only part of what Lady Bird Johnson had in mind. Driving or walking along America's roadways in the mid-1960s was like driving through a landfill. Her legislation instituted fines for littering, provided money for scenic enhancement, offered incentives for the cleanup of city parks, and helped hide junkyards. It also established a national expectation that Americans should not be walled off from their country's natural beauty.

Initially, Johnson put his political muscle behind his wife's pet project in the interest of maintaining domestic tranquility in his own home. But as official Washington knew, when LBJ set his mind to something, especially if that something was ramming legislation through Congress, he could be a force of nature. With his remarks at the bill-signing ceremony, he signaled that when it came to enhancing America's beauty the president was all in.

"As I rode the George Washington Memorial Parkway back to the White House only yesterday afternoon, I saw nature at its purest," Johnson said. "I looked at those dogwoods that had turned red, and the maple trees that were scarlet and gold. In a pattern of brown and yellow, God's finery was at its finest. And not one single foot of it was marred by a single, unsightly, man-made construction or obstruction—no advertising signs, no old, dilapidated trucks, no junkyards. Well, doctors could prescribe no better medicine for me, and that is what I said to my surgeon as we drove along."

In her diary, Lady Bird was equally eloquent. "The subject of beautification is like a tangled skein of wool," she wrote. "All the threads are interwoven—recreation and pollution and mental health and the crime rate and rapid transit and highway beautification and the war on poverty and parks...everything leads to something else."

October 23, 1963

Changing Times

Bob Dylan was in a Columbia Records studio on this date recording a song that would serve as a lyrical warning to the established order. The title song off an album that would be released in January 1964, it has been called a generational anthem, which was precisely its intent. "I knew exactly what I wanted to say," Dylan later said, "and who I wanted to say it to."

Come gather 'round people
wherever you roam

Infused with Scottish and Irish folk tunes as well as Biblical allusions, "The Times They Are A-Changin'" sounded simultaneously old and new. It was, music critic Evan Schlansky wrote, a carefully crafted battle cry advocating "compassion over complacency, action over inaction, courage over fear."

As Dylan told rock chronicler Cameron Crowe, "This is definitely a song with a purpose." That aim was achieved. Both the music and the message are so evocative that the song has been covered by everyone from the Byrds and Bruce Springsteen to Flogging Molly, a Celtic punk band. The second verse was used by Steve Jobs to unveil a long-awaited computer at an Apple shareholders meeting in 1984. Did that take it too far? Probably not; the song was always about more than politics. Yet its backdrop was the civil rights movement, and it was released in an election year. In case anybody missed that fact, Dylan spelled it out for them:

Come senators, congressmen
Please heed the call...

But times do change and in 2010, with an African-American as president, Dylan performed this song at the White House, in a less angry and less urgent tempo.

October 24, 1861

Linking Up

The irony was palpable. Only six months after starting a destructive Civil War that divided families, America became a place where people could communicate with each other across a sprawling continent in real time. Until then, those on the West Coast were living, in the words of telegraph pioneer James Gamble, "beyond the pale of civilization." But when Western Union Telegraph completed a link in Salt Lake City, California, was connected to the great cities of the East Coast. The first message from San Francisco to Washington, D.C., was sent on this date from California Supreme Court Justice Stephen J. Field to Abraham Lincoln.

Constructing the telegraph line eastward from Carson City, Nevada, to Utah necessitated shipping wire and insulators from the East Coast around South America to California, where they were then carried by wagons over the Sierra Nevada Mountains. When the crews descended the high country, they faced the prospect of erecting six hundred miles of telegraph poles through a treeless desert. For the western segment of the line, Mormon settlers (led by telegraph company official James Street) helped workers scour arroyos for usable wood, but when it came to the portion being constructed from Omaha, Nebraska, to Salt Lake, Sioux Indians cut the wire down to use it for bracelets. But as the arduous summer turned to fall, the eastern section was finally completed.

One striking aspect is how quickly Americans embraced the new technology—and how fast their thoughts turned to the rest of the world. Writing in the all-caps style that would dominate Western Union dispatches for more than a century, Brigham Young sent a message on this date to H. W. Carpentier, president of the Overland Telegraph Company (which would later be absorbed into Western Union):

DEAR SIR: I AM VERY MUCH OBLIGED FOR YOUR KINDNESS... IN GIVING ME PRIVILEGE OF FIRST MESSAGE TO CALIFORNIA. MAY SUCCESS EVER ATTEND THE ENTERPRISE. THE SUCCESS OF MR. STREET IN COMPLETING HIS END OF THE LINE UNDER MANY UNFAVORABLE CIRCUMSTANCES IN SO SHORT A TIME IS BEYOND OUR MOST SANGUINE ANTICIPATIONS. JOIN YOUR WIRES WITH THE RUSSIAN EMPIRE, AND WE WILL CONVERSE WITH EUROPE.

That would soon happen. American technology would continue to link the human race ever more tightly: 134 years later to the day, a newly formed U.S. government agency, the Federal Networking Council, passed a resolution formally defining the term *Internet*.

October 25, 1942

The Alcan

In one sense, it was a photo of a ribbon-cutting ceremony. It was also an example of what President Franklin D. Roosevelt called "American know-how"—a sign of who would win the war Japan started. Two months after Pearl Harbor, FDR ordered the immediate construction of the Alaska-Canada Highway, a 1,650-mile road from Dawson Creek to Fairbanks.

The stated rationale for the "Alcan" was resupplying U.S. military forces in Alaska. But FDR also wanted a big, visible project that would demonstrate that Americans would do whatever it took to defend North America. So, on March 9, 1942, seven regiments of the U.S. Army Corps of Engineers, supplemented by hundreds of locals hired as contractors, began a seemingly impossible task—finishing the road before winter set it.

Surveyors ventured ten miles into the wilderness to lay markers, and crews with bulldozers blasted away at the trees, brush, and rocks in their path. Learning on the fly, the soldiers and the engineers learned how to build roads over permafrost. They erected bridges over unnamed streams only to have those wash away months later because they didn't comprehend the power of the spring thaw in the Yukon. They learned how to keep trucks and tractors running at fifty below zero—and how to keep themselves alive. The most valuable lesson they learned was tolerance: Three of the seven units building the Alcan were African-American. These men, most of them from the South, were sent into the Arctic wilderness because their (white) officers weren't sure how they'd perform in battle. The answer was that they performed heroically, working tirelessly, sixteen hours a day alongside—and in competition with—white servicemen.

On this date, a black corporal was pictured shaking hands with a white private after their units had linked up and finished the Alcan. The photograph was taken by Harold Richardson of the *Engineering News-Record*, and transmitted around the world. The African-American soldier is smiling and extending his hand. The white soldier is smiling too, a cigarette dangling from his lips. In Tokyo, the propaganda office issued a cheeky statement thanking the U.S. for building a road the Japanese Imperial Army could use after it invaded, but both sides knew this was bluster. U.S. officials also knew that Richardson's photograph had a powerful message. Among other things, it implied that a cohesive USA could accomplish anything. "That's the sort of thing," mused Alaska territorial secretary Bob Bartlett, "we're fighting for."

October 26, 1940

Flying Mustangs

Vance Breese was already an accomplished test pilot when he took a remarkable little airplane out for its maiden spin. The aircraft, developed by North American Aviation, was the P-51 Mustang. Its creation was a joint effort of American technological skill and British grit—an aeronautical innovation that saved countless Allied lives and helped win a war.

The plane's genesis came in March 1940 when Henry Self, who was in charge of production and procurement of new aircraft for the Royal Air Force, asked American aviation executive James "Dutch" Kindelberger if he would build a fleet of Curtiss P-40 fighters for the RAF. Kindelberger, the president of North American Aviation, replied that NAA could build and produce a superior fighter plane, with the same engines, in less time than it would take to set up a mass production line for the P-40. All right, said Sir Henry, but you have 120 days.

Exactly 117 days later, the first P-51 rolled off the assembly line. And on this date, Vance Breese took it into the sky and reported back that it performed well. Guarding its turf, the U.S. Army kept two of the planes. The rest were delivered to Great Britain under the terms of Lend-Lease and thrown into the war effort against Germany.

The new fighter had a longer range than its predecessors, and better maneuverability. It flew at a higher altitude and was faster, although not quite fast enough against the Luftwaffe fighters. That changed in 1942, when the old Allison engines being used in the Mustangs were replaced with the Rolls-Royce Merlin V-12 engine. The P-51 could now fly an astonishing 440 miles per hour. A new design wrinkle was added, too: a bubble canopy. Now the Allies had a lethal weapon that could not only protect the long-range bombers being deployed over Germany, but also hunt enemy fighters in the air and shoot them out of the sky.

The Americans' B-17 fleet had suffered frightful losses up to that point. In the U.S. Army Air Corps, October 14, 1943, was known as "Black Thursday." That was the day when sixty American bombers were shot down by German fighters. And each B-17 had a crew of ten. To the rescue came the single-seat P-51 Mustang. The bomber pilots took to calling the fighter "my little friend." By spring 1945, the Mustang had proved a friend indeed. Its crews had destroyed 4,950 enemy planes and played an instrumental role in bringing the war in Europe to an end.

October 27, 1838

Learning from Our Mistakes

It was one of the most notorious orders issued by a governor in the history of the United States. Its official name was Missouri Executive Order 44, and it was directed to Gen. John B. Clark of the state militia by Gov. Lilburn W. Boggs on this date.

"The Mormons must be treated as enemies and must be exterminated or driven from the state if necessary for the public peace," it read. "Their outrages are beyond all description."

Yes, a sitting U.S. governor gave an order with the word *exterminated* in it—directing against adherents of an entire religion, and a homegrown sect at that. This edict, which became known as "the extermination order," achieved its desired result: Followers of the Church of Jesus Christ of Latter-day Saints were forced out of Clay County, Missouri, just as they had been driven out of Jackson County—where their newspaper was destroyed by a mob—five years earlier, and driven from New York and Ohio before that.

Missouri's "Mormon War," as it was known, began on August 6, 1838, in the town of Gallatin when LDS members tried to vote. Although many of the Mormons were immigrants from Northern Europe, their church was all-American. Yet its devotees were drawn into armed conflict with their fellow citizens for daring to vote (and for publishing a newspaper and insisting on bearing arms for their protection). How subversive of them: They wanted to exercise their constitutional rights. As for the extermination order, it came amid the fog of war. At the Battle of Crooked Creek, state militiamen disarmed Mormons and took three prisoners. An armed Mormon rescue party freed the captives, but in the skirmish three Mormons and one member of the militia were killed. Given wildly inaccurate reports that almost all the Missourians had been slaughtered, Boggs issued his notorious order.

It wasn't rescinded when Joseph Smith was taken from his jail cell and murdered by an Illinois mob in 1844. It wasn't rescinded when "the Saints" removed to the Utah territory under the leadership of Brigham Young. It wasn't rescinded when Utah was admitted to the Union in 1896. It was finally withdrawn by another Missouri governor, Republican Christopher "Kit" Bond, but not until 1976.

"We cannot change history," Bond explained. "But we certainly ought to be able to learn from it and, where possible, acknowledge past mistakes."

October 28, 2003

"We Have a Donor!"

Wendy Marx, a native New Yorker, found personal love and professional success in San Francisco. She also found hepatitis B, or rather it found her. It was a foe she would battle most of her adult life. Wendy was born in 1967, the same year hepatitis B was identified. On Thanksgiving Day in 1989, the disease attacked her liver, leaving her in a coma. Her parents and two brothers were told that, barring a miracle, it was only a matter of hours. What ensued next was a miracle *and* a tragedy—the death of a nine-year-old boy in a traffic accident. Facing despair, the Marx family heard a doctor pronounce the fateful words: "We have a donor!" What Wendy and her brother Jeffrey, a Pulitzer Prize–winning journalist, did with this gift of life—joined by Olympian Carl Lewis— was devote themselves to the cause of organ transplantation.

In 1989, when doctors in San Francisco brought Wendy Marx back from the brink of death with a liver transplant, eighteen thousand Americans were on organ donor waiting lists. Five or six of them died each day. The next year, Wendy and Jeff formed the Wendy Marx Foundation for Organ Donor Awareness. With help from Jeff's speaking and with the publicity garnered because of Carl Lewis's involvement, the foundation worked with established organizations including the American Liver Foundation and the Transplant Recipients International Organization. In 1990, Wendy Marx and Carl Lewis teamed with the National Kidney Foundation to inaugurate the U.S. Transplant Games in Indianapolis. Some 400 athletes participated.

In August 2018, the Transplant Games of America will host thousands of athletes and their families in Salt Lake City. As donor awareness has risen, so have the number of donors and transplants. In 1989, some 13,000 transplants were performed in this country. In 2018, the number will be closer to 35,000. But as awareness and transplant technology have improved, so has the need, which has grown exponentially. In 1989, a handful of people died each day awaiting organs they never got. Today, that grim number is closer to twenty-one—and the waiting list has more than 120,000 names. One of those who died while waiting was Wendy Marx. The hepatitis that destroyed her first liver returned and attacked the replacement organ.

She needed a second transplant, but the miracle of a last-minute donor was not repeated. On this date, at age thirty-six, Wendy Marx took her final breath. "She was," recalled her brother, "a woman of passion and purpose."

October 29, 1962
"Let's Go Surfin' Now"

When the Beach Boys released their first album, kids growing up in California suddenly had something other than the Giants and Dodgers to occupy their imaginations. *Surfin' Safari* was released on this date. Rock music now officially had a new genre: beach music.

The most influential pioneer in developing the surf sound was a young guitarist who went by the name of Dick Dale. In the late 1950s, he began playing dance music at a seaside venue near Newport Beach, California, called Balboa's Rendezvous Ballroom. Dale, whose real name was Richard Anthony Monsour, had moved to Southern California from New England with his family after World War II. Dick graduated from Washington High School in Inglewood in 1954, moved to Orange County, learned to surf, and took up the guitar. His influences included a new form of music being pioneered by an array of guitar players ranging from Chuck Berry to Elvis Presley. Dale learned Arabic scales from his Lebanese-American father, adopted a rapid-fire picking style he thought captured the rhythms of the Pacific Ocean waves, and experimented with an amplifying technology he developed with Leo Fender—as a way of being heard over the crowds that packed the Balboa.

Among those who came to hear him perform were Jimi Hendrix, who, like Dale, was left-handed, and sometimes played his guitar upside down, and three brothers—Brian, Dennis, and Carl Wilson, along with their cousin Mike Love—all of whom hailed from the nearby town of Hawthorne. Although Dennis was the only one of the Wilson clan who actually surfed, they named their new group the Beach Boys. Later, after they hit the big time, they played homage to Dick Dale by covering his legendary 1958 tune, "Let's Go Trippin'."

"Surfing music is a sound that is copied from the power you get by surfing in the ocean," Dick Dale said later. "It's a machine-gun staccato sound that doesn't break rhythm. Surf music is actually just the sound of the waves played on a guitar."

If Dick Dale was "the king of surf guitar," as he was called, the Beach Boys became the new genre's face—and voice. They helped create a sound that would be drowned out by the British Invasion, but which never really disappeared. Like other rock acts, the Beach Boys went on a fiftieth anniversary tour. They didn't have their original players, but it was an impressive run of longevity just the same—due in part to the timeless nature of the source of surf music's inspiration: the sea itself.

October 30, 1953

Statesman

The Nobel Peace Prize had never been awarded to a career military man—until this date—when George C. Marshall was announced as the recipient. A five-star general during World War II while serving as U.S. Army chief of staff, Marshall's contribution to the Allied war effort earned this succinct praise from Winston Churchill: "The organizer of victory."

But it was his work as secretary of state, specifically his oversight of the program that still bears his name—the Marshall Plan—that earned him the peace prize. The Norwegian Nobel Committee made this clear, although his Oslo presenter freely acknowledged the obvious paradox: had it not been for the armies directed by Marshall, there wouldn't have been any free Europe for the Marshall Plan to rescue in 1948.

We tend to think of George C. Marshall as a Virginian, as he is the scion of a prominent Virginia family, attended Virginia Military Institute, and is buried in Arlington National Cemetery. But Marshall was born in Pennsylvania, and he spoke with a flat and unaffected accent that conveyed modest Midwesterner more than chivalrous Southerner.

In his Oslo acceptance speech, Marshall discussed the danger of disarmament—unusual for a Nobel laureate—mentioning how America's abrupt demilitarization after World War II made the circumstances ripe for South Korea to be invaded. Marshall described the U.S. Army as a "vast power for maintaining the peace." He acknowledged, in his straightforward way, that his honor had made some people uneasy. "There has been considerable comment over the awarding of the Nobel Peace Prize to a soldier," he said. "I am afraid this does not seem as remarkable to me as it quite evidently appears to others." Marshall also discussed that massive aid effort in Oslo, referring to it, as he invariably did, by its formal name, the European Recovery Program.

Marshall's humility was the genuine article. So was the affection for him among free people around the world. In his book on the Nobel Peace Prize, Jay Nordlinger recounts an anecdote that underscores both propositions:

> In June 1953—six months before he received the Nobel prize—he attended the coronation of Queen Elizabeth II, as the American representative. When he entered Westminster Abbey, unannounced and, as usual, unassuming, the entire congregation rose. Marshall, aware that people were standing, looked around to see who had entered. It was he.

October 31, 1926

The Great Houdini

On this date in 1926, a president died. He was foreign-born, ran for office under an assumed name, and was killed by a Canadian.

Budapest-born Harry Houdini (born Erik Weisz), was elected in July 1926 to his ninth consecutive term as president of the Society of American Magicians. The son of a rabbi, and the fourth of seven children, our protagonist was brought to America from Hungary when he was four, settling initially in Appleton, Wisconsin, which he would claim as his hometown. In 1887, the family moved to New York City, which is where Ehrich Weiss, as he then spelled his name, became a skilled acrobat and trapeze performer. He joined the circus, taught himself how to be a professional magician, took the stage name Harry Houdini in homage to two performers he admired, and earned world renown as an escape artist.

Houdini scoffed at the mediums who populated county fairs and traveling shows in those days, but sometimes he couldn't resist their tricks. In 1914, while aboard a ship sailing to Europe, he was asked to entertain the passengers. Among them was Theodore Roosevelt, who was writing a book about his recent trip to Brazil's River of Doubt.

"I offered to summon the spirits and have them answer any questions that might be asked," Houdini recalled. "Roosevelt wanted to know if they could tell him where he had spent Christmas Day. I brought forth a map...which indicated the spot where he had been on the famous River of Doubt. That map was an exact duplicate of one that was to appear in his book, which had not been published. I had never seen the map and, to make my case stronger, the name of W. T. Stead, the English spiritualist and writer who lost his life on the *Titanic*, was signed below the map in a handwriting which one man present instantly recognized as that of Stead. And I might add that I was unfamiliar with Stead's signature."

"Is it really spirit writing?" asked the astonished Roosevelt.

Houdini never explained his trick, but left no doubt that was what it was. Three years later, he registered for the military draft as "Harry Handcuff Houdini." He died of peritonitis poisoning after a student in Montreal punched him in the stomach during a demonstration. Perhaps the student meant no harm, but Houdini hadn't time to flex his strong abdominal muscles, and the punches apparently ruptured his appendix. He was taken to a Detroit hospital, where he was conscious to the end. He passed on to the great beyond on Halloween.

November 1, 1872

Susan B. Anthony

By 1872, the Fourteenth Amendment had been ratified, Reconstruction was underway, and wildflowers grew in the fields that had been covered with the dead and wounded in the previous decade. After such a cataclysm, fought on the Northern side under the banner of ending slavery, many Americans found it obscene that half the adults in the country couldn't participate in the most basic democratic exercise—because of gender, not race. The women who pressed this case were called suffragists (or "suffragettes") and they had no more eloquent a champion than Susan B. Anthony.

Before the war, she had been an abolitionist and prohibitionist. The temperance movement radicalized Susan Anthony, though not in the way its leadership intended. Barred by men from speaking at antidrinking rallies, she turned her intellect and her ire away from the distillers and toward a bigger target: America's male-dominated political system. And so, on this date, she and three other women talked their way into registering to vote in a barbershop in the Eighth Ward in Rochester, New York. The male registrars didn't want to do it, but Anthony threatened to sue them personally. Elsewhere in the city, as part of a plan, several groups of women attempted to register to vote, several of them succeeding.

The ballots they cast four days later were secret, but the women's sympathies were not: President Grant and his Republican Party was more receptive to women's rights than Democrats. A Democratic Party poll watcher named Sylvester Lewis didn't want to accept the votes, but the two Republican registrars did; so on a 2–1 vote, it went in the hopper. Pettiness and pettifoggery characterized the response of the city's male burghers to this affront. "Citizenship no more carries the right to vote than it carries the power to fly to the moon," harrumphed the *Rochester Union and Advertiser*, the city's leading Democratic newspaper. "If these women in the Eighth Ward offer to vote... they should all be prosecuted to the full extent of the law."

This advice was duly followed. Sylvester Lewis registered a formal complaint. The local U.S. attorney's office charged Anthony with a federal crime. This was precisely the discussion she hoped to launch, and after being indicted (by an all-male grand jury) on January 24, 1873, she embarked on a speaking tour in every corner of Rochester, trying to open the minds of anyone who might happen to be seated on her jury. Her reasoning was forceful, but basic: Voting was an inherent right of every citizen and couldn't be taken away by voting registrars, courts, state legislatures—even by Congress. Anthony wasn't coy about the result she was trying to bring about: jury nullification, and eventual ratification of her view by the U.S. Supreme Court.

"We ask the juries to fail to return verdicts of 'guilty' against honest, law-abiding, tax-paying United States citizens for offering their votes at our elections," she said. "We ask the judges to render true and unprejudiced opinions of the law, and wherever there is room for a doubt to give its benefit on the side of liberty and equal rights to women."

In response, the prosecutor convinced a judge to move the trial to another county and delay the trial until June. This gambit offered Anthony the opportunity to proselytize prospective jurors in another venue, which she did with gusto, speaking for twenty-one consecutive days before concluding with a passionate oration in the county seat the night before her trial.

The presiding judge was Ward Hunt, whom Anthony seems to have considered a dim-witted political hack. She was right, but he was a high-level hack: friends with New York political boss Roscoe Conkling, Judge Hunt had at the time of Anthony's trial been nominated to the U.S. Supreme Court where he would serve, with little distinction, for nine years. In the months between Anthony's arrest and her trial, in fact, the Supreme Court undercut her legal rationale by issuing two very narrow interpretations of the Fourteenth Amendment. The *New York Times*, for one, couldn't hide its glee—or its hostility to Anthony's cause.

"Miss Anthony is not in the remotest degree likely to gain her case, nor if it were ever so desirable that women should vote, would hers be a good case," the *Times* editorialized. "When so important a change in our Constitution as she proposes is made, it will be done openly and unmistakably, and not left to the subtle interpretation of a clause adopted for a wholly different purpose." For his part, Judge Hunt essentially rigged the trial against Anthony, ruling that she could not testify in her own behalf, then reading a handwritten ruling from the bench—

apparently penned before the trial—directing the jury to render a guilty verdict.

Anthony later revealed her own views of the trial judge, describing him as "a small-brained, pale-faced, prim-looking man, enveloped in a faultless black suit and a snowy white tie." After Hunt pronounced his sentence (a $100 fine, no jail time), Susan B. Anthony stood and denounced his verdict, despite the judge's repeated attempts to make her sit down and be quiet. She did neither, not until she was good and ready. The fine and court costs have gone unpaid to this day.

November 2, 1783

Band of Brothers

It was time for their commanding officer to bid his soldiers and officers adieu. Pursuant to an act of Congress upon the completion of the Continental Army's mission, which was achieving victory over the British troops sent to quell rebellion on these shores, George Washington painstakingly wrote out the orders to his men from his headquarters in New Jersey.

Referring to himself as "Commander-in-Chief," his official title before the new nation ever had a president, General Washington said he was using the prerogatives of rank to wish his soldiers a "long" and "affectionate" farewell. In his nearly 1,600-word order, Washington sounded as though he could scarcely believe what he and his troops had accomplished.

"The unparalleled perseverance of the armies of the United States through almost every possible suffering and discouragement for the space of eight long years," he wrote, "was little short of a standing miracle."

Warming to his key point, Washington asked rhetorically: "Who has before seen a disciplined army formed at once from such raw materials? Who that was not a witness could imagine, that the most violent local prejudices would cease so soon, and that men who came from the different parts of the continent, strongly disposed by the habits of education to despise and quarrel with each other, would instantly become but one patriotic band of brothers?"

George Washington was doing more than flattering his officers and soldiers. He was reminding them of the regional, sectarian, and political differences they had set aside, while imploring them to retain the spirit of unity that had made such a disparate group into an effective fighting force. In this, he was foreshadowing his farewell address as president—and he was doing so in vain.

Civil War was in the new nation's future, and neither Washington's foreboding nor his impassioned entreaties could forestall it. Putting aside our provincial and partisan differences comes hard to Americans, a truth underscored as recently as the aftermath of 9/11, when our national concord proved fleeting. But as the widespread national discord that followed the 2016 presidential election reminded us anew, GW's advice is as valid now as it was on this date when he implored his soldiers—and, by extension, the people of the United States of America—"that with strong attachments to the Union, they should carry with them into civil society the most conciliating dispositions."

November 3, 2016

We Ain't Afraid of No Goats

For many, if not most, Americans, the 2016 presidential election was a disheartening civic exercise—regardless of who they ended up voting for. Briskly selling T-shirts for sale outside Wrigley Field during the 2016 World Series caught the nation's mood just right. "Nobody for President" they declared. By contrast, what took place inside the stadium *was* uplifting, especially for Chicago Cubs fans. On this date, for the first time since October 14, 1908, the Chicago Cubs could rightly claim to be the best team in organized baseball.

It was a World Series with many heroes on the Cubs' side, starting with team president Theo Epstein, who built a powerful roster, along with Anthony Rizzo, the Cubs' man-child first baseman; veteran catcher David Ross; Series MVP Ben Zobrist, and the good Lord himself. Yes, finally taking pity on the Cubbies, He ordered up a seventeen-minute rain delay that allowed the shell-shocked Cubs to regroup after blowing a lead in Game 7 against the Cleveland Indians.

As exciting for baseball fans as the games, the atmospherics surrounding the 2016 Series were just as evocative. Whether it was Indians' fans holding signs that said NOT IN MY TEPEE, or the *Ghostbusters*-themed T-shirts for sale outside Wrigley Field reading WE AIN'T AFRAID OF NO GOATS, baseball fans reminded us that they can laugh at themselves, their opponents, and their own team in ways that, well, political junkies often cannot.

That "goats" curse stems from the 1945 World Series—yes, that was the last time the Cubbies were in it—when a Chicago saloonkeeper was escorted out of Wrigley because he brought a smelly pet goat to the park and other fans objected to the odor. The tavern owner was heard on his way out to mutter something about how the team would never win. And they hadn't until this date. Professional baseball players these days (the average salary is over $4 million a year) can seem mercenary, but Cubs players got into the spirit. As Game 7 reached its climax, twenty-seven-year-old slugger Anthony Rizzo turned to catcher David Ross, a team father figure playing his last game and said, "I'm an emotional wreck." It seemed an uncommonly candid admission, until Rizzo added, "I'm in a glass case of emotion right now."

Then it was clear that Rizzo was quoting Will Ferrell's character in *Anchorman*, a movie that came out when Rizzo was fourteen. Actually, he was channeling most of the city of Chicago—and every Cubs fan who'd visited Wrigley Field since 1908.

November 4, 2008

The Voters Have Spoken

The tradition of holding elections on the first Tuesday in November means that November 4 has been a witness to many memorable elections, none more historic than the one culminating on this date in Chicago's Grant Park with the election of Barack Obama.

Hillary Clinton's presidential ambitions were believed to be over, the "Arab Spring" had not occurred, and Dmitry Medvedev had succeeded Vladimir Putin as Russian president—or so it seemed. Democrats had swept to power in Washington, not just in the White House. Capitol Hill was firmly in their control, while liberal academics and much of the media relegated the Grand Old Party to the dustbin of history. WE ARE ALL SOCIALISTS NOW, exclaimed *Newsweek*. ABC News warned about "the end of the Republican Party," while *Time* magazine wondered in print: "So are the Republicans going extinct?"

About the only thing conservatives had going for them, it seemed to many observers, was the cable news supremacy of conservative-leaning Fox News and its entrenched network chieftain, Roger Ailes. Even in the heart of the conservatives' castle, however, the election of a freshman senator, a biracial African-American with the name Barack Hussein Obama, was a historic and an inspirational benchmark—as Fox anchorman Brit Hume noted poignantly.

"Tonight is a night of victory, and a night of hope, when all things seem possible," Hume said as his network's camera panned Grant Park. "It really seems possible that this remarkable man will be someone truly and remarkably different, who can lift us out of the partisan differences that divide us, the ideological divisions that keep us apart. Who can change the atmosphere in Washington, as his predecessor had hoped to do but could not. Who can somehow find a set of policies that are right for the time. Who can fight the war on terror in some different way perhaps, that will be at least as successful and maybe more so. These are the things that people can hope tonight—because Barack Obama has been elected—an African-American, the son of immigrants—the forty-fourth president of the United States of America. What a story!"

But elections have consequences, as President Obama told Republican congressional leaders days after being inaugurated. As do the machinations and imperfections of man. Brit Hume went into semiretirement, leaving a vacuum at Fox. The careers of Roger Ailes and top-rated Fox host Bill O'Reilly were derailed by serial accusations of sexual harassment. President Obama gave Hillary Clinton a lifeline by tapping her as secretary of state. Democrats overplayed their hand in Congress. It turned out that reports of the GOP's demise, to quote Mark Twain about premature reports of his own death, "was an exaggeration." Although Obama had carried all the "swing" states against John McCain in 2008, the following year Republicans won governor's races in two states he carried—Virginia and New Jersey. In the 2010 midterms, partly because *Obamacare* had replaced *Romneycare* in the long-standing national debate over medical insurance, Republicans won back the House of Representatives.

"After what I'm sure was a long night for a lot of you—and, needless to say, it was for me—I can tell you that some election nights are more fun than others," the president noted the following day. "Some are exhilarating; some are humbling."

Democrats knew what he meant, as did Republicans two years later when Obama won reelection over Mitt Romney. The bitterly contested and historically close 2016 election that produced Donald Trump as president took this lesson to a whole new level for Democrats. Many of them could relate to the words uttered by progressive legend Morris K. Udall after losing the 1976 presidential nomination to Jimmy Carter: "The voters have spoken—the bastards."

This quip was borrowed from legendary liberal gadfly Dick Tuck, who delivered that pithy assessment after losing a 1966 California state senate primary. Tuck was a notorious political prankster who worked on campaigns, usually behind the scenes and surreptitiously, sometimes without bothering to coordinate with the Democrat he was trying to help. It was mostly innocent stuff, compared to what came later, such as spoofing the Republicans' treacly 1968 campaign slogan by hiring obviously pregnant young women to show up at a Nixon rally carrying placards saying NIXON'S THE ONE.

Although it seems like innocent fun now, both Nixon and Tuck saw such antics in a more serious light. "I always used to hate the word 'prank,'" Tuck told the *Christian Science Monitor* in 1982. "I don't consider the Boston Tea Party a prank." Tuck characterized it instead as an important, albeit staged, event with a political message. For his part, Nixon grudgingly admired Tuck, and can be heard on the White House tapes comparing his own staff's dirty tricks unfavorably to Tuck's pranks. "Shows what a master Dick Tuck is," Nixon said.

"I've made a lot of candidates look foolish," Tuck noted in that 1982 interview. "Usually with a lot of help from the candidates themselves."

November 5, 1912

Tyranny of the Majority

With William Howard Taft and Theodore Roosevelt splitting the Republican vote, Woodrow Wilson was elected on this day in 1912. A fourth candidate, Socialist Party nominee Eugene Debs, garnered just over 900,000 votes—good for 6 percent of the popular vote.

Eugene Victor Debs was born in Terra Haute, Indiana, the son of immigrants from the Alsace region in France. Leaving school at fourteen, he went to work on the railroad. He rose through the ranks of the Brotherhood of Locomotive Firemen, where he became editor of the union magazine, and was elected a member of Indiana's state legislature in 1884. By then he was too radical for the Democratic Party—and his old union.

Ten years later, he was at the center of an American Railway Union strike against the Pullman Palace Car Company, a fight pitting Debs against the federal government and the liberal establishment. "The truth is that every labor union man in the city of New York knows that he becomes a criminal the moment he puts himself on the side of Debs," brayed the *New York Times*. "He is a lawbreaker at large, an enemy of the human race."

To his followers, Debs was a great friend of the human race. They believed he was the enemy of a corrupt political system that sustained itself by crony capitalism and stepping on the throat of the workingman. In 1900, he ran for president as a Socialist. The 1912 presidential election was not his last campaign; nor was unionism his last cause. In 1916, he ran for Congress for an open Indiana seat, mainly on the same platform Woodrow Wilson was using in his reelection campaign: keeping America out of the First World War.

Debs lost, while Wilson won—then promptly steered the United States into war. Outraged, but unsurprised, Debs began giving antiwar speeches. After one of them, delivered in Canton, Ohio, he was arrested for violating the notorious Espionage Act of 1917. Tried in federal court in Cleveland, he was sentenced to ten years in prison. Even this shameful episode in American jurisprudence didn't silence Eugene V. Debs. He ran for president again in 1920, again polling more than 919,000 votes—this time from a prison cell in Atlanta.

"While there is a lower class, I am in it," he proclaimed at his trial. "While there is a criminal element, I am of it. While there is a soul in prison, I am not free." Debs added another point, one still relevant nearly a century later: "When great changes occur in history, when great principles are involved, as a rule the majority are wrong," he said. "The minority are right."

Gallant and Meritorious Service

Abraham Lincoln also won a four-man race for the White House on this date. Precisely forty years later, William McKinley was elected the twenty-fifth U.S. president. These two men, along with a third popular Republican president—James A. Garfield—are woven together in America's historical tapestry by tragedy. In a thirty-six-year period, all three men were assassinated. But they were connected in life as well as death. The Lincoln-Garfield connection is well-known: Garfield was a successful Union general whom Lincoln persuaded to run for Congress in 1862. But the Lincoln-McKinley link is obscure. It, too, took place in the Civil War.

William McKinley won the presidency in 1896 by jettisoning Republicans' traditional anti-Catholic bias, encouraging blacks to vote, and reassuring working-class voters that the GOP didn't care only about business owners. He first answered his nation's call at eighteen, a teenager so tender and green that he was assigned to be a private in a Union Army commissary unit. He didn't stay a private for long. At Antietam, he loaded up a wagon train with supplies including hot coffee and food, and braved withering Confederate fire while crossing an open field to resupply starving Union soldiers two miles away. One wagon was blown up, but McKinley made it safely to the men, who greeted him with "tremendous cheers," an eyewitness said.

After the war, when McKinley ran for office, the "coffee incident" was derided by one political opponent. But to his comrades in arms, McKinley was a hero; a statue commemorating his bravery still stands at Antietam. He performed similar feats repeatedly, once crossing a field at the Battle of Kernstown to deliver word to an isolated regiment to fall back, saving hundreds of lives. He kept getting promoted, to sergeant, to lieutenant, to captain—all by twenty-one. At Kernstown, the officer who sent him into harm's way (another future president, Rutherford B. Hayes) was overjoyed when he made it back alive. Before the war was over McKinley was made a major. To the end of his days, this was the honorific he preferred.

"I earned that," he'd say. "I'm not so sure about the rest."

McKinley received that brevet commission a month before President Lincoln was killed. That document was one of his most prized possessions. It stated matter-of-factly that he was being promoted for "gallant and meritorious services at the battles of Opequon, Cedar Creek, and Fisher's Hill." It was signed, "A Lincoln."

November 7, 1837

Threat from Within

Elijah Parish Lovejoy, a native of Maine, graduated first in his class at Waterville College and headed west, to St. Louis, where he opened a school and purchased an interest in a local newspaper, the *St. Louis Times*. By 1832, he was the editor, but his passions were caught up in a religious revival called the Second Great Awakening. His faith rekindled, Lovejoy attended Princeton's theological seminary, emerging two years later as an ordained Presbyterian minister.

The West beckoned again, this time in the form of a group of St. Louis civic leaders who asked him to edit a periodical promoting "religion, morality and education." So he returned to St. Louis to pastor a small Presbyterian Church while editing the *St. Louis Observer*.

Although it all sounded innocent enough, it wasn't. When his former newspaper endorsed mob action against a woman who had formed a Sunday school for slaves, Lovejoy joined the fray. Lovejoy's initial essay sought a middle ground. But slavery did not lend itself to moderation, and as his antislavery writing escalated, so did the threats. Three times his printing presses were destroyed by mobs. After a white mob broke into a local jail and burned a black man alive, the abolitionist press was outraged. A St. Louis judge with an apt name (Luke Lawless) directed a grand jury to indict no one in the lynching. Lawless then embarked on a rant against the abolitionist press in general, and Elijah Lovejoy, in particular. With mob rule essentially endorsed by Missouri courts, he moved across the river to Alton, Illinois.

Lovejoy was now in a free state, but not in a safe city. There, on this date, a fourth printing press was delivered. A mob congregated at the warehouse to seize it. This time, he stood his ground. But he and other armed men were overwhelmed. Lovejoy was cut down by gunfire, the Alton warehouse torched, and his presses thrown into the Mississippi. These events galvanized state legislator Abraham Lincoln. "At what point shall we expect the approach of danger?" Lincoln said. "By what means shall we fortify against it? Shall we expect some transatlantic military giant, to step the ocean, and crush us at a blow? Never! All the armies of Europe, Asia and Africa combined, with all the treasure of the earth (our own excepted) in their military chest; with a Bonaparte for a commander, could not by force, take a drink from the Ohio, or make a track on the Blue Ridge, in a trial of a thousand years."

No, they couldn't, Lincoln said, but the problem was that the danger lay within.

I'm Your Huckleberry

John Henry Holliday was a well-educated dentist from Georgia, thin, handsome and physically frail. Like many others, he gave himself a makeover in the American West. He abandoned dentistry for the more stimulating vocation of gambling. Compensating for his slight frame, he became proficient with knives and guns. Well brought up, his main love interest was a Hungarian immigrant who was likely a prostitute. He answered not to "John," but to a handle that generations of pulp fiction writers and moviemakers would make famous: "Doc" Holliday. The legends of his life are manifest, but here's a fact: On this date, he died of tuberculosis in a Glenwood Springs, Colorado, sanitarium at age thirty-six.

Of all the impressions created in biographies and films invariably glorifying Doc Holliday's life, none were more indelible than those created by Val Kilmer in the 1993 Hollywood production *Tombstone*. "I'm your huckleberry," Holliday's character keeps saying, and also: "You're a daisy if you do." According to contemporary newspaper accounts, the "daisy" line is accurate. It seems that Frank McLaury told Holliday at the O.K. Corral shootout, "I've got you now"—and that Holliday replied, "Blaze away, you're a daisy if you have"—before shooting McLaury dead. But the inquest following the Tombstone gunfight was notable for the conflicting accounts of the eyewitnesses, and the stories of Doc Holliday and Wyatt Earp morphed into fact-challenged legends partly because Earp and his brothers ably assisted their hagiographers. Once Hollywood got into the act, all bets were off. Over the years, Doc was played by Cesar Romero (1939), Victor Mature (1946), and Dennis Quaid (also in 1993).

Two traits come through in these films, as in the recollections of those who knew him: Doc Holliday was both smart and tough. As Virgil Earp told one biographer, "He was a slender, sickly fellow, but whenever a stage was robbed or row started, and help was needed, Doc was one of the first to saddle his horse and report for duty."

That dramatic scene in *Tombstone* where Doc and Johnny Ringo speak Latin to one another in the Oriental Saloon? That feels about half right. Although Ringo was a thuggish inebriate, Holliday was educated in the classics—and did know some Latin. But one character trait seems to be lost in all the dramatic re-creations of his life: Doc Holliday was not an unfeeling killer.

According to his common-law wife, Kate Horony, after the shootout at the O.K. Corral Holliday put his head in his hands and told her, "That was awful—awful."

November 9, 1731

Your Most Obedient Servant

In his impassioned 1963 "I Have a Dream" speech, Martin Luther King Jr. reminded Americans they had fallen short of the "magnificent words" of the Constitution and Declaration of Independence. Those documents, King said, were promissory notes, to which every American, white or black, was a rightful heir. In 1791, sixty-year-old Benjamin Banneker made the same point, just as eloquently—in a letter to the author of the Declaration.

He was born on this date on a Maryland farm to Robert and Mary Bannaky. Mary was half white and half black, Robert a freed slave. They named their son Benjamin. At some point, the name was altered to Banneker, and it is a name to be remembered. Benjamin Banneker grew up to become a citizen of the new country arising around him, a renowned scientist, a fluid writer, and the quiet conscience of a continent. On August 9, 1791, he sent an almanac he'd written to a man whose approval could open many doors: Thomas Jefferson, then secretary of state. Banneker noted bluntly that blacks' reputation in the white world was that of a race "considered rather as brutish . . . and scarcely capable of mental endowments." Writing in elegant prose that Banneker hoped would belie that reputation, he said he'd heard that Jefferson was more charitable in his assessments "and that you are willing and ready to lend your aid and assistance to our relief, from those many distresses, and numerous calamities, to which we are reduced."

So what did Banneker ask of Jefferson? Generally, help correcting the prevailing opinion of the intellectual capacity of African slaves and their descendants. Specifically, in furtherance of that goal, he wanted Jefferson's help in publicizing his almanac. He also reminded Jefferson of his own synthesis of natural rights in the Declaration of Independence, saying bluntly that blacks' "captivity and cruel oppression" was at odds with Jefferson's views about freedom being an "unalienable" right. He noted the irony that the Framers were "guilty of that most criminal act, which you professedly detested in others, with respect to yourselves."

Jefferson replied the following day. Although he ignored the question of his own hypocrisy, he was responsive to Banneker's aspirations. Jefferson said he was eager to see proof of the talents of "our black brethren" exhibited for all the world to see, writing that he had forwarded Banneker's almanac to the French Academy of Sciences in Paris.

He signed off this way: "I am with great esteem, Sir, Your most obedt. humble servt. Th. Jefferson."

November 10, 1975
For Whom the Bell Tolls

A Great Lakes freighter, the *Edmund Fitzgerald*, reported her position and the weather conditions on Lake Superior. The big ship was twenty miles south of Isle Royale, steaming through ten-foot waves and experiencing winds of more than fifty knots. November storms are not unknown in that region, but the National Weather Service had predicted that this one would pass south of Lake Superior. That forecast was wrong.

The day before, when the *Edmund Fitzgerald* set out from its Wisconsin port with a crew of twenty-nine and a cargo of twenty-six thousand tons of iron ore pellets, Superior was already starting to roil. The ship's captain, Ernest McSorley, opted for a northern route, hugging the Canadian coast. That night, he turned the big freighter south, heading across Superior toward Whitefish Bay. From there, the planned route would take them through the straits of Sault Ste. Marie, and down the length of Lake Huron to a port near Detroit called Zug Island. At dawn, however, snow was blowing and visibility was difficult. At 7 a.m. on this date, the giant freighter sent another weather report. Later in the morning, she went down with all hands.

The lake, it is said, never gives up her dead
When the skies of November turn gloomy.

Those lines come from Gordon Lightfoot's 1976 ballad, "The Wreck of the *Edmund Fitzgerald*." It was an unlikely hit, but Lightfoot's haunting melody and narrative tale of the doomed ship and crew were mesmerizing. At first, the families of the lost seamen didn't care for this tune. Who, they wondered, was this Canadian troubadour to profit on their pain? The passage of time gradually won most of them over, for good reason: The song is a tribute to the men who lost their lives.

It was more than that, as well. The wreck of the *Edmund Fitzgerald* wasn't the worst maritime tragedy in the history of the Great Lakes. Another early November storm in 1913 took a dozen ships and more than 250 sailors' lives. The bodies of the *Fitz*'s crew were never recovered, but the ship's bell was. And when it is tolled twenty-nine times every November 10, it will be for those men—and for the twenty-five thousand other seamen and passengers who have lost their lives in those waters down through the centuries.

Our Gallant Dead

The First World War ended on this date when a cease-fire was signed between the Allies and Germany at the eleventh hour of the eleventh day of the eleventh month of the year. In 1919, Armistice Day was observed in the United States, Great Britain, and France.

"To us in America, the reflections of Armistice Day will be filled with solemn pride in the heroism of those who died in the country's service and with gratitude for the victory," proclaimed President Wilson.

Those who most appreciated the 1918 cease-fire were the men about to go into battle. One of them, Army combat veteran Andrew Johnson, related in a 1930s oral history project how his unit was poised for what promised to be a costly assault on the fortified French city of Metz near the German border. "We were waiting to storm a great walled city," he recalled, "which would have cost us many men, as we would have to cross a level plain about two miles long."

Today, Woodrow Wilson is associated with the phrase "the war to end all wars," but those are words he never uttered. That phrase itself is a slight corruption of British writer H. G. Wells's phrase, contained in the title of a 1914 book, *The War That Will End War*. Wilson did tell Congress of his hope that the Great War, as it was called, would be "the final war." But in his April 2, 1917, speech to a joint session of Congress that brought America into the conflict, Wilson uttered a sentiment many presidents have invoked since that time.

"The world," he said, "must be made safe for democracy."

Wilson also noted that the United States wasn't out to take land for itself or subjugate other people. "We have no selfish ends to serve," he said. "We desire no conquest, no dominion."

Other nations do not always believe this, but American soldiers point to the U.S. military cemeteries in Europe to make their point. Colin Powell made it in 2003, and Gen. Mark W. Clark did in 1950. Clark returned to Italy after World War II was won. It was Memorial Day, as it happened, and Clark was with his wife. "We visited the American cemetery at Anzio and saw the curving rows of white crosses that spoke so eloquently of the price that America and her Allies had paid for the liberation of Italy," he wrote. "If ever proof were needed that we fought for a cause and not for conquest, it could be found in these cemeteries. Here was our only conquest: All we asked of Italy was enough of her soil to bury our gallant dead."

November 12, 1815

Oh, My Daughter!

Daniel Cady was a Federalist Party lawyer serving in Congress when his daughter Elizabeth was born on this date. Daniel was a self-made man, originally a farmer. His wife, Margaret Livingston Cady, came from a prominent political family, too. Her father had served with distinction in the Revolutionary War.

Elizabeth and her sisters were raised in a family in which reading and thinking were encouraged and discussions of civic life were always in the air. But she was a girl, and the limitations imposed on her because of her gender in the early nineteenth century were not imaginary. Women could not vote or run for office or even inherit property. The injustice of this system came crashing down on Elizabeth amidst a family tragedy.

Two of the Cady boys had died young. Now, when she was eleven, her parents were thrown into despair by the death of their last remaining son, Eleazar, who had just graduated from Union College.

"We early felt that this son filled a larger place in our father's affections and future plans than the five daughters together," Elizabeth would write later. Daniel Cady's inconsolable grief was not something his eleven-year-old girl knew how to assuage—but she tried. On the day of Eleazar's funeral, she came across her father in a darkened room, sitting beside her brother's body.

"As he took no notice of me, after standing a long while, I climbed upon his knee, when he mechanically put his arm about me and, with my head resting against his beating heart, we both sat in silence, he thinking of the wreck of all his hopes in the loss of a dear son, and I wondering what could be said or done to fill the void in his breast," Elizabeth wrote in her autobiography.

"At length, he heaved a deep sigh," she continued, "and said: 'Oh, my daughter, I wish you were a boy!' Throwing my arms about his neck, I replied: 'I will try to be all my brother was.'"

It was a well-intentioned promise, and Elizabeth Cady did not disappoint her family. Over time, her crusade became more ambitious, and more universal. As suffragist leader Elizabeth Cady Stanton, she dedicated her life to a proposition that is pretty simple when you think about it: Girls in this country should be afforded the same opportunities in life as boys.

November 13, 1982

This Hallowed Wall

In 1980, five years after the fall of Saigon, Congress set aside a three-acre site for a memorial for the veterans who had participated in the Vietnam War. Nothing about that conflict was ever easy, so it was inevitable, and perhaps fitting, that the process of creating a proper tribute to the soldiers, sailors, airmen, and Marines who had fought there was itself fraught with bitter controversy.

It was a complicated process, but with many years' perspective, the most salient detail is that the design competition was an open one. How very American of us. Egalitarian, too, which meant that the competition wasn't preordained to be won by the great Frederick Hart (he finished third), but instead by a Yale University architecture student named Maya Lin. The daughter of Chinese immigrants, Lin produced a design that was shocking in its simplicity, its starkness, and its emotional power. The monument, in black marble, is essentially a time line of American fatalities, with every name listed. It shocked many of the organizers and some of the memorial commission's key backers, including Ross Perot, who demanded changes, and James Webb, who called it "a nihilistic slab of stone."

Nonetheless, on this date the Vietnam Veterans Memorial was officially unveiled on the National Mall. It has proven itself a tour de force. In time, even most of its critics were won over. In part, this was done through compromise, which is something of a lost art in Washington: A more traditional statue of three soldiers was added adjacent to the memorial, and Frederick Hart was chosen to cast them.

What really happened was that the public voted with its feet on Maya Lin's daring design. Visitors just kept coming, and coming and coming. Almost immediately, they began tracing the names of their loved ones on pieces of paper. Soon, the National Park Service began helping people do it.

These pilgrims to the monument Vietnam veterans simply took to calling "the Wall" also leave flowers, letters, American flags, photographs, baseball caps, and other personal memorabilia.

What they are really doing is leaving little pieces of their hearts.

November 14, 2013

People of America!

José Ramón Andrés Puerta and his wife, Patricia, awoke in their Washington, D.C., home on this date, logged on to Twitter and resumed the activity that had consumed much of their time the day before: answering congratulatory tweets from friends, customers, and acquaintances—some famous, some not—who were responding to the news José had shared on social media.

"People of America! 4 hours ago, my wife and I became AMERICAN CITIZENS," he had tweeted, "thanks to all for being part of our world."

Born in Spain in 1969, José Andrés first laid eyes on the United States as a young sailor. "The first time I saw America was from my perch on the mast of a Spanish naval ship, where I could spot the Statue of Liberty reaching proudly into the open, endless American sky," he recalled. "At night, I would often wonder whether that sky was the explanation for the stars on the American flag—put there so the world would know that this is a place of limitless possibility, where anyone from anywhere can strive for a better life."

Andrés certainly found the life he was looking for. He opened Jaleo, a tapas restaurant in the nation's capital that introduced Washingtonians to small-plate dining, and went on to open other successful restaurants in Beverly Hills, Las Vegas, Miami Beach, and Puerto Rico—becoming a celebrity chef in the process. Three weeks after becoming an American citizen, José Andrés wrote about his feelings for his adopted homeland.

"I recalled that starry sky on Nov. 13, when after 23 years in America, my wife, Patricia, and I were sworn in as United States citizens," he wrote in the *Washington Post*. "The naturalization ceremony in Baltimore, attended by 72 other tearful immigrants from 35 countries, was a moment I had dreamed about since the day I arrived in America with little more than $50 and a set of cooking knives, determined to belong."

In mid-2016, Andrés backed out of a restaurant deal at a new Trump Hotel in Washington because of statements Donald Trump made on the campaign trail about Mexican immigrants. Although Trump sued for breach of contract, the episode only seemed to bind Andrés even more closely to his adopted country: A week before Trump's inauguration, Andrés proposed settling it by donating the money he was supposed to pay in rent to veterans' groups. Like any trendy American (and as Trump often does), Andrés made his offer on Twitter.

November 15, 1806

Pikes Peak

As the Lewis and Clark expedition was winding down, a third U.S. Army officer, Lt. Zebulon Montgomery Pike, was tasked with delving deeper into the vast expanse of the Louisiana Purchase. On this date, Pike and a cadre of fifteen men were traversing the Rocky Mountains in what we now know as Colorado when they discovered the mountain so high in the sky that they initially mistook it for a cloud.

It's problematic to think of "discovering" a geological edifice as imposing as Pikes Peak (yes, the accepted spelling omits an apostrophe). The mountain, obviously, was there for many millennia before Zebulon Pike and his small band encountered it. The Utes who lived in the area since about AD 500—and Pike encountered a settlement of three thousand Utes—called it "Sun Mountain." Their oral history says that the local band referred to themselves as Tabeguache, which means "the people of Sun Mountain." Spanish explorers also named it "El Capitan" before Pike ever saw it, and when the Arapaho arrived in the region after Pike, they started calling the place Heey-otoyoo, which translates as "Long Mountain."

Pike's first reaction was simply awe of what he called "Grand" Peak. "I thought I could distinguish a mountain to our right, which appeared like a small blue cloud," he wrote in his journal. "Their appearance can easily be imagined by those who have crossed the Alleghenies; but their sides were whiter, as if covered with snow, or a white stone."

Actually, these mountains could scarcely be imagined back East. It took ten days on the march just to reach the peaks Pike had spotted. "The sky was always climbing" is how Pike biographer John Patrick Michael Murphy put it. When Pike and three of his men began their ascent, they weren't even on the right mountain. When they reached the summit two days later, Pike saw he'd been deceived by a phenomenon that still amazes modern visitors to the Rockies: the difficulty of accurately determining distances amid that vast landscape.

"The summit of the Grand Peak, which was entirely bare of vegetation and covered with snow, now appeared at the distance of fifteen or sixteen miles from us," he wrote. "It would have taken a whole day's march to arrive at its base." By February 1807, Pike had left Colorado, never to return. But his journals would be published in 1810, and his mountain, and the possibilities it implied, would make their way into the consciousness of a new nation.

Captain Molly

The Americans had built several forts around New York and the British were never quite aware precisely where George Washington's troops were garrisoned. But on this date, a Continental Army fort in Hudson Heights in present-day Upper Manhattan, was overwhelmed by a huge force of eight thousand British and Hessian soldiers. It was almost as if the British had inside information, which they did. The traitor's name was William Demont, and he apparently traded his honor for money.

Whatever Demont's motivation, he did real damage. American casualties in the surprise attack included fifty-three dead and ninety-six wounded, with 2,800 taken prisoner, many of whom would not live out the war. Among the dead was a Continental soldier named John Corbin. His wife was one of the wounded.

Margaret Corbin was an orphan. Her father had been killed during an Indian raid in Pennsylvania in 1756, and her mother had been carried off into captivity, never to be seen again. The little girl grew up with a tough hide, and when her husband enlisted in a Pennsylvania regiment to fight for independence, his childless bride followed along. Such wives were called "Captain Molly" or "Molly Pitcher," for the water they would bring men in battle, but Margaret Corbin went them one better. When her husband fell at her feet to a British musket, she began loading the cannon he had manned. When the fort fell, Margaret was found among the injured, her shoulder mangled by grapeshot, her face and arm lacerated.

To New York state historian E. F. DeLancy, Margaret Corbin's valor reminded him of a poem by Byron, celebrating Agustina of Aragon:

> *Her lover sinks—she shed no ill-timed tears;*
> *Her Chief is slain—she fills his fatal post;*
> *Her fellows flee—she checks their base career;*
> *The Foe retires—she heads sallying host;*
> *Who can appease like her a lover's ghost?*

Margaret Corbin was the first female combat veteran in U.S. history. No Purple Hearts were pinned on the jackets of wounded heroes in those days, but Corbin's disabilities did earn her a pension, the first awarded to a female fighter.

Today, she is buried behind the Old Cadet Chapel at West Point, one of only two Revolutionary War soldiers interred at the military academy.

November 17, 1734

Freedom of the Press

William Cosby, a petty autocrat dispatched from London to serve as colonial governor of New York, didn't know how to silence John Peter Zenger, a German immigrant who published an uncompliant newspaper. Zenger's *New York Weekly Journal* was New York's first opposition newspaper—created in opposition to Cosby. Anticipating such intransigence, the *Weekly Journal* also positioned itself on the side of press freedom.

"No nation ancient or modern has ever lost the liberty of freely speaking, writing or publishing their sentiments," Zenger wrote, "but forthwith lost their liberty in general and became slaves." Deaf to such argument, Cosby tried to shutter the paper. On this date, he ordered Zenger's arrest. The governor had misjudged his man. From his jail cell, Zenger penned an apology. Not to Cosby, but to his readers—for missing the November 18 edition.

The case came to trial eight months later (Zenger was incarcerated the entire time), with the defendant represented by a "smart Philadelphia lawyer," as he was described, named Andrew Hamilton—the third immigrant to enter this drama. A native of Scotland, Hamilton represented the family of William Penn, had served in the Pennsylvania Assembly, and supervised the construction of Philadelphia's Independence Hall. He *was* smart, and highly esteemed.

The prosecutor argued that the libel laws of England were the de facto libel laws of New York and therefore, any defamation against the crown or its agents was merely a matter of proving the identity of the author. In other words, insofar as the jury was concerned, truth was no defense. There *was* no defense. Hamilton challenged this logic. Without exactly explaining why, he argued that the laws of England should not apply in New York. The trial judge didn't buy it, but the defense strategy was to talk past him, straight to the jury and, by implication, the court of public opinion. Hamilton addressed his argument to John Peter Zenger's peers. He was going for jury nullification. In his closing argument, he did not mince words about what was at stake.

"The question before the court and you, gentlemen of the jury, is not of small or private concern," he said. "It is not the cause of the poor printer, nor of New York alone. No! It may in its consequence affect every free man that lives under a British government on the main of America. It is the best cause. It is the cause of liberty." When the jury returned from its deliberations, the foreman called out the verdict: "Not guilty!"

Hurrahs rang out through the courtroom, drowning out the judge's call for order. Something had been started that would be hard to quell. Nearly half a century later, Gouverneur Morris, one of the Founding Fathers, would write: "The trial of Zenger in 1735 was the germ of American freedom, the morning star of that liberty which subsequently revolutionized America."

November 18, 1863

Gettysburg Address

Secretary of War Edwin Stanton booked Abraham Lincoln on a 6 a.m. train, figuring that was plenty of time for a wartime president to travel the 120 miles to a planned noontime speech in the village of Gettysburg. Had Lincoln adhered to that schedule, historian Garry Wills believes, he wouldn't have been there in time to deliver it. But Lincoln personally altered Stanton's plan. "I do not like this arrangement," he said. "I do not wish to so go that by the slightest accident we fail [to arrive] entirely." So Lincoln left the night before, on this date.

After Lincoln captured the heart of the matter in 272 words—speaking for about three minutes—various accounts arose about the provenance of the Gettysburg Address: Lincoln's black servant helped him write it; he dashed it down on the train on the back of an envelope; he wrote it in his head while the featured speaker, Edward Everett, droned on for two hours.

Garry Wills, author of *Lincoln at Gettysburg: The Words That Remade America*, calls these fanciful tales "silly, but persistent" myths. He points out that William Herndon, Lincoln's friend and longtime law partner, said Lincoln was a slow speechwriter, and a careful one. Wills cautions us that the haphazard way Lincoln was invited to speak at Gettysburg should not be confused with Lincoln's well-conceived plan for what he hoped to accomplish from the dais that day. Lincoln not only memorialized a deadly battle and paid tribute to those who died in those Pennsylvania fields, but he redefined the meaning of the Civil War—and of America itself. Lincoln traced the nation's birth to the Declaration of Independence, with its bold declaration that all men were equal, instead of the Constitution, with its requisite political compromises.

"I should be glad," Everett wrote Lincoln the next day, "if I could flatter myself that I came as near to the central idea of the occasion, in two hours, as you did in two minutes."

"I am pleased," Lincoln replied graciously, "to know that, in your judgment, the little I did say was not entirely a failure."

Dickens in America, Part I

Charles Dickens arrived in the United States four years to the day after Lincoln's Gettysburg Address. The Civil War had ended and Lincoln martyred. The famous writer's first port of call on this date was Boston, as it was twenty-four years earlier. That visit did not end well for the acclaimed fiction writer, so let's use a novelist's device, the flashback, to set the scene: Dickens arrived in Boston on January 22, 1842, two weeks shy of his thirtieth birthday. He was already famous on both sides of the Atlantic, primarily for *Oliver Twist* and *The Pickwick Papers*. That celebrity would mar the visit.

At first, he waltzed happily through snow-covered streets, reading shop signs aloud and reveling in his surroundings. He was feted at the White House. A New York dinner in his honor was the social event of the season. But Dickens began to find the adulation excessive. "If I turn into the street," he confided in a letter to his friend John Forster, "I am followed by a multitude."

There were other irritations. He didn't care for the personal habits of his American cousins. In Cleveland, he was repelled by Midwestern table manners. In Washington, it was men spitting tobacco in the street, which he described as "an exaggeration of nastiness." Unfortunately, the line did not appear in a private letter, but in a travelogue called *American Notes*. In the book, Dickens described American politics thusly: "Despicable trickery at elections; under-handed tamperings with public officers; and cowardly attacks upon opponents, with scurrilous newspapers for shields, and hired pens for daggers." That sounds contemporary.

Charles Dickens, concluded University of Kentucky literary scholar Jerome Meckier, found Americans "overbearing, boastful, vulgar, uncivil, insensitive and above all acquisitive." This last word is key. At first, he was amused by phenomena such as Tiffany's selling a Dickens bust in its jewelry shop. But as he realized how popular he was in the United States, it dawned on Dickens that the absence of international copyright standards was costing him money: American printers were free to publish his books and keep the profits, and this was what they were doing.

He brought this topic up gingerly in his talks with his

American hosts, but to no avail. Upon returning home, Dickens took out his frustrations in *American Notes* and a novel, *Martin Chuzzlewit*. Across the sea, Dickens's scorn was perceived, understandably, as ingratitude. Hurt feelings prevailed. Prominent U.S. newspapers turned on him, as did some of the Americans who had personally extended themselves. Charles Dickens was as dead to them as Jacob Marley.

November 20, 1963

"If Ever I Would Leave You..."

Lyndon Johnson, a vice president with too much energy and too little to do, spent this date making sure his ranch house was ready for a presidential visit. It was a full-court press. Lady Bird Johnson was involved, too. Jacqueline Kennedy, who'd never been to the Southwest, was accompanying her husband on this trip, and Mrs. Johnson wanted to make sure the First Lady enjoyed herself. So, the terry-cloth towels that Jackie liked after her bath were procured by the Johnsons, along with the Salem cigarettes she smoked and the French champagne she liked to sip. The president's favorite Scotch, Ballantine's, was also brought to the Johnson ranch, along with the Poland water JFK liked as a mixer.

Presidential press secretary Pierre Salinger informed the White House press corps about the Texas trip on November 7. The big news was that Jackie was going. As William Manchester noted in *The Death of a President*, not only had Jackie never been to Texas, she hadn't been west of Middleburg, Virginia, since moving into the White House. It seems clear now that the Kennedy brain trust didn't appreciate what they had in Jackie, politically speaking, until it didn't matter. Americans loved her, and crowds strained to see her and her dashing husband together. After Salinger made his announcement, Lady Bird penned Jackie a letter.

"The President's on page five, Lyndon's on the back page, but you're on the *front* page," she wrote delightedly. There was more to this expression of solicitude than sisterly solidarity. In August, the Kennedys had lost a son, Patrick Bouvier Kennedy, two days after his birth. For most Kennedy confidants, it was the only time they'd seen him cry—as he'd done in the hospital, again while informing his wife, and a third time at the home of Boston's Cardinal Richard Cushing. In his grief, John F. Kennedy had wrapped his arms around the tiny coffin until the old prelate told him, "Jack, you better go along. Death isn't the end of all, but the beginning."

After the baby's funeral, Kennedy lingered at the gravesite, murmuring to Dave Powers, his closest personal aide, "It's awful lonely here." Then, as Manchester noted in a haunting passage, "he returned to his wife, to comfort her after what had been the penultimate misfortune which can come to a woman." That was certainly Jackie's view. As Kennedy comforted his wife during her convalescence that autumn, she had told him, "There's just one thing I couldn't stand—if I ever lost you..."

November 21, 1963
The Wonders on the Other Side

Texas governor John Connally was the one who suggested that President Kennedy bring his wife to Texas. Connally was insistent, and since the entire trip was designed to unite the feuding factions of Texas's Democratic Party, this request was honored.

JFK's schedule had him speaking at three separate stops over the two days. The first was the dedication of the School of Aerospace Medicine at Brooks Air Force Base outside San Antonio. The base was named for a World War I–era pilot who was killed flying a biplane the year Kennedy was born. The new facility was envisioned as a place where the effects of space travel would be studied extensively. Kennedy sounded like a science fiction buff as he mused aloud on this date about the possibilities of space medical research. He simultaneously came across as a dreamy literary romantic. To explain his curiosity about the heavens, Kennedy invoked the imagery of Irish writer Frank O'Connor, who once wrote that while walking the countryside as a boy, if he and his friends came across an orchard wall that seemed too high to risk scaling, they'd toss their caps over the wall—leaving them no choice but to climb over.

"This nation has tossed its cap over the wall of space, and we have no choice but to follow it," Kennedy said in his last official act as president. "With the vital help of this Aerospace Medical Center, with the help of all those who labor in the space endeavor, with the help and support of all Americans, we will climb this wall with safety and with speed—and we shall then explore the wonders on the other side."

That night in Houston, Kennedy attended a dinner in honor of Texas congressman Albert Thomas. Representative Thomas had served in the House for nearly twenty-seven years, and during his speech, Kennedy again donned his science fiction writer's hat, imagining the world twenty-seven years in the future, in 1990. The young president expressed the hope that Americans in 1990 would look back fondly on the officeholders of 1963, "and say that we made the right and wise decisions." He added, " 'Your old men shall dream dreams, your young men shall see visions,' the Bible tells us, and 'where there is no vision, the people perish.' "

Jack Kennedy perished the very next day, and his brothers have joined him on the other side as well. But Kennedy's visions about space were realized. Meanwhile, NASA engineers have set their caps on Mars.

November 22, 1963

Oswald's Other Victim

The images from Dallas on this date long ago fade incrementally with each passing year. The faces of the Dealey Plaza crowd turning instantly from happy to horrified; the mortally wounded president lurching forward in his convertible; the protective reaction of the First Lady in her suddenly blood-spattered pink suit; the rush of the motorcade toward the hospital; the stunned vice president taking the oath of office aboard Air Force One; and the sad realization of an entire nation that two small children back in Washington would never see their father again.

But Jacqueline Kennedy was only one of two women widowed in Dallas that day. Caroline Kennedy and John F. Kennedy Jr. were just two of five children left to grow up without a father. J. D. Tippit had grown up on a farm in rural East Texas. In 1944, he answered his nation's call, joining the U.S. Army. Before he turned twenty, J.D. was on his way to earning his wings as a paratrooper in the Seventeenth Airborne Division. His unit was dropped into fierce fighting in Germany, sustaining heavy casualties. The young soldier refused a Purple Heart for a minor injury, but was awarded a Bronze Star for valor in battle. Like the president he had voted for—and who would be murdered by the same gunman—J. D. Tippit was a war hero.

His death touched a chord. Thousands of Americans sent letters of condolence. Among those who were moved were the Kennedys. Bobby Kennedy phoned the family, and in a poignant touch, Marie Tippit ended up consoling the attorney general: "They got killed doing their jobs," she told him. "He was being the president, and J.D. was being the policeman he was supposed to be." A letter arrived from Jackie Kennedy offering help. Marie replied that she and J.D. had loved the president: could she get a portrait of the Kennedy family? Days later, a framed photo arrived with an inscription reading: "For Mrs. J. D. Tippit, with my deepest sympathy, and the knowledge that you and I now share another bond—reminding our children all their lives what brave men their fathers were. With all my wishes for your happiness, Jacqueline Kennedy."

But even though she remarried twice, happiness proved elusive for Marie Tippit. In a rare interview on the fortieth anniversary of the assassination, she told Michael Granberry of the *Dallas Morning News* that no amount of time could take away the pain she felt for the man she loved. "And for anyone who thinks she's 'over it,'" Granberry wrote in November 2003, "well, she says, they never really knew J. D. Tippit."

Not-So-Silent Cal

Calvin Coolidge was a twenty-year-old Amherst College junior when he was tapped on this date to give a humorous speech at the Class of 1895's Plug Hat Dinner. He performed well and afterward the lads patted him on the back, started calling him "Cooley," and invited him to pledge a fraternity. After college, Coolidge went into government, ascending the ladder of Republican politics until he was governor of Massachusetts and later vice president under Warren G. Harding. It was then that the "Silent Cal" reputation took root.

At that time, vice presidents were *supposed* to be seen and not heard. And when Coolidge took the top job after Harding's death, he gave all the speeches required of early-twentieth-century presidents. He ran for a full term in 1924, winning easily, and would have likely won reelection four years later. He had other plans, however, which he indicated in August 1927 to the reporters who traveled with him on vacation. "I do not choose to run for president in 1928," Coolidge said simply. He took no follow-ups. So no, his terseness was not a myth.

Coolidge came by this reticence naturally. His father was a dignified Yankee public servant, and Calvin had lost his mother and a sister—experiences contributing to his emotional restraint. Then, early in his White House tenure, his son and namesake died from an infection that today would be a minor medical event cured in days with antibiotics. Coolidge also understood the political value of silence, especially in service of conservatism. This didn't set well with everyone. Alice Roosevelt said his facial expression looked like he was "weaned on a pickle." Upon hearing that Coolidge had died in 1933, Dorothy Parker reportedly quipped, "How could they tell?" Partly, this was politics. Coolidge was a popular president, but the onset of the Depression a year after he left office had cast a pall on his hands-off approach to governing.

"Nero fiddled," groused H. L. Mencken, "but Coolidge only snored."

When Coolidge's name is invoked today, it is usually done so critically—and for something he did not really say: "The business of America is business." These words are invoked, without amplification, as an example of what's wrong with (a) America, (b) capitalism, or (c) the Republican Party. Newspaper columnists can't get enough of this line—which is a sad commentary on the media, because Coolidge made those comments to American newspaper executives while explaining that he, and the country, realized that media owners answered to a higher calling than just turning a profit. In other words, Coolidge was making the opposite point—and he was talking to journalists about journalism when doing so.

Speaking on January 17, 1925, at the National Press Club the president did say, "After all, the chief business of the American people is business." But he quickly followed it with this: "Of course, the accumulation of wealth cannot be justified as the chief end of existence. . . .

"It is only those who do not understand our people, who believe that our national life is entirely absorbed by material motives," Calvin Coolidge added. "We make no concealment of the fact that we want wealth, but there are many other things that we want very much more. We want peace and honor, and that charity which is so strong an element of all civilization."

In conclusion, this taciturn Yankee offered one of the sunniest appraisals of the American Identity ever formulated by a U.S. president. "The chief ideal of the American people is idealism," he said. "I cannot repeat too often that America is a nation of idealists. That is the only motive to which they ever give any strong and lasting reaction."

November 24, 1864

Thanksgiving

It was a minor problem, considering the gruesome war the president was overseeing, but there was a nagging question about the timing of Thanksgiving Day. George Washington had proclaimed a national day to thank the Almighty for Americans' blessings, not the least of which was throwing off the British yoke and creating a nation. Washington chose November 26, 1789, which was the last Thursday of the month.

John Adams followed suit, but mostly Americans celebrated on their own without instructions from presidents—at least until Abraham Lincoln brought it back officially, in 1863, designating the last Thursday in November as Thanksgiving. As luck would have it, that date was also November 26, the original date picked by George Washington. But the last Thursday in 1864 fell on November 24, so Lincoln went with that day instead.

It turns out Americans didn't care one way or the other—at least until Franklin Roosevelt was president and a dispute broke out about whether Thanksgiving should be the fourth Thursday in November or the last one. (Roosevelt was president so long that twice while he was in office, November had five Thursdays.) This led to a comical impasse in 1940, when thirty-two states followed FDR's example and used the fourth Thursday, while sixteen states celebrated it on the fifth Thursday—a Republican Thanksgiving and a Democratic one.

Congress stepped in the following year (but not before the House and Senate disagreed as well) and the modern holiday was settled. As for two familiar customs—Thanksgiving Day parades and pro football—those traditions date to 1920, courtesy of Gimbels department store in Philadelphia and the Canton Bulldogs, a team coached by the great Jim Thorpe.

November 25, 1849

Heart and Hearth

Writing from his new digs in Sacramento, a merchant named Franklin A. Buck wrote a homesick letter on this date to his sister Mary. Born in Maine, Buck was only twenty-three and working in New York City when he felt the siren call of the California gold fields. The Panama Canal had not yet been built, so sailing from New York to San Francisco entailed traveling, as Magellan had done, around Cape Horn. Once on the West Coast, these "Forty-Niners" faced many hardships, not the least of which was missing their families during the holidays.

As a way of staving off those feelings, Buck put up a brave front in the letter to his sister. "I have not come 20,000 miles," he wrote, "to turn around and go right back again like some persons who have been here and gotten homesick."

He was no kind of hard-rock miner, but Frank Buck knew an opportunity when he saw it. In October, he made his way from San Francisco to the boomtown of Sacramento City, where he and his friends opened a supply store for prospectors. The miners needed everything, and they needed it fast. Markups were high. Think of his store as a "Black Friday" sale—in reverse.

"Week before last, we sold out of our little store $1,500 worth of goods," he informed his sister. "All cash trade in one day. . . . The flour that I bought in San Francisco for $18 per sack (200 lbs.) we sold for $44 and are all out."

Buck also boasted about California's mild weather, as residents do today when talking with their kith and kin living in less pleasant climes. "Today is Sunday," he wrote. "Gloomy November, probably, with you, but here the weather is splendid, not cold enough to need a fire."

Yet there were longings in California in 1849—as there are in all places in all times—that neither money nor temperate weather can cure. One of them is the desire to be with loved ones during the holidays. That hearth that he needn't fire up, in other words, was also a reminder of what he'd left behind. "I should like to be at home on Thanksgiving Day," he wrote. "I suppose you have had or will have one about this time. (Bake me a turnover!)"

"Be sure and write me all about it. I look forward with great pleasure to spending a Thanksgiving with all the family once more in my life," he added. "We were blessed, Mary, with the best of parents and a happy home. Probably they were the happiest years of our lives—those that we spent at home."

We'll Always Have Morocco

As U.S. involvement in World War II deepened, Army Chief of Staff George C. Marshall urged a counteroffensive in Western Europe. Winston Churchill and his generals did not agree. Preconditioned by the horrors of World War I trench warfare and chastened by the success of Erwin Rommel's Panzer divisions, the British high command insisted that the Allies first break Nazi control over the Mediterranean. This meant invading North Africa. This dispute was resolved by FDR, who ordered his commanders to accede to Churchill's wishes.

This was a fortuitous decision for one Hollywood movie studio. Warner Bros. had just completed a picture set in the coastal Moroccan city of Casablanca. The film managed simultaneously to be wartime propaganda and a stirring dramatic tale. Starring Ingrid Bergman and Humphrey Bogart, it premiered on this date, Thanksgiving Day, in New York City.

Nominated for eight Academy Awards, *Casablanca* won for best picture, best director, and best screenplay. The writing Oscar went to Julius Epstein and his twin brother Philip, along with Howard Koch. They certainly deserved it: Lines from that movie are still used in everyday American idiom. But the inspiration for the picture, along with its plot, setting, theme music, and memorable characters goes to a New York City vocational school teacher who went to Europe in the summer of 1937 to help Jewish relatives emigrate. His name was Murray Burnett, and after visiting a nightclub run by an American ex-pat in the south of France, he returned to the United States with an idea for a play. He cowrote it with a friend named Joan Alison. Its main character was an outwardly cynical but inwardly idealistic American saloon keeper, Rick Blaine. Their story featured his doomed love affair with a married woman, a daring escape from Nazi-occupied Casablanca, even the playing of the 1931 hit "As Time Goes By."

Their unpublished play, titled *Everybody Comes to Rick's*, came to the attention of Hollywood story editor Irene Lee Diamond. She took it to Warner Bros., which purchased the rights for $20,000. It was money well spent, not just for Jack Warner, but for three generations of moviegoers. Among the early viewers delighted by the film was Franklin Roosevelt, who screened it at the White House on New Year's Eve in 1942.

Two weeks later, FDR sat with Churchill and other Allied leaders at a January conference held—well, where else?—in Casablanca. "Of all the gin joints, in all the towns, in all the world..."

Breakfast of Champions

William Howard Taft never got stuck in a bathtub, as legend has it, but he could have. A binge dieter whose weight would yo-yo in accordance with the stress of his job and his ability to find time to exercise, Taft knew to avoid some foods—especially fatty meats—but he couldn't always manage to do it.

"The President weighs 332 pounds," White House housekeeper Elizabeth Jaffray wrote in her diary on this date, "and tells me with a great laugh that he is going on a diet but that 'things are in a sad state of affairs when a man can't even call his gizzard his own.'"

In some ways, Taft was a man ahead of his time when it came to his girth, and in his attempts to control it. For years, a la Weight Watchers, he kept a written diary of what he consumed, and he dutifully climbed on the scale each day to check his progress. He sought the services of a personal trainer and learned through trial and error that the key to daily exercise was finding a regimen he enjoyed—in his case, horseback riding.

But as anyone who has struggled with being heavy knows, it's not easy. In one letter to his long-distance mentor, British physician and weight-loss guru Nathaniel Yorke-Davies, Taft noted that he was "continuously hungry."

For Taft, the problem started at breakfast. Thanks to Elizabeth Jaffray's diary, we know what Taft consumed in the morning when he went off the wagon: "two oranges, a twelve-ounce beefsteak, several pieces of toast and butter and a vast quantity of coffee with cream and sugar."

That's an impressive morning meal, but it pales in comparison to that legendary—and almost certainly apocryphal—daily repast once described by gonzo journalist Hunter Thompson.

"I like to eat breakfast alone, and almost never before noon; anybody with a terminally jangled lifestyle needs at least one psychic anchor every twenty-four hours, and mine is breakfast," Thompson wrote.

He then described the contents of the meal itself: "The food factor should always be massive: four Bloody Marys, two grapefruits, a pot of coffee, Rangoon crêpes, a half-pound of either sausage, bacon, or corned-beef hash with diced chilies, a Spanish omelet or eggs Benedict, a quart of milk, a chopped lemon for random seasoning, and something like a slice of key lime pie [and] two margaritas...for dessert."

November 28, 1912

Jim Thorpe, All-American

Thanksgiving Day came late in the 1912 football season, and at the Carlisle Indian Industrial School in Pennsylvania the coaches knew what they were thankful for: that five years earlier, Hiram Thorpe had sent his son to their school. On this date, Jim Thorpe played his last football game for Carlisle. The weather was unusual—a driving snowstorm—but the result was typical: a 32–0 drubbing of Brown. Led by Thorpe, their transcendent star, the Indians won twelve games that year. The most satisfying win was Carlisle's 27–6 trouncing of Army.

Many myths attend to that game, some of them dubious: Did Carlisle's coach Glenn "Pop" Warner stoke his players' passions by telling them these West Point cadets were the sons of U.S. Army officers who'd destroyed their tribes? That seems doubtful, since Warner himself was the son of a Union Army officer. Did star Army halfback Dwight Eisenhower hurt his knee tackling Thorpe? Ike emphatically denied that in a 1967 interview with Thorpe's biographer, Robert W. Wheeler. "I was not hurt at all in the Carlisle game," he said. "As a matter of fact, I was thoroughly enjoying the challenge that Jim was presenting. Except for him, Carlisle would have been an easy team to beat. On the football field there was no one like him in the world."

In 1912, Jim Thorpe achieved athletic success that has never been equaled. Earlier in the year, he'd sailed to Sweden with the U.S. Olympics team that included West Point cadet George Patton and Hawaii swimming star Duke Kahanamoku. All Thorpe did once he got to Stockholm was dominate track and field, earning the famous pronouncement from Swedish King Gustav V as he placed gold medals for the pentathlon and decathlon around his neck, "You, sir, are the greatest athlete in the world."

Both his parents were of mixed heritage, so Thorpe was baptized a Catholic and given a "white" name, James Francis Thorpe, as well as an Indian one, Wa-Tho-Huk, which means "Bright Path." The path wasn't bright right away. His mother passed away while he was a boy. His father died soon after, but not before sending his son to Carlisle. There, he starred in track, football, basketball, and lacrosse, and played semiprofessional baseball one summer in North Carolina in 1909. For that transgression—it would be legal today—the International Olympic Committee stripped Thorpe of his medals. He went

on to play professional baseball for six years while also playing pro football—he's a Hall of Famer in that sport—and helped create the National Football League. In 1950, the Associated Press ratified King Gustav's pronouncement by naming Thorpe the greatest athlete of the first half of the twentieth century.

In 2012, sports journalist Sally Jenkins reviewed his performance a century earlier, noting sports fans' fondness for comparing decathletes from different eras and speculating who would win if all the Olympic champions could compete head to head. "The numbers Thorpe posted in Stockholm give us a concrete answer," Jenkins wrote. *"He would."*

Ike's Promise

Dwight Eisenhower didn't wait to be inaugurated to fulfill the campaign trail pledge he'd made in the waning days of his presidential election to personally go to Korea. Ike went there as president-elect, on this date, to view the situation firsthand. He spent three days meeting with his former World War II comrades, including Gen. Mark Clark, sharing C-rations with his old infantry regiment, and flying in a small plane along the Thirty-Eighth Parallel, the line demarking the two Koreas. From the air, Eisenhower eyeballed the formidable defensive positions of the Chinese forces supplementing the North Koreans.

As historian Jean Edward Smith noted, Ike came away with two strong impressions. First, prevailing on the battlefield would entail incurring enormous casualties. "It was obvious that any frontal attack would present great difficulties," Eisenhower told aides. "Small attacks on small hills would not win this war."

The president-elect's second perception flowed from the first. "We cannot tolerate the continuation of the Korean conflict," he confided to his advisers. "The United States will have to break this deadlock." On July 27, 1953—six months after he took office and three years after the war began—the United States, China, and both Koreas agreed to an armistice.

"After Eisenhower made peace in Korea, not one American serviceman was killed in action during the remaining seven and a half years of his presidency," Jean Smith wrote in 2009. "No American president since Ike can make that claim."

November 30, 1995

Blessed Are the Peacemakers

I didn't know much about my family background—not because of a lack of interest, but because my father was orphaned before he was six years old," President Reagan told the residents of a town called Ballyporeen when he visited Ireland in June 1984. "Now, thanks to you and the efforts of good people who have dug into the history of a poor immigrant family, I know at last whence I came. And this has given my soul a new contentment. And it is a joyous feeling. It is like coming home after a long journey."

In his visit to his ancestral homeland, Reagan was faithfully following a tradition started by John F. Kennedy. The Irish were warm enough to Reagan—that's their way—but it's long been believed that no presidential trip to Erin could rival JFK's nostalgic visit to his family's ancestral homeland. The trip, the *Cork Examiner* observed, was "a union of hearts."

Yet, new memories are made as well. President Obama trekked to the County Offaly, a place where the grandfather of his maternal grandfather, a man named Falmouth Kearney, lived as a boy in a village called Moneygall. There Obama charmed an impassioned crowd of twenty-five thousand, beginning with a self-deprecating quip that immediately connected him to the audience.

"I'm Barack Obama—from the Moneygall O'Bamas," the president said smilingly. "And I've come home to find the apostrophe we lost along the way."

Bill Clinton played the ethnic card, too. With White House encouragement, the Cassidy Clan produced a supposed presidential cousin, a sixty-five-year-old farmer from Northern Ireland named Mick Cassidy, whom the Genealogy Office in Dublin discovered was probably *not* related by blood to Clinton at all. But Clinton had actual business in Ireland. Reminiscent of Eisenhower's promise about Korea, Clinton honored his 1992 vow to involve himself in negotiations to quell the conflict in Northern Ireland. The Irish people were grateful for Clinton's attention and in 1995, when he visited Derry, a huge throng assembled at Guildhall Square.

Seeing him on the dais next to John Hume, a prominent Catholic statesman from Northern Ireland, the crowd began to chant, "Bull! Bull! Bull!"

Perplexed, Clinton turned to Hume. "Why are they saying that?" he asked.

Hume, familiar with the local dialect, smiled and replied, "They are saying your name."

They were saying, "Bill! Bill! Bill!"

December 1, 1917

New World Order

Alice Paul and her army of demonstrators had marched for months in front of the White House, their demands expressed simply: "Mr. President, what will you do for women's suffrage?" Initially, Woodrow Wilson was chivalrous. If he encountered the female demonstrators, he'd tip his cap and say hello. By summertime, however, with American doughboys fighting in France, his heart hardened toward them. With Wilson's acquiescence, authorities began citing the women, ostensibly for blocking sidewalk traffic along Pennsylvania Avenue. On August 28, 1917, police arrested ten suffragists and took them away to jail. If Wilson thought Alice Paul was missing the big picture, she thought the same of him.

"There never will be a new world order," she said, "until women are a part of it."

Of the 218 women arrested outside the White House in 1917, half were incarcerated in the D.C. jail or a women's prison called the Occoquan Workhouse. In prison, the women launched hunger strikes. Fearing they would have female martyrs on their hands, authorities force-fed them through tubes. This violent procedure helped turned public opinion in the women's favor once again.

"When the forcible feeding was ordered, I was taken from my bed, carried to another room and forced into a chair, bound with sheets and sat upon bodily by a fat murderer, whose duty it was to keep me still," Miss Paul explained. "Then the prison doctor, assisted by two woman attendants, placed a rubber tube up my nostrils and pumped liquid food through it into the stomach." This was done twice a day for a month, finally ending on this date.

Although no scientific polls yet existed to measure the effect news of such treatment was having on public opinion, none were needed. The brutal treatment of the arrested women was duly reported in the press. By

January 1918, Wilson reversed field, and lined up in support of a constitutional amendment giving women the right to vote. It was, he said, "an act of justice to the women of the country and the world."

August 18, 1920, is celebrated each year as Women's Equality Day to commemorate passage of the Nineteenth Amendment. But the bravest and most dangerous work was not done in the halls of Congress or the state legislatures. It was done in the streets and jail cells by what were now platoons of women led by the intrepid Alice Paul.

December 2, 1963

The President and the Widow

Lyndon Johnson and Jacqueline Kennedy had never been close, and were as different as people could be. Yet the assassination that made LBJ president and Jackie Kennedy a widow had bound them forever in history. A poignant telephone exchange between them on this date, captured on tape and stored at the University of Virginia's Miller Center, reveals each of them at their best. Although Johnson could be crude and bullying, on this occasion he was paternally protective. And the often-shy and reserved Mrs. Kennedy came out of her shell to make a subtly risqué witticism she knew LBJ would appreciate. Johnson began the call to Jackie Kennedy by saying, "I just want you to know that you are loved by so many—and so much—and I'm one of them." Jackie, who had sent Johnson a letter, said she doesn't want to bother him with too many such missives. He cut her off gently, saying, "Listen, sweetie. Now, first thing you've got to learn...is that you don't bother me. You give me strength." When Mrs. Kennedy suggested that it was an imposition on Johnson's time to write her back, he reassured her again:

"Don't send me anything," he said. "You just come on over and put your arm around me. That's all you do. When you haven't got anything else to do, let's take a walk...and just let me tell you how much you mean to all of us..." But Jackie was thinking of something else—how much she cherished the letter Johnson sent her, and wishing she had more letters from her husband.

"I know how rare a letter is in a president's handwriting," she said. "Do you know that I've got more in your handwriting than I do in Jack's now?"

This sentiment seems to throw Johnson off, and reminds him of his own family.

"My mother and my wife and my sisters and you females got a lot of courage that we men don't have," Johnson replied. "And so we have to rely on you and depend on you, and you've got something to do. You've got the president relying on you. And this is not the first one you've had! So there're not many women, you know, running around with a good many presidents. So you just bear that in mind. You've got the biggest job of your life!"

This comment made Jackie laugh. "She ran around with two presidents," she quipped, "that's what they'll say about me!" It was now the president's turn to chuckle, and he signed off: "Goodbye, darlin'."

"Thank you for calling, Mr. President," she replied. "Good-bye."

December 3, 1867

Dickens in America, Part II

In the twenty-four winters since Charles Dickens had last set foot on American soil, the country was much changed. The same was true of Dickens. No longer the spry young man who had dashed around Boston streets in the snow, he was now in his mid-fifties, and in poor health.

His fame, however, had increased exponentially. *A Tale of Two Cities* and *Great Expectations* had been published in the ensuing years. So had the little book that had rekindled affection for Dickens on this side of the ocean. *A Christmas Carol* had been written in 1843, the year he returned from America the first time, and what was clear by the time of Dickens's second U.S. visit was that this tale, along with Americans' own mercantile spirit, had helped transform how the birth of Jesus was celebrated in this country.

Word that the author would read *A Christmas Carol* at Boston's famed Tremont Temple rippled through the city. "Dickens has arrived for his readings," wrote Henry James. "It is impossible to get tickets."

Those willing to wait hours in line for the $2 tickets or who were lucky enough to have friends or connections, were rewarded with a vintage performance. The author read his entire morality play aloud, adopting different voices for the narrator and the famous characters: Ebenezer Scrooge, Jacob Marley, Bob Cratchit, and, of course, Tiny Tim. A-listers in attendance for the premiere included the triple-named luminaries of New England's world of arts and letters: Henry Wadsworth Longfellow, Ralph Waldo Emerson, Oliver Wendell Holmes, James Russell Lowell, and Charles Eliot Norton. One Boston newspaper review, which ran on this date—the morning after the performance— noted puckishly that all the "poets, philosophers, sages and historians of this city and vicinity were mingled like plums in a Christmas pudding."

It also said that Dickens's show was "unlike anything we have ever seen in this country." That performance, and the seventy-five that followed it, healed the rift between the beloved British author and his American public. At a New York banquet held in his honor on April 18, 1868, Dickens made further amends to his American cousins by promising to issue an appropriate appendix to future editions of *American Notes*, his less-than-complimentary account of his first trip. Like Scrooge at the end of *A Christmas Carol*, he "was better than his word.

"He did it all, and infinitely more."

December 4, 1915

Santa Claus Ship

There weeks after the "guns of August" heralded the onset of the First World War, New York writer Lilian Bell tossed and turned one night in the summer heat as she contemplated the suffering. "I walked the floor, blinded by my tears," she later wrote. "I forgot the heat—I forgot everything except that I must think of a way. The burden was laid on my heart in that very hour, and has never lifted since—the burden of the hapless orphans of the war!"

The specter of a hapless holiday season flashed before her eyes: "Not a smile on the face of any child in the length and breadth of that devastated land! How I wished that I could send all Europe a Christmas!" But Lilian Bell was an American, so she came up with a plan. Even better, she was a native of Chicago, so she knew who to turn to for help in carrying it out: a newspaper editor in that news-crazed town. She wrote a letter to James Keeley, the British-born publisher of the *Chicago Herald*. Keeley asked her to take a train to her hometown, which she did. Hours later, they'd put the plan in motion. What was that plan? It was to ask American children to give toys and other presents to European children—and send them overseas for Christmas.

"I knew President Wilson would give us a ship," Bell said. "I knew the railroads and express companies would carry the gifts free. I knew that not a facility which could be utilized would be withheld by the grand and glorious Americans who make this country of ours the most wonderful land in the world." Mostly, she wrote, she trusted the children of this country. "I knew if I asked them to load a ship with Christmas toys for the little orphans of the war I would present an idea which would capture the imagination of every child who heard the plan."

It all came true. More than two hundred newspapers joined the *Herald*'s crusade. Eight thousand tons of toys were collected, and a U.S. Navy ship, the USS *Jason*—dubbed the "Santa Claus Ship"—set sail for Europe in mid-November. On this date, the London *Daily Telegraph* carried a story on page ten with instructions on how and where families would obtain toys from the Santa Claus Ship.

Before it left, Woodrow Wilson sent a telegram wishing it a safe voyage, adding, "May the good ship carry comfort and relief to the distressed and suffering." Because America was still neutral in that war, after off-loading many of the presents in the UK, the Santa Claus Ship sailed for Marseilles and Genoa to deliver presents to German and Austrian children. Some gifts were transferred to another ship and taken to Russia. God bless us, everyone.

December 5, 1950

Give 'Em Hell, Harry

Singing a program of classical music, Margaret Truman packed Constitution Hall on this date for an audience that included her parents—the President and First Lady—as well as Paul Hume, the accomplished music critic for the *Washington Post*.

Harry Truman was reviled while in office for some of the same traits he is admired for today, among them his unvarnished candor and everyman manner of communication. Both were on display the following morning at 5:30, when he saw Hume's review in his morning newspaper—the one in which the *Post* critic said Miss Truman "cannot sing very well."

So the president penned a response.

"Mr. Hume, I've just read your lousy review of Margaret's concert," it began. "It seems to me that you are a frustrated old man who wishes he could have been successful....

"Someday I hope to meet you," Truman continued. "When that happens you'll need a new nose, a lot of beefsteak for black eyes, and perhaps a supporter below!" Truman went on in this vein for a while, concluding by saying that he wanted to call Paul Hume a son of a bitch, but felt constrained from going that far.

A gentle soul—he was a conscientious objector in World War II—Hume was stunned by this letter, and urged his editors to publish it. That idea was vetoed by *Post* publisher Philip L. Graham, who had received several angry Truman missives himself and never run them. Complicating the situation was the sudden death of White House press secretary Charles G. Ross, a close Truman confidant, who had suffered a heart attack hours before Margaret's concert. This may have been a factor in the president's outburst. At the least, Ross might have prevented the letter from being mailed.

Nonetheless, after Hume mentioned the letter to a music critic at a rival newspaper, Truman's outburst did make it into the national press, causing a brief furor. Years later, while in Kansas City to review a Maria Callas concert, Hume decided to drive out to Independence to see the Truman Library—and make amends with the former president. The men did not fight that day. That was not Paul Hume's way, and the feisty president had mellowed considerably. Truman spent an hour with Hume, proudly showing him the presidential library.

Then the two men played the piano together.

December 6, 1941

Dark Clouds

War had been raging in Europe for two years, but American public opinion had not reconciled itself to joining the fight, despite the interventionist impulses of a popular U.S. president. In the Pacific, Gen. Douglas MacArthur expressed confidence that he could repel any Japanese invasion of the Philippines. In Hawaii, Adm. Husband E. Kimmel spent this day, a Saturday, wondering if he should order the U.S. Navy Seventh Fleet to disperse from Pearl Harbor.

The USS *Enterprise*, its biggest aircraft carrier, had been due back in port, but bad weather had delayed her: As the winter sun slipped down over the horizon, the ship was still 250 nautical miles away—out of harm's way, as it would turn out.

In Washington, Franklin D. Roosevelt began his day with back-to-back White House meetings with Supreme Court Justice William O. Douglas and budget director Harold D. Smith. After lunch with trusted aides Harry Hopkins and Grace Tully, FDR met with Secretary of State Cordell Hull and Attorney General Francis Biddle. He discussed the war in Europe with Lord Halifax, the British ambassador, at 4:50 p.m. and kept a 6 p.m. doctor's appointment before a predinner cocktail with philanthropist Vincent Astor. Thirty-four guests attended dinner at the White House. Violinist Arthur LeBlanc provided the entertainment. Afterward, as his last act of the day, FDR dictated a cable to Emperor Hirohito imploring him to choose peace.

"I address myself to Your Majesty at this moment in the fervent hope that Your Majesty may, as I am doing, give thought in this definite emergency to ways of dispelling the dark clouds," FDR wrote. He added that the two had "a sacred duty" to do all they could to "prevent further death and destruction in the world."

Roosevelt was not naïve. He knew Japan still occupied Manchuria, that thousands of Japanese troops had been pouring into Indochina, that Australia was anticipating an attack. What the president did not know was that Adm. Isoroku Yamamoto's fleet had already crossed the Pacific and was amassed near Pearl Harbor. Later that night, FDR was given an intercepted message from Tokyo to the Japanese Embassy in Washington titled "Final Communication to the United States." The cable did not declare war or call for the breaking of diplomatic relations. But its tone was menacing, and the U.S. Navy lieutenant who delivered the decoded document to the White House recalled Roosevelt's terse reaction: "This means war," he said simply.

December 7, 1941

Prisoner of War No. 1

Pearl Harbor was devastated in a Sunday morning surprise air attack launched from Japanese aircraft carriers that had crossed the Pacific Ocean undetected. For the United States armed forces the loss of life was frightful: 2,400 men killed, nearly half of them aboard the USS *Arizona*, and 1,200 wounded. Casualties among the invaders were light: sixty-four aviators killed, one sailor captured. But that one prisoner lived to tell a tale.

Kazuo Sakamaki was one of ten Japanese sailors manning five minisubmarines that slipped into Pearl Harbor the day of the attack. All five were destroyed and the other nine sailors killed. The lone survivor didn't want to be taken alive. As instructed, Sakamaki tried to blow up his grounded sub, but the charges didn't detonate. When he dove underneath to try and fix the problem, he lost consciousness. When he awoke in custody, he burned his face with cigarettes in shame and begged his captors to allow him to commit suicide. They refused, so Lieutenant Sakamaki became the first U.S prisoner of war in the Pacific Theater.

He was sent to the mainland and eventually taken by train to a Tennessee prison camp. Like other Axis prisoners, Sakamaki was surprised by the lack of brutality at the hands of his captors, and by the quality of medical care and food he was provided—and his access to news accounts of the war. All these amenities were denied prisoners taken by the Japanese, as Sakamaki knew. He began to rethink what he had been taught. In 1942, when they heard about the great American victory at the Battle of Midway, other Japanese POWs disbelieved it. Not Kazuo Sakamaki. As historian John Toland, who interviewed Sakamaki, wrote in *The Rising Sun*, the young Japanese officer had reason to believe what he read in U.S. newspapers.

"On his long journey to Tennessee he had seen countless factories and endless fields and he knew that tiny Japan had yet to feel the full might of the United States," Toland wrote. "Midway was just the beginning of the end of Japan's hope of conquest."

But it was not the end of Sakamaki's life. He began counseling other Japanese POWs not to commit suicide, and by the time he returned home, he was a pacifist. He revealed why in his 1949 memoir, *Four Years as Prisoner of War No. 1*, which was published in both Japanese and English. In his book, and in his 1960 interview with Toland, Sakamaki told of his transforming experience among the Americans. "It was," he said, "a rebirth of reason."

December 8, 1941

The Day After

Franklin Roosevelt had gone to bed about thirty minutes after midnight, knowing that the morning would be a momentous one. At midday, he went to the Capitol to address a joint session of Congress, entering that chamber no longer as the partisan architect of a controversial New Deal but as a wartime commander in chief of a unified, aggrieved, and galvanized nation.

Speaker of the House Sam Rayburn announced his entry simply: "The president of the United States," which precipitated a wildly enthusiastic standing ovation, followed by a six-and-a-half-minute address that formally put the nation in a war posture.

"Yesterday, December 7, 1941—a date which will live in infamy—the United States of America was suddenly and deliberately attacked by naval and air forces of the Empire of Japan," President Roosevelt began.

In an address consisting of fewer than five hundred words, the president eschewed the traditions associated with asking for a declaration of war: He didn't dwell on the constitutional justification for such a step—didn't mention it, actually—let alone the moral justification for entering the conflict. In reciting Japan's list of aggressions, Roosevelt didn't mention a single event that was more than twenty-four hours old. Using mesmerizing repetition and a martial cadence that reflected his anger, Roosevelt wasn't trying to talk his fellow Americans into war. He knew, and they knew, that war had come to them. What FDR was doing was trying to inspire his countrymen. That was why he spoke of the "inevitable triumph" ahead, adding this line: "No matter how long it may take us to overcome this premeditated invasion, the American people in their righteous might will win through to absolute victory."

The first person to witness FDR's instant metamorphosis into a wartime president was the First Lady, Eleanor Roosevelt. The Roosevelts had dinner plans the night before with Edward R. Murrow and his wife, Janet. The Murrows had recently returned from Great Britain, where Edward had made a name for himself broadcasting during the Blitz. Hours after Pearl Harbor was attacked, Mrs. Murrow telephoned the White House to say that she understood that dinner was now impossible. But Eleanor, displaying the grace under pressure that epitomized that family, waved her off.

"We still have to eat," Mrs. Roosevelt said simply. After dinner, which was a less formal affair than originally planned, Janet Murrow left the White House. Her husband remained, at the president's request. Hours later, Murrow was still there as FDR ushered him into his personal study. Sandwiches and beer were served, and the visiting broadcaster saw that the president was still seething over Japan's perfidy.

"Our planes were destroyed on the ground!" Roosevelt said, pounding his desk. "By

God, on the ground!" The commander in chief was angry, but focused, as his wife and Murrow could see. Eleanor later noted that the president was "deadly calm...like an iceberg."

Other meetings were taking place in the White House that night, as the capital converted instantly to wartime footing. Among the members of the congressional leadership who arrived was Hiram Johnson of California, a Progressive Party stalwart and one of the most prominent isolationists in the Senate. The isolationists had opposed Roosevelt on the military draft, on Lend-Lease, on so much. They couldn't oppose him now.

"What a sight!" *Christian Science Monitor* correspondent Richard Strout wrote in a dispatch to his office. "The great isolationist, Hiram Johnson, grim-faced, immaculately dressed, stalks across our little stone stage on the White House portico. All the ghosts of isolationism stalk with him, all the beliefs that the United States could stay out of war if it made no attack.... [He] walks by, refusing to comment, looking straight ahead through the crowd of reporters, who are silenced for a minute with the sense of history passing and a chapter closing."

As this was happening, Franklin Roosevelt was planning what he would say to all of Johnson's colleagues in the Capitol—and a waiting world—the following morning.

"Roosevelt often wrote his own speeches, or at least provided substantial edits," wrote Craig Shirley, author of *December 1941: 31 Days That Changed America and Saved the World*.

"The president's original manuscript of his address revealed the sheer power of words," Shirley continued. "He initially wrote December 7, 1941 would live in 'history,' but he later crossed out that word, inserted a proof-reader's caret, and scribbled 'infamy.' As Mark Twain once said, 'The difference between the almost right word and the right word is really a large matter—'tis the difference between the lightning bug and the lightning.'

"In his speech to Congress on December 8," Shirley added, "the president had captured lightning in a bottle."

December 9, 1941

Wartime Rumors

In the aftermath of the attack, Americans were jittery, especially on the West Coast. As the government kept mum on the Navy's losses at Pearl Harbor, gossip and half-baked news reports about supposed impending new attacks by the Japanese filled the vacuum. In many places, these rumors induced full-out panic, and it dawned on policymakers inside the White House that President Roosevelt would have to reveal more details to the American people than he had in his brief "date which will live in infamy" speech the day before to Congress. Steve Early, the president's press secretary, announced that FDR would take to the radio waves at 10 p.m. Eastern time to provide "more complete documentation" of what had occurred in Hawaii.

At the White House, reporters peppered the president with questions implying that the government had to have been aware that attacks on Pearl Harbor were in the works. Remember those hateful (and invented) rumors about Jews who supposedly took the day off on 9/11? Reporters asked FDR about similar rumors about Navy personnel on December 7 as FDR—a former assistant secretary of the Navy—bristled with resentment.

Meanwhile, West Coast cities imposed mandatory blackouts at nightfall. In Seattle, the windows of thirty or forty shopkeepers who didn't comply were smashed by an angry mob.

In San Francisco, a member of the California State Guard opened fire on a car driven by a man named Don Sayre as it approached the Golden Gate Bridge. Sayre apparently didn't see the guardsman waving him over; his wife was hospitalized with a gunshot wound. Air raid drills were ordered in New York City and a million schoolchildren were sent home, as were fourteen thousand shipyard workers in Quincy, Massachusetts. Warnings of the supposed approach of a squadron of enemy planes were broadcast over the radio in Boston.

"Remember," cautioned Massachusetts public safety official J. Wells Farley, "panic is the worst danger." Here, Farley was channeling FDR, who'd issued the same warning to the American people eight and a half years earlier in the context of the Depression. But Roosevelt was in the process of forgetting his own lesson: One rumor making the rounds on this day was that the government was collecting the names of Japanese immigrants and Japanese-Americans living on the West Coast. Some news accounts suggested that the FBI had a plan to incarcerate them. These rumors were true.

December 10, 1869

State of Equality

Remember the ladies," Abigail Adams had written to John Adams in 1776 when he represented Massachusetts in the Continental Congress in Philadelphia. Nearly a century later, Julia Bright made the same case to her husband, Wyoming legislator William Bright, stressing her view that voting was a foundational right of citizenship. Bright came to concur, and drafted the legislation that made history.

In the aftermath of the Civil War, the nation was in the process of extending the franchise to African-Americans—provided they were male. If freed slaves could vote, why not women? Edward M. Lee, appointed territorial secretary by President Grant, made this point during the low-key debate in Cheyenne.

The women's vote passed the twenty-man Wyoming territorial legislature with little fanfare and, on this date, John Allen Campbell, Wyoming's first territorial governor, signed a bill extending the vote to women—the first jurisdiction to do so. Self-interest played a role in their enlightenment: One reason Wyoming's male populace was receptive to granting women the vote was to encourage women to move to the territory, as a dearth of female settlers made it hard to find wives. This rationale was anticipated by none other than Mark Twain.

"What, sir, would the people of the earth be without woman?" Twain quipped in a January 1868 speech. "They would be scarce, sir, almighty scarce." Twain had other observations about women, few of which would pass muster in our more sensitive age. ("There is nothing comparable to the endurance of a woman," he wrote in his autobiography. "In military life she would tire out an army of men, either in camp or on the march.")

Feminists of the time believed their sisters should literally march to Laramie. Susan B. Anthony suggested that women in the East relocate to Wyoming as a political statement. That didn't happen, but Anthony and Elizabeth Cady Stanton took a trip in 1871 on the newly completed transcontinental railroad to the place they called "the land of freedom." Two decades later, opposition to Wyoming statehood arose in Congress because of Wyoming's voting laws. Territorial legislators sent a defiant telegram proclaiming that they would happily remain out of the Union for one hundred years rather than regress on the issue of women's suffrage. Congressional opponents backed down, and on July 10, 1890, President Benjamin Harrison signed into law a bill admitting Wyoming into the Union, recognizing it as the nation's "Equality State."

December 11, 2016

God Is with Us

Wednesday evenings is when Emanuel African Methodist Episcopal Church in Charleston, South Carolina, holds Bible study classes, and this date was no exception. The day before, the gunman who'd come to Bible study a year and a half earlier and taken nine precious lives had been sentenced to death at trial. But there was no hate in the hearts of the Christians who met in the lower level of the church.

It's been that way for two centuries at the church on Calhoun Street. In 1818, two preachers from Charleston—Morris Brown, a free man of mixed race, and former slave Henry Drayton—launched the church and affiliated it with the African Methodist Episcopal denomination. What took place in Charleston over the river of years reminds us that the oldest foundational legacy in Christianity is suffering. In 1821, fiery and charismatic former slave Denmark Vesey began preaching at the Charleston church, and fomenting revolution as well. Vesey was arrested, tortured, tried, and hanged along with three dozen of his coconspirators—and the church was burned to the ground by a white mob. Morris Brown and Henry Drayton decamped to Philadelphia, but the good Lord was not done with their former church. It was reconstructed in 1834, though most worshiping was done in secret.

Church life there rose, Lazarus-like, after the Civil War, and a new word was incorporated into its name: Emanuel, which means "God is with us." Soon, it earned the same moniker as the original AME church in Philadelphia, which is called "Mother Bethel"— the Charleston church became known as "Mother Emanuel." After an earthquake destroyed the wood church in 1872, a grander and more durable brick and marble structure arose in its place.

Among those who preached love and liberation there over the ensuing decades were Booker T. Washington, Martin Luther King Jr., and Clementa C. Pinckney, a fixture in modern South Carolina politics. Pinckney was leading worship there on the fateful Wednesday night in June 2015, along with two other ordained pastors of the church: Daniel L. Simmons Sr. and DePayne Middleton-Doctor, the mother of four daughters. Pinckney, Simmons, and Middleton-Doctor all lost their lives there, along with six other apostles, when a young man with a warped brain and a cancerous heart entered Emanuel with a .45-caliber handgun.

He did not get the last word.

December 12, 1917

Love, Actually

On this date, Irish-born Catholic priest Edward J. Flanagan opened his heart and his Omaha, Nebraska, parish to six wayward kids. It was the beginning of Boys Town. "There are no bad boys," Father Flanagan said, in both real life and in the movie in which he was played by Spencer Tracy. Fifty years later to the day, another movie featuring Spencer Tracy opened in theaters—and opened Americans' hearts in another way.

Guess Who's Coming to Dinner was ostensibly about color-blindness, but really it was about love, and all the more poignant because it was the last time Katharine Hepburn and Spencer Tracy would grace the big screen together. Hepburn and Tracy played a liberal couple in San Francisco whose daughter brings home her love interest, an African-American doctor played by Sidney Poitier. For moviegoers, even those who considered themselves enlightened on race, director Stanley Kramer included a twist that challenged audiences—white or black—to confront their own prejudices: Sidney Poitier's parents were just as upset as their white counterparts.

The film arrived in theaters months after the Supreme Court unanimously declared in *Loving v. Virginia* that race-based restrictions on marriage were unconstitutional. Fittingly, perhaps, during the tenure of a U.S. president with a white mother and a black father, the Court again expanded the definition of marriage. Meanwhile, a popular new pope set a more welcoming tone for divorced Catholics, even while not officially altering church doctrine, which was one of the factors that kept the real-life Tracy-Hepburn romance in the shadows (the other being that marriage held limited appeal for the independent-minded actress).

The political system also adapted. In 1964, Nelson Rockefeller's presidential ambitions were compromised, in part, by his divorce. By 1980, voters flocked to the polls to support divorced former movie actor Ronald Reagan. His cause was helped by a pivotal moment in a New Hampshire debate, when a moderator tried to cut him off and Reagan barked, "I paid for this microphone, Mr. Green." It was a dramatic scene, notwithstanding the moderator's name being *Breen*, but it wasn't original. Reagan borrowed the line from Spencer Tracy, who played a GOP presidential candidate in the 1948 film *State of the Union*. As his wife (yes, played by Katharine Hepburn) looks on, Tracy sets in motion the movie's denouement as his handlers try to shush him: "Don't you shut me off!" Tracy roars. "I'm paying for this broadcast!"

December 13, 2000

Concession

The presidential election held on November 7, 2000, produced an anomaly that had happened three previous times in U.S. history: The winner lost. The most notorious instance came in 1824. In a four-man race, Andrew Jackson won the popular vote *and* bested John Quincy Adams in the Electoral College. He lacked a majority of electors, however, so the issue was thrown into the House of Representatives, which chose Adams. This result infuriated Jackson supporters and galvanized Old Hickory to win the presidency handily four years later.

In 1876, Rutherford B. Hayes prevailed in the Electoral College by the whopping margin of one electoral vote, while losing the popular tally to Samuel J. Tilden. The same fate befell incumbent President Grover Cleveland in 1888, although he won the rematch four years later in the only presidential campaign featuring two candidates running for reelection.

For Al Gore, the loss was triply painful. First, he lost in the Electoral College by a margin so narrow that a switch of even the smallest state from Bush to Gore would have made the difference. Second, it seemed apparent that third-party candidate Ralph Nader cost him a win in New Hampshire—and certainly in Florida, where a razor-thin recount result (and the Supreme Court) decided the outcome. Third, Gore won the popular vote by some half-million ballots.

The result of the 2000 campaign revealed something to Americans that neither Al Gore nor George W. Bush had given much thought to at the outset of the contest: The concession speech is not merely good manners. It is an essential part of the democratic process. It signifies to partisans that the election is over. On this date, it was time for Gore to send that signal. He did not shy from his civic duty.

Speaking from the vice president's office on this date, Gore began with a lighthearted quip: "I promised him that I wouldn't call him back this time," a reference to the election-night concession to Bush that Gore had retracted an hour later.

"I offered to meet with him as soon as possible so that we can start to heal the divisions of the campaign and the contest through which we just passed." In prose that evoked Lincoln, Gore added: "Neither he nor I anticipated this long and difficult road; certainly neither of us wanted it to happen. Yet it came, and now it has ended—resolved, as it must be resolved, through the honored institutions of our democracy."

When it came time to accept victory, Bush, too, subtly invoked Lincoln, saying in a speech in Austin that the nation "must rise above a house divided."

"Americans share hopes and goals and values far more important than any political disagreements," Bush added. "Republicans want the best for our nation, and so do Democrats. Our votes may differ, but not our hopes."

Bush went out of his way to pay homage to his rival. "Vice President Gore and I put our hearts and hopes into our campaigns," said the Texas governor. "We both gave it our all. We shared similar emotions, so I understand how difficult this moment must be for Vice President Gore and his family. He has a distinguished record of service to our country as a congressman, a senator and a vice president."

The president-elect added a verbal "salute" to Al Gore, and wished him every success.

That success came, too, for both men, along with setbacks. George W. Bush served two terms in office, teamed up as an ex-president with Bill Clinton in fighting AIDS in Africa and raising money for victims of a tsunami in Asia, and taught himself to paint after leaving office. Gore became a spokesman for our Earth's ecology, an Academy Award winner, and a Nobel laureate. In other words, when it came to Albert Gore Jr., F. Scott Fitzgerald wasn't just wrong about there being no second acts in American life, he was conspicuously wrong: There are second, third, and fourth acts.

Yet the defeat stung—they all do.

Sometime after the 1984 presidential campaign, Walter F. Mondale—"Fritz" Mondale to his friends—sought the counsel of fellow former Democratic senator George McGovern. Mondale had carried only one state against incumbent Republican president Ronald Reagan; McGovern had carried only one state against incumbent Republican president Richard Nixon.

"Tell me, George, when does it stop hurting?" asked Mondale.

"When it does, I'll let you know, Fritz," McGovern replied. "I'll let you know."

Is it worse to lose in a landslide, or narrowly? Anecdotally, the answer might be the latter. Nearly four years later, at the 2004 Democratic National Convention, Gore described his own election this way: "You know the old saying, 'You win some, you lose some'? And then there's that little-known third category."

It was a laugh line, although Gore didn't seem particularly amused by it. The Democratic delegates could feel his pain. Then, sixteen years later, it happened to them all over again.

December 14, 1799

First in War, First in Peace

After bringing the Revolutionary War to its victorious conclusion, General Washington repaired to Mount Vernon for what he hoped would be a long and peaceful retirement. In a February 1, 1784, letter to Lafayette, Washington invoked the imagery of the Old Testament in outlining his plans: "At length, my Dear Marquis, I am become a private citizen on the banks of the Potomac, and under the shadow of my own vine and my own fig tree, free from the bustle of a camp and the busy scenes of public life."

Instead, he remained in government service for another eight years. George Washington had one last duty: inventing the office of the presidency. In *The Federalist Papers*, Alexander Hamilton had called for a "vigorous" and "energetic" executive branch, arguing persuasively that this was possible only if the authority was invested in a single person. And as they met in Philadelphia in the sweltering summer of 1787 to draft the Constitution and create the presidency, the Framers struggled with the concept.

"Shall we have a king?" asked John Jay. While no one in Philadelphia wanted monarchy, everyone knew who—and who alone—had the stature and the temperament to be the new country's first non-king. To this day, anyone who studies the presidency is struck by how many of the customs and protocols of the office were established by the first man to hold it. Washington knew this, too. "I walk on untrodden ground," he said. "There is scarcely any part of my conduct which may not hereafter be drawn in precedent."

After eight years in office, Washington refused a third term, wrote a prescient farewell address and finally began his long-delayed life on his Virginia estate. This idyll lasted a little less than three years, ending on this date. Washington had gone for a five-hour ride in miserable weather the day before and was taken ill. His friend and doctor James Craik attended him, although in an age before antibiotics, that attention did not prolong his life. Like most professional soldiers, Washington had seen death and contemplated his own mortality. Three months earlier, after he learned of the death of his brother Charles, he wrote: "When the summons comes I shall endeavour to obey it with a good grace."

"When the summons came the following December," historian Frank E. Grizzard noted poignantly in his biography of the great man, "Washington was busy planning for the future."

December 15, 1944

Bugle Call

Glenn Miller was a high school football star in Fort Morgan, but by the time he was seventeen neither the gridiron nor the classroom held his attention. Glenn Miller's passion was music. When he skipped his graduation ceremony for a gig in Laramie, the principal handed his diploma to his mother, with the wry observation, "Maybe you're the one who should get it anyway—you probably worked harder on it than he did."

Miller attended college for two years at the University of Colorado, drifted up to Chicago where he roomed with Benny Goodman, and gravitated to New York where he and the Dorsey brothers helped perfect the Big Band sound. The Glenn Miller Orchestra was at the height of its popularity when the U.S. entered the Second World War. Besides regularly churning out gold records, Miller landed movie roles in 1941 and 1942 and was signed up for a third. But like Hollywood leading man Jimmy Stewart (who would later star as the bandleader in *The Glenn Miller Story*), Miller was itching to do his bit.

Every bit as popular as Elvis Presley would be a generation later, the Glenn Miller Orchestra played its last concert under Miller's direction in September 1942. Commissioned as an Army officer, he performed hundreds of times over the next two years. "Next to a letter from home, Captain Miller, your organization is the greatest morale builder in the European Theater of Operations," Lt. Gen. James Doolittle told him. On this date, Miller boarded a small plane at a British air field on a foggy and freezing morning. He was flying to Paris for a Christmastime show for the troops who had liberated France. He never made it across the English Channel.

Because the plane was never found, Miller's disappearance fueled speculation, even conspiracy theories. The Germans peddled a fanciful story that Miller survived, and subsequently died of a heart attack in a Paris bordello. This was meant to be spiteful, but it's kind of a comforting thought. Yet that shouldn't be our last one about the Glenn Miller Orchestra. "It's not an exaggeration to say that Glenn Miller and other American jazz bands had a pivotal effect on the morale of our European Allies in World War II," Bill Clinton said years later.

"It's probably not wrong to say," President Clinton added, "that Elvis Presley did more to win the Cold War when his music was smuggled into the former Soviet Union than he did as a GI serving in Germany."

December 16, 1965

Jingle Bells

For just a second, the ground crews at Mission Control heard something from outer space that made them fear a UFO was stalking Gemini 6, which carried astronauts Walter Schirra Jr. and Thomas P. Stafford. The day before, Gemini 6 had rendezvoused in space with Gemini 7, which was carrying Frank Borman and Jim Lovell. The exercise had required meticulous pilot control and utmost computer precision—and its success left NASA officials in Houston feeling good about the mission. But as Gemini 6 was about to reenter Earth's atmosphere, Stafford contacted Mission Control to report something strange in the night sky.

"We have an object, looks like a satellite going from north to south, probably in polar orbit," he reported on this date. "Looks like he might be going to reenter soon.... You just might let me pick up that thing."

Wally Schirra later reported that they could hear the tension in the breathing of the guys at Mission Control—until Stafford added the punch line: "I see a command module and eight smaller modules in front. The pilot of the command module is wearing a red suit." With that Schirra pulled out the harmonica he had snuck onboard and played the chorus of "Jingle Bells."

It was, as far as anyone knows, the first Christmas song played in outer space.

"Jingle Bells" was submitted for publication in 1857 by a man named James Lord Pierpont, a thirty-five-year-old organist and youth choir director at a Unitarian Church in Savannah, Georgia. Its initial title was "The One Horse Open Sleigh" and in the original version, the chorus is a bit slower with a more classical melody, apparently inspired by Johann Pachelbel's Canon in D Major.

In choosing "Jingle Bells," Wally Schirra picked a popular, and utterly secular, holiday tune. James Pierpont's lyrics don't reference Jesus's birth or God—or even Santa Claus. That's not Saint Nick guiding that one-horse sled—it's a young man out squiring a young woman.

Why is a resident of Savannah writing about joy-riding over snow-covered fields ("hills" in the original score) anyway? Well, that's a story in itself.

James Pierpont was born April 25, 1822, in Boston, the scion of well-connected New England patriots on both sides of his family. His father, the Rev. John Pierpont, was the pastor at Boston's famed Hollis Street Church. It originally was associated with the Congregational denomination; later it affiliated with the Unitarian Church. In both incarnations, Hollis Street Church was a hotbed of abolitionism.

As a boy, James Pierpont was sent away to boarding school in New Hampshire. He apparently didn't like it, running away at fourteen to sign up on a whaling ship. Before leaving, he penned a nostalgic letter to his mother about sleigh riding in the woods. At some point in his seafaring life, he joined the U.S. Navy and sailed into San Francisco.

That port town must have been more agreeable to James, because when the Gold Rush began he headed back there, leaving behind his wife and children. Pierpont did not strike it rich out West. Quite the contrary: His first known song is a cheeky 1852 ditty, "The Returned Californian." (Its first lines give the flavor of the song: "Oh! I'm going far away from my creditors now. I ain't the tin to pay 'em and they're kicking up a row.")

James' life went from farce to tragedy—his wife died in 1853. Looking for a new start, he joined his older brother, John Pierpont Jr., who had followed in his father's footsteps and had been called to Savannah to take over the city's Unitarian Church.

John Jr. shared his father's politics, but abolition wasn't a popular stance in Savannah at the time, and by 1860, the Unitarian congregation had closed its doors and John had moved back North. James Pierpont did not accompany his brother. By then he had a new family. His second wife was Eliza Jane Purse, the daughter of Savannah's mayor, and the sister of John Pierpont's friend Thomas Purse Jr. When war broke out, James Pierpont—the son and brother of Northern abolitionists and a man of God—enlisted in the Confederate cause, serving as a clerk in a Georgia cavalry regiment. His talent was songwriting, not fighting, and he penned several songs for the Southern army.

It's a cliché to say that the Civil War pitted brother against brother and fathers against sons, but in the case of the Pierponts it was literally true: John Pierpont Sr. served as a Union Army chaplain.

After the war, James seems to have lost his zest for writing music: no new songs by him appear after that time. He died in Florida in 1893, and is buried, per his request, in Savannah's Laurel Grove Cemetery next to his brother-in-law, Thomas, who was killed in 1861 in the earliest days of the Civil War, at the First Battle of Bull Run.

Also on This Date: December 16, 1943
White Christmas

If you only went by its sheet music, this long-forgotten song first recorded on this date by a popular crooner might have seemed a minor ditty. Consisting of only fifty-four words, its opening line, set to a melancholy strain, was "I'm dreaming of a white Christmas."

Except that the author of the tune was Irving Berlin and the singer was Bing Crosby. So maybe "White Christmas" wasn't an unlikely hit after all. Like "Jingle Bells," it cut across the grain in several ways. For starters, popular Christmas carols tended to be religious anthems. This was a secular song, which makes sense because it was written by a Russian-born Jew—the son of a cantor—whose first language was Yiddish. Also, it was a sad song, not a happy one.

Apparently set in Southern California, the song's narrator is ostensibly missing the snow of the holiday season, but what he's really missing are his family and childhood memories.

Finally, America had been at war for two years by December 1943, which "White Christmas" doesn't so much as acknowledge. There was a reason for that, too: It was written before the United States entered World War II, and pulled out of Irving Berlin's filing cabinet for a movie called *Holiday Inn*. That film was in production when Pearl Harbor was bombed, which changed everything about "White Christmas." Or maybe it changed nothing.

In the 1930s, Bing Crosby was America's biggest star. He described himself, his daughter Mary Crosby recalled later, as "an ordinary guy who could carry a tune." He was much more than that, of course. He sounded, as jazz writer and film critic Gary Giddins wrote, "like the guy next door." By that Giddins meant Bing didn't affect some big, operatic voice. He just unpretentiously, and beautifully, sang songs for American audiences. Roy Harris Jr., another chronicler of American music, dubbed Crosby's style "casual romantic."

Whatever you called it, radio audiences loved the guy. Crosby turned NBC's floundering *Kraft Music Hall* into a variety show that set a template that would last more than half a century. Hollywood producers discovered that moviegoers adored Crosby, too. Film directors discovered, to their initial surprise, that the singer could also act. He starred with his pal Bob Hope and Dorothy Lamour in seven "Road" musical comedies (*Road to Singapore, Road to Zanzibar,* etc.) while also excelling in serious motion pictures. He won an Academy Award for his performance in the 1944 hit *Going My Way*, and would be nominated for Best Actor again the following year for *The Bells of St. Mary's*.

Bing first sang "White Christmas" on Christmas Eve, 1941, for his *Kraft Music Hall* audience. It was neither hyped nor recorded, which is why the December 16, 1943, version, which *was* recorded, is a collector's item.

Having Crosby perform the number was Irving Berlin's own idea. Berlin knew it was going to be popular—he once quipped that it was not only "the best song I ever wrote, it's the best song anybody ever wrote"—but he maximized his chances by saving it for Bing.

Despite being Jewish, Berlin appreciated the Christmas season, resenting only that it was often a busy time for him professionally when he would have preferred being home with his family. Berlin biographer Philip Furia theorized that Berlin's imagery in the song was inspired by the Robert Frost poem, "Stopping by Woods on a Snowy Evening." Perhaps, but the melancholy subtext of "White Christmas" was also certainly infused by the death of his infant son, Irving Berlin Jr., on Christmas Day in 1928.

In a less polarized political environment, nobody complained about a "war on Christmas" when Bing Crosby sang a Christmas song that never hints at the birth of Jesus. And the success of "White Christmas" inspired other secular numbers. One of them, "I'll Be Home for Christmas," was released in 1943 by Crosby. This was definitely a wartime song ("Danny Boy" was on the flip side of the single) and Crosby often sang it to the troops himself.

The following year, "Have Yourself a Merry Little Christmas" was released. It was first sung by Judy Garland in the 1944 Christmas movie, *Meet Me in St. Louis*, and later interpreted skillfully by Frank Sinatra. Late in life, Bing recorded another secular Christmas song, a cross-generational duet with David Bowie.

As for "White Christmas," Irving Berlin's tongue-in-cheek boast notwithstanding, no one could have known in the early 1940s that audiences would still be listening to that song so many years later. But it outlived World War II, and other wars, too. Maybe that's the point. Carl Sandburg, writing on the first anniversary of Pearl Harbor, took a stab at explaining it:

"We have learned to be a little sad and a little lonesome, without being sickly about it," he wrote. "This feeling is caught in the song of a thousand juke boxes and the tune whistled in streets and homes, 'I'm Dreaming of a White Christmas.' When we sing that song we don't hate anybody. Away down under, this latest hit of Irving Berlin catches us where we love peace."

December 17, 1862

Grant's Folly

The most inexplicable thing about the ill-considered order issued by General Ulysses S. Grant on this date is how out of character it was. It nearly derailed his meteoric rise through the Union Army's officer corps.

As late as April 1861, Grant was a cashiered U.S. Army captain and undistinguished West Point graduate whose dismal failures in the private sector left him working, at age forty, for his two younger brothers in the family leather business in Galena, Illinois. Twenty months later, Grant was leading a huge army that was trying to take Vicksburg, and with it, the Confederacy's access to the Mississippi River. Commander of a region that included much of Tennessee, Mississippi, and Kentucky, Grant was chagrined by the profiteers who'd come from the North to make a quick buck off cotton seized by the Union Army. When Grant's father visited his son's Oxford, Mississippi, headquarters with a group of such hustlers, several of whom were Jewish, Grant acted impulsively. On this date, a week before Christmas Day, he issued an edict banning Jews from the territory. He would regret it the rest of his life.

To be sure, in the long litany of abuses, calumnies, injustices, pogroms, and persecutions already committed against the Jewish people—and this was nearly a century before the Holocaust—Ulysses S. Grant's General Orders No. 11 was one of the least harmful. A minor footnote in the Civil War, it was also a minor footnote in American Jewish history: No one was killed; homes and property were not seized. A handful of people reported indignities. Two or three said they were jailed overnight; another was forbidden to change out of wet clothes—that sort of thing. As for the Jews living in Paducah, Kentucky, where Grant's order was most resented, they don't seem to have left the city during the short time the order was in effect.

One Jewish merchant did depart Paducah, however, and he did so in a hurry. His name was Cesar Kaskel, and he took off for the nation's capital. Outraged that such an order would emanate from a U.S. Army officer, Kaskel intended to lodge his protest directly with the commander in chief. Religious freedom was guaranteed by the Constitution, and had been affirmed—directly to the Jewish community—by no less an American eminence than George Washington. It was why people of Cesar Kaskel's faith had come to these shores, why there were Jews in Paducah, Kentucky, in the first place.

Now, in a war being fought to free the slaves, no less, President Lincoln's favorite general was causing offense by using the words *profiteer* and *Jew* interchangeably, and issuing edicts forcing them to be refugees in their own land. What the hell was going on? That was what some of Grant's fellow officers wanted to know. Brig. Gen. Jeremiah C. Sullivan, the Union commander stationed in Jackson, Tennessee, groused that he was "an officer of the Army and not of a church." And as Cesar Kaskel raced toward Washington, Abraham Lincoln was preparing the Emancipation Proclamation. News of Grant's order had been slow to reach Lincoln, but when it did he wasn't pleased. Meanwhile, Kaskel was proving himself a dynamo. In the capital he morphed into an instantaneous, one-man lobbying outfit who planted stories in the press, stirred up Congress, and secured an audience with the president. Kaskel's account of their White House meeting is the only one that survives, and ought to be taken with a grain of salt, but the conversation as he later rendered it included this exchange:

LINCOLN: And so the children of Israel were driven from the happy land of Canaan?

KASKEL: Yes, and that is why we have come unto Father Abraham's bosom, asking protection.

LINCOLN: And this protection they shall have at once.

Making allowances for Kaskel's purple prose, the line about the "happy land of Canaan" does sound like the sixteenth president. However disappointed he was with Grant, Lincoln loved a pun, and his habit of invoking Biblical allusions was perfectly apropos. In any event, on January 4, 1863, Lincoln ordered Grant to revoke what the general's own wife, Julia, called "that obnoxious order." The upshot is that Grant's original order, and its subsequent rescission, serve as unlikely bookends to the Emancipation Proclamation.

Later, Grant's imprudence briefly became a campaign issue when he ran for national office. He overcame it by apologizing publicly and privately. As president, Grant appointed more Jews to positions in his administration than any previous president, spoke out against European persecution of Jews, and sent an envoy to Bucharest to support victims of anti-Jewish persecution. By the time he died in 1885, Ulysses S. Grant's reputation in the nation's Jewish community had been restored, and he was mourned in synagogues all over this country.

For modern presidents or other politicians inclined to use social media to hurriedly impart intemperate ideas on how the United States should treat refugees or religious groups, Grant's own words offer a caution: "I do not sustain that order," he wrote later. "It would never have been issued if it had not been telegraphed the moment it was penned, and without reflection."

Runyonesque

Famed aviator Eddie Rickenbacker flew one of his last missions on this date. It was also illegal. Flying over Manhattan, Rickenbacker was carrying a passenger, Damon Runyon Jr., who scattered the ashes of his famous father over Broadway.

Guys and Dolls is part of the Runyon legacy, as was his career as a sportswriter, Hearst newspaper columnist, poet, and playwright. He mentored young reporters, spawned many imitators, and lent glamour to the craft of journalism. Born in Kansas and raised in Colorado, Runyon barely went to school. Yet he not only taught himself to write, he invented a literary style. To this day, *Runyonesque* describes not a style of prose, but a way of looking at life.

Although he loved saloons, Runyon quit drinking after his first wife died battling alcoholism. He never gave up the Turkish cigarettes that would give him throat cancer, take his voice, and end his life. Yet he retained his sense of style to the end: the tailored suits, silk ties, spats, and fedoras we associate with the characters in his stories. His second wife was a Spanish dancer he'd met in Mexico while writing about the Army's fruitless search for Pancho Villa. Runyon ran into the Mexican revolutionary himself in a Texas bar while covering spring training. Things like that often happened to him. It was Runyon who dubbed his pal Jimmy Braddock, the heavyweight boxing champion, the "Cinderella Man."

His short stories and plays were written in the first person, in the voice of a narrator who combines gangster patois and stilted English that makes it seem real and is simultaneously chilling and comical. ("Well, besides black hair, this doll has a complexion like I do not know what, and little feet and ankles, and a way of walking that is very pleasant to behold.")

Writing in the *New Yorker* decades later, Adam Gopnik deconstructed the genius of this writing: "The Narrator's half-conscious knowledge that there are rules out there that you've got to respect leads him to overcompensate by respecting the wrong rules; that is, using formal diction where there ought to be vernacular idioms and vernacular idioms where there ought to be formal diction."

Cosmic, and comic, juxtapositions came naturally to a man born in Manhattan, Kansas, and made famous in Manhattan, New York. Who else but Damon Runyon could paraphrase Ecclesiastes into a racetrack idiom: "The race is not always to the swift, nor the battle to the strong, but that's how the smart money bets."

Jolly Old St. Nick

Santa Claus is an amalgamation. He was also originally an immigrant. He comes originally from Greece (though his village lies in modern-day Turkey), and his magical persona has been overlaid with the merging of two cultural forces of enduring power: ancient Nordic mythology and modern American marketing.

Santa Claus is an Anglo-Germanic rendition of "Saint Nicholas," which is fitting enough, because the original inspiration is a man named Nicholas who was a saint in the early Christian Church. He is believed to have been born in a Mediterranean village then called Patara and now known as Demre. Nicholas's wealthy family raised him in the faith—one of his uncles was a priest—and when his parents died, he followed his uncle's career path while using his inheritance to help the needy. Nicholas became a bishop in the church, which had not yet undergone the split between Roman Catholicism and Eastern Orthodox.

Under the reign of Roman Emperor Diocletian, Christians were widely persecuted; Nicholas was among those imprisoned. He was not martyred, however, as were so many early saints. One aspect of his life that would lend itself so easily to mythmaking was that he apparently died of old age, beloved by his fellow believers, and universally revered for his generosity. In later years, Nicholas would be claimed as a patron saint by many people, most especially sailors, as the miracles and good deeds credited to him piled up. In one act of kindness, he threw three bags of gold through the window of a house where a poor widower lived with three daughters who needed a dowry in order to marry. It is said that the bags of gold landed in stockings hanging by the chimney. Perhaps you see where this is going.

Nicholas is believed to have died on December 6 in the year 343 (December 19 on the Julian calendar). It is this anniversary that became a day of celebration: St. Nicholas Day. In the ensuing centuries, Christianity spread through the remnants of the Roman Empire, and by the end of the first millennium Nicholas was Christendom's most popular saint, celebrated—as was Jesus—for his many miracles and love of children. By 1100, notes writer Jason Mankey, French nuns were leaving gifts in St. Nicholas's name at the homes of poor children on the night of December 5.

St. Nick wasn't done evolving, though. He'd scarcely begun. As Christianity spread northward, local peoples merged his legend with those of other sovereigns and deities. The death of Nicholas (and the birth of Christ) became infused with the Norse and Germanic celebrations of the winter solstice known as Yule.

For all we know, Nicholas of Patara was walking down the lane on foot when he anonymously tossed those bags of gold into another man's house. But the St. Nicholas of

Northern Europe was given a horse—one previously ridden by the Norse god Odin. This steed, by the way, could land on rooftops. As it happens, Odin also had a naughty list. Elsewhere in Scandinavia, a god named Thor seems to have added to Santa's transportation options: Thor had a cart, pulled by goats. (In Holland, where the "Sinterklaas" tradition remains strongest, he still rides a white horse named Schimmel).

It is the Dutch who brought this tradition to America. Here, it was refined many times, first in books, later in movies, and ultimately by tens of thousands of shopping mall Santas in identical red suits. Santa makes his first appearance in a New York newspaper in 1773, three years before Thomas Jefferson penned the Declaration of Independence. Washington Irving, writing under the satirical pseudonym Diedrich Knickerbocker, furthers the legend. Irving's 1809 book, *A History of New-York from the Beginning of the World to the End of the Dutch Dynasty*, is intended as a Federalist Party send-up of Jefferson. But the satire is lost on a mass audience more enthralled by stories of a guardian saint, Nicholas, who slides down chimneys to give kids presents at Christmastime.

By 1821 an anonymous poem reaffirms the gift-giving proclivities of "Santeclaus," while replacing Odin's goats with reindeer. Two years later, Clement C. Moore's *The Night Before Christmas* is published. By the 1850s, America's preeminent cartoonist and illustrator, Bavarian-born Thomas Nast, is drawing on his native culture to flesh out the images of Santa that dance in our heads to this day—regardless of one's politics or faith.

"His Santa Claus wasn't a bishop," noted Jason Mankey (who himself is a paganist), "but a man of the people."

"In a world that so often lacks any magic, Santa provides a doorway into a realm of imagination and wonderment," Mankey wrote. "A world without Santa is a world I don't want to live in. We share so little myth these days, and what myth we do share rarely transcends religious boundaries, but Santa is different. With his origins in Greek myth, Catholic tradition, Norse paganism, and the wilds of the human imagination, he's capable of not just magically jumping down chimneys, but of jumping into the hearts of whoever will have him."

December 20, 1946

Movie Action Hero

It was always a bit of an in-joke, casting Jimmy Stewart as the older brother who flunks his Army physical and doesn't go to war. Stewart didn't mind. He was glad to be reunited with director Frank Capra, whose new motion picture had a plot familiar to moviegoers: It was a mid-twentieth century reinterpretation of *A Christmas Carol*.

Starring Stewart, Donna Reed, and Lionel Barrymore, *It's a Wonderful Life* premiered on this date at New York City's Globe Theatre. The Sicilian-born Capra had volunteered for military service in his adopted country when the United States entered World War I, and he almost died from influenza. A few days after Pearl Harbor, at age forty-four, Capra volunteered again, resigning as president of the Screen Directors Guild—but not forsaking his craft.

During World War II, Capra created an amazing series of films for the military called *Why We Fight*. Jimmy Stewart went him one better: In 1941, Stewart was the most bankable leading man in Hollywood. In 1939, he'd starred in *Mr. Smith Goes to Washington*, and in 1940 had won an Oscar as best actor for *The Philadelphia Story*. By the time Pearl Harbor was attacked and hundreds of thousands of American men were being drafted into the service, Jimmy Stewart was already in uniform, pulling duty at Moffett Field, south of San Francisco, as a corporal in the Army Air Corps.

In *It's a Wonderful Life*, the fictional George Bailey misses out on the war because a childhood mishap left him deaf in one ear. In real life, the man who played George Bailey had problems passing the minimum weight requirement, as he carried only 130 pounds on his six-foot-four-inch frame. The official version of what happened, which can be found on his hometown's website, was that Stewart ate and ate until he just got over the 138-pound limit.

The unofficial story, as Stewart cheerfully recalled later, was that when his local draft board realized this movie star wanted *in* the military instead of out, they simply told him, "We just won't weigh you, and we'll put down any weight you want!" By war's end, Jimmy Stewart had flown twenty combat missions in a B-24 Liberator, become a squadron leader, won a passel of medals, and risen through the ranks from corporal to colonel. As he explained later, the men in his family had left their small hardware store in Indiana, Pennsylvania, to serve their country in every American war since 1861—and he just wanted to do his part.

December 21, 1853

Thoreau's Drumbeat

We are tempted to call these the finest days of the year," Henry David Thoreau's diary entry from this date reads. Writing on the first day of winter, he was searching for why he loved it so. Part of it was the solitude of this solitary man. But it was more than that.

"We sleep, and at length awake to the still reality of a winter morning," he wrote weeks later in contemplation of the change of seasons. "Now commences the long winter evening around the farmer's hearth, when the thoughts of the in-dwellers travel far abroad, and men are by nature and necessity charitable and liberal to all creatures."

Thoreau's brand of liberalism, however, would be largely unrecognizable in twenty-first-century American politics. In today's parlance, he might be called a classic Libertarian.

"I heartily accept the motto, 'That government is best which governs least,'" he wrote in *Civil Disobedience*. "Carried out, it finally amounts to this, which also I believe— 'That government is best which governs not at all.'" He wasn't kidding: Thoreau viewed government with such suspicion that he didn't favor a standing army. Thoreau would also find much common ground with fiscally conservative Republicans. He surely didn't like taxes. "When I meet a government," he wrote, "which says to me, 'Your money or your life,' why should I be in haste to give it my money?"

Yet he was certainly a racial liberal, a committed abolitionist who was jailed in 1843 for not paying his poll tax—not as a tax protest, but as a remonstration against slavery. He wasn't a big law-and-order man, either. "Under a government which imprisons any unjustly," he wrote, "the true place for a just man is also a prison."

It's also clear that Thoreau would be a dedicated environmentalist today, as this was true in his day as well. "If a man walks in the woods for love of them half of each day, he is in danger of being regarded as a loafer," Thoreau wrote in *Life Without Principle*. "But if he spends his whole day...shearing off those woods and making earth bald before her time, he is esteemed as an industrious and enterprising citizen."

One thing is sure: He'd be his own person, and never worry about poll numbers. "If a man does not keep pace with his companions, perhaps it is because he hears a different drummer," he wrote in *Walden*. "Let him step to the music which he hears, however measured or far away."

December 22, 1970

Viva La Huelga!

It was the first time Cesar Chavez had ever been incarcerated. Jailed for contempt of court by Superior Court Judge Gordon Campbell for refusing to call off a secondary boycott against a local lettuce grower, the United Farm Workers' leader was taken to the county jail on Alisal Street in Salinas. Built during the Depression, the jail had a Gothic-revival façade that resembled a mission. But it was a drafty and damp old lockup with lousy lighting. The light was an issue for Chavez, because his wife, Helen, had brought a book on Gandhi for him to read behind bars.

Union activists decked out a flatbed truck with flowers, added an Our Lady of Guadalupe statue in back and parked it across the street from the jail. At sunset, they'd light votive candles to illuminate this makeshift shrine. On Chavez's third night in jail, Robert Kennedy's widow, Ethel, came to Salinas. She marched in a candlelight procession down Alisal Street, where a Mass was held at the shrine. When counterdemonstrators chanted, "Carpetbagger Go Home!" the farmworkers and their sympathizers sang, "De Colores," the UFW anthem. As the farmworkers took communion, Mrs. Kennedy headed to the visitors' entrance to the jail, passing through a phalanx of dueling protesters: UFW members and their sympathizers on one side of a police cordon; Teamsters and growers' loyalists opposite them. If Mrs. Kennedy was rattled by any of this she didn't show it. Seeing Chavez, she quipped, "You throw some weird parties."

As the case generated national attention—most of it sympathetic to Chavez—Coretta Scott King came, too. "As my husband often said, you cannot keep truth in jail," she told the farmworkers. "Truth and justice leap barriers and in their own way reach the conscience of the people."

In his cell, Cesar received a letter from Helen on this date. "The kids are out of school for two weeks," she wrote. "Christmas vacation. Take care and we are praying so that you will be home soon."

Whether it was those prayers, or the bad publicity the growers were getting, or just the requirements of the law, after twenty days behind bars Chavez was released the next night on orders of the California Supreme Court. He thanked his supporters, mentioned that it was only hours until Christmas Eve, pointed out that the "Prince of Peace" blessed those who fight for justice, and went home to Delano to spend Christmas with family.

He did not call off the boycott.

December 23, 1937

Yes, Virginia

All children want to believe they are loved unconditionally. And what says that more than an unseen benefactor who surreptitiously places the very toy they most desire under the family Christmas tree in the middle of the night? Yet, any intellectually robust child of eight or nine puzzles over the scientific and logistical obstacles of delivering gifts via an airborne sleigh with flying reindeer to every hearth and home in the world—on the same evening.

In the nineteenth century, when poets such as Samuel Taylor Coleridge and William Wordsworth ushered in the Romantic Movement as an antidote to the Industrial Revolution, they realized that adults faced a similar dilemma. It was Coleridge who produced the most famous formulation for reconciling our hearts and heads. He called it the "willing suspension of disbelief which constitutes poetic faith." Part of the magic of Christmas is how willing adults are to help children retain their "poetic faith." Encouraging it is what prompted the editors of the *New York Sun* to reply to a youthful reader in 1897. "Dear editor," wrote Virginia O'Hanlon a few days after her birthday. "I am 8 years old. Some of my little friends say there is no Santa Claus. Papa says, 'If you see it in The Sun it's so.' Please tell me the truth; is there a Santa Claus?"

"Virginia, your little friends are wrong," the *Sun*'s editors replied on September 21, 1897.

They have been affected by the skepticism of a skeptical age. They do not believe except [what] they see. They think that nothing can be which is not comprehensible by their little minds....

Yes, Virginia, there is a Santa Claus. He exists as certainly as love and generosity and devotion exist, and you know that they abound and give to your life its highest beauty and joy. Alas! How dreary would be the world if there were no Santa Claus. It would be as dreary as if there were no Virginias. There would be no childlike faith then, no poetry, no romance to make tolerable this existence. We should have no enjoyment, except in sense and sight. The eternal light with which childhood fills the world would be extinguished....

No Santa Claus! Thank God! he lives, and he lives forever. A thousand years from now, Virginia, nay, ten times ten thousand years from now, he will continue to make glad the heart of childhood.

This missive is the most oft-republished editorial in American newspaper history. Forty Christmases later—on this date—a grown-up Virginia O'Hanlon Douglas, married and with children of her own, read the letter aloud on WNYC radio in New York City.

December 24, 1923

Let There Be Light

Until the late nineteenth century, no American had ever seen electric lights on a Christmas tree. During the 1880 Christmas season, Thomas Edison strung a strand of electric lights on an outdoor tree that could be seen by rail passengers passing by his lab in Menlo Park, New Jersey. Christmas trees were then typically illuminated by candles, which led to many home fires. In 1889, the first Christmas tree inside the White House was decorated by President Benjamin Harrison with just such candles. This could have been the second time the White House burned to the ground, but that calamity was avoided, and five years after that, Grover Cleveland thrilled his daughters with electric lights on their family Christmas tree.

Two decades later, President Coolidge expanded this tradition to the entire nation. Electric lights were no longer a novelty in 1923, but to anyone of Calvin Coolidge's generation they were a marvel. Think about it this way: When Coolidge illuminated the National Christmas Tree on this date by hitting a switch, his Vermont hometown of Plymouth Notch still lacked electricity altogether. One other thing can be said as well: Calvin and Grace Coolidge knew how to keep Christmas. The original plan was to light the tree on the White House lawn, but First Lady Coolidge was doing another caroling event there. In the days leading up to the holiday, newspapers were full of the First Lady's activities. She went shopping for her two sons, away at college, but as the *Washington Post* noted, "What she bought is being kept a secret as though the boys were of the Santa Claus age."

Grace Coolidge sent Christmas bouquets to every clerk who waited on her while she shopped. She spent Christmas Eve volunteering at the local Salvation Army headquarters, helping distribute some five hundred gift baskets to needy families. On Christmas Day, the First Family went to Walter Reed General Hospital to visit wounded soldiers. Mrs. Coolidge, it was reported, was especially tender toward the injured men. So it has gone through the years. In 2010, First Lady Michelle Obama announced a White House Christmas theme of "Simple Gifts."

"The greatest blessings of all are the ones that don't cost a thing," Mrs. Obama explained. "The time that we spend with our loved ones, the freedoms we enjoy as Americans, and the joy we feel from reaching out to those in need."

December 25, 1776

Tally Ho!

As 1776 wound to a close, George Washington was in search of a victory to convince his men they were fighting for a cause that could prevail, and so he conjured up a daring plan.

At 11 p.m. on this date, he gathered his force of 5,400 men, divided them into three groups and led them across the icy cold Delaware River. The next morning, Washington realized that the only forces to make it to the staging area were those he led himself. Two divisions, with 3,000 men, hadn't made it. But time was of the essence, so this cold and hungry force of 2,400 citizen-soldiers marched on Trenton, surrounding the town and trapping the Hessians in their garrison. Casualties were small by the standards of modern warfare: 21 Hessians killed, 83 wounded, another 800 captured. The Americans lost only two men in the fighting.

If the victory was complete, it was also temporary. Without the two other divisions and his artillery, Washington couldn't hold the town. Even after his strategic retreat, British general Charles Cornwallis was determined to trap the Americans in their encampment on Assunpink Creek. On the night of January 2, 1777, as Cornwallis prepared to attack in the morning, one of his officers urged a nighttime assault. "We may easily bag the fox in the morning," he demurred.

At that moment, "the fox" was having midnight counsels with his own officers. Should they defend the ground they occupied, cross the Delaware for the third time in ten days, or slip away via back roads and attack Princeton? It was this last option, the most audacious, that Washington chose. Leaving five hundred troops at Assunpink with campfires burning as a feint, the wagons and artillery were wrapped in cloth to stifle the sounds of their evacuation. Cornwallis sent his troops on January 3 to meet the Americans, but they were gone.

Outside Princeton, the American army overran the British rear guard. Now it was George Washington who employed hunting metaphors. "It's a fine fox chase, my boys," he called out as the redcoats broke ranks.

To the British, Trenton and Princeton were minor setbacks. But Washington's victories convinced his troops, and his fledgling nation, that America could win the Revolutionary War. In time, this came to be the English view, too. A century later, Sir George Trevelyan summarized the two battles by writing words that foreshadowed Winston Churchill's famous ode to the Royal Air Force in World War II. "It may be doubted," said Trevelyan, "whether so small a number of men ever employed so short a space of time with greater and more lasting effects upon the history of the world."

December 26, 1949

"And Away They Go..."

What do you open the day after Christmas?"

Southern Californians who love horse racing know this line. It was an ad campaign for Santa Anita Park, which on this date began a tradition of opening its winter meet on Boxing Day. For Californians of Japanese ancestry, however, the beautiful track at the foot of the San Gabriel Mountains long had a more sinister association: Santa Anita was the largest processing center for those incarcerated during World War II because of their race. Santa Anita was where two future U.S. congressmen, Norman Y. Mineta and Robert Matsui, and actor George Takei were taken.

"We showered in the horse paddocks," Mineta noted. "Some families lived in converted stables, others in hastily thrown together barracks. We were then moved to Heart Mountain, Wyoming, where our entire family lived in one small room of a rude tar paper barrack."

From those camps emerged thousands of volunteers—young men willing to enlist in the armed forces of the country that had deemed them disloyal. One of them, Kazuo Masuda, was killed in Italy while covering the retreat of other men in his unit. His family was incarcerated at the time in Arizona. The injustices didn't end then. His sister was threatened when she returned to her Orange County farm after the war. A local cemetery refused to accept Masuda's remains. This infuriated the Army brass, who by then knew what they'd had in the legendary all-Nisei 442nd Regimental Combat Team. Gen. Joseph W. Stilwell went to Orange County, and pinned Kazuo Masuda's Distinguished Service Cross on his sister Mary Masuda in a public ceremony. Show business personalities attended, too, including Will Rogers Jr. and a thirty-four-year-old film star serving as stateside Army captain.

"Blood that has soaked into the sands of a beach is all of one color," the actor said that day. "America stands unique in the world: the only country not founded on race but on an ideal. Not in spite of, but because of, our polyglot background, we have had all the strength in the world. That is the American way."

The actor's name was Ronald Reagan. Years later, he recalled those remarks at the signing ceremony for the Japanese-Americans redress law. "And, yes, the ideal of liberty and justice for all—that is still the American way," he said.

As for Santa Anita, it still opens its winter meet on December 26, but it has a more recent tradition, too. It's a springtime event built around the Tokyo City Cup: Japan Family Day.

December 27, 1968

The Good Earth

Apollo 8 splashed down in the Pacific Ocean with Frank Borman, James Lovell, and William Anders safe and in good spirits. The three astronauts had been the first explorers to achieve lunar orbit and had taken an iconic photograph of an "earth rise." They were picked up by the USS *Yorktown* after splashdown on this date after having literally been to the dark side of the moon.

When Neil Armstrong and Buzz Aldrin stepped out of the Apollo 11 lunar landing craft in 1969, they became the first human beings to set foot on the moon. But it was the Apollo 8 mission seven months earlier that truly convinced NASA engineers that John F. Kennedy's famous goal was within their reach. This spaceship lifted off from the Kennedy Space Center on December 21, 1968, at 7:51 a.m. with Borman in command.

Much had happened in the years since President Kennedy had committed the United States to landing astronauts on the moon by the end of the decade. Much had happened in 1968 itself. Five years after President Kennedy was taken from us, his brother Robert and Martin Luther King were both martyred. The Vietnam War was spinning out of control, racial tensions were at a boiling point, and for many Americans the world seemed a dangerous and uncertain place.

It was then that three brave astronauts left Earth's orbit while simultaneously entering Americans' living rooms to help us put it all in perspective. "The vast loneliness is awe inspiring," Jim Lovell exclaimed in a Christmas Eve broadcast, "and it makes you realize just what you have back there on Earth."

The crew, starting with William Anders, then took turns reading the first few chapters of the Book of Genesis. "In the beginning, God created the heaven and the earth," he began. "And the earth was without form, and void; and darkness was upon the face of the deep."

The broadcast concluded with Borman reading his verses, ending with "and God saw that it was good." Then he signed off: "From the crew of Apollo 8, we close with good night, good luck, a Merry Christmas, and God bless all of you—all of you on the good Earth."

Time magazine subsequently chose the crew, understandably, as their "Men of the Year."

One man, a stranger to the astronauts, spoke for millions of Americans in a brief telegram he sent to Commander Borman. "Thank you, Apollo 8," it read. "You saved 1968."

December 28, 1793

Paine and Suffering

Thomas Paine considered himself safe in Paris, even during the French Revolution. A radical thinker and lover of liberty, he'd gone to France to encourage rebellion, as he had done in America. Paine had initially been embraced by French revolutionaries, but as *la révolution* morphed into *la terreur*, Paine's opposition to capital punishment put him out of sync with the Reign of Terror's architects. On this date, Paine was tried for treason and imprisoned—not in that order—and sent to Luxembourg Palace, which had been converted to a prison.

Word of his incarceration roiled public opinion in the United States. The French didn't get this at first. They claimed Paine, who'd been born in Britain and was living in France prior to his arrest in Paris, was an Englishman, not an American—and France was at war with Britain. The point wasn't contested by the U.S. ambassador to France, Gouverneur Morris, a Federalist, who considered Paine, well, a pain. The author of *Common Sense* and other tracts that inspired George Washington's troops had also written *The Rights of Man*, a book declared seditious in Britain. Avoiding prosecution, paradoxically, was why Paine had come to France in 1793.

Paine referred to himself as a "citizen of the world." Even those who locked him up called him an "apostle of liberty." While at Luxembourg, Paine was working on another book, *The Age of Reason*, that was making waves even before it was published. This work was viewed by many critics—and Paine himself—as an attack on religion, which was one reason Morris balked at helping him. Although the French let him write it while under arrest, Paine was in peril. Realizing this, James Monroe, the U.S. ambassador who replaced Morris, worked hard for his release. Monroe told French officials that it was absurd not to consider Paine an American, an argument that eventually prevailed. Monroe was correct on the merits. Yes, Tom Paine was born in England. And yes, he'd gone to live voluntarily in France. But his opening line of the introduction to *Age of Reason* addresses the citizenship question directly.

"To My Fellow-Citizens of the United States of America, I put the following work under your protection," it began.

"You will do me the justice to remember," Paine continued, "that I have always strenuously supported the right of every man to his own opinion, however different that opinion might be to mine. He who denies to another this right, makes a slave of himself to his present opinion, because he precludes himself the right of changing it."

December 29, 1763

Mickey's Mantle

Horace Walpole, a British politician and man of letters, had an interesting eye for detail, which he shared in an entertaining missive to his cousin, the Earl of Hertford. Penned on this date, the letter covered the goings-on in Parliament around the holiday season. If you change some proper nouns and update a word two, it could have been modern Washington, D.C., he was writing about.

"We are a very absurd nation," Walpole tells his cousin. "The Parliament opens; everybody is bribed and the new establishment is perceived to be composed of [stubborn hardheads]. Christmas arrives; everybody goes out of town. Parliament meets again; taxes are warmly opposed."

It's a lively epistle, but why do we care? Here's why: His book, *The Letters of Horace Walpole, Volume 1*, documents early usage of a quote usually attributed to New York Yankee's centerfielder Mickey Mantle two centuries later: "If I had known I was going to live this long, I'd have taken better care of myself." Arthritis in his knees hobbled Mantle, who once ran like a cheetah. But the reference wasn't to his training methods; it alluded to his four decades of abusing alcohol. Mantle himself attributed the pithy line to his friend, Pro Football Hall of Fame quarterback Bobby Layne, another legendary carouser. But where did Layne come by it?

Various quotation compilations place the words in the mouths of labor leader George Meany, comedian George Burns, and Mark Twain. The evidence for Twain is weak, but as quote sleuth Ralph Keyes documented, many Americans used the line—just not first. That distinction may belong to Robert Henley, the first Earl of Northington. In that letter to his cousin, Horace Walpole describes Henley's escapades, which also were fortified by adult beverages.

In a footnote to *Letters of Horace Walpole, Volume 1*, the anthology's editor, Charles Yonge, adds a vignette of his own: "Lord Northington had been a very hard liver. He was a martyr to the gout; and one afternoon, as he was going downstairs out of his Court, he was heard to say to himself, " 'Damn these legs! If I had known they were to carry a Lord Chancellor, I would have taken better care of them.' "

It's not a straight line from Lord Northington to Mickey Mantle, but as Yogi Berra liked to say (others said it first), it's difficult to make predictions, especially about the future. Charles Yonge, who died in 1891, would have enjoyed Yogi's wit. He'd have appreciated Berra's and Mantle's baseball talent, too. Besides being a historian and a classicist at Oxford College, Yonge was an accomplished cricket player.

December 30, 1940

First Freeway

On this date, California opened its first freeway. It was a six-lane, six-mile stretch of road connecting Pasadena to Los Angeles. It was named the Arroyo Seco Parkway. Governor Culbert Olson attended the ribbon-cutting, hailing the road as "the first freeway in the West."

In 1940, it took an average of twenty-seven minutes to drive a car from Pasadena to downtown Los Angeles. This was not progress. More cars on the road meant more congestion, and the commute times were getting longer. Plans for a dedicated roadway between the two cities predated the internal combustion engine. In 1897, dueling proposals were floated by civic leaders in the two burgs: one dedicated to horse-drawn wagons, the other for a newfangled technology called the bicycle. Given the bicycle craze sweeping the country, the latter trail made more sense, and a private firm called California Cycleway purchased a right-of-way from Pasadena to Avenue 54 in the Highland Park neighborhood of Northeast Los Angeles. The company then constructed an elevated wooden bikeway along the route. It opened on January 1, 1900, but what it really did was connect Pasadena to South Pasadena.

When the bike fad ebbed, a local utility called Pacific Electric Railway constructed a streetcar connecting the two cities and the wooden bikeway was torn down. Meanwhile, California's obsession with the automobile had begun. From 1914 through 1922, vehicle registrations in Los Angeles County quadrupled. The region's transportation problems were only beginning. In the 1920s and 1930s, the population of Los Angeles County would increase from just under 1 million to nearly 3 million. Car registrations all over California were increasing at twice the national average, and all of this was taking place before the huge boom in growth that would hit the state after World War II. New roads were needed, badly.

In 1924, famed landscape architect Frederick Law Olmsted Jr. and noted urban planner Harland Bartholomew produced a report, "Major Street Traffic Plan for Los Angeles." Among other projects, it called for a new parkway between Pasadena and LA that would reduce congestion while also affording motorists "a great deal of incidental recreation and pleasure."

The freeway's name has varied over the years. What began as the Arroyo Seco Parkway was immediately shorted by locals to "Arroyo Parkway," then "Arroyo Freeway," and in time "Pasadena Freeway." Bowing to custom, highway administrators renamed it the Pasadena Freeway in 1954. Because all its original bridges are intact—and because no trucks are allowed on it—the road was designated a national scenic byway in 2002. On December 30, 2010, it officially got its old name back.

Today, the Arroyo Seco Parkway carries 125,000 cars a day on lanes designed for 27,000. For two miles, there's a bike path, and although California Cycleway is long gone, efforts are afoot to expand it.

December 31, 1988

Shining City upon a Hill

Ronald Reagan spent his last New Year's Eve as president in Palm Springs, California. It was a Saturday, so he delivered his weekly radio address, a custom he borrowed from Franklin Roosevelt. Reagan also did a photo opportunity showcasing a free trade pact, telephoned Canadian prime minister Brian Mulroney, who was in Florida getting ready to take his family to Disney World, and played eighteen holes of golf in a foursome with Secretary of State George P. Shultz and professional golfers Lee Trevino and Tom Watson. Reagan did "a little desk work," he wrote in his diary, before preparing for a New Years' ball at the home of wealthy friend Walter Annenberg. Bob Hope was the evening's emcee. Reagan didn't turn in until 1:30 a.m.

Back in Washington, White House speechwriter Peggy Noonan wasn't interested in revelry. With an eighteen-month toddler at home, she didn't stay up late. Noonan had spent the day working on Reagan's farewell address as president. The first draft would be delivered on Tuesday to Reagan—who was working out of the Bel Air home where he and Nancy Reagan would be moving after the inauguration of George H. W. Bush. The speech Reagan would deliver on January 11, 1989, reprised the highlights of his political career, including his belief in limited government.

"There's a clear cause and effect here that is as neat and predictable as a law of physics: As government expands, liberty contracts," he said. Reagan added that he believed the leaders of the Soviet Union had come to a point where they realized they needed to change accordingly, but that when it came to the Russians he retained his mantra of "trust, but verify." Looking into the camera for his final Oval Office address, Reagan also spoke of the need for "an informed patriotism," while gently deflecting the notion that he was a gifted orator.

The fortieth U.S. president also told his countrymen how he often went to a favorite window in the White House residence to look out at people driving to work, going about their everyday lives, and occasionally seeing a sailboat on the Potomac River. He invoked a "a small story" he'd heard "about a big ship, and a refugee, and a sailor." The sailor was a U.S. Navy crewman aboard the USS *Midway*, patrolling the South China Sea at the height of the exodus of what were called the Vietnamese boat people.

"The sailor, like most American servicemen, was young, smart, and fiercely observant," Reagan said. "The crew spied on the horizon a leaky little boat. And crammed inside were refugees from Indochina hoping to get to America. The *Midway* sent a small launch to bring them to the ship and safety. As the refugees made their way through the choppy seas, one spied the sailor on deck, and stood up, and called out to him. He yelled, "Hello, American sailor! Hello, freedom man!"

Reagan continued: "The past few days when I've been at that window upstairs, I've thought a bit of the 'shining city upon a hill.' The phrase comes from John Winthrop, who wrote it to describe the America he imagined.... He journeyed here on what today we'd call a little wooden boat; and like the other Pilgrims, he was looking for a home that would be free."

Winthrop was a Puritan, not a Pilgrim, a mistake the *New York Times* also made during Reagan's presidency. (Such misconceptions are commonplace. In 1984, Walter Mondale invoked Winthrop during the waning days of his campaign against Reagan, erroneously calling him "Reverend Winthrop." Actually, he was a lay leader in the church, a lawyer by trade, and a natural politician, who became Massachusetts's first governor.) In any event, the ideas Winthrop conveyed in the famous sermon he delivered either on the docks in Britain or while crossing the ocean are equally applicable as theology or a guiding principle of civil society.

"*The eyes of the people are upon us.*" Yes, this one of the most famous invocations in Christianity. "You are the light of the world," Jesus advised his followers. But this is also a founding American ideal in a secular context. The United States wouldn't be formed for a century and a half after the Pilgrims and Puritans landed in the New World in the early 1600s, but the core idea Winthrop expressed was that America is more than a physical place, it's *an idea*. Remember, John Winthrop had yet to lay eyes on the New World when he espoused it. John F. Kennedy invoked this concept in his farewell speech as a senator to the people of Massachusetts—as he prepared to become president.

"During the last sixty days, I have been engaged in the task of constructing an administration," Kennedy said. "I have been guided by the standard John Winthrop set before his shipmates on the flagship *Arabella* 331 years ago, as they, too, faced the task of building a government on a new and perilous frontier."

At its core, the idea that America is the light of the world means that we must behave in a way that reflects well on democracy. That was what Kennedy and Reagan were saying, and this idea guides millions of Americans every day, even in our current hyperpartisan political environment. It also strongly implies an obligation that America be a welcoming place to new (small *p*) pilgrims. Near the end of his farewell address, Reagan circled back to this concept.

"I've spoken of the shining city all my political life, but I don't know if I ever quite communicated what I saw when I said it," Reagan said. "But in my mind, it was a tall, proud city built on rocks stronger than oceans, windswept, God-blessed, and teeming with people of all kinds living in harmony and peace; a city with free ports that hummed with commerce and creativity. And if there had to be city walls, the walls had doors and the doors were open to anyone with the will and the heart to get here. That's how I saw it, and see it still."

Photo Credits

Jan 1, Jan 29, Feb 14, Feb 16, Feb 19, Feb 22, March 31, April 8, April 16, May 3, July 3, July 11, Aug 5, Aug 9, Aug 11, Aug 24, Sept 11, Oct 6, Nov 28, Dec 1: **Library of Congress**

Jan 6, March 26, April 3, May 13, May 21, June 6, June 10, June 18, July 14, Nov 1, Nov 19: **US National Archives**

Jan 27: **NASA.gov**

March 20: **Courtesy of C-Span**

April 13: **Courtesy of the Franklin D. Roosevelt Presidential Library and Museum**

May 17: **Courtesy of the New York Public Library**

May 19: **Courtesy of the Smithsonian Library**

June 19: **Eric M. Durie/US Navy**

June 30: **"Yosemite Valley in Winter" by George Fiske, courtesy of the California Historical Society**

July 28, Aug 1: **US Naval Institute**

Sept 9: **Courtesy of the National Baseball Hall of Fame**

Oct 3: **Lauren Gerson/Flickr**

Dec 2: **Courtesy of the John F. Kennedy Presidential Library and Museum**

Index

426

About the Author

Carl M. Cannon is the Washington Bureau Chief of RealClearPolitics and a past recipient of the Gerald R. Ford Journalism Prize for Distinguished Reporting and the Aldo Beckman Award, the two most prestigious awards for White House coverage. Previous positions include Executive Editor of *Politics Daily*, Washington Bureau Chief for *Reader's Digest*, White House correspondent for both the *Baltimore Sun* and *National Journal*, a fellow-in-residence at Harvard University's Institute of Politics, and a past president of the White House Correspondents' Association. He is the author of *The Pursuit of Happiness in Times of War*, co-author of *Reagan's Disciple: George W. Bush's Troubled Quest for a Presidential Legacy* with Lou Cannon, and *Circle of Greed* with Patrick Dillon. Carl was also a member of the *San Jose Mercury-News* staff awarded a Pulitzer Prize for the paper's coverage of the 1989 Loma Prieta earthquake.

Mission Statement

Twelve strives to publish singular books, by authors who have unique perspectives and compelling authority. Books that explain our culture; that illuminate, inspire, provoke, and entertain. Our mission is to provide a consummate publishing experience for our authors, one truly devoted to thoughtful partnership and cutting-edge promotional sophistication that reaches as many readers as possible. For readers, we aim to spark that rare reading experience—one that opens doors, transports, and possibly changes their outlook on our ever-changing world.

12 Things to Remember about TWELVE

1. Every Twelve book will enliven the national conversation.
2. Each book will be singular in voice, authority, or subject matter.
3. Each book will be carefully edited, designed, and produced.
4. Each book's publication life will begin with a month-long launch; for that month it will be the imprint's devoted focus.
5. The Twelve team will work closely with its authors to devise a publication strategy that will reach as many readers as possible.
6. Each book will have a national publicity campaign devoted to reaching as many media outlets—and readers—as possible.
7. Each book will have a unique digital strategy.
8. Twelve is dedicated to finding innovative ways to market and promote its authors and their books.
9. Twelve offers true partnership with its authors—the kind of partnership that gives a book its best chance at success.
10. Each book will get the fullest attention and distribution of the sales force of the Hachette Book Group.
11. Each book will be promoted well past its on-sale date to maximize the life of its ideas.
12. Each book will matter.